toddler care
book

toddler care
book

A Complete Guide
from 1 to 5 Years Old

Dr. Jeremy Friedman MB.ChB, FRCP(C), FAAP

The Hospital for Sick Children

Robert
ROSE

Toddler Care Book
Text copyright © 2009 The Hospital for Sick Children
Cover and text design copyright © 2009 Robert Rose Inc.

For a complete list of photo credits, see page 432.
For complete cataloguing information, see page 433.

This book is a general guide only and should never be a substitute for the skill, knowledge, and experience of a qualified medical professional dealing with the facts, circumstances, and symptoms of a particular case.

    The nutritional, medical, and health information presented in this book is based on the research, training, and professional experience of the author, and is true and complete to the best of his knowledge. However, this book is intended only as an informative guide for those wishing to know more about health, nutrition, and medicine; it is not intended to replace or countermand the advice given by the reader's personal physician. Because each person and situation is unique, the author and the publisher urge the reader to check with a qualified health-care professional before using any procedure where there is a question as to its appropriateness. A physician should be consulted before beginning any exercise program. The author and the publisher are not responsible for any adverse effects or consequences resulting from the use of the information in this book. It is the responsibility of the reader to consult a physician or other qualified health-care professional regarding his or her personal care.

Editor: Bob Hilderley, Senior Editor, Health
Copy editor: Sheila Wawanash
Proofreader: Sue Sumeraj
Indexer: Gillian Watts
Design and production: PageWave Graphics Inc.
Illustrations: Kveta/Three in a Box
Sam's Diary blocks illustration: © iStockphoto.com/Dave Hopkins
Front cover: © 2009 Jupiterimages Corporation
Back cover: © The Hospital for Sick Children

The publisher acknowledges the financial support of the government of Canada through the Book Publishing Industry Development Program (BPIDP).

Published by Robert Rose Inc.,
120 Eglinton Ave. E. Suite 800, Toronto, Ontario, Canada M4P 1E2
Tel: (416) 322-6552 Fax: (416) 322-6396

Printed and bound in Canada

1 2 3 4 5 6 7 8 9 TCP 17 16 15 14 13 12 11 10 09

To toddlers and their parents everywhere . . .

And to the best pediatrician, colleague, and mentor, Dr. Norman Saunders, whose wisdom, wit, and friendship is so sorely missed by so many.

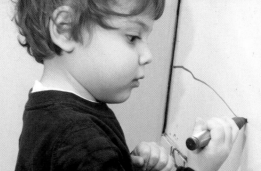

Contents

Introduction. 10

PART 1
Your Young Toddler
(Age 12 to 24 months)
Growing by leaps and bounds 14
Doctor, doctor 29
Vaccinations 33
Challenging behaviors. 41
Pacifying habits. 52
Grooming your toddler 56
Teething time 57
Equipping your toddler 60
Choosing a good caregiver 66
Let's play ball 72
Sun, cold, and bugs 76
Twin care. 81
Dad's role 85
Frequently asked questions. 88

PART 2
Feeding Your Toddler
The "right" diet. 94
Healthy eating habits 100
Eating skills development 105
Beverage options 107
Essential vitamins and minerals. 109
Organic foods 117
Vegetarian diets 119
Food allergies and intolerances. 121
Eating issues. 125
Frequently asked questions 131

PART 3
Your Older Toddler
(Age 2 to 3 Years)
Thriving during the terrible twos 138
Visiting the doctor again 143
Temper, temper. 145
Disciplining your toddler. 150
Teaching your child to share. 155
Talking with your child. 157
Private parts. 159
Television time. 161
Welcoming a new sibling. 165
Traveling with your toddler. 169
Dental care. 179
Right to play. 182
Dad's role 190
Frequently asked questions 193

PART 4
Toilet Training Your Toddler
Independence day 200
Toileting without tears. 203
Children with special needs 208
Troubleshooting 211
Frequently asked questions 215

PART 5
Your Preschooler
(Age 4 and 5 Years)
Big enough to go to school. 220
Routine visits to the doctor. 234
Preschooler behavior. 240

Disciplining your preschooler 244
Helping your child cope with loss 248
Parenting an adopted toddler.........251
School readiness 253
Recreation options...................259
Dad's role 262
Frequently asked questions 265

PART 6
Helping Your Toddler Sleep
Understanding sleep 272
How much sleep does my child
        need? 275
Secrets to a good night's sleep.......280
Problematic sleep behaviors..........284
Solving sleep problems...............287
Frequently asked questions 300

PART 7
Protecting Your Toddler
Accidents don't just happen 306
Safety at home 307
Safety on the road...................314
Water safety.........................322
Playground safety 324
Winter sports safety for
        colder climates 327
Frequently asked questions 328

PART 8
First Aid for Toddlers
Basic life support....................334
Choking, drowning, and poisoning 335
Cardiopulmonary resuscitation........342

First aid for major injuries 346
First aid for minor injuries 350
Creating a first aid kit................357
Frequently asked questions 358

PART 9
Caring for Your Sick Toddler
Recognizing illness 364
Managing a fever....................365
Remedying a cold 369
Resolving skin problems..............372
Treating eye problems 381
Dealing with ear, nose, and
        throat problems.................383
Managing chest and breathing
        problems 390
Treating heart conditions.............394
Taking care of stomach conditions....395
Addressing genitourinary problems ...400
Managing neurological conditions.....404
Recognizing musculoskeletal
        conditions 410
Giving medicine to your toddler.......412
Preparing your child for surgery 414
Caring for a child with a chronic
        illness..........................415
Complementary and alternative
        medicine 421
Frequently asked questions 425

Toddler Care Resources..............428
Acknowledgments 430
Index...............................434

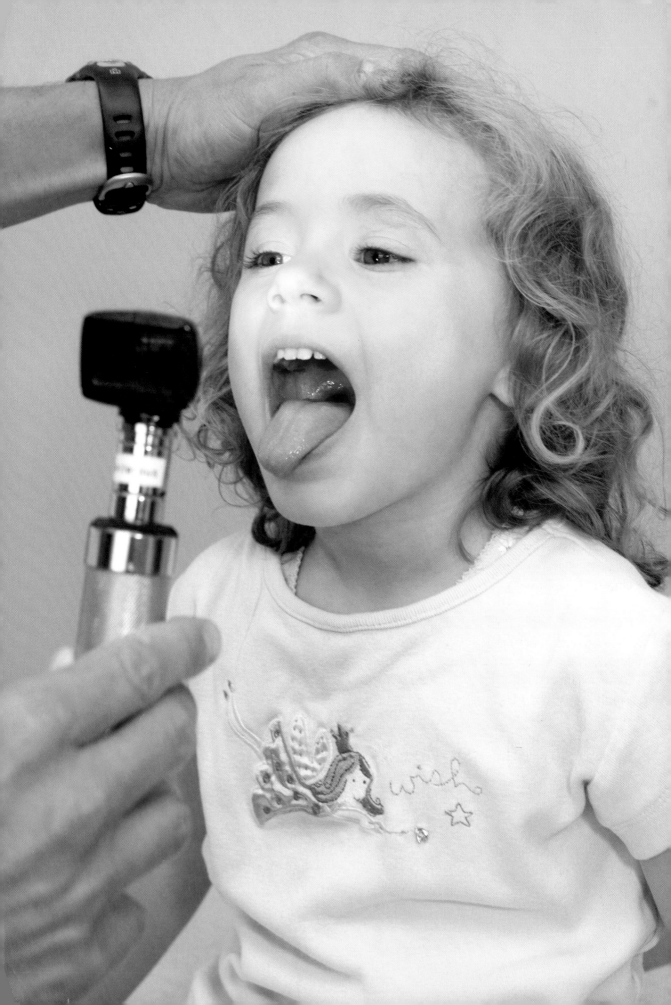

Contributing Authors

Sherri Adams, RN, MSN, CPNP
Division of Paediatric Medicine
The Hospital for Sick Children
Faculty of Nursing
University of Toronto

Carolyn Beck, MSc, MD, FRCP
Division of Paediatric Medicine
The Hospital for Sick Children
Assistant Professor
Faculty of Medicine
University of Toronto

Stacey Bernstein, MD, FRCP
Division of Paediatric Medicine
The Hospital for Sick Children
Assistant Professor
Faculty of Medicine
University of Toronto

Catherine Birken, MSc, MD, FRCP
Division of Paediatric Medicine
The Hospital for Sick Children
Assistant Professor
Faculty of Medicine
University of Toronto

Jeremy Friedman, MB, ChB, FRCP, FAAP
Chief, Division of Paediatric Medicine
The Hospital for Sick Children
Associate Professor
Faculty of Medicine
University of Toronto

Sheila Jacobson, MB, ChB, FRCP
Division of Paediatric Medicine
The Hospital for Sick Children
Assistant Professor
Faculty of Medicine
University of Toronto

Michael Peer, MD, FRCP
Division of Paediatric Medicine
The Hospital for Sick Children
Assistant Professor
Faculty of Medicine
University of Toronto

Michelle Shouldice, MD, FRCP
Division of Paediatric Medicine
The Hospital for Sick Children
Assistant Professor
Faculty of Medicine
University of Toronto

Michael Weinstein, MD, FRCP
Division of Paediatric Medicine
The Hospital for Sick Children
Assistant Professor
Faculty of Medicine
University of Toronto

Introduction

The stores are full of books devoted to parenting and children's health, and the Internet has a vast variety of resources devoted to toddlers — so why did we go to the effort of writing this new book on toddler care?

I attended medical school for 6 years and, after a year of internship, spent a further 4 years as a resident specializing in pediatrics. These were long days and nights filled with learning. I then had the opportunity to work as a general pediatrician at the world-famous Hospital for Sick Children for about five years before my first child was born. Sam is now 9, and his sister, Danielle, is 7. You'll read a little about Sam in the diary that my wife kept of his toddler years, reproduced in installments at the end of most chapters in this book. What you'll quickly realize is that fully qualified pediatricians who are also first-time parents are not quite sure what to make of the trials and tribulations of raising a toddler. My wife — who also works with young children as an occupational therapist — and I were often perplexed, sometimes frustrated, and frequently dismayed as a result of the wide variety of issues that seemed to crop up around every corner during the toddler years. At the same time, it was an incredibly exciting, wonderful stage in our lives. All in all, it was fun.

With this experience fresh in my mind, and after recovering from the stress of sleepless nights and challenging days, I felt that the time was right to put together a guide for parents of toddlers between their first and fifth birthdays that would answer many of the questions we had, as well as those I am frequently asked in my practice as a pediatrician.

If I was going to go to the effort of writing a book, I was determined to make it the most comprehensive source of information available. No one wants to have to buy a bunch of different books for each different stage or issue. So it would need to cover growth and development, behavior, nutrition, sleep, safety, medical issues, and everything in between. And it needed to be easy to read, readily applied, and, above all, practical. What parent of a toddler has more than a few minutes here and there to look for guidance on the particular issue at hand? There are lots of books that go into lengthy theoretical and philosophical detail but don't give any practical advice or simple strategies to use. So this book focuses on succinct and very practical answers to your questions.

Written by faculty members at one of the most highly respected children's hospitals in the world, this book is based on the best scientific knowledge available. The Hospital for Sick Children is an iconic institution in Canada, with an international reputation, built over more than a century, for the very best in caring for children, educating the next generation of pediatricians, and conducting cutting-edge research. To help write this book, I enlisted

the best help I could find at Sick Kids: health-care professionals who are not only highly respected for their care of young children in their practices but are also parents of young children. The result is eight contributors who between them have 18 children under the age of 9, with two more on the way. Many of these children are featured in the beautiful pictures illustrating this book. Who better to understand what parents need to know than a group of pediatricians and a nurse practitioner experiencing what they are writing about in real time? As a result, this book is an authoritative source any parent can trust, just as you would entrust us with the care of your children in our offices, clinics, and hospitals.

This toddler care book is a companion to the baby care book I co-authored with Dr. Norman Saunders. That book quickly became a bestseller after its release in 2007. I was so encouraged by the tremendously positive feedback from our readers that it made sense to continue with the same accessible and attractive, full-color, illustrated format this time around.

Tragically, since the publication of our last book, my co-author, great friend, and mentor, Norm Saunders, passed away after a long and brave fight against cancer. His influence has been with me through the process of putting this book together, and I hope that I have done justice to our partnership.

I hope that you find this book helpful. I wish you and your toddler much health and happiness in the years ahead. These are wonderful years — so make sure you enjoy them!

— *Jeremy Friedman*

Your Young Toddler

(Age 12 to 24 months)

Growing by leaps and bounds 14

Doctor, doctor 29

Vaccinations 33

Challenging behaviors 41

Pacifying habits 52

Grooming your toddler 56

Teething time 57

Equipping your toddler 60

Choosing a good caregiver 66

Let's play ball 72

Sun, cold, and bugs 76

Twin care 81

Dad's role 85

Frequently asked questions 88

Growing by leaps and bounds

The second year of life is an exciting period of growth and development marked by many wonderful achievements. Your toddler will learn to walk and run, begin to dress herself and feed herself (albeit messily) with a fork and spoon, and her language ability will begin to flourish. As your young toddler exerts independence and discovers the world around her, a whole host of interesting toddler behaviors will emerge, such as temper tantrums and separation anxiety — to name just a few! Your parenting skills will be challenged in a whole new way, but the rewards of parenting a toddler are great. These are exciting years.

Physical growth: 12 to 24 months

Your toddler is a dynamic, constantly changing individual who will undergo a fairly orderly and predictable sequence of growth and development. The rate of growth and development will vary between children, however, even within the same family. This rate depends on many things, including internal factors, such as the child's own genetic characteristics and temperament, as well as outside forces, such as a caregiver's personality and the surrounding environment.

Growth curves

Growth is the most predictable of all milestones, but it must be considered in the context of each child's specific genetic and ethnic background. At your child's checkups, your health-care provider will weigh your toddler and measure her height and head circumference. Don't be shocked if this simple task seems like a tall order for your toddler. The head circumference is generally measured until 2 years of age, while weight and height will continue to be monitored until adolescence.

PLOTTING THE MEASUREMENTS

These measurements are plotted on standard height, weight, and head circumference growth curves. Growth curves describe the range of normal weight, height, and head circumference at all ages. There are separate growth curves for boys and girls.

By plotting the measurements on a curve, your health-care provider will determine whether your child falls within the typical range and is growing proportionately at the expected rate.

Deviations from these expectations may mean that your child is simply expressing her own unique growth pattern. However, poor growth can sometimes indicate a problem, such as poor nutrition or an illness. Your physician may give you nutritional guidance, recommend some tests, or follow your child's growth more closely for a period of time.

READING GROWTH CURVES

The growth curves shown on pages 16–21 are provided by the United States National Center for Health Statistics and the National Center for Chronic Disease Prevention and Health Promotion (NCCDPHP) and are based on measurements from a North

Did You Know?

Physical growth facts

An infant typically triples his birth weight by 1 year of age. At 1 year, the average height is 30 inches (76.2 cm) and the average weight is 22 pounds (10 kg). By 2 years, the average height is 35 inches (89 cm) and the average weight is 27 pounds (12 kg) — four times the birth weight! Growth is occurring incredibly fast, although it has slowed down somewhat from the first year of life. Teeth are coming in quickly too. Your toddler will, on average, get his first molar at 14 months, his first canine tooth at 19 months, and his second molar at 24 months.

American population. Children of other ethnic backgrounds may have slightly different growth patterns that may be better reflected by growth curves produced by the World Health Organization (WHO). There are also specific adjusted growth curves for children with medical conditions, such as Down syndrome or Turner syndrome.

Developmental milestones: 12 to 24 months

Developmental milestones provide a timetable to observe the progress of your child's language skills, gross and fine motor skills, and activities of daily living. New skills build on the achievement of earlier skills. As the old saying goes, you can't run before you learn to walk.

While each milestone is important, don't overlook your child's development as a whole. Each child's development is unique, so the timing of milestones will differ from child to child. Some children will walk or talk months before others, but this does not mean that they are going to be more athletic or smarter.

This section will outline some of the important growth and developmental milestones in children 1 to 2 years of age, as well as identify some red flags or worrisome signs that might signal a developmental problem. If you have concerns about the timing of your child's developmental milestones, or if your child seems to lose previously attained milestones, discuss this with your child's health-care provider.

Did You Know?

Normal range

On standard growth curves, the 50th percentile describes the average weight, height, or head circumference measurement at each age. The range of normal falls between the 3rd and 97th percentiles. If your child was born prematurely (before 36 complete weeks of pregnancy), a correction will be made until the age of 2 years when plotting the values.

CDC Growth Charts

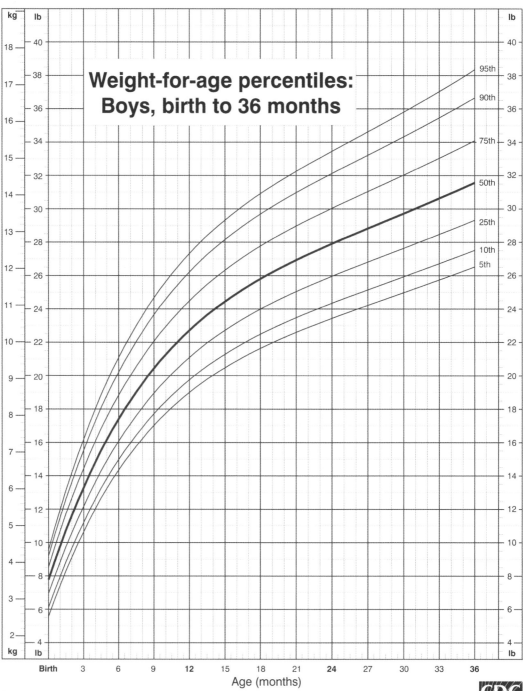

**Weight-for-age percentiles:
Boys, birth to 36 months**

Age (months)

Published May 30, 2000.
SOURCE: Developed by the National Center for Health Statistics in collaboration with
the National Center for Chronic Disease Prevention and Health Promotion (2000).

SAFER·HEALTHIER·PEOPLE™

CDC Growth Charts

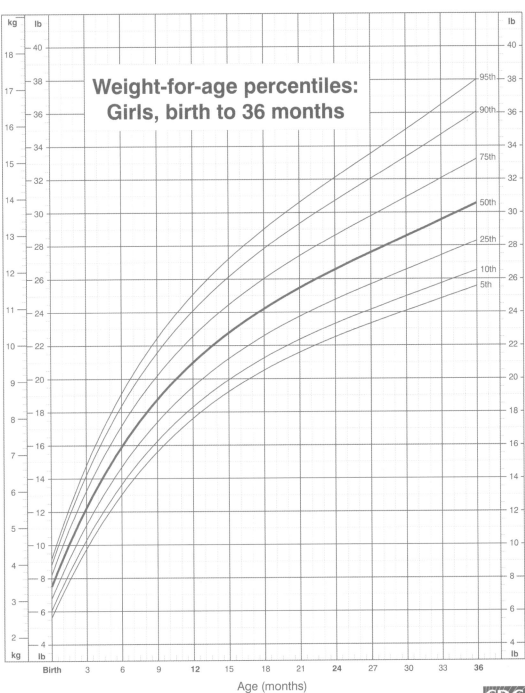

Weight-for-age percentiles: Girls, birth to 36 months

Age (months)

Published May 30, 2000.
SOURCE: Developed by the National Center for Health Statistics in collaboration with
  the National Center for Chronic Disease Prevention and Health Promotion (2000).

SAFER · HEALTHIER · PEOPLE™

CDC Growth Charts

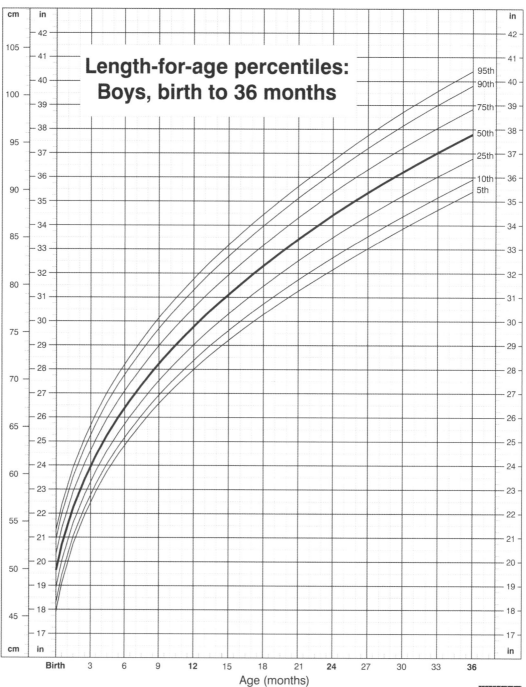

Length-for-age percentiles: Boys, birth to 36 months

Published May 30, 2000.
SOURCE: Developed by the National Center for Health Statistics in collaboration with
the National Center for Chronic Disease Prevention and Health Promotion (2000).

SAFER · HEALTHIER · PEOPLE™

CDC Growth Charts

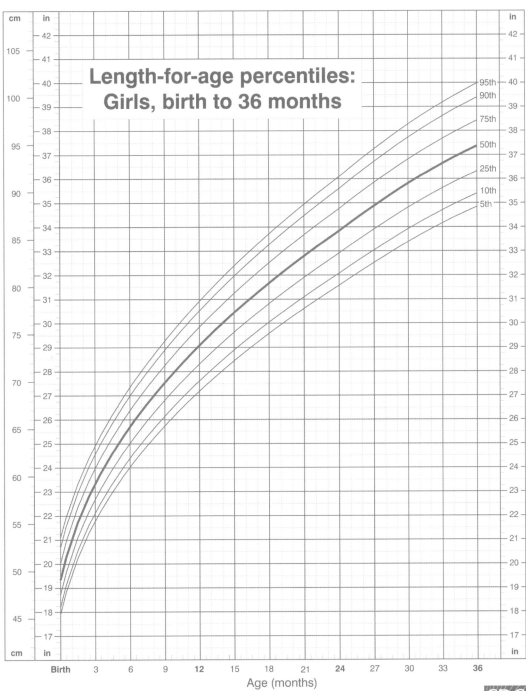

Length-for-age percentiles: Girls, birth to 36 months

Age (months)

Published May 30, 2000.
SOURCE: Developed by the National Center for Health Statistics in collaboration with
the National Center for Chronic Disease Prevention and Health Promotion (2000).

SAFER・HEALTHIER・PEOPLE™

CDC Growth Charts

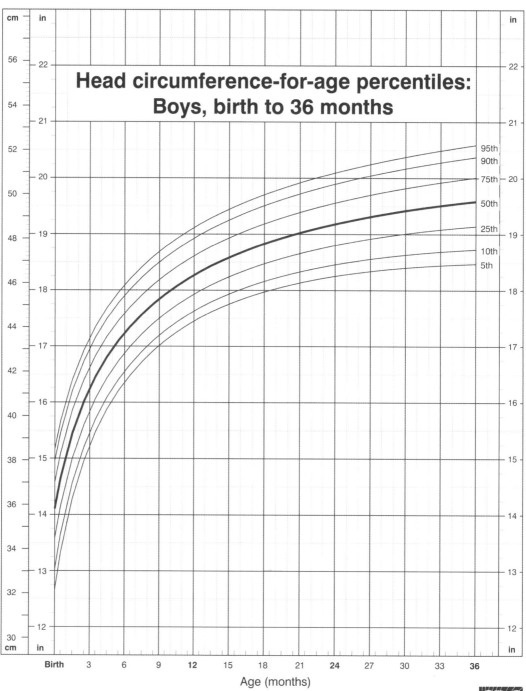

Head circumference-for-age percentiles: Boys, birth to 36 months

Published May 30, 2000.
SOURCE: Developed by the National Center for Health Statistics in collaboration with
the National Center for Chronic Disease Prevention and Health Promotion (2000).

SAFER · HEALTHIER · PEOPLE™

CDC Growth Charts

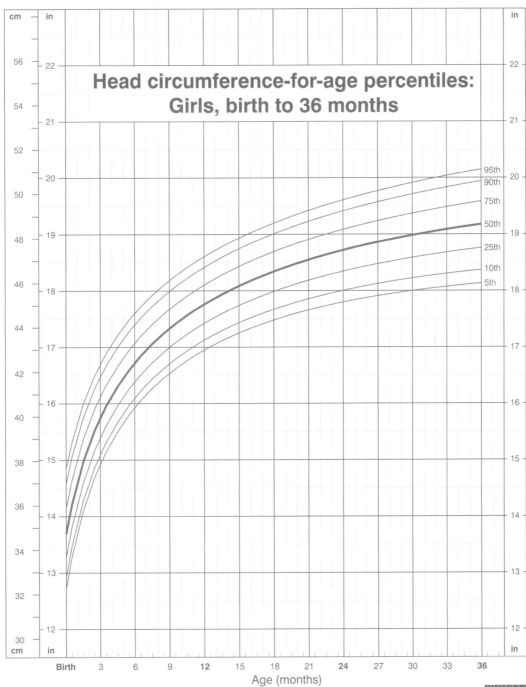

Head circumference-for-age percentiles: Girls, birth to 36 months

Published May 30, 2000.
SOURCE: Developed by the National Center for Health Statistics in collaboration with
the National Center for Chronic Disease Prevention and Health Promotion (2000).

SAFER·HEALTHIER·PEOPLE™

Different skill sets
It may be surprising to see two children of the same age playing side by side in the park with completely different skill sets.

Try not to compare your child with others too much. If you are concerned about your child's growth or development, seek advice from your health-care provider.

Gross motor development

Gross motor development refers to skills, such as crawling and walking, achieved through development of the large muscles of the body. In the second year of life, gross motor development proceeds through a sequence of milestones, from standing to walking and running.

Initially, the toddler walks on a wide base, with legs shoulder-breadth apart and hands held out in front for balance (a bit like Frankenstein). With time — and many tumbles — the movements become more fluid, the base narrows, and the arms begin to swing. By 18 months, toddlers run stiffly, and in the following few months, they will walk up stairs one at a time while holding the rail. By 2 years, they can climb onto small furniture but usually can't come down safely on their own. Supervision and babyproofing are even more important during this period, when your toddler has this newly discovered mobility. She is testing new skills but is unaware of her own limitations, and the chances of injury are increased.

RED FLAG
If your child is not taking steps before 18 months or can't walk up stairs at 24 months, draw this to the attention of your health-care provider.

Fine motor development

Fine motor development refers to skills, such as building a tower of blocks, achieved through development of the small muscles of the hand. At 18 months, toddlers can usually stack four blocks and scribble spontaneously. By 2 years, they can stack a larger tower of six to seven blocks and copy straight or circular strokes with a crayon.

Handedness, or hand dominance, should not really develop before 18 months. If you note a preference for the use of one hand before this age, bring this to the attention of your health-care provider; it may be a sign of weakness on the other side.

Language development

We tend to think of language in terms of the number of spoken words a toddler can say, but language is much more than that. Language skills can be divided into receptive language, which is the ability to understand language, and expressive language, which is the ability to make thoughts, ideas, and desires known to others. Expressive language can take the form of speech, gestures, sign language, and writing.

Toddlers have the ability to communicate expressively long before they speak; for example, they can understand and point to indicate what they want. When a proud parent exclaims, "Show me the light," toddlers love to look up and point at the fixture on the ceiling. They can raise their hands to say, "Pick me up," and point at the door from their crib as if to say, "Get me out of my room!"

During the second year of life, your child will expand her vocabulary. She will point to a few body parts and to pictures on request. She will start to realize that people and objects have names and to recognize her own name. Toddlers at this stage should understand the meaning of "no" — even if they don't always listen! You may hear your child stringing long nonsensical "sentences" together with the normal musical sounds of speech and an embedded word here or there.

Did You Know?

Play tools

Now that your child can reach for, grab, transfer, and pick up increasingly small things, he is able to play with objects in ways that he was unable to in the first year of life. In the second year of life, your child will learn how to use objects as tools during play. Instead of banging or mouthing a play brush to explore it, he will place it on his hair in a meaningful action. Problem-solving and fine motor skills develop together and complement each other. When your child sees a pop-up toy, he will press on the buttons to create the desired effect.

Guide to

Second-year developmental milestones

BY 18 MONTHS, YOUR CHILD

Understands

- Follows simple instructions ("Show me the teddy" or "Give me the cup")
- Can point to three body parts when asked
- Understands more words than he can say
- Knows the meaning of "no" and shakes his head

Expresses

- Uses at least 10 words or word attempts ("Mama" for Mommy or "ba" for ball)
- Can say "No"
- Asks for what he wants by pointing to objects and using sounds or words such as "uhuh" or "baba"
- Makes gestures or asks for "more" or "again"

Ask your health-care provider for help if your child

- Is not trying to talk
- Does not like to play with toys that make sounds and do things
- Does not like to move to music
- Does not make gestures or sounds like you do
- Started to use words but stopped

What you can do

- Take turns banging on pots and pans with your child
- Talk about too big/too small or my shoes/your boots
- Put objects in plastic containers: shake them, open and close them, take things out and put things in
- Add words like "in," "out," "more," "shake"
- Go for a walk and point to and name trees, birds, and other objects
- Show your child picture books and talk about what you see

BY 24 MONTHS, YOUR CHILD

Understands

- Searches with his eyes when asked, for example, "Where is the book?"
- Understands more words than he can say
- Points at body parts and familiar objects when asked, "Show me your nose" or "Where is the ball?"
- Responds to pictures of familiar people and things
- Responds to questions correctly by saying, "Yes," "Yup," "Yeah," or "No"

Expresses

- Produces animal sounds
- Tries to say words but may not always be clear
- Says two words together, such as "More milk"
- Uses some describing words, such as "hot" and "cold," "big" and "small"
- Asks, "What's that?" (May sound like "Wha dat?" or "Whatssat?")

Ask your health-care provider for help if your child

- Has repeated ear infections (an audiologist should check a child's hearing if fluid has remained in his ear for more than 2 months)
- Lacks awareness or interest in others
- Cannot make you understand what he is saying
- Uses very few words or does not put words together

What you can do

- Take turns tickling, feeding, and rocking dolls or teddy bears
- Sing simple songs with actions, such as "Itsy Bitsy Spider" or "Round and Round the Garden"
- Correctly repeat back what a child is trying to say (Child: "Mommy work." Adult: "Yes. Mommy is at work.")
- Use two to four words when talking, such as "Look up!" or "I see a cat"
- Hide objects under or behind pillows, blankets, or furniture and ask: "Where's the ball?" or "Find the teddy"
- Point to and talk about people and things when looking at books with large, clear pictures
- During everyday activities, use short sentences to talk about what you are doing
- Expand your child's world by introducing new people and places and by asking him to share toys with friends
- Look at your child when you talk to each other

Adapted by permission from Toronto Preschool Speech and Language Services information documents.

Problem-solving

Your child's ability to solve problems depends on a combination of developmental skills, including vision, fine-motor coordination, and cognitive processing. A 1-year-old child recognizes objects and associates them with functions, leaving behind purely sensory motor play and entering into functional play. When toddlers pick up a rattle, instead of exploring it orally by jamming it into their mouth, they will use it the way it is meant to be used, by shaking it. Your 1-year-old uses toys in actions directed toward herself; for example, by putting a toy telephone to her own ear.

During the second year, she also uses toys in actions toward dolls; for example, putting a toy tea cup to the doll's mouth (symbolic play). Imaginary play develops only after 24 months of age.

Developmental Milestones: 12 to 24 Months
Motor, Language, and Problem-Solving Skills

Months	Gross Motor	Fine Motor	Language	Problem-Solving
12	• Takes independent steps	• Grasps objects between thumb and index finger • Turns pages a few at a time	• Speaks two to three words • Points in response to words	• Removes lid on a container to find a toy
14	• Walks independently	• Builds tower of two blocks • Makes marks with a crayon	• Names one object • Follows command without gestures or prompts; e.g., "Bring me the book"	• Puts two blocks into one hand to take a third one with the other hand
18	• Pushes and pulls large objects • Seats self in small chair • Runs stiffly	• Builds tower of four blocks • Scribbles with a crayon • Dumps small objects from a bottle	• Speaks 10 to 25 words • Points to self and at least three body parts	• Shows symbolic play with a doll • Matches pairs of objects
22	• Walks up stairs one at a time holding rail	• Builds tower of six blocks	• Speaks 25 to 50 words • Points to three or four pictures and six body parts	• Deduces location of hidden objects
24	• Jumps in place • Throws and kicks ball • Walks down stairs one at a time holding rail • Climbs on furniture	• Builds tower of seven blocks • Imitates a straight or circular line with a crayon • Makes a train out of blocks	• Speaks 50+ words and two- to three-word sentences • Refers to self by name • Words can be understood by others 50% of time • Follows two-step commands	• Sorts objects, matches objects to pictures

Did You Know?

Peek-a-boo

Developing a sense of object permanence — the recognition that even when an object moves out of sight, it is still present — is an important aspect of problem-solving in the second year of life. Development of this skill begins with peek-a-boo play and separation anxiety when a loved one leaves the room. Later on, toddlers will experience success in finding an object that dropped out of sight and landed with a sound, and then gradually even one that landed silently. They will find an object that they saw you hide under a cup. By the end of the second year, toddlers will look for and often find a hidden object without observing it being hidden.

Psychosocial development

Emotional, social, and adaptive (self-help) developmental milestones are more variable than motor milestones because of the greater influence of the environment in which your child develops. An infant is born with a set of emotional-social characteristics and a style of interacting, and these are modified by parenting style and social and cultural environment. Both nature and nurture are at play.

Emotional development includes the child's feelings and the expressions of those feelings.

Social development includes the steps needed to form interpersonal relationships.

Adaptive development involves the skills required for independence in feeding, dressing, toileting, and other activities of daily living. Skills in this domain are influenced by social environment, as well as by motor and cognitive skills. You can imagine, for example, that if your mom always puts your coat on for you, it may be a while before you learn how to or want to do it for yourself. You can foster adaptive skill development by encouraging your toddler's independence in using skills, such as self-feeding and dressing. This is often quite messy and time-consuming, but your patience will be rewarded.

Developmental Milestones: 12 to 24 Months
Psychosocial Development

Months	Emotional	Social	Adaptive
12–15	• Exhibits shyness • Displays empathy • Provides self-comfort	• Plays mostly alone (solitary play) • Separation anxiety continues • Begins forming relationships	• Cooperates with dressing • Drinks from cup
15–18	• Feels shame and guilt	• Self-conscious period (coy) • Hugs parents	• Removes socks and shoes • Uses spoon
18–21	• Associates feelings with verbal symbols • Begins to have thoughts about feelings	• First application of attributes to self (good, naughty) • Kisses with a pucker	• Moves around house independently • Starts to remove clothing
21–24	• Begins to change reaction to events and emotions based on social influences of others	• Imitates others to please them • Plays next to but not with another child (parallel play) • Begins to tolerate separation • Has tantrums when frustrated • Resents attention shown to others	• Removes clothes without buttons • Opens door by turning knob • Unzips zippers • May indicate toileting needs

Doctor, doctor

Some new parents wonder whether it is best to see a family doctor (a general practitioner) or a pediatrician (a doctor who specializes in the care of children). The advantage of seeing a family doctor is that the whole family can be cared for by the same individual, so your "doc" will get to know all of you. Others argue that pediatricians have extra specialized training and their offices are geared specifically to young children. In many areas, particularly outside of larger cities, you may not have a choice between a family doctor and pediatrician.

Routine checkups

Recommendations will vary, but most healthy toddlers are seen by their doctor at 12, 18, and 24 months, and then on an annual basis thereafter. Some doctors like to see their patients at 15 months as well.

The 12-month well-child checkup

There are a number of guidelines for doctors to follow in conducting the various checkups. In the United States and Canada, guides for infant and child health maintenance visits have been endorsed by the national societies for pediatricians and family physicians. In Canada, for example, doctors generally use the Rourke Baby Record.

Growth: During all visits in the first two years, your child should be weighed and her height and head circumference

---

Guide to

Choosing a doctor

No doubt there are excellent family doctors and excellent pediatricians — and probably some not-so-excellent examples from both groups. In choosing a doctor, you may want to consider some practical issues, such as proximity to your home, accessibility — which would include the availability of public transportation and/or parking — convenience of office hours, and weekend and after-hours care. But the most important question is the "fit."

- Do you feel comfortable with your doctor?
- Do you trust her?
- Does she give you enough time and listen to your concerns?
- Does your toddler seem to like her?

  If your answers are yes, yes, yes, and yes, you are probably seeing the right individual.

  If you haven't found a doctor yet or are considering a switch, word of mouth is often the best way to go. Ask family, friends, and neighbors for recommendations. If this doesn't help, ask the obstetrician who delivered your baby. Otherwise, in most jurisdictions, the medical licensing colleges can provide a list of doctors who are taking on new patients.

HOW TO
Maximize the value of medical checkups

At each routine checkup, you need to feel comfortable with your child's doctor. You should never feel rushed — the idea behind every visit is to discuss any issues, questions, or concerns you may have at that point. You can maximize the value of these sessions by making a few preparations.

1. Make a list of questions
Many parents find it helpful to make a list of issues and questions ahead of time. Take this list with you so you don't forget something in the hustle and bustle, only to remember it just as you are leaving the building. As doctors, we are taught that there are no "stupid" questions, and as parents ourselves, we have probably been anxious about similar issues at one time or another.

2. Plan the timing of the visit
If possible, set up appointments for a time that works for your little one; for example, when he is less likely to be tired or hungry. Some doctors' offices always seem to be running late — you may have better luck if you choose the earliest available time in the morning or directly after the lunch break, before the office starts to get backed up!

3. Enlist support from family or friends
Having someone accompany you to these appointments can be really helpful. If your partner comes with you, he can ask his own questions, take part in the discussion of current issues, and benefit from the anticipatory guidance component of the checkup. An extra pair of hands to keep your toddler happy will also allow you to give your full concentration to making sure you come away from the visit with all the necessary information. Bring along a favorite toy or activity to help keep your child occupied during the talking part of the appointment.

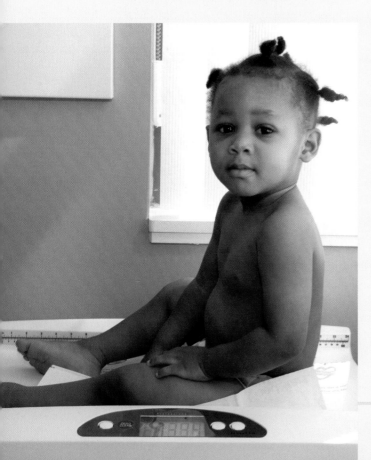

measured. These values are then plotted on the growth curve charts to identify any anomalies in the rate of weight gain or physical growth.

Development: Your doctor will ask you a number of questions to assess whether your toddler is achieving her developmental milestones and will observe her closely to confirm this.

Physical examination: A general physical will likely involve a head-to-toe examination, including a check of the eyes, ears, teeth, heart, chest, tummy, hips, and genitalia.

Discussion: You should then have an opportunity to discuss any particular concerns or questions you may have. This is the cue to bring out your prepared list so you don't forget anything in the heat of the moment.

Vaccinations: Most doctors will wait until close to the end of the appointment to give the needles — for obvious reasons!

Did You Know?

Education

At some point in your toddler's checkup, your doctor will want to spend a bit of time on education, giving advice on some common yet important issues.

Nutrition

- Continuing breast-feeding if possible and desirable
- Changing from formula to homogenized (full-fat) milk, limited to less than 20 ounces (625 mL) a day (see page 107)
- Limiting juice to a maximum of 4 to 6 ounces (125 to 175 mL) a day
- Switching from a bottle to a cup for feeding
- Watching for choking hazards (see page 128)
- Recognizing problematic reduced appetite and picky eating (see page 100)
- Brushing teeth for dental care (see page 58)

For more information on nutrition, see Part 2

Safety

- Using car seats correctly (see page 314)
- Turning down the temperature on your hot water tank (see page 309)
- Locking medications and toxins away (see page 310)
- Avoiding the dangers of second-hand smoke
- Testing smoke and carbon monoxide detectors regularly

For more information on safety, see Part 7

Other Issues

- Sleep problems, including frequent night waking (see Part 6)
- Child care and return to work (see page 66)
- Complementary and alternative medicine (see page 421)
- Pacifier use (see page 52)
- Reading to your child (see page 75)

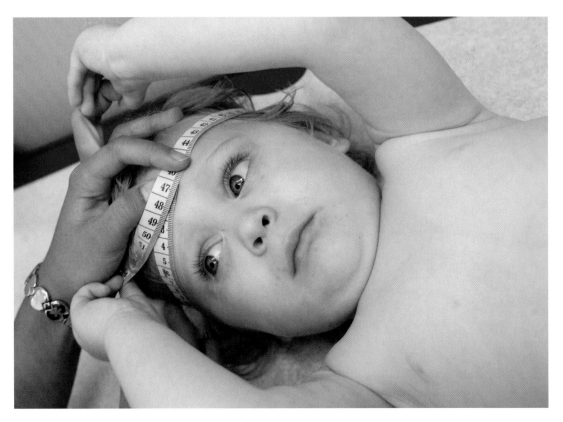

Vaccination schedules vary widely from place to place, both in terms of timing and in the specific vaccines administered. In most jurisdictions, a number of different vaccinations may be given between 12 and 24 months of age. These generally include the MMR (measles, mumps, and rubella), chicken pox (or varicella), and PCV (pneumococcal conjugate vaccine) vaccinations. A booster shot for DTaP-IPV (diphtheria, tetanus, acellular pertussis, and inactivated polio virus) and Hib (*Haemophilus influenzae* type B), given as one combined shot in Canada, may also be given between 12 and 18 months, depending on the jurisdiction. It is recommended that children receive the influenza vaccine annually in the fall after the age of 6 months. Finally, health authorities in the United States recommend the hepatitis A, or HepA, vaccine, and their counterparts in Canada recommend that the meningococcal conjugate vaccine be given in the second year of life.

The 18-month visit

This is very similar to the 12-month visit, with a few additional topics for advice and discussion — and a few more vaccinations! The topics you may consider reviewing include discipline and setting limits, as well as your toddler's interactions with her peers. This is also a good time to discuss how you are coping. The additional vaccinations may include DTaP-IPV, and Hib, and perhaps influenza if your visit takes place in the fall.

Vaccinations

Few issues in children's health care have aroused more study and debate in the last few years than immunizations. On the one hand, there is convincing evidence to suggest that the introduction of vaccinations was probably the greatest advance in pediatric health care in the 20th century. On the other hand, there are minor side effects and some more serious but very rare risks associated with some of the vaccines.

Disease prevention

For many diseases, vaccinations have been so successful that most of us have never seen children die from tetanus, diphtheria, or polio, nor have we seen children born deformed because their mothers had German measles (rubella) during pregnancy. Since the introduction of the Hib and pneumococcal conjugate vaccines in the past 10 to 20 years, there has been a dramatic drop in the number of children dying or being permanently brain damaged from bacterial meningitis.

In poorer developing countries, which cannot afford to immunize their children universally, many hundreds of thousands are still dying from these diseases, and with increased foreign travel and immigration, we occasionally still see an isolated outbreak in North America.

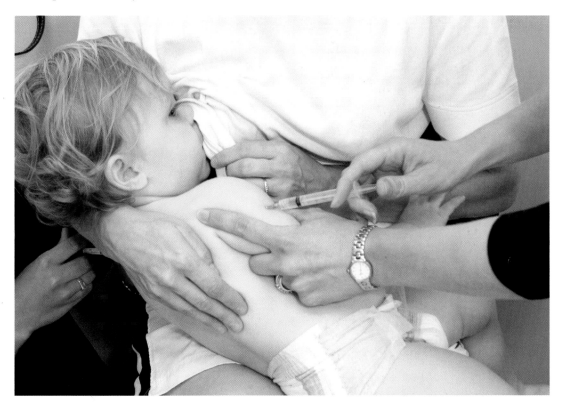

Did You Know?

Pain reduction

Vaccinations can be painful for your child, but this can be managed effectively. A very popular option is to give your toddler a dose of acetaminophen or ibuprofen about 1 hour before you anticipate that the needle will be given. Make sure that you give an adequate dose as recommended on the bottle. You will likely need to give a second dose 4 to 6 hours later, again as recommended on the bottle.

Topical local anesthetics are becoming increasingly popular. These are applied to the skin and cause dulling of the pain receptors, resulting in numbness. They are available from your local pharmacy in the form of creams, gels, or patches. You will need to ask your doctor or her nurse ahead of time exactly where the shot will be given, as you need to apply the medication over the "badge" area on the upper arm about 30 to 60 minutes before the shot will be given. These numbing creams can be pretty pricey, so be sure to find out what they cost before you're at the cash register.

Side effects

Mild side effects, such as temporary redness, swelling, pain, and fever, are common, but serious side effects from vaccinations are rare. Other side effects are conjectural. For example, there has been conjecture that the measles-mumps-rubella (MMR) vaccine is associated with the onset of autism, but several large, population-based studies have failed to show any connection between this vaccine and autism. Another vaccine-related concern has been raised in regard to thimerosal, a mercury-containing compound used as a preservative in vaccines. In 2001, thimerosal was removed from most vaccines but can still be found in some HepB and influenza vaccines.

Risks and benefits

Despite possible side effects, vaccinations are generally much safer than the risk involved in contracting the disease itself.

Many parents will likely decide to proceed as advised by the regulatory bodies in their particular country or jurisdiction, which have examined the evidence in detail and obtained many expert opinions. And some school districts will not allow children to attend without proof of vaccination status.

If you want to know more about these issues, many reliable sources of information can be accessed through the American Academy of Pediatrics or the Canadian Paediatric Society. Discuss your questions with your doctor. If you decide to go to the Internet, be selective about the sources you use. There is some very helpful information out there, but also some theories that are misrepresented as facts. Becoming educated on the pros and cons of any treatment or prescribed therapy allows you as parents to make an informed decision about what is in the best interest of your child.

Guide to

Vaccinations

MMR VACCINE

What?

This 3-in-1 vaccination protects against measles, mumps, and rubella. Before this vaccination was introduced, many children contracted these diseases.

Why?

Death used to occur in about 1 out of every 1,000 cases of measles, and 1 out of every 100 affected children required hospitalization. More than 90% of those who haven't been immunized will contract measles if exposed to the virus through sneezing or coughing. Symptoms of measles include high fever, runny nose, cough, red eyes, rash, and ear pain.

Mumps is also caused by a virus and results in fever, headache, muscle aches, and swelling of the salivary glands, which makes the cheeks puff out. It can unfortunately also cause meningitis and deafness and (rarely) lead to infertility through swelling of the testicles.

Rubella, or German measles, causes a mild rash, fever, swollen glands, and muscle aches. The most serious risk is if a pregnant woman is infected in the first trimester, when it can result in serious damage to or even death of the fetus.

When?

This vaccine needs to be given twice: the first shot is given between 12 and 15 months, with a booster at least 1 month later, but usually before your child starts school, between 4 and 6 years of age.

Side effects?

These are generally very mild. A bit of redness, swelling, and pain may occur at the injection site. Fever, and much more rarely (in 2%) a rash, may be seen 8 to 10 days after vaccination. These can last for 24 to 48 hours. Encephalitis (inflammation of the brain) may be seen in 1 per 1 million cases (but occurs in 1 in 1,000 cases of measles).

During the past decade, there has been some controversy linking the vaccine to the onset of autism. Despite media reports and concerns raised by anti-vaccination groups, this has not been scientifically proven. Multiple research studies, performed by different researchers in various countries, have strongly supported the lack of a link or association between the MMR vaccine and autism or other developmental problems.

CHICKEN POX (VARICELLA) VACCINE

What?

This vaccine protects against chicken pox and shingles.

Why?

Chicken pox causes fever, headache, muscle aches, and a typically itchy rash. Before the vaccination was introduced, chicken pox resulted in thousands of hospitalizations and even some deaths every year. While it is true that chicken pox is usually a mild disease, it is very contagious, and prior to the vaccine, most children contracted it before the age of 15, resulting, on average, in at least 3 missed school days. Rare serious complications include skin infections, "flesh-eating" disease, and inflammation of the brain. Even after being vaccinated, it is possible to get chicken pox, but the symptoms tend to be very mild.

When?

The vaccine is given sometime after the first birthday. It can be given together with any of the other shots. If not given at the same time as the MMR, you should wait at least 1 month so that the immune response to the MMR does not weaken the immune response to the varicella vaccine.

Side effects?

Reactions are usually mild. Soreness, redness, swelling, or rash at the injection site can occur in about 20% of children. A low-grade fever occurs in less than 15%, and a mild chicken pox–like rash may be seen in less than 5%.

PNEUMOCOCCAL CONJUGATE VACCINE
What?

This vaccination protects against infection by seven different types of the *Streptococcus pneumoniae* bacterium.

Why?

This type of streptococcus can infect many parts of the body, the most serious effect being on the brain (meningitis). One out of five children with pneumococcal meningitis will die from their illness, and many others will be left with permanent brain damage. These common bacteria are also often responsible for blood infections, pneumonia, and ear infections.

When?

The vaccine is given at 2, 4, and 6 months, with a booster between 12 and 15 months of age. It can be given at the same time as the other vaccines.

Side effects?

Mild redness, swelling, and tenderness at the injection site occurs in about 10% to 20% of children.

MENINGOCOCCAL CONJUGATE VACCINE
What?

This vaccination protects against infection caused by the *Neisseria meningitides* bacterium.

Why?

This infection causes meningitis and blood infections, leading to death in about 10% of cases.

When?

The recommended schedule varies in different jurisdictions. In Canada, for example, some regulatory bodies recommend giving three shots at 2, 4, and 6 months of age; others recommend a single shot after the first birthday. In the United States, this vaccination is generally given after the second year. It can be given at the same time as other shots.

Side effects?

There are mild local reactions lasting 24 to 48 hours in 10% to 20% of children.

DTaP-IPV AND Hib VACCINE
What?

In the United States, this is given as two separate needles that protect against diphtheria, tetanus, acellular pertussis (DTaP), polio (IPV, or inactivated polio virus), and *Haemophilus influenzae* type B (Hib) infections. In Canada, this is given as a 5-in-1 needle (DTaP-IPV-Hib).

Why?

Most parents are not familiar with and have never seen "old" diseases such as polio, diphtheria, or tetanus. This is a great thing! What it means is that the vaccinations have successfully eradicated them, but all of these diseases used to kill or permanently damage children who had severe episodes in years gone by.

Diphtheria results in a sore throat, fever, and serious breathing problems. One out of 10 children who had it used to die from it.

Tetanus, or lockjaw, enters through a break in the skin and releases a nerve toxin. This results in paralysis and painful muscle spasms, which can result in death.

Pertussis, or whooping cough, causes severe coughing spasms that can last for weeks or months. It can cause brain damage and even death, especially in young babies.

Polio can cause fever, headache, vomiting, and muscle pains. One out of every 100 infected children will be severely paralyzed, and some may even die.

Haemophilus influenzae type B (Hib) can infect many parts of the body, but the most dangerous result is meningitis, which may cause brain damage, deafness, and even death. The number of cases of meningitis due to Hib has dropped dramatically since the introduction of the vaccine just over 20 years ago, but in the U.S., 20,000 children under the age of 5 became seriously ill with Hib and 1,000 died every year before the vaccine was given.

When?

The primary series of shots is given at 2, 4, and 6 months of age. A booster is required between 12 and 18 months in the United States and usually at 18 months in Canada. This is repeated at 4 to 6 years, without the Hib.

Side effects?

Pain, tenderness, and redness may occur at the site of the injection and are a bit more common with the booster shot than with the primary shots in the first year. Since the introduction of the acellular pertussis (aP) component, replacing the older pertussis (P) part of the vaccine in 1997, side effects are much less frequent and less severe. High fever may occur in less than 1 in 3,000 cases, prolonged crying in 1 in 300, and severe fussiness in about 1 in 100. Allergic reactions, most commonly hives, can occur in rare cases.

INFLUENZA VACCINE
What?
This protects against the influenza virus, which causes "the flu."

Why?
The real influenza is very different from what most people call the flu, which is usually just the common cold. Influenza causes a sudden onset of high fever, often with chills, headache, sore throat, cough, muscle aches, and in rare cases even inflammation of the brain (encephalitis) and pneumonia. As you can see, a bad cold is generally not the flu.

When?
This needle is required every year in the fall because there are minor changes in the virus every season, which means that the immune system doesn't recognize the virus from year to year and needs to be reminded with the latest version of the flu vaccine. It is recommended for all children with chronic illnesses, and for healthy children between the age of 6 months and 5 years, at the time of the influenza season. In the summer of 2008, the American Academy of Pediatrics approved recommending annual influenza vaccination up to the age of 18.

Side effects?
More than half the children receiving the vaccine will have soreness at the injection site for 1 to 2 days. Mild fever, muscle aches, and fatigue may also last for a day or two. Despite many people's concerns that they "got the flu" from the vaccine, this is not really possible because the vaccine contains a killed virus that cannot actually cause influenza.

HEPATITIS A (HepA) VACCINE
What?
This vaccine protects against hepatitis A, one of the group of hepatitis viruses that can infect the liver. The virus can be picked up from contaminated food or water and is very easy to pass on to other people.

Why?
Symptoms can include fever, fatigue, nausea, vomiting, diarrhea, loss of appetite, tummy pains, and yellow skin and eyes (jaundice). These may last several weeks. Most people recover completely, although in very rare cases hepatitis A can cause severe damage to the liver. One in five people may require hospitalization, and 3 to 5 out of every 1,000 cases may die from the disease.

When?
In the United States, the HepA vaccine is recommended for all children between 12 and 23 months. The two doses in the series must be given at least 6 months apart.

Side effects?
Mild pain and redness may occur at the injection site in about 20% of children, and headache, mild fever, and tiredness may occur 3 to 5 days after the shot.

Challenging behaviors

The terrible twos! How come nobody told us they could start so early? Whoever coined the term "the terrible twos" either had an angelic 1-year-old or was playing a cruel trick on parents to catch them by surprise.

Do not be at all shocked if your sweet, compliant infant adopts some monster-like behavior almost overnight at the time of her first birthday. Temper tantrums may arrive on the scene much sooner than you anticipated. Be prepared with a few tricks up your sleeve so you can take the edge off this somewhat painful developmental milestone.

Breath-holding spells

Just when you thought life was interesting enough, you find your toddler flat out on the floor after a breath-holding spell.

During breath-holding spells, just as the name implies, your toddler involuntarily holds her breath. While these spells are generally very scary to observe, they are quite common and not at all dangerous. The condition is frequently seen between 6 and 18 months of age and is observed in as many as 5% of children. It resolves on its own, certainly by age 5, without causing any lasting damage or effects. Nevertheless, to put your mind at rest, you will likely want to see your doctor the first time it happens to be sure this is not a seizure disorder or an entirely different problem.

Did You Know?

Blue and pale spells

There are two forms of breath-holding spells: blue (cyanotic) and pale (pallid), with the former being much more common than the latter.

Blue breath-holding spells

These spells are preceded by an intense exchange, crying episode, or angry outburst, usually after a child has not gotten his way. The child cries vigorously, exhales, then stops breathing and turns red, blue, or purple in the face, especially around the lips. He may even pass out or have a short seizure (a few jerks of the arms and legs) due to a very brief lack of oxygen to the brain. Once the child falls to the floor, he will usually recover spontaneously in a matter of seconds to minutes. Nevertheless, these seconds will seem like years to the frightened parent.

Pale breath-holding spells

These spells are usually precipitated by a frightening or painful experience (for example, catching his finger in the door). Instead of turning blue, your toddler turns a whiter shade of pale, usually after a reflex slowdown in his heart rate. The sequence of events thereafter is the same as in blue spells.

Guide to

Managing breath-holding spells

When your toddler has a breath-holding spell, make sure he is in a safe environment in case he falls. Beyond this, try not to pay too much attention to the event — which is easier said than done!

Do not reinforce the behavior. This is especially challenging. Not surprisingly, some parents will go to great lengths to give in to their toddler rather than encounter another dreaded breath-holding spell. This puts the wrong person in control and paves the way for absolute toddler mayhem.

Use techniques for avoiding temper tantrums that do not involve giving in to your toddler (see page 146).

See your doctor if

- Breath-holding episodes are not precipitated by crying, frustration, or pain.
- They last longer than 1 minute.
- They occur in infants before 6 months of age.
- They are severe.
- You are not really sure that they are breath-holding spells.

Fears and phobias

The following scene may sound familiar. You are going about your daily routine, business as usual. Suddenly, your toddler becomes hysterical, shrieking and crying, petrified by a common household object that she has not so much as blinked at in the past — a loud noise (such as the vacuum cleaner), a dog barking, the dark, bathtub drains, a balloon, or a plastic toy snake. Fears and phobias are commonplace in the life of a toddler. With understanding and patience, adults can help children deal with their fears.

Separation anxiety

You are about to leave and are pulling out of the driveway. You glance back and see and sometimes hear your toddler shrieking at the window, red-faced, with huge tears streaming down her face. She hasn't yet developed a sense of time or an understanding of when or even whether you will return. It is scary for her to be in the great wide world "on her own."

It may help alleviate some of the guilt to know that this behavior is common in the toddler years. Separation anxiety is a normal developmental milestone that peaks at 10 to 18 months and, fortunately, fades toward the end of the second year. Your toddler will come to understand the concept of object permanence — when something or someone is out of sight, they do still exist.

With a few simple strategies, you can help your toddler overcome this fear.

Comfort objects

Many children become attached to an object, such as a blanket or stuffed toy, that comforts them when they are away from their parents, falling asleep, or feeling sad or scared. Comfort objects help toddlers feel secure as they independently explore the world, and they represent a normal, healthy developmental stage.

HOW TO
Tame the monsters

Do not shrug off, dismiss, or ridicule your child's fears. Take them seriously — they are very real to him.

1. Avoidance
Avoid contact wherever possible during the phobia phase. Put away that toy snake so his brother can't lurk unsuspected around corners and frighten him. Vacuum while he is napping or out of the house. Leave the dinosaur exhibit … even if you just paid admission for the whole family. Limit your child's exposure to scary media. Some things are hard to avoid entirely, such as the dark or balloons at birthday parties, but do try!

2. Alleviation
Try to solve problems together. Go out with your toddler and purchase a night light so his room is not too dark at night, or make a sign that says, "No monsters allowed!" and pin it up on the door.

3. Reassurance
You can't stop the thunder during a storm or even the fireworks on the Fourth of July, but you can cuddle your toddler and reassure him that everything will be all right. Model calm, confident behavior when confronting the source of the fear. Let him know that you're not afraid. Purchase or make a worry doll or other comforting object he can hold when he is afraid. Make up a story or read a book about the topic that will help reassure him that there is no need to be frightened.

4. Desensitization
Don't push your child into getting over his fears before he is ready. Once you think he can handle it, take small steps. For example, if he's afraid of dogs, start off by looking at pictures of dogs together, then visit a pet store to see some cute puppies behind the glass.

HOW TO
Beat the bye-bye blues

As a parent, it is difficult to know what to do in this distressing situation. Is it better to sneak away without saying goodbye while your child is distracted? Is it easier to stay home and avoid the theatrics? Here are some tips for managing separation anxiety:

1. **Establish routines wherever possible.** Daily routines are the equivalent of wristwatches for young children. Toddlers are usually better at managing situations that are predictable for them. They are also likely to be more tolerant when they are not hungry, tired, or sick.

2. **Create a goodbye ritual.** This builds trust. Downplay the departure, reassure your child, and tell him that "Mommies and daddies always come back." It is generally not a good idea to sneak away. It may be more confusing and anxiety-provoking for your child. It may also lead to his getting anxious any time you are out of sight, panicking that you may have left.

3. **Say a confident, quick goodbye.** Try not to prolong the agony. If your child knows you will not leave while he is crying, he will continue to cry longer and louder to get you to stay.

4. **Create a diversion.** Find some interesting and fun activity that will distract his attention after you say your goodbye.

5. **Help him get used to new situations.** Invite the babysitter to come a bit early, while you are still there, or stay at a friend's home for a bit to give him a chance to get comfortable before you leave.

6. **Know that he will be okay after you leave.** It defeats the purpose if you dissolve into tears and are sick with guilt, worrying about your child the entire time you are gone. It may help to have a mutually agreed-upon call-in time with the caregiver, if that will make you feel better. Be prepared for the fact that your toddler may cry again upon your return when he "remembers" that he was left. This too is completely normal.

You can help your child develop a comfort toy by providing her with a particular stuffed animal or blanket every time you put her to sleep. Toddlers have a mind of their own, though, often picking a comfort object themselves, and not the one we would have chosen for them. Make sure the object is not one that is physically attached to you, such as your hair. This can tie you down in more ways than one.

If possible, it is a good idea to buy a duplicate: the object will occasionally require cleaning, will inevitably be misplaced, and may even get lost. Unfortunately, identical-looking comfort objects may not feel or appear identical to the discriminating toddler, especially as an object becomes more tattered and loved with age.

Diaper care

Diapers can cause toddlers — and their parents — considerable discomfort. Some children never get a diaper rash, while others are constantly battling them, often with similar diaper care routines. Some children wear their diapers happily, while others pull at and tear back the tabs. Diapering can become a source of contention.

To reduce any physical or behavioral issues, be sure the diaper area is kept as dry and clean as possible to reduce irritation from the urine and stool and the various germs that accompany them. To prevent diaper rash, you can apply a barrier protectant, such as petroleum jelly or various types of zinc ointment, but for many toddlers this is not necessary. A good cleaning and regular diaper changes should keep the area clean and dry.

Toddlers don't need to be changed in the middle of the night now that they are (or should be!) sleeping through. If your little one wakes up wet in the middle of the night or in the morning, try reducing the amount of fluid right before bedtime, change her immediately before bed, or upsize the diaper you use at night.

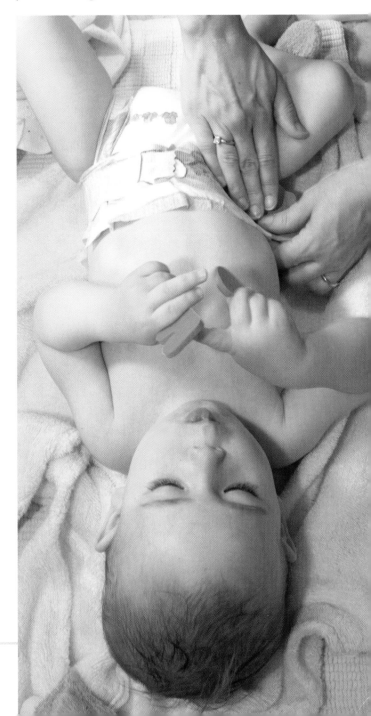

Guide to

Defeating diaper dilemmas

Toddlers often go through frustrating phases where they suddenly challenge and refuse to cooperate with certain everyday routines. This can be especially trying when it comes to the frequent and potentially messy business of diaper changing. Fortunately, these behaviors can disappear as abruptly as they begin.

REFUSING A CHANGE

Here are some tips for surviving the stage when your toddler writhes, screams, and rolls around trying to escape during his diaper change:

- Avoid the change table. You don't want to get into a battle in the middle of a diaper change with the added threat of a fall from a height.
- Try distraction. Use books, toys, food or music.
- Try a different method, such as changing your toddler while he is standing up.

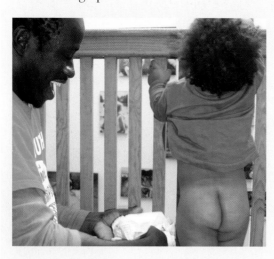

- Get your toddler to help. Have him hold the diaper cream or wipes or choose the diaper.
- Change less frequently. It's no crime if your toddler spends a bit of extra time in a wet diaper (as long as he doesn't develop a diaper rash).
- Finally, sometimes you gotta do what you gotta do. There are certain things that are not negotiable. Get an extra set of hands if you need the help, secure your toddler, and get on with it.

DIAPER DROPPING

Toddlers love to pull open their diaper tabs and smile broadly as the diaper drops to their ankles. This tends not to be as amusing for the parent, especially if the diaper is full. To prevent this from becoming a recurring behavior, try the following methods:

- Use pull-ups. They tend to be more difficult for the toddler to remove.
- Keep the diaper covered as much as possible. You can use tights, pants, pajamas, one-pieces, or underwear. If you're desperate, try duct tape, but be aware that it may be just as hard for you to remove as it is for your toddler!
- Put the diaper on backwards. Tabs in the back are more difficult to access.
- Consider toilet training if you think your child is exhibiting readiness to come out of diapers and not just playing a game.
- Minimize your reaction to his behavior. Creating a hoopla will only reinforce the activity.

HOW TO
Manage messy eating and food throwing

Feeding your toddler can be a very messy experience. Like most aggravating toddler behavior, this too shall pass. In the meantime, here are some survival tips:

1. Expect the worst. If you expect and prepare for it, you will be less frustrated and upset. Much of the behavior represents a normal developmental stage. Part of the process of experiencing and experimenting with different textures and tastes involves squashing them, wiping them all over the table, chewing them, and spitting them out. When toddlers first learn to feed themselves using utensils, it is a hit-and-miss situation. Favorite foods, such as watermelon and spaghetti sauce, inevitably leave their mark. Invest in a good stain remover.

2. Keep mealtime as short as possible. Get all the food ready before your toddler is seated, and make sure he is hungry when you put him into his seat. Take the food away when he is done eating.

3. If he tends to throw food on the floor, try putting small amounts in front of him at a time.
Avoid getting into the game where you are retrieving everything he is throwing on the floor. He is going to get more fun out of it than you are. Save cleanup for after the meal.

4. Try using special equipment.
Sectioned plates with suction cups at the bottom can stick to your tabletop and won't be easily overturned. Sippy cups and developmentally appropriate stubby utensils or dippers make less mess. Try using a bib that has a reservoir at the bottom to catch stray food. Whatever ends up in there is that much less to clean off the chair or floor after a meal.

5. Use neater food. Thicker-textured foods, such as oatmeal and applesauce, are less likely to fall off the spoon. Finger foods work well too.

6. Let your toddler hold one set of utensils. While he feeds himself, you can feed him with another set.

7. Clear the area. Make sure the area is mess-friendly. You may need to move the high chair or booster seat to a place where the floor is easy to clean or spread out a garbage bag below to catch the droppings. Keep the vacuum cleaner close by.

8. Stay calm and model positive behavior. Instead of getting frustrated and angry, try, if possible, to model what you would like him to say; for example, "All done" or "No thank you, Mommy."

HOW TO
Prevent your child from eating non-food items

1. Make sure that toys are age-appropriate, do not have small parts, and are not subject to a safety recall. When toys are labeled "Not suitable for children under 3," this often means that they have small parts, not necessarily that they are developmentally inappropriate. Keeping unsafe toys away is especially challenging when there are older siblings around. In this case, if possible, try to keep some items in a separate play area that is out of reach for your toddler.

2. When your toddler puts something in his mouth, discourage him by repeating a simple warning phrase such as, "We don't put things in our mouth."

3. Childproof your home. Your toddler may still be crawling close to the ground, only an arm's length from lost magnets, spare change, stray buttons, pen caps, and batteries. He may be cruising or walking around with newfound freedom and access to previously unreachable items. Put up safety gates. Clean your home, especially in those places that toddlers like to explore — under the couch or between sofa cushions.

4. Learn basic first aid and stay up to date. Be familiar with what you would need to do in case of a choking episode (for first aid information, see Part 8).

Eating other stuff

Toddlers put non-food items in their mouths for many reasons. They may be teething, curiously exploring an object, or just doing it to test your response. On rare occasions, toddlers do odd things, such as sucking on shoelaces or eating dirt, a behavior known as pica. Pica can sometimes be a sign of anemia. Non-food items are potentially dangerous because they may be choking hazards or toxic.

Bathing the beast

Bath time should be fun, but that's not always the case. To make bath time fun, follow a predictable routine, sing, play music, use bath toys, and enjoy this time when your toddler is well contained in an enclosed space! It may also be an opportunity to let your partner take ownership of this particular piece of the routine.

Your child may go through a phase when she refuses to take a bath. Like most toddler behavior, this too shall pass; before you know it, she will be refusing to come out of the bath! Try enticing her with novelties — a shower, a new bath toy, or bath crayons. If all else fails, try sponge bathing or decreasing the frequency of baths for a while. You don't want to get into the dangerous situation where your child is thrashing around and having a tantrum in the water.

Frequency

How often should you bathe your toddler? Good question, but unfortunately there is no correct answer. If the weather is warm and your toddler is covered in greasy sunscreen and is dirty from playing outside, she probably needs a bath. If the weather is cold and your child's skin is dry, bathing every other day will likely suffice from a cleanliness perspective. Mealtimes and diaper changes may sometimes create an unanticipated need for a bath. Some parents prefer to maintain the routine of a daily bath.

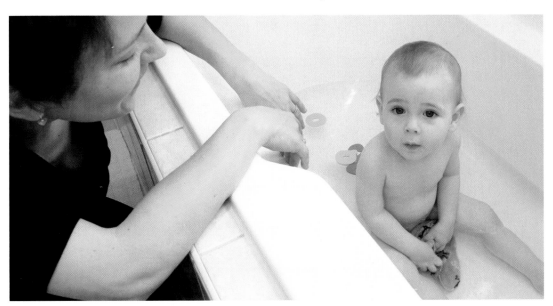

Did You Know?

Bath water temperature

Most homes have their hot water set at 140°F (60°C), but for bathing your child, the ideal water temperature should be no higher than 97°F to 100°F (36°C to 38°C) and at a level that is comfortable for your child. Reset your water heater to 120°F (49°C) or lower —140°F (60°C) water can burn a child's skin in seconds

Anti-scald devices that reduce the flow of water to a trickle when the water is hot can be placed on your faucets. Some parents purchase water thermometers to measure the bath temperature. You can use your hand to test the water before allowing your toddler to get in. If you have a single faucet, after you run the bath, run cold water through the tap so the spout is no longer burning hot in case your toddler inadvertently touches it. It can be fun to place a bright, colorful cover over the faucet to prevent burns or bumps. Do not run the water while the child is in the bath.

Guide to

Bathing safety

Toddlers can drown quietly and quickly in as little as 2 inches (5 cm) of water. Once your child is in the bath, you should never leave him unsupervised; in fact, you should be within one arm's length at all times.

- Prepare everything in advance. Assemble all the equipment you might need while your child is in the bath: towel, pajamas, soap, shampoo, washcloth, and diaper, even the telephone, but nothing electrical, such as a radio or heater. If the doorbell or the telephone rings and you need to answer it, take your toddler out of the bath, wrap him in a towel, and take him with you.
- Make sure the environment is safe. Use a small amount of warm water at waist level when your child is sitting. Put a non-slip mat on the bottom of your tub. Do not use bath seats or rings in the tub. Toddlers can topple over or try to climb out and get stuck. Many drownings and near drownings have occurred when parents assumed that their toddlers were safe in a bath seat or ring without appropriate supervision.
- Take proper care of squeeze toys. These toys can retain water inside, which can lead to the development of fungus. Make sure you squeeze all the water out of them after the bath.

Self-care

There is a wide range of self-care behavior that you may encounter in your child's second year. "Me do it" may be a commonly heard anthem in your home as your toddler adamantly refuses all help and struggles to put on her socks.

Initially, it is hard to adjust to the fact that your dependent infant may be capable of starting to care for herself. You may just naturally perform the activities of daily living for your toddler without even thinking. This way, you are less likely to encounter inside-out shirts and ghastly color combinations. And, of course, it will allow you to stay on schedule. Nevertheless, even though it might complicate your day, it is important to start encouraging and fostering independence.

Keep in mind the following tips when promoting self-care skills:

- **Have realistic expectations.** Your toddler should be able to help with undressing. She will be able to use utensils, but it will be a messy business.
- **Take turns.** Let your toddler practice brushing her teeth, then let Mommy or Daddy have a turn. Toddlers still need lots of supervision and attention and are not capable of doing an adequate job of brushing their teeth without help. Keep a watchful eye as she experiments with her newfound independence.
- **Facilitate the process.** Slip-on pants, Velcro fasteners on shoes, shirts without buttons, and disposable electric toothbrushes can help put your toddler on the road to self-sufficiency.
- **Provide encouragement.** Resist the urge to jump in and help, take over, and redo the job. These are proud moments in your toddler's life — even if the moments seem like hours!

Pacifying habits

Now is the time to evaluate the habits your child has developed to pacify herself, including the use of a pacifier and thumb sucking.

Pacifiers

Surveys show that more than 50% of babies use pacifiers. If your toddler is still using a pacifier, you have undoubtedly experienced the ups and downs of pacifier life. You survived the first few months, when you had to get up a few times every night specifically to find the pacifier and put it back in her mouth. You may have found yourself driving the car with one hand and reaching blindly around the back of your seat with aching arm muscles to search for a dropped pacifier. You have most certainly had to unexpectedly and creatively replace a missing pacifier or clean a dirty one.

So what now? What are the risks and benefits of using a pacifier? And when and how do you get rid of it?

Guide to

Pacifier care

- To prevent choking caused by placing the entire pacifier in the mouth, make sure that the pacifier is the correct size for your toddler's age.
- Now that your child has teeth, he may chew on the pacifier. Discourage this behavior and check pacifiers for holes. Throw them out if they are perforated.
- Remove hair, lint, and cotton caught at the base by stretching out the nipple. This is also a good way to look for perforations and tears.
- Sterilize new pacifiers by placing them in boiling water for 5 minutes and then letting them cool down before they are used. After that, wash them under hot soapy water or run them through the dishwasher to clean them. Do not clean them by putting them in your own mouth, which is full of germs.
- Never tie a pacifier around a child's neck, because this can cause accidental strangling. If necessary, you can use a clip with a short ribbon.
- Do not dip the pacifier in sugar or honey. This can contribute to the development of cavities.

HOW TO
Wean your toddler from a pacifier

There is no right or wrong way or exact time to get rid of your child's soother. Many parents start planning to get rid of it after their child's first birthday. For those who are taking their time, be sure to do away with the pacifier well before the permanent teeth arrive.

Once you decide to take the pacifier away, you will usually need to endure a few difficult days and nights. When you decide to do it, make sure you are ready to deal with the potential fallout. For example, you may want to wait until you are not too stressed, and well in advance of the arrival of a new sibling.

1. Cut back the settings in which your toddler is allowed to use the pacifier. For example, don't permit him to use it outside the house, or restrict use to times when he is in bed.

2. Get rid of all the soothers stashed away around the house and in pockets of clothing.

3. Use a reward chart or star calendar for positive reinforcement.

4. "Trade" the soothers in at the toy store, leave them under the pillow for the tooth fairy, or cut off the tips and claim they are broken.

5. Go cold turkey.

6. Do not tease or embarrass your child into getting rid of the pacifier.

7. Do encourage him and tell him how proud you are of this significant achievement.

8. Once you've got rid of them, don't give in to the inevitable request to get them back!

Risks and benefits

There is considerable controversy about the value and safety of using pacifiers. Sucking on a pacifier is clearly helpful during painful procedures and for self-soothing. Sucking on a pacifier is less problematic than thumb sucking because it causes fewer dental problems and you can more easily wean a child from the habit when the time is right. Recent evidence also suggests that pacifier use when an infant is falling asleep does appear to reduce the risk of sudden infant death syndrome.

Some authorities suggest, however, that pacifiers can increase the risk of health complications. Current studies indicate that long and frequent use may be one of many risk factors for ear infections. Dental cavities are associated with pacifier use beyond age 5, or at any age if inappropriately sweetened. Dental associations recommend that, at the very latest, the pacifier habit should be stopped around age 4 or 5, before the permanent teeth arrive (around age 6 or 7). Frequent pacifier use may cause the top two front teeth to protrude (buck teeth) or may open the gap between the upper and lower teeth (overbite). Pacifiers can also be contaminated with germs and yeasts, but there is no good proof that they actually cause infections in children.

Thumb sucking

Like sucking on a pacifier, thumb sucking can cause buck teeth and an overbite. Chronic thumb suckers may also develop thickened skin on their thumbs. None of these complications are permanent. They will go away once your toddler stops sucking.

You can't really control the fact that your child decided to suck her thumb, nor can you get rid of her thumb like you can a pacifier! You will need her cooperation to kick the habit. The good news is that most children stop sucking on their own due to peer pressure once they are in school. If your child doesn't stop on her own, you should try to break the habit around age 4 or 5, before the permanent teeth come in (around age 6 or 7).

Guide to

Stopping thumb sucking

- Never coerce your child to cooperate. Do not press the issue by using forceful methods, such as pulling the finger out of your child's mouth. This will only reinforce and encourage the behavior.
- Avoid teasing or embarrassing your child to try to get him to stop thumb sucking.
- Use encouragement and positive reinforcement, such as a reward chart or star calendar. Every day that he refrains from sucking is rewarded with a star. Discuss an appropriate reward for when he has gone for a few weeks with stars pasted on every day of the calendar.
- Try to distract your child and keep him busy. Some children suck their thumb when they're bored. Avoid activities that stimulate the behavior, such as watching television.
- Many children are not even aware of the fact that they're sucking their thumb. Use an adhesive strip or bitter-tasting medicine to remind him not to suck his thumb.

- Nighttime sucking will be difficult to stop. You can try applying a sock or glove to the child's hand.
- Enlist the help of your doctor or dentist to encourage your child to give up the habit because he is "growing up."
- Buy a book or take one out from the library that you can read to him about breaking the habit.
- As a very last resort, your dentist can make a plate that prevents thumb sucking.

Grooming your toddler

You may have personal and religious preferences about the timing and approach to the first haircut, but toddlers may need a haircut around their first birthday. Regardless of when you decide or need to cut her hair, your toddler may not be as thrilled by the experience as you are. She may be afraid of being in a foreign place and hearing other children crying or the howl of the dryer.

Haircut options

To avoid a hair-raising experience, you may want to go to a shop that specializes in children's haircuts. These shops usually have toys, books, and videos to distract your toddler, and the employees won't be disturbed by crying. You can also try taking her with you when you get your own hair cut. Some adult salons or barbers will cut children's hair for free or at a reduced rate.

Some parents cut their own children's hair — the price is certainly right, even if the bangs aren't always exactly straight! And chances are that at least once or twice an unscheduled snip will be performed by a friend or a sibling.

Guide to

Your toddler's first haircut

- Give your toddler a preview. Take him along for the ride when you get a haircut, pretend to cut a doll's hair, or just explain the process.
- You may want to call it a trim rather than a cut, which may sound painful to a toddler.
- Make sure you take your toddler to the shop at a time when he isn't overtired or hungry, and make an appointment, so you aren't sitting around waiting.
- You may need to have him sit on your lap to keep him still.
- Bring an extra shirt for him because he may refuse to wear a smock, and the hair fragments can be very itchy.
- Bring a small envelope to keep a lock of hair.
- Bribery is sometimes helpful. You may want to promise a small reward for when he is done.
- Communicate clearly with the hairdresser about what you are looking for — not everyone has the same definition of "short."
- Be prepared for an immediate transformation of his appearance and say farewell to his baby look.
- Don't be disappointed if it's not the greatest haircut. Cutting the hair of a moving target is no easy feat.

Teething time

During your toddler's second year, it may seem like the tooth fairy is working overtime and that your child is forever teething. Rest assured that she is getting close to having her full complement of 20 baby (primary) teeth, 10 on top and 10 on the bottom. This usually happens by the end of the third year of life.

Teething patterns

Like all aspects of your toddler's development, there is wide variation in the timing of when teeth appear. On average, the first tooth appears at about 7 months. If there is no sign of any teeth after the first birthday, this is worth discussing with your health-care professional at the 1-year checkup.

The following table shows the age at which the primary teeth usually erupt.

Eruption pattern

Upper jaw

Tooth	Eruption
Central incisor	7–12 months
Lateral incisor	9–13 months
Canine	16–22 months
First molar	13–19 months
Second molar	25–33 months

Lower jaw

Tooth	Eruption
Central incisor	6–10 months
Lateral incisor	7–16 months
Canine	16–23 months
First molar	12–18 months
Second molar	20–31 months

Teething symptoms

Many doctors have said words to the effect that teething produces nothing but teeth. This may not be entirely true, but it speaks to the fact that teething has been incorrectly blamed for all kinds of symptoms and behaviors in the first few years of life. Some symptoms commonly attributed to teething include diarrhea, fever, drooling, irritability, sleep disturbances, runny nose, congestion, flushed cheeks, and rashes. And the list of symptoms goes on.

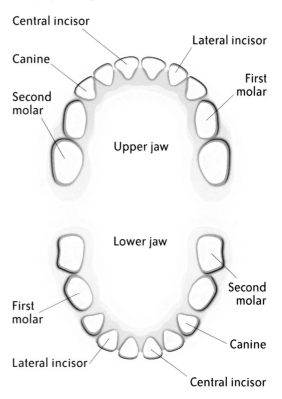

Central incisor
Lateral incisor
Canine
First molar
Second molar
Upper jaw

Lower jaw
First molar
Second molar
Lateral incisor
Central incisor
Canine

Part of the challenge is that colds, fevers, and diarrhea are so common in toddlers that they can coincide with tooth development purely by chance. Studies have looked at large groups of teething children to see what symptoms can be attributed to the teething process. These studies have shown varying results, but one thing is clear: no toddler had a high fever or was very sick from teething alone. If your child seems ill or feverish, do not delay in seeking medical attention, and don't feel comfortable attributing her symptoms to teething.

Tooth care

Even though the baby teeth will ultimately be replaced by the permanent teeth, they still need to be very well cared for. The primary teeth are important for giving shape to a child's face, helping her learn to eat and speak, and guiding the permanent teeth into the proper position.

Early hygiene habits set the stage for a lifetime of good oral health. Inadequate care of the teeth at this early age can lead to painful complications, such as cavities and dental infections, as well as poor aesthetics.

Brushing technique

Brush the teeth "2 for 2" — twice a day for 2 minutes each time. Brush the tongue too — this helps get rid of bacteria that accumulate there. Use a toothbrush with soft, rounded bristles that is the right size

---

Guide to

Treating teething symptoms

Here are a few basic do's and don'ts for managing teething time.

DO
- Nothing at all if your child is not bothered by teething. Many parents look in their child's mouth only to discover that they have acquired a new tooth without a single symptom.
- Massage the gums with a clean finger or a wet gauze pad to encourage tooth eruption . . . if your child permits!
- Soothe the gums with cold items, such as a teething ring, a small cool spoon, or a clean wet washcloth placed in the freezer for 30 minutes.

- Give acetaminophen or ibuprofen occasionally if you think your child is uncomfortable. If you are giving it at night, make sure to give it before he brushes his teeth.

DON'T
- Apply topical painkillers, such as teething gels. They have potential side effects and are not very effective.
- Give teething biscuits. They may contain sugar.
- Use homeopathic teething therapies unless you know exactly what they contain. Their contents are not always clearly stated and they may contain toxic elements, such as mercury and lead.
- Ignore serious medical symptoms because you attribute them to teething.

for your child's mouth and replace it three to four times a year, especially if the bristles are flattened out.

Some experts recommend not using toothpaste with fluoride until your child is 2 or 3 years old, while others are okay with it as long as you use only a small, pea-sized amount and encourage your toddler to spit it out rather than swallowing. Too much fluoride can cause fluorosis (for more information, see page 180). If you wish, you can purchase a fluoride-free toothpaste. If your child doesn't like the taste of toothpaste, you can simply wet the bristles of the brush with water alone.

Did You Know?

Bottle caries

Dental caries, also known as cavities, can develop predominantly in the upper two front teeth and primary molars in toddlers who bottle-feed. Prolonged contact with the sugar in milk and juices can cause decay. This common condition can seriously affect a child's appearance and dental function.

To prevent this serious health problem, try these strategies:

- No bottle, no caries. Try to wean your child from the bottle to a cup as soon as possible, ideally by the first birthday. You can go straight from the breast to a cup.
- No bottle in bed. If your toddler lies with the bottle in his mouth, the sugar in the milk or juice will cause his teeth to decay. If your child really needs a bottle in bed, just give him plain water.
- Brush his teeth before bed. Make sure not to give him anything but water after you brush his teeth. This includes breast milk. If you breast-feed, try to brush your toddler's teeth before he goes to sleep.
- Reduce the juice. Juice — including the "all natural, no added sugar" kind — is very high in sugar. Dentists call it liquid candy! Give juice in a cup only, and try to restrict consumption to no more than 4 ounces, or $\frac{1}{2}$ cup (125 mL), a day. You can dilute juice to half- or even quarter-strength with water to cut down on the sugar content.
- Never sweeten a soother or put a child's soother in your own mouth.

Equipping your toddler

When it comes to making sure that you have all the paraphernalia required to look after your toddler, the options can be overwhelming — and expensive! Those responsible for marketing these products know that as parents we only want the best for our children, and they're not afraid to use a little emotional blackmail to encourage you to buy, buy, buy. Nevertheless, you shouldn't have to build up credit card debt in the process. A few tips will help you make sure that your purchases will be smart, safe, and economical.

Sleeping

The importance of a good night's sleep cannot be overemphasized. Both parent and toddler will be far better off if sleep is undisturbed. This is so important that we have devoted a full chapter (see Part 6) to dealing with some of the common problems that crop up. What follows gives a bit of guidance on choosing a crib or a bed and keeping your toddler in it.

Cribs or beds

When should you move your toddler into a bed? Not until you absolutely have to! A crib is the best way to contain a very active toddler during the quiet time of sleep and naps. Do not succumb to peer pressure. Most toddlers make this move sometime

between 18 months and 3 years. There is no age limit for this transition, but parental guidance is required.

CONSIDER MAKING THE TRANSITION FROM CRIB TO BED

- When your toddler can get out of the crib by herself or you catch her straddling the crib rail. Make sure you have lowered the crib mattress as far as it will go. You can eliminate bumper pads and stuffed toys from the crib if your toddler climbs on them to help her escape. You might also consider acquiring a crib tent that stretches over the top of the crib.
- When your child exceeds the weight and height limit set by the manufacturer. This is usually around 50 pounds (23 kg) in weight and 36 inches (91 cm) in length.
- When your child is toilet trained, if she is going to the bathroom without assistance.
- When your child repeatedly expresses a desire to move into a bed.
- When you have another baby on the way. Most parents do not want to buy a second crib — they're expensive.

HOW TO
Keep your toddler in bed

Some children don't realize that they can get out of a bed on their own and will still call a caregiver to come get them when they wake up. Other children are very quick to get out of bed and reluctant to stay put. Here are some strategies to deal with this challenging problem:

1. Provide positive reinforcement with star calendars and rewards.

2. Consistently condition the child's behavior by taking him back to his room every time he gets up and making it clear that he must sleep in his new bed.

3. Fasten a gate to the child's bedroom door to prevent him from leaving, or simply close the door.

Some parents feel comfortable bringing their child into their own room to sleep. If you choose to take this route, it may be a tough habit to break.

Making the transition from crib to bed

Make the transition as exciting as possible. Involve your child. Let him help select the bed and new bedding, get a book on moving to a new bed, have a party celebrating the change, or make a big deal about having your toddler show guests his new "big-boy bed."

Consider the timing. Try not to piggyback the move from crib to bed onto other firsts, such as the first day of preschool. If you are expecting a new baby, try to make the change a few months in advance. Your child may be changing rooms, as well as graduating to a big bed.

Stick with the usual bedtime routine. Now that accommodations are more spacious, avoid the temptation to lie down with your child while he falls asleep. This is an incredibly hard habit to break once the routine gets established.

Choosing a bed

As an initial move, you can take out the crib mattress and place it on the floor. This can be especially helpful if you were caught off guard when your child climbed out of her crib on her own and you don't have an alternative bed or bed rail. Some cribs will transform into daybeds.

Beds specifically designed for toddlers are also available. They are lower to the ground than standard beds and are smaller (good only up to 50 pounds/23 kg), less expensive intermediary beds that have built-in side rails. While they are fun to look at, it won't be long before your toddler has outgrown the bed and you need to make another big purchase.

If you buy a twin or double bed, be sure to purchase a guardrail for each side of the bed that is not adjacent to a wall to prevent the child from rolling off the bed. Children should not sleep on the top level of a bunk bed until they are 6 years old.

Walking

Toddlers' shoes can be very cute — and pricey. Remember, these shoes were made for walking!

Choosing shoes

Children do not need to wear shoes until they are walking well. Shoes are not necessary for arch support or foot development. Barefoot certainly works well in the house and helps develop good toe grip and muscle strength. Non-slip socks or soft-soled, flexible, slip-on baby moccasins work well until you need to invest in the first pair of walking shoes. When she is taking her first steps, footwear is only required to keep the feet protected, dry, and warm. You'll be spending plenty on footwear in the years to come, so don't waste too much at this stage.

Traveling

You and your stroller are going to be spending a lot of time together. You need this to be a happy relationship free of frustration and hassle. Here are a few things to think about before you make your choice.

Guide to

Buying the first pair of shoes

- Bring your toddler with you when you're buying shoes.
- Buy the proper size. Children's feet grow quickly, and shoes should fit properly. When standing up, there should be about $\frac{1}{2}$ inch (1 cm) between the big toe and the tip of the shoe. Children often need a full size larger in boots than they need in shoes.
- Try not to buy shoes to "grow into" because they may make it easier for him to trip. Remember that children's feet grow quickly. They will often need a few pairs of shoes a year, so take this into consideration when you're thinking of purchasing an expensive pair.
- Avoid used shoes that have lost their shape.
- Ankle boots do not necessarily provide more support than low-cut shoes, but they are more difficult for your child to remove.
- Avoid laces whenever possible. They often untie and are a tripping hazard.
- Be prepared. Your toddler may not share your excitement about this milestone.

Choosing a stroller

This is a costly item, so don't rush into making a decision. Go to the store and try out a few for size. Think about where you are going to use it most and which features are most important to you. No particular stroller will meet all your needs, so make sure you are buying the right one for your family. If you have more than one child, you may want to consider buying a double stroller.

WHEN CHOOSING A STROLLER, CONSIDER

- **Portability and bulkiness:** Are you going to take it shopping? If so, is it easy to navigate in the aisles of stores, or will it behave like a bull in a china shop? If you want to take it in your car, does it fit easily without requiring dismantling and causing unnecessary frustration and stress? Are you going to use it for air travel? If so, is it easily collapsible with one hand so you can take it all the way to the gate? How big is it? Will it fit in your trunk if you have lots of other luggage?
- **Size:** How heavy is it to push or pick up? Some strollers can weigh as much as 35 pounds (16 kg). What is the size limit? Make sure that your toddler is not going to grow out of it anytime soon.
- **Wheels and maneuverability:** Do you need all-terrain wheels? Will you be using it on sandy or snowy surfaces? Can you push it with one hand? How does it take corners? Is the handle bar adjustable?
- **Price:** There isn't a great market in used strollers, so you may not want to pay any more than you have to. How expensive is it? Take into consideration all the extras, such as a rain shield, the adapter for a car seat (if there is one), and cupholders.
- **Storage room:** Make sure you have room somewhere in the stroller to store

what you will need to carry — especially if you use it for shopping. You don't want to have to be a pack mule in addition to concentrating on safely maneuvering your family through doors and along aisles.

- **Safety and durability:** Check consumer reviews. Is the fabric stain-resistant? Is the seat cover removable and washable?

WHEN CHOOSING A DOUBLE STROLLER, CONSIDER

- **Fit:** Will your older child still go into the stroller? If not, does your single stroller have a buggy board attachment that your older child can stand on if she gets tired of walking? Are there other vehicles that would better suit your needs, such as a wagon or a double jogging stroller?
- **Price:** Consider buying a secondhand stroller if price is an issue, especially if you don't think you will need it that often.
- **Seating:** Do you want a side-to-side or front-to-back (tandem) stroller, with or without upper and lower levels (stadium seating)? Side-to-side strollers can be difficult to fit through doors, although they will generally squeeze through most doors. Some parents say that front-to-back strollers are more difficult to maneuver and are challenging because children argue about who gets the front seat. Double umbrella strollers are the most portable and compact if this is an issue.

Eating

You need the right equipment to maximize your chances of transferring the meal you have lovingly prepared (or at least some of it) from table to tummy.

Booster seats

Your toddler may be getting too big for or may be refusing to sit in her high chair. If so, a booster seat is a practical next step. These seats attach securely to a regular kitchen or dining-room chair. They often have a removable tray. Security straps are a must for safety. The seat can be pulled up to the dinner table so your child can join the rest of the family at mealtime. They are much more portable and easier to clean than a high chair — some trays go straight into a dishwasher. And when you're eating out, the booster seat is easy to pack in with the rest of your equipment.

Dishes, cups, and cutlery

Think non-breakable, easy to clean, and not dangerous as your three basic principles in this department. Choices are wide-ranging. The bowls, plates, and cups should have a broad base to minimize unintentional flipping over, but there isn't much you can do to avoid the intentional flips! Some parents like to try dishes with suction cups on the bottom to stabilize the dish on the tray, but be warned that many suction cups don't stick particularly well.

The most important component of the toddler's cutlery set is undoubtedly the spoon — a nice short handle and a biggish bowl tend to work best, and you'll need a few of them. The knives and forks are less useful; just make sure that they're blunt and can't do any damage.

Perhaps the most useful piece of equipment is the newspaper or plastic sheet you lay out under the chair to catch all the spills and minimize the cleanup after meals!

Choosing a good caregiver

It may be hard to believe that the time has come for you to return to work — work outside the home, that is! There is no question that being at home with your toddler is one of the most demanding jobs around. While some parents are able to stay home with their children, many return to work on either a full- or part-time basis at some point in their child's early years. Some parents feel ready to go, craving uninterrupted adult conversation and a hot cup of coffee on their own time. Other parents wish they could extend their leave, unable to imagine leaving the important task of child rearing in someone else's hands.

Parents' separation anxiety

Finding an appropriate child-care provider for your toddler often causes more anxiety and guilt than your actual return to work. This is natural. We all want the best for our children and view their separation from us as caregivers with trepidation.

Rest assured that no one can ever take your place as your toddler's parent. After all, you're not looking for someone to replace you. Rather, your goal should be to find a person or service to complement your parenting by providing a loving, caring, stimulating environment, with learning opportunities appropriate to your toddler's age, for the hours that you cannot be with her.

There's no "best" child-care option. There are many choices. Parents are generally very creative in finding a unique solution that works for them.

Family members

Some people are lucky enough to have a grandparent or other family member willing to care for their child while they are away at work. This situation can be ideal: the financial savings are considerable, the schedule of child care can potentially be very flexible, and you can feel confident that love, devotion, and common values are being shared.

Did You Know?

Grandfather knows best

You need to clearly explain your philosophy of child rearing to caregivers, especially if your caregiver is also a family member. This is where working with a relative — mixing family with business affairs, so to speak — can be tricky. The grandparent may believe he knows what is best for your toddler. Yes, he may have some helpful tips, but he may have ideas about discipline, for example, that don't match yours. You are, after all, his daughter and have no doubt had disagreements with him in the past, but the bottom line is that you are your child's parent. Your wishes need to be respected for this working relationship to thrive.

There are, however, several factors to consider before asking a family member to provide daycare.

Is the family member physically able to look after a toddler? Toddlers are busy bees, taking a physical and emotional toll even on the most youthful caregiver. It may have been a long time since grandparents cared for a little one. Suggest that they take a course on first aid and refresh their knowledge of how to treat mild illnesses. These practices have changed over time. If your child's time will be split between two different relatives, ensure that there is consistency in the "rules."

Making arrangements

Determine ahead of time where your toddler will be cared for. Will you drop her off at Grandma's house in the morning, or will Grandma arrive at your door? If the care is to be provided at the caregiver's home, help her childproof it to your standards. Make sure that she is equipped with the toddler essentials: a bed for napping, appropriate toys, a booster seat for the table, a potty, and anything else required for a typical day.

It is also wise to provide your relatives with a daily routine, as well as a list of activities and facilities, such as drop-in centers, music classes, and the like, where they can take your child to play and learn. For the grandparent, a schedule may be most welcome.

Transition time

Consider creating a transitional period from your care to your relative's care. Your toddler's relationship with "Grandma who sees me occasionally and who spoils and loves me" will inevitably be different from the relationship with "Grandma who cares for me daily, disciplines me appropriately, and still loves me!" Ensure that both parties are accustomed to each other before your return to work. If handled properly, their new relationship will be a special one and your mind will be at ease, knowing that your toddler is being cared for by a loving member of the family.

Nannies

Hiring a nanny to care for your little one is a popular option among families with two working parents. The nanny cares for your toddler within your own home, eliminating the need for hectic drop-offs and pick-ups at the beginning and end of each day. Your toddler receives one-on-one care, and the nanny is often able to help with light housework and some meal preparation.

Benefits

The one-on-one care provided by a nanny means that your toddler will benefit from the security and consistency derived from individual attention. By the age of 2 to 3 years, your little one needs to be comfortable playing with other youngsters and stimulated with age-appropriate activities. Many experienced nannies are aware of the developmental needs and capabilities of the children under their care. They often become friendly with other nannies in the neighborhood, ensuring that your toddler participates in informal play dates and is exposed to books and toys to stimulate all areas of her development.

Many families like to supplement this activity with music or sports classes, library programs, or other community offerings. Consider how far these programs are from your house to ensure that your nanny will be able to walk or take public transit with your toddler. Additionally, some parents enroll their toddler in a preschool or other more formal prekindergarten learning program, which usually begins at age $2\frac{1}{2}$ or 3 years. Make sure it is realistic for your nanny to bring your toddler and pick her up. You may also want to factor the cost of preschool and other community programs into any economic comparison of child-care options.

Live-in nannies

An important decision prior to hiring a nanny is whether she will live in your house. A live-in nanny is a considerably less expensive option because you are providing her with room and board in partial lieu of payment. You must, however,

Did You Know?

Employer obligations

Remember that even though a live-in nanny is sharing your home, she is not working for you 24 hours a day, 7 days a week. Make sure that you negotiate her work hours and make expectations clear. As with any employee, she should always be treated with respect and compensated appropriately if you return home late at day's end or if she agrees to babysit for you in the evening.

HOW TO
Hire a nanny

Here is a basic job description and employment questionnaire you can use when interviewing nannies. These questions cover not only previous work experience, but also child-rearing and disciplinary techniques and problem-solving skills. Providing your potential employee with a few mock scenarios and assessing her response will give you insight into how she might handle situations that arise in your home. Remember that personal references from someone you trust are very helpful but may not always be available.

Job description
- State number, age, and sex of your children. Note any special needs.
- Specify working hours and any need for flexibility or overtime.
- List key child-care responsibilities (e.g., walking to school, taking to play group).
- List non-child-care responsibilities (e.g., cooking and cleaning), if applicable.
- State preference for a live-in or live-out arrangement.
- Specify vacation time (number of weeks, coincident with employer vacation).
- Request willingness to travel with the family, if applicable.

Employee questionnaire
1. What is your employment history? Dates, employers' names, telephone numbers? Available references? Age of the children looked after? What did you like best and least about those jobs? Why are you leaving your current job?

2. How do you manage common child-care situations? Discipline philosophy and strategies? Present specific scenarios: for example, what would you do if the child was in the bath and you forgot his favorite towel in his bedroom? What would you do if the child didn't want to put her coat on for school and it was cold outside?

3. Do you have first aid and CPR training? Have you ever had an emergency situation while babysitting? How did you handle it? Can you swim?

4. What is your educational background? High school, college, degree in early childhood education?

5. What is your family background? Do you have children of your own? If so, what is your backup care plan for them?

6. What are your recreational interests? How do you spend your free time? Hobbies, sports, clubs?

7. Do you have any health issues? Do you smoke? Do you have any allergies?

8. Where do you live? If you live out, how would you get to work? Will you need a bus pass? Parking space? Do you have a driver's license?

9. What are your salary and benefits expectations? Would you be willing to come for a (paid) trial?

10. Can we call your references? Can we check for any criminal or driving offenses?

be able to provide her with appropriate living conditions (her own bedroom and bathroom, at a minimum) and be comfortable with this living arrangement.

Most people find nannies via word of mouth or through advertisements or reputable agencies. Most live-in nannies are sponsored from other countries, arriving in North America to work, with the ultimate goal of bringing their own families to join them. Many have prior experience working with young children. If you don't have the luxury of meeting the nanny prior to her arrival, be equipped with a list of questions you can ask during a telephone interview.

Live-out nannies

Generally speaking, the role of a live-out nanny is similar to that of a live-in, with the exception that she travels from her home to yours each morning and returns home in the evening. A live-out nanny is generally more expensive than a live-in caregiver, though if you have more than one child, this option may, in fact, be less expensive than daycare arrangements for two.

The nanny's roles should be clearly negotiated and appropriately respected. Will she be able to reach your house each morning in time for you to travel to work? Will you be able to relieve her at day's end in time for her to get home? Is she expected to do housework? Will she make dinner for the kids and get them ready for bed, or is this something that you'd prefer to do once you're home?

Live-out nannies are generally hired locally, allowing you to interview them in person and have them meet your toddler. In addition to considering their answers to

your questions and their discussions with you, note how they interact with your little one. After all, it's your toddler the nanny is being hired to take care of!

Home daycare

An alternative to family care and nannies, home daycare provides care for a small group of children at the care provider's home. Government-licensed home child-care agencies approve home daycare providers. If you find a nurturing care provider who suits your requirements and meets your toddler's needs, a home daycare arrangement can be a wonderful blend of a group care environment and an intimate home setting.

If you go this route, contact licensing agencies in your area to ensure that the center you are considering meets all the required standards. Visit the home with your child to see if there is a good fit — between your child and the caregiver, between your child and other children in the home, and between yourself and the caregiver. Ensure that she has a backup child-care plan to cover her own vacation time or illness. Ask about the age range of the other children and consider whether they will provide an age-appropriate peer group for your toddler. Inquire about the range of activities provided and whether the physical space and equipment is conducive to naps and meals or snacks.

Daycare centers

Daycare centers are popular options for working families. A quality daycare center provides a safe and nurturing environment where children of different ages have the opportunity for play, socialization, exploration, and developmentally appropriate learning. Children are usually separated into age groups, each with legislated caregiver-to-child ratios. The toddlers category, for example, usually encompasses children between 18 months and $2\frac{1}{2}$ years of age, with a ratio of at least one caregiver for every five children. The preschoolers category may cover children from $2\frac{1}{2}$ to 4 years of age, with a lower ratio of one to eight. Provided that the daycare meets quality standards, most parents view this arrangement as an alternative to activities within the community and even to preschool, in effect providing an all-in-one child-care solution. Even a large daycare center can feel very comfortable and warm, while a smaller facility may just not feel right.

Guide to

Choosing a daycare center

CONSIDER THESE ISSUES:
You will need to drop off and pick up your child within the stipulated hours of operation. On the one hand, a facility close to your house will allow either you or your partner to participate in pick-ups and drop-offs. This will mean less time in transit for your toddler. On the other hand, a location close to your workplace will mean you are closer if you receive a call that your little one is sick. If you anticipate that time may be tight at the end of the day, being closer to work may also make it easier to pick up your toddler with time to spare.

If your child is sick and unable to attend the child-care center, you will need to have a backup plan if you can't take time off.

In many communities, the demand for daycare spots is often larger than the supply. Place your name on several waiting lists well in advance of the time you will require care.

Daycare centers can be expensive, but the cost usually decreases as your child gets older. If you are eligible, subsidies or financial assistance may be available at licensed child-care centres. Inquire through your local municipality.

ASK THE DAYCARE MANAGER QUESTIONS ABOUT:
- Licensing (ask to see a copy of the license)
- Adherence to the legislated child-to-caregiver ratios (some centers may even exceed the requirement)
- Requirements for caregiver training, with particular attention to formal schooling in early childhood education
- Staff turnover versus consistency
- Schedules, including at least daily opportunities for outdoor play and an allowance for a naptime, or a quiet time for older toddlers
- Food choices and general nutrition
- References (you may want to speak with other parents whose children now attend the daycare center)

Apart from being armed with appropriate questions, trust your natural instinct about the facility.

Let's play ball

Trying to keep your toddler entertained may sometimes seem like hard work. Here are some tips for easy, safe, economical play options that are fun.

Play groups, play dates, and programs

Community play programs offer an opportunity to get out of the house — which may require motivation when the weather gets cold — meet other caregivers and children in the neighborhood, and build skills. Find out what programs are available in your community — at the library, community center, indoor playgrounds, and play places. Community centers generally have very affordable programs in music, art, and swimming, for example. These are often in high demand, so enroll early. Make sure you choose a time of day that works well for your toddler's schedule. This can be challenging at the toddler stage, when children can be unpredictable about dropping the morning nap. If you have a group of children in your neighborhood, you may want to set up a program that will come to you, such as music classes in the home.

Guide to

Choosing toys

Choose toys for your toddler that are:

- **Safe:** Toys need to be free of small parts, which are significant choking hazards. Small toy pieces, balloons, and marbles are the perfect size to lodge in a child's airway and cause breathing problems that are potentially life-threatening. Toddlers still tend to put things in their mouth as a method of exploration or for relief of teething discomfort. The problem tends to improve a bit when toddlers start to "toddle" and spend more time upright, away from the floor, which can be a minefield of spilled food, lost change, and pieces of toys. Be especially cautious with an older sibling who cannot realistically be expected to keep choking hazards out of reach. Make sure that toys are in good condition, especially if you buy or obtain them secondhand. Toys that are well loved may have sharp broken edges or missing pieces.

- **Developmentally appropriate:** Read the age range listed on the packaging and make sure that toys are developmentally appropriate. Popular toys for this age group include balls, dolls, stacking toys, wooden blocks, telephones, musical instruments, ride-on toys, shape sorters, books, large, non-toxic crayons, cars, trucks, trains, and pop-up toys. Every child's interests are unique. Let your toddler find his own favorites and play with what he finds fun. You do not need to discourage toys that you feel are not gender-appropriate.

Did You Know?

Free from recall

Toys may be recalled by the manufacturer at any time due to safety issues; examples include the presence of lead in the paint or parts that are found to break off easily. Try to stay current on product recalls. In the United States, the Consumer Safety Product Commission (CSPC) can be located at www.cpsc.gov. In Canada, consult Health Canada's consumer product safety website at www.hc-sc.gc.ca.

Less is more

There is considerable pressure today to pack in as many programs as possible to ensure that your toddler is fully stimulated and exposed to all opportunities. However, sometimes less is more. There is nothing wrong with good old-fashioned solo play and play dates, where toddlers get to learn how to entertain themselves and function in a less structured setting. As in most cases, moderation is the key.

Reading

Reading is an important play activity for many different reasons. It develops your toddler's language skills, prepares her for reading by herself, and increases her chances of success at school. Reading requires minimal equipment and can be done in any setting at any time. Best of all, it is a fun activity and a great way for both parents and grandparents to spend quality time with the toddler.

Try to incorporate bedtime stories into your regular nighttime routine. Go on outings to your local library. You can save money and always have a nice variety of books by borrowing from the library. Even babies can get a library card. Public libraries often have excellent children's programs as well. Spend time in your neighborhood bookstore. Many of them have play areas for children with books to read.

Screen time

The American Academy of Pediatrics recommends that children under the age of 2 not watch television. They suggest that children spend time interacting with their caregivers and doing activities that promote brain development, such as talking, playing, singing, and reading. You will likely find this advice challenging in a media-saturated environment, where an abundance of products are marketed to and targeted specifically at this young age group.

If you decide to let your toddler watch television at this age, make sure to practice good habits. Watch the program with her and ensure that the content is appropriate. Discuss with her what she is watching. Never put a television in the child's bedroom. Media should not be used to help a child fall asleep, reward good behavior, or act as a babysitter. Television should not be playing in the background during meal- or playtime — this counts as screen time too.

Did You Know ?

Risks and benefits

There is no good evidence to date about the effect that screen time (television, videos, DVDs, and computer games) has on toddlers — and there's certainly no guarantee that a show will make your child smarter if it has the word "genius" in the title or plays classical music in the background!

Watching educational shows has potential benefits, including role modeling of good behaviors, such as cooperation, manners, and sharing. Simple arithmetic and the alphabet are often nicely presented. But these benefits must be weighed against what we know about the many negative effects of excessive screen time on older children, including obesity, reduced physical activity, and possibly poorer school performance.

HOW TO
Read to your toddler

Choose appropriate books

1. Chunky board books are less likely to get ripped and torn, the pages are easy to turn, and the books are small enough for a child to carry.

2. Books that have only a few words per page and choruses that repeat and rhyme predictably are good choices.

3. Books with favorite characters, baby faces, and pictures of children performing the routine activities of daily living — taking a bath and brushing teeth, for example — are always appealing.

4. Books with durable peek-a-boo flaps or different textures to feel are often a hit.

Encourage reading

1. Let your toddler pick the book and control the pace of the story.

2. Get comfortable with your toddler's short and unpredictable attention span. It may be awhile before you can read a book cover to cover. Be persistent and keep reading as part of your routine. He will get the hang of it eventually.

3. Be prepared to read the same books over and over. Children tend to have favorites and seem never to tire of them!

4. Keep books in an area that is easily accessible to your toddler. If he can reach books, then he may spontaneously bring you one to read — or "read" to his stuffed toys and dolls.

5. Encourage language development while reading by asking questions such as, "What's that?" or "Point to the ducky." As he becomes more familiar with the book, leave out words when you're reading and let him fill in the blanks.

6. Use books and DVDs to facilitate transitions — for example, *Elmo's Potty Time* or *Show Me Your Smile!* (Dora the Explorer goes to the dentist).

Sun, cold, and bugs

If you play with your toddler outdoors, be sure to protect her from the sun, the cold, and the bugs.

Sun

The sun is fun to play in but can also burn a child's vulnerable skin. Bad sunburns and long-term sun exposure without protection have been linked to a higher risk of skin cancer later in life. Children spend lots of time outdoors — 60% to 80% of the cumulative lifetime sun exposure happens before age 18 — and your skin remembers every suntan and burn it ever gets. You will need to protect your toddler's skin during this critical period.

Guide to

Safe fun in the sun

Avoid sun exposure during the peak hours between 10 a.m. and 2 p.m. Stay indoors or in the shade. Encourage your child to drink lots of water to avoid dehydration. Here are a few other tips for safely enjoying time in the sun:

- **Proper attire:** Cover up with sun hats that have wide brims and back flaps, swimwear that has built-in UV protection, and cotton clothing with a tight weave. Bring an extra T-shirt to the pool for your child to wear in the water. Sunglasses should have 100% UVA and UVB protection. Wraparounds are best.

- **Sunscreen:** Apply sunscreen 15 to 30 minutes before you go outside or in the water, and use an SPF (sun protection factor) of at least 15 that has UVA and UVB protection. Cover all sun-exposed areas. Don't forget the tip of the nose, tops of the feet, ears, and the back of the neck. Reapply every 2 hours or after sweating, swimming, or playing with water. Ideally, use a waterproof brand that is designed specifically for children. Apply on cloudy days too — 80% of the sun's rays can penetrate light clouds, mist, and fog. Don't forget that the sun can bounce off surfaces, such as snow and water.

- **Sun shield:** Use a stroller with a canopy, buy a mesh sun net, and attach an umbrella to the stroller or, if at the beach, stick an umbrella in the sand.

- **Lead by example:** Practice safe sun habits yourself! Make sun protection a regular family activity. You can help each other apply sunscreen to various hard-to-reach spots.

HOW TO
Keep warm in winter

Here are some tips for staying warm in cold weather:

1. Dress your toddler in loose layers of safe, warm clothing. If you have layers, you can always take off or add an extra one as the need arises. Try to use an absorbent synthetic fabric next to the skin, then a warmer middle layer, and finally an outer layer. Keep a warm blanket at the bottom of your stroller.

2. Avoid using scarves and remove drawstrings from clothing — they are a risk for strangulation. If you need to use a scarf, tuck it into your child's jacket. It is preferable to use a balaclava or a neck warmer.

3. Protect your child's head, hands, and feet. These parts are especially susceptible to the cold. Buy warm waterproof boots that are not too tight. The boots will likely be a size larger than the child's shoes — the toes should have wiggle room, and you don't want them to be outgrown too quickly. Dry the boots between outings. Avoid extra-thick socks, because they can cut off circulation. Wool or wool blend socks are better than cotton. Choose mittens over gloves because they tend to keep the hands warmer. Mittens have a habit of getting lost, so you may need to buy an extra pair. Attach mittens through the jacket with a string or with mitten clips. Lots of heat gets lost through the head, so it is important to wear a warm hat that is close-fitting and covers the ears. Function before fashion definitely applies when it comes to cold weather!

4. Prepare for the elements. Buy a rain or weather shield for the stroller and have an umbrella handy for protection.

5. Make sure you leave extra time to get out of the house. Winter gear inevitably slows you down, especially at the beginning of the season, when your child may be resistant to getting into a snowsuit or wearing a hat.

6. Stay inside if the weather is extreme; for example, if the temperature is below −13°F (−25°C) or the wind chill is below −15°F (−28°C). To prevent frostbite, watch for signs of it in areas that are particularly vulnerable, such as the cheeks, ears, nose, hands, and feet. Get toddlers out of their clothes and boots quickly if they are wet.

7. Make sure your toddler doesn't stick his tongue on cold metal (yes, it does happen from time to time!).

8. Apply sunscreen to exposed skin, even when it's cloudy or cold.

Cold

At the other end of the heat spectrum, little ones get chilled quickly when out in the cold, especially when they are sitting still in a stroller. They need special protection from the cold.

Bugs

And then there are the bugs. How do we protect our defenseless toddlers from bothersome and potentially dangerous insect bites? Protect, avoid, and repel! In most cases, bites result in an annoying but relatively harmless itchy reaction, but these bites sometimes become infected if scratched, allowing germs to enter through the skin. And some mosquitoes carry an infection called West Nile virus (WNV). If they bite us, they can transmit this infection to humans. While WNV infection is rare in children, it can cause flu-like symptoms or, very rarely, a serious infection, including inflammation of the brain. The peak WNV season in North America is from May to the end of October — just when many families like to go camping.

In tropical countries, the most dangerous and common disease carried by mosquitoes is malaria. You will need to discuss precautions with your doctor if your toddler will be traveling to a country where malaria is a concern.

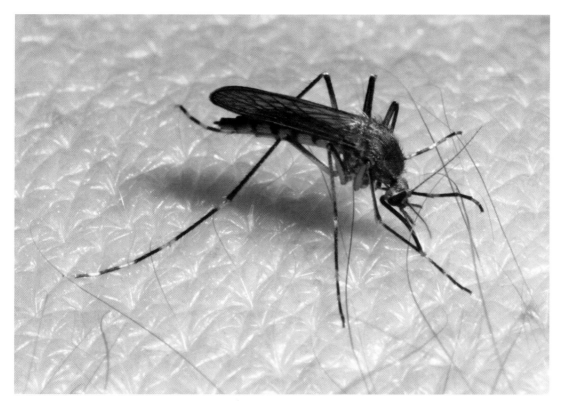

Guide to

Protecting against insect bites

Here are some tips for avoiding insect bites:

- **Choose protective clothing.** Whenever possible, dress your toddler in light-colored, long pants tucked into socks, with a long-sleeved shirt if you anticipate that he will be exposed to mosquitoes or other biting insects.
- **Avoid biting bugs.** Try not to be outdoors during peak mosquito activity time, specifically dusk and dawn. Avoid places where mosquitoes breed and live, such as areas with standing water. Make sure to avoid creating your own breeding grounds. Keep play swimming pools, pails, and other toys that collect water indoors or overturned when not in use. Make sure your windows and doors have tight-fitting screens. Mosquito nets or screens are available if necessary for strollers.
- **Apply insect repellent.** Repellents don't actually kill the mosquitoes, but they do make humans less appealing to the pesky creatures. Make sure to use insect repellent properly. Apply it lightly on healthy exposed skin and not on irritated or sunburned areas. Do not use it under clothes. Apply it in well-ventilated areas. To avoid irritation and ingestion, do not apply on children's hands, mouth, or the area surrounding the eyes. When using it on a child's face, do not spray it on directly but place it on your hands and then apply it. After returning indoors, wash off the repellent with soap and water.

Did You Know?

DEET safety and effectiveness

Insect repellents containing DEET (N,N-diethyl-meta-toluamide) have been proven to be effective for long periods. DEET is available in varying concentrations. The greater the concentration, the longer the duration of action: 10% DEET is effective for about 2 hours, and 24% will protect for as long as 5 hours. Based on American Academy of Pediatrics recommendations, DEET can be used on babies over 3 months of age. Use the lowest concentration necessary to cover your child for the time he will be outdoors. To avoid toxicity, DEET should not be applied more than once a day. Avoid citronella products, products containing lavender oil, and products that combine DEET and sunscreen.

Twin care

For parents of twins, the toddler years are doubly dynamic. Many of the parenting strategies used in caring for single toddlers apply to the care of twins, but there are a few other questions that arise as your twin toddlers show their independence, not only from you, but also from their twin.

Double trouble

Twins generally pick up on each other's emotional cues, so you should expect emotional reactions when one child's behavior sets off similar behavior in the other child. One child seems to get the other child going, potentially resulting in concurrent tantrums, fears, anger, crying, or silliness.

One toddler throwing food can turn into a messy food fight when the other joins in!

Many parents of twins recount how as soon as one child gets upset over something, the other twin often reacts similarly. Dropping twins off at a daycare center can be no hassle until one twin saddens and cries, then the other one cries too.

In these situations, try to address each child's needs, one child at a time. Calm will eventually be restored.

There are also certain benefits to your twins copying each other's behavior when it comes time to learn new developmental skills, such as potty training, writing, reading, and counting. One twin will often help teach the other.

Taking turns

Be prepared to repeat activities, whatever they may be, a second time. Expect that each child will want her turn at switching the lights on or off, shutting or opening the door, and putting the key in the keyhole. You may end up taking two elevator rides up to the doctor's office so that each child can push the button. This can be exasperating.

To avoid doubling your effort, try assigning duties to each child before you begin the task at hand. For example, let one help by planting the flowers while the other one waters the soil, and then switch. Explain to your twins that this time Kim gets to ride next to the window, but on the way home Kelly gets her turn. Whatever the strategy used, and no matter how many times each child wants her turn, remain calm and patient. You are teaching your twins to share your attention and to respect each other's wants. In fact, you may notice that your twins become more willing to share and take turns than singletons of their age because this behavior was instilled so early on.

Separation options

As each twin's unique personality begins to develop and shine, parents are faced with many challenges, including the question of whether to keep their twins together or separate them. There really is no right or wrong answer to this question, but bear in mind the following considerations.

Together

Many twins at this age will play very nicely with each other and remain very close, often complementing each other's personalities. In this case, families may decide to keep them close together, sharing the same room, toys, and clothes (if the same gender) — even sleeping side by side. If the home does not have enough bedrooms for each child, the parents will have no choice but to keep the two together. In preschool or programmed activities, keeping the twins together may make the transition to a new school or program easier for both.

Apart

For other twins at this age, the relationship may diverge. One child may boss the other one around, and regular conflicts may arise. As new friendships with other children develop, one twin may dominate the friendships, leaving the other out. In this case, it may be best to separate the two at home and at preschool.

Parents may feel it is more beneficial to each twin's growth and development if each is given the chance to develop relationships with others without feeling the force of their twin. At home, parents may choose to separate the twins into their own bedrooms, perhaps because they are different genders or because the parents feel it makes the bedtime or sleeping routine less challenging.

HOW TO
Supervise twins in the playground

With toddler twins, venturing out for any occasion can be an exhausting experience for all involved, but a trip to the playground can present quite a challenge. Allow lots of time for getting dressed and loading the kids into a stroller. At this stage, toddlers generally need one-on-one supervision at the playground, so, if possible, bring along someone to help or solicit help from others at the park. Since another pair of hands and eyes may not always be available, you may find some of these strategies useful.

1. Stand back and watch from a distance. Position yourself so you can keep an eye on both children. As one father remarked, "Never get in the middle of them, for you quickly lose sight of the one behind you." He laughs that he lost 10 pounds the summer his twin boys were 2 years old, simply from chasing after them.

2. Avoid open-space parks where you can quickly lose sight of your busy toddlers, as well as parks near bodies of water, unless you have one-on-one supervision. Look for playgrounds that are smaller and perhaps enclosed by a fence.

3. Consider using a stroller harness or leash. A double stroller may be more useful than a wagon at this stage because of the security of the harness straps. If one twin wants to rest, you can strap him in safely while you are with the other one, without worrying about a twin on the loose. For very active twins, some caregivers may opt for the body harness and leash. Although many feel that this is too restrictive, remember that you know your children best of all, and if you feel that a leash will keep them safe, do what's best based on your experience.

When the twins are a bit older, usually at 3 or 4 years, you will find that trips to the playground and park become more manageable, even with one caregiver. Your toddlers can now climb and swing freely without much assistance, and you may even feel that the outing is somewhat relaxing!

Dad's role

As a dad, you want to do something fun with your child. But what exactly can you do with a 1-year-old? Surprisingly, there is a lot to do, and the more you do it outside, the better. Getting out of the house is fun for your child, fun for you, and especially fun for Mom, who gets a break at home. Here are a few ideas of where you can go.

Parks

God bless whoever created parks. Swings and slides, tunnels and sand — kids can play endlessly at your local park. Throw a ball into the mix and your child is good for the morning. You will get bored long before she does.

While playing at the park, some safety rules have to be followed. Your toddler is still learning to walk, so she may not be as good a climber as you think she is.

Swimming

Most parents want their children to learn to swim and not be afraid of the water. You can start taking your child swimming at as early an age as possible. You don't have to swim laps, just have fun in the water. You can carry your child around and splash together, treating the pool like a big bath.

Make sure to bring a couple of swimming diapers. A regular diaper is not an adequate substitute, and, if you use one, your child's bathing suit will swell up like a beach ball.

Despite liking the water, your child cannot swim — she can only

just walk — so hold on to her tightly in and around the pool. Pay attention and don't slack off. Make sure to have a nice warm towel and snacks ready for afterward.

Walk around the block

A walk around the block does wonders. Kids like to explore, and your very own neighborhood is a treasure trove of new sights and sounds. With a bit of luck, you will find another little girl or boy your child's age to play with. Bring the stroller, but try to get your child to walk as much as possible. Don't be surprised, though, if you end up being one of those dads who carry their child while pushing an empty carriage. If you are an energetic dad who likes to exercise, you can multitask by investing in a running stroller and take your little one along as your running partner.

Work as play

Dads need to find at least one particular activity or chore to claim as their own, where they are the go-to guy. One suggestion is the bath. It's easy, especially as your child can now sit and stand independently. You run the bath, make sure that it isn't too warm or too full. Add one child, some soap, and a bunch of toys, and you can't go wrong.

Just be sure to stay vigilant to avoid risks, such as bumping, falling, and even drowning. Give 100% of your attention to this playtime, with absolutely no distractions.

Guide to

Playing at the park

- Always keep your toddler within an arm's length. Don't even think about goofing off with the sports section. At this age, it is unsafe not to be beside your child.
- Make sure your child is protected from the sun. A good hat that doesn't come off easily, long sleeves and pants, and some suntan lotion, preferably applied before you leave, will protect your toddler.
- Don't go to the park without a supply of drinks and snacks. A hungry child is an unhappy child.
- Bring diapers and lots and lots of wipes. While most moms can clean the messiest bums with only a quarter of a wipe, dads may need a few more.

Frequently asked questions

As family doctors and pediatricians, we answer many questions from parents. Here are some of the most frequently asked questions. Be sure to ask your health-care providers any other questions that may arise. If they don't have the answers, they will refer you to a colleague who does.

Q: My 18-month-old daughter likes to play mostly by herself. Is she antisocial?

A: This is completely normal toddler behavior. Typical play at this age is described as solitary play. In the second year of life, most toddlers have little interest in playing with other children. They explore and experiment with the world around them on their own. Toward the end of the second year, they will partake in parallel play. On a "play date," they may stand next to another child, but each one will likely be doing her own thing. Cooperative play — two children playing a game together — will come later. As with all toddler development, it is normal to witness a wide range of behavior when it comes to play. It depends on many factors, including your child's temperament, interests, place in the birth order, and what she's been exposed to.

Q: How do we care for our son's foreskin?

A: The uncircumcised penis does not require any fancy care. Clean the outside of the penis during diaper changes and with soapy water during the bath. It is normal to see a white cheesy discharge (smegma) coming from beneath the foreskin. This is just excess dead skin cells that have sloughed off. Gently wipe it away. Do not retract the foreskin or try to clean underneath with cotton swabs or cleansing agents. This can cause trauma and bleeding. With time, usually by the age of 2 to 5, the foreskin will separate on its own.

Q: Can I use bubble bath with my toddler?

A: Toddlers — and parents — enjoy soaking in bubbly, soapy baths, but bubble bath can dry out and irritate a young child's skin, particularly the outside of the vagina (vulva). Many physicians recommend avoiding bubble bath if your child is prone to urinary tract infections, although there is no medical proof that bubble bath actually causes urinary tract infections. It should also be avoided for children who have eczema or vulval irritation. Use your discretion. If you are using bubble bath, follow the directions and use the appropriate amount rather than letting your toddler control things.

Q: What can I do when my child cries when I try to get the shampoo out?

A: Try the following tips to avoid this common bath scenario:
- Make sure you are using a baby shampoo that won't burn the eyes.

- Have him lie on his back while you get the soap out.
- Try a bath visor or a shampoo rinse cup that forms a tight bond against the forehead.
- Have your child hold a washcloth near his face to absorb any water that rolls down.

Q: When is a good time to introduce a new pet into the family?

A: Having a pet can be rewarding, educational, and fun for children. Make sure the time is right for your family. Be certain you are ready to add the responsibility of another new family member. This will inevitably involve time, money, and dedication for years to come. Avoid transitional periods. It might be overwhelming for a 2-year-old to get a new sibling and a dog at the same time. Avoid impulse buys when it comes to pets, and select a pet that is safe and appropriate for children. Take phobias, allergies, and asthma into consideration. Outline responsibilities at the outset, but it is unrealistic to imagine that your 2-year-old is going to clean the hamster cage or walk the dog. Nevertheless, involve your child in a developmentally appropriate way.

Q: When should we pierce our child's ears?

A: The decision to pierce your child's ears is based on personal choice and cultural practice. Some physicians recommend waiting until your child is at least a few months old and has had her first few shots. Others suggest waiting until the child is between 4 and 8 years of age and can help with self-care. At this age, children are also less likely to choke on small earring parts. You might also consider waiting until your toddler is old enough to decide for herself.

If you decide to go ahead with piercing her ears, make sure to go somewhere reputable that uses sterile equipment and has experience with children. Clean newly pierced ears daily with alcohol applied on a cotton swab and twist the earring to keep it mobile. Keep an eye open for any sign of infection, especially if your child is too young to communicate. Things to look out for include fever, redness, tenderness, or a yellow sticky discharge from around the earring. It takes about 6 weeks for the opening to develop fully.

Q: Is it safe for my toddler to wear jewelry?

A: Make sure you use jewelry safely to avoid choking and strangling hazards. Children should not wear jewelry when they are unsupervised, while sleeping, or in a car seat. Costume jewelry should not be sucked or chewed on, due to the risk of choking and lead contamination. Earrings should be well fastened so that young children can't pull them off, put them in their mouth, and choke. They should not be tight enough to cause pressure and trauma on the earlobe. Hoops and dangling earrings should be avoided, because they can get pulled or catch on things and lead to a torn earlobe. Use good-quality earrings to prevent infection and allergic reactions. Take earrings off at night before the child goes to sleep.

Sam's Diary

February 20 (1 year old)

Sam, new things are happening almost daily now. You are such a smart little guy!

You've cut three new teeth all at once with no problem and will soon have 10 teeth in total. You've suddenly decided that you love climbing the stairs — you've been up and down all day long. You can point out Mom, Dad, and yourself in photos and already know some of your body parts:

hair, head, eyes, ears, teeth, toes. If you're holding a toy while we're putting on your top, you put it in the hand we aren't busy with and then change it over. You also try to pull on your shoes. It's amazing that you're already helping with dressing!

You are determined to feed yourself with your spoon and get extremely frustrated and mad when we try to help you.

You really want to be independent. You're showing your frustration these days by banging yourself on the head. We feel so helpless watching you, as you won't accept help and we can see how desperate you are to be able to achieve your goals. At times, you prostrate yourself on the floor and just cry. We know it's very important to you, and we feel sad that you're so frustrated.

You're having just one nap a day now, and it seems to help you sleep longer at night. The last couple of mornings you've slept until 7 and then been happy to play in your crib for a while after that. It's so nice for Mom and Dad on the weekends!

March 15 (13 months old)

Yesterday you became aware of the moon for the first time. Now that the weather's a bit warmer and it's getting darker later, we've been going for walks in the early evening before your supper. You are enthralled by the moon, pointing and nodding your head and saying "Mmm."

This evening you found your push car and were very proud to show Mom and Dad how you could "walk" it all over the house. You seem much closer to walking these days — you stand for long periods on your own and will walk holding on to one finger. Today, you actually took one and a half steps by yourself!

Other things you love to do: play with your cars, driving them back and forth, making car sounds. Pointing out airplanes and birds. Dancing — Mom loves this! These days you love having a bath — you now use a non-slip mat rather than a bath seat. You give us a sweet, funny smile when we ask you to, and you do a funny thing with your eyes to attract attention, almost like looking up into your head. You are such a nut! You do action songs — even "crying" when one song says, "You can cry if you want to."

April 6 (14 months old)

Well, last week you took your first steps!!! And you're very proud of yourself. You still use your preferred method (walking on your knees) to get around most of the time, but you're taking more and more steps all the time. When we ask you to walk and you don't want to, you sink to your knees. If we try to get you to stand, you shake your head and say "Da." You do best in your own time, with no expectations and when you're unaware that you're being watched.

Feeding Your Toddler

The "right" diet 94

Healthy eating habits 100

Eating skills development 105

Beverage options 107

Essential vitamins and minerals 109

Organic foods 117

Vegetarian diets 119

Food allergies and intolerances 121

Eating issues 125

Frequently asked questions 131

The "right" diet

As the well-known saying puts it, there's some bad news and some good news about feeding your toddler. The bad news is that there is no simple, universal diet guide to feeding an individual child "properly." The good news is that the majority of children will, if offered a range of healthy foods, eat appropriate amounts and extract the nutrition they specifically need to grow and meet their potential. Simply put, a toddler who is active, energetic, and meeting his individual growth pattern is receiving the "right" amount of nutrition — even if his grandmother complains that he never eats!

Nutritional needs

Humans require food for two basic reasons:

1. To provide the fuel our bodies need to perform our daily activities.

2. To provide the building blocks our bodies need to grow.

Like adults, different toddlers require different amounts of food. Unlike adults, who are fully grown, children use nutrients as the building blocks that allow for normal growth. Toddlers are able to extract the nutrients they need — including carbohydrates, protein, fats, minerals, and vitamins — from their food. A caregiver's responsibility is to offer, never force, a balance of healthy foods.

Food as fuel

Rarely do parents complain that their toddler lacks energy. To spend a few hours with a busy toddler is to envy and marvel at his remarkable zest, spirit, and curiosity. The fuel that propels toddlers comes from their diet, which may explain why they have such an affinity for carbohydrates, which are an excellent energy source.

Special toddler needs

It is ironic that during the toddler years, when so much physical and developmental growth occurs, many children become picky

and difficult to feed. Despite this common eating behavior, undernutrition is rarely seen in the developed world. Overnutrition (obesity), however, is becoming a significant health challenge that many people feel will be one of the major health issues in this and future generations. As parents, we want our children to eat as much as we think they should eat — which may be too much. And this can lead to problems.

A toddler has a small stomach, so smaller but more frequent meals may be more appropriate. Children must eat nutrient-rich foods to receive the vitamins and minerals they need to thrive and fend off disease. Sometimes, despite how much our children eat, it is not adequate for their growth and development.

Food guides

One of the best ways to ensure that your toddler has a healthy, balanced diet with the appropriate portion, or serving, size is to follow the nutritional advice in the United States Department of Agriculture (USDA) MyPyramid guidelines or in Eating Well with Canada's Food Guide. MyPyramid divides food into five groups — grains, vegetables, fruits, milk, and meat and beans — while Canada's Food Guide identifies four groups — vegetables and fruit, grain products, milk and alternatives, and meat and alternatives. Canada's Food Guide also provides a list of the recommended number of daily servings from each food group for children age 2 to 3 and age 4 to 8 years.

Eating Well with Canada's Food Guide

Recommended Number of *Food Guide Servings* per Day

	Children			Teens		Adults			
Age in Years	2-3	4-8	9-13	14-18		19-50		51+	
Sex	Girls and Boys			Females	Males	Females	Males	Females	Males
Vegetables and Fruit	4	5	6	7	8	7-8	8-10	7	7
Grain Products	3	4	6	6	7	6-7	8	6	7
Milk and Alternatives	2	2	3-4	3-4	3-4	2	2	3	3
Meat and Alternatives	1	1	1-2	2	3	2	3	2	3

The chart above shows how many Food Guide Servings you need from each of the four food groups every day.

Having the amount and type of food recommended and following the tips in *Canada's Food Guide* will help:

• Meet your needs for vitamins, minerals and other nutrients.
• Reduce your risk of obesity, type 2 diabetes, heart disease, certain types of cancer and osteoporosis.
• Contribute to your overall health and vitality.

For the full guide, please contact Health Canada or visit their website.

What is One Food Guide Serving?
Look at the examples below.

Fresh, frozen or canned vegetables
125 mL (½ cup)

Bread
1 slice (35 g)

Bagel
½ bagel (45 g)

Milk or powdered milk (reconstituted)
250 mL (1 cup)

Cooked fish, shellfish, poultry, lean meat
75 g (2 ½ oz.)/125 mL (½ cup)

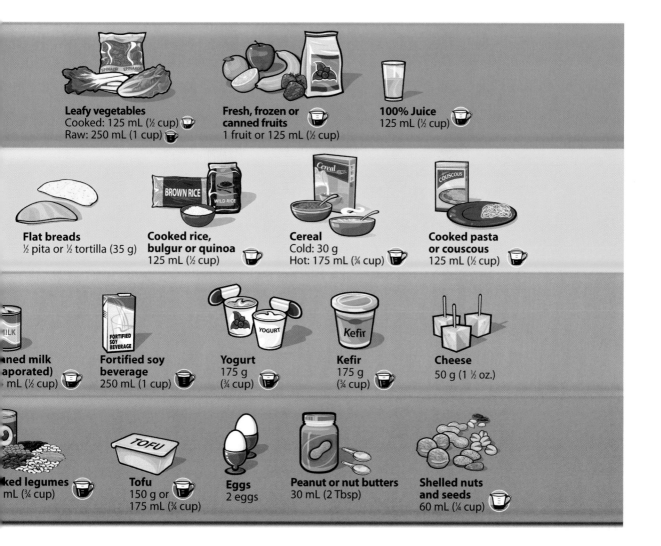

Leafy vegetables
Cooked: 125 mL (½ cup)
Raw: 250 mL (1 cup)

Fresh, frozen or canned fruits
1 fruit or 125 mL (½ cup)

100% Juice
125 mL (½ cup)

Flat breads
½ pita or ½ tortilla (35 g)

Cooked rice, bulgur or quinoa
125 mL (½ cup)

Cereal
Cold: 30 g
Hot: 175 mL (¾ cup)

Cooked pasta or couscous
125 mL (½ cup)

...ned milk (...aporated)
... mL (½ cup)

Fortified soy beverage
250 mL (1 cup)

Yogurt
175 g
(¾ cup)

Kefir
175 g
(¾ cup)

Cheese
50 g (1 ½ oz.)

...ked legumes
... mL (¾ cup)

Tofu
150 g or
175 mL (¾ cup)

Eggs
2 eggs

Peanut or nut butters
30 mL (2 Tbsp)

Shelled nuts and seeds
60 mL (¼ cup)

MyPyramid
STEPS TO A HEALTHIER YOU
MyPyramid.gov

GRAINS	VEGETABLES	FRUITS	MILK	MEAT & BEANS
GRAINS Make half your grains whole	**VEGETABLES** Vary your veggies	**FRUITS** Focus on fruits	**MILK** Get your calcium-rich foods	**MEAT & BEANS** Go lean with protein
Eat at least 3 oz. of whole-grain cereals, breads, crackers, rice, or pasta every day 1 oz. is about 1 slice of bread, about 1 cup of breakfast cereal, or ½ cup of cooked rice, cereal, or pasta	Eat more dark-green veggies like broccoli, spinach, and other dark leafy greens Eat more orange vegetables like carrots and sweetpotatoes Eat more dry beans and peas like pinto beans, kidney beans, and lentils	Eat a variety of fruit Choose fresh, frozen, canned, or dried fruit Go easy on fruit juices	Go low-fat or fat-free when you choose milk, yogurt, and other milk products If you don't or can't consume milk, choose lactose-free products or other calcium sources such as fortified foods and beverages	Choose low-fat or lean meats and poultry Bake it, broil it, or grill it Vary your protein routine — choose more fish, beans, peas, nuts, and seeds

For a 2,000-calorie diet, you need the amounts below from each food group. To find the amounts that are right for you, go to MyPyramid.gov.

Eat 6 oz. every day	Eat 2½ cups every day	Eat 2 cups every day	Get 3 cups every day; for kids aged 2 to 8, it's 2	Eat 5½ oz. every day

Find your balance between food and physical activity

- Be sure to stay within your daily calorie needs.
- Be physically active for at least 30 minutes most days of the week.
- About 60 minutes a day of physical activity may be needed to prevent weight gain.
- For sustaining weight loss, at least 60 to 90 minutes a day of physical activity may be required.
- Children and teenagers should be physically active for 60 minutes every day, or most days.

Know the limits on fats, sugars, and salt (sodium)

- Make most of your fat sources from fish, nuts, and vegetable oils.
- Limit solid fats like butter, stick margarine, shortening, and lard, as well as foods that contain these.
- Check the Nutrition Facts label to keep saturated fats, *trans* fats, and sodium low.
- Choose food and beverages low in added sugars. Added sugars contribute calories with few, if any, nutrients.

MyPyramid.gov
STEPS TO A HEALTHIER YOU

U.S. Department of Agriculture
Center for Nutrition Policy and Promotion
April 2005
CNPP-15

USDA

Healthy eating habits

It is never too early to start building healthy eating habits. How you prepare food and conduct yourself at mealtime will be closely watched by your toddler. Set a good example.

When to eat

There is no "correct" schedule for eating that should be followed by all families. Establishing and maintaining a rigid "three square meals a day" schedule may be difficult. For many families, the pace of life seems to be speeding up. Besides, many toddlers like to graze — that is, eat frequent smaller meals rather than fewer larger meals. This makes sense when you consider that they tend to have smaller stomachs and a faster metabolism than adults. Whatever schedule a family follows, offering a variety of healthy options is more important than when or how often meals occur. Don't be tempted to solve a scheduling problem with prepackaged processed foods; they offer lower-quality nutrition than fresh foods.

Where to eat

Eating meals together as a family offers parents an opportunity to model healthy eating behavior and choices. Toddlers shouldn't be fed while they're running around and playing, as this presents a risk of choking. Food should also not be consumed in front of the television, which has been associated with overeating.

Picky eaters

One of the most common challenges faced by families during the toddler years and beyond is the "picky eater." Many infants are avid eaters. Between 6 and about 12 months of age, they visibly enjoy their meals and will generally welcome new foods into their diets. For many toddlers, this can change quite suddenly at around 12 to 24 months of age. Not only do they seem to be too busy to sit and eat, but the actual amount of food intake decreases. To make things even worse, healthy, nutritious foods, such as fruits, vegetables, and meat, are often rejected for less nutritious refined carbohydrates, such as white bread, crackers, and plain pasta. These picky toddlers often play with their food and eat very slowly.

Does this sound familiar? Your toddler's seemingly low appetite and narrow range of food preferences often become a source of

Did You Know?

First rule for picky eaters

Rest assured that for most toddlers, picky eating behavior is normal. Picky eating requires no intervention, apart from some parental education and understanding. The first rule in handling picky eaters is: Never force your child to eat.

ongoing tension not only between parents and their toddler but also within the extended family. Family members and well-intentioned friends often have strong opinions about how to handle picky eaters!

Appetite changes

There are many reasons why appetite changes in the toddler years. Here are a couple of potential explanations:

GROWTH CHANGES

In the first year of life, children grow very rapidly. In fact, it is considered normal for average-size newborns to triple their birth weight by their first birthday! Thankfully, at no other time in life does weight increase so quickly.

It stands to reason that during this first year of rapid growth and weight gain, appetite is healthy. Simply put, the parts of the brain that control appetite are sending "keep eating" signals to help fuel the growth.

During the next several years, however, weight gain slows considerably. Yearly weight increases of 2 to 4 pounds (1 to 2 kg) are normal. It is reasonable to assume that the parts of the brain that control appetite and satiety — the feeling of fullness — begin to change their message to "slow down eating."

Guide to

Healthy eating habits

While there are no road maps to feeding toddlers, these 12 tips can help them develop good eating habits:

- Be a role model of healthy eating habits. Take the lead and most toddlers will follow.
- Eat meals together as a family. In addition to encouraging good eating habits and allowing you to model eating behaviors, this provides some wonderful family time. Mealtimes should not involve chasing your toddler around with a spoonful of food.
- Whenever possible, serve homemade meals rather than prepared or convenience foods. Encourage eating and snacking on fresh fruit and vegetables by having them cut up, ready to eat, and easily accessible.
- Offer your toddler a variety of healthy foods, regardless of your own likes and dislikes. This is important for maintaining a balanced diet.
- Introduce your toddler to new foods gradually. Studies have shown that some children will eat a new food only after tasting it five or more times.

- Limit your toddler's juice intake: 4 ounces, or $\frac{1}{2}$ cup (125 mL), a day is plenty. Water is a healthy option if she's thirsty.
- Adjust portions to suit your child's comfort level. She can always come back for seconds.
- Don't coerce or force-feed your toddler — this is likely to have the opposite effect of the one you intend. Recognize that needs vary between children, and between meals for a particular child.
- Ensure that you are providing an adequate source of iron in your child's diet, particularly in the case of big milk drinkers. Milk is low in iron, and the iron it does contain is poorly absorbed.
- To minimize overweight and obesity, model healthy, active living by walking, playing, bicycling, or swimming together as a family.
- Don't stand for distractions. The television should not be on during mealtimes.
- Make mealtimes fun. Don't worry about the mess. Get your toddler involved in meal planning and preparation. Ask her to decorate a menu in crayon. Appoint her as the official taster.

BEHAVIOR CHANGES

As most parents are acutely aware, toddlers are stubborn. And part of this stubbornness and defiance is the desire to be independent ("I want to do it myself!") and have some control over their lives. The choice of how much or what they eat is one area over which this control can be exercised. A wise parent will choose not to fight on this battleground.

Did You Know?

Full signals

Some authorities worry that pressuring children to keep on eating ("Please, just finish your plate for Mommy," or "Just one more piece") beyond their point of fullness will, over time, teach them to ignore their satiety signals. This may play a role in the markedly increased rate of obesity we are seeing in children.

Red flags

If your child is active, energetic, and able to keep up with normal activities, he is almost certainly receiving adequate nutrition. And if your child is growing and developing normally, he is almost certainly getting adequate nutrition.

A parent and health-care provider should become concerned when a child's overall energy level decreases or his growth and development decreases abnormally. A chubby infant who has grown into an active yet thinner toddler is not a cause for concern.

Eating skills development

Understanding what your toddler is capable of developmentally will help you manage your expectations when feeding him.

Developmental Milestones

Age	Motor Skills	Social and Personal Skills
1 to 2 years	• Starts to use a spoon and fork • Spills most of his food • Uses his fingers to pick up food (so serve finger foods!) • Drinks from a cup	• May want to feed you • Becomes more independent; too busy to eat • By 18 months, able (and likely) to say "No!" • Able to gesture or ask for food if hungry • Appetite may seem to decrease
2 to 3 years	• Holds cup • Puts spoon in his mouth • Spills a lot • Chews better, but choking is still a concern	• Has definite likes and dislikes • Demands to do things "by myself" • Dawdles over food • May eat only a few different types of foods at times
3 to 4 years	• Holds cup by the handle • Uses a fork • Starts to pour • Can chew most foods	• Appetite may improve • Requests favorite foods • Likes different shapes, colors • Influenced by television ads • Likes to help in the kitchen
4 to 5 years	• Becomes quite good at feeding himself • Uses a knife and fork	• Prefers talking to eating • Peer influence becomes important • Is interested in where food comes from

Adapted by permission from Daina Kalnins and Joanne Saab, *Better Food for Kids* (Toronto: Robert Rose, 2002).

Developing preferences

Parents with strong preconceptions about what their child "should" be eating often struggle as they butt heads with a stubborn toddler whose taste may be vastly different. This is a battle that should not be fought — there won't be any winners.

Each child has his own nutritional requirements and taste preferences. Still, at this stage in your child's development, you may want to expand his food horizons to ensure a well-balanced diet and begin to instill some good eating habits. Bear in mind that it has been shown that some toddlers may need to be offered a new food five or more times before they decide to eat it.

Guide to

Introducing new foods

Here are a few tips to help you convince even the most stubborn toddler to try something new:

- Make the new food look appealing and interesting. Be creative — try different colors, shapes, and sizes. Give it an interesting name, such as "broccoli trees."
- Be a role model. Make sure your toddler sees you and other family members eating and enjoying the new taste of the day.
- Try offering the new food at the beginning of the meal, when your child is likely to be most hungry.
- Add cooked vegetables to a soup; serve raw vegetables with a bit of salad dressing or a dip.
- Offer the new food in small servings to start. Too much of a new food can be intimidating for a little stomach.
- Don't give up too easily! Many children will reject a new food the first time it is offered. Wait a week and try again, or try preparing it in a different way or cut into a different shape. Never force or coerce your child into trying something she doesn't want.

Beverage options

Despite their smaller body size, toddlers have higher fluid requirements than adults. While two-thirds of an adult's body weight is made up of water, three-quarters of a younger child's weight is water. In other words, drinking the "right" amount of liquids is even more important for children than it is for their parents.

Many parents lament the fact that their children don't seem to drink enough. Fortunately, the human body carefully regulates fluid balance to ensure that the right amount of fluid is consumed. The only situation when fluid intake may be less than adequate is during an acute illness, such as gastroenteritis (stomach flu), when vomiting, diarrhea, and fever lead to higher than usual fluid losses. For management of these problems, see Part 9.

Best beverages

Milk, juice, and water are the basic options we have. But some drinks are better than others.

Milk

Milk is an excellent source of protein, as well as key minerals, such as calcium and vitamin D. However, excessive milk intake is associated with iron deficiency and anemia, which is yet another example that too much of a good thing is not a good thing.

Most authorities recommend a maximum of 16 to 20 ounces (500 to 625 mL) of milk daily for toddlers. Note that there is no minimum milk requirement. A child who doesn't like milk should not be forced to drink it, but will need an alternative source of calcium and vitamin D. While full-fat milk (homogenized, or 3.25% milk fat) is generally advised for children between 1 and 2 years of age, parents can choose any milk (2%, 1%, or non-fat) for their children beyond 2 years of age.

Juice and soft drinks

Juice is frequently perceived as healthier than water because it contains vitamins and nutrients not found in water alone. Unfortunately, even natural unsweetened fruit juices generally contain large amounts of sugar, which contributes to dental caries (cavities) and in some toddlers and children

Did You Know?

Thirst center

Parents must trust their toddler's "thirst center," located in the brain. Combined with healthy kidneys, this will regulate the body's fluid status. Just as a healthy child won't forget to breathe, so will a child not forget to drink. The body requires oxygen — we can't survive for more than 3 to 4 minutes without it. Likewise, the body requires water. Without this crucial element, we cannot survive beyond a few days.

Did You Know?

Toddler formulas
Recently, toddler formulas have been introduced to the marketplace. These formulas are meant to follow the infant formulas that are recommended for children under 1 year of age. After 1 year of age, most authorities recommend regular homogenized milk for children. There is no need for healthy children to continue consuming these formulas unless specifically advised to do so by their health-care providers.

may play a role in obesity. The American Academy of Pediatrics recommends *no more* than 4 to 6 ounces (125 to 175 mL) of juice per day for children between 1 and 6 years of age. There is more nutritional value in

eating the whole fruit and drinking regular water than in consuming fruit juice. If you are going to serve juice, consider letting your toddler get used to the taste of it diluted with water from the get-go. Even if you dilute the juice, it is not a good idea to let your toddler sip on it constantly. It is better to drink the full 4 to 6 ounces in one serving and be done with it for the day.

Soft drinks are very high in sugar, as well as other unhealthy ingredients — such as caffeine — and should not be given to young (and even older!) children.

Water

Water is the most suitable thirst-quenching beverage for children. Water will meet a child's fluid requirements without filling them with calories, which are better obtained from eating a variety of healthy foods, such as fruits and vegetables. A child who refuses water is most likely not thirsty — or is attempting to manipulate his parent in the hope of obtaining juice, a soft drink, or milk.

There is no evidence that bottled water is healthier than municipal water supplies (tap water). In addition to having no health advantage, bottled water is clearly less friendly to the environment and a lot more expensive!

Essential vitamins and minerals

The terms "vitamin" and "mineral" refer to parts of the diet that are essential for healthy growth and development. Because the human body cannot make these nutrients, they must be provided in the diet or, in some cases, as supplements. While they account for a very small fraction of a child's total daily food intake, they have many important roles in various body systems. At this age, calcium, vitamin D, and iron are especially important in promoting growth and preventing vitamin and mineral deficiency diseases, such as rickets and anemia.

The ABCs of vitamins and minerals
Essential nutrients at a glance

Vitamin/mineral	Type	Assists in	Sources
Vitamin A (from beta-carotene)	Fat-soluble	Vision, growth, bone development, healthy skin	Liver, eggs, whole milk, dark green leafy vegetables, yellow and orange vegetables, and fruit
Vitamin B_1 (thiamin)	Water-soluble	Enzyme activity, metabolism of nutrients	Oatmeal, enriched breads and grains, rice, dairy products, fish, pork, liver, nuts, legumes
Vitamin B_2 (riboflavin)	Water-soluble	Growth, metabolism of nutrients	Dairy products, eggs, organ meats, enriched breads and grains, green leafy vegetables
Vitamin B_3 (niacin)	Water-soluble	Tissue repair, metabolism of nutrients	Organ meats, peanuts, brewer's yeast, enriched breads and grains, meats, poultry, fish, and nuts
Vitamin B_6 (pyridoxine)	Water-soluble	Metabolism of nutrients (primary role)	Brewer's yeast, wheat germ, pork, liver, whole-grain cereals, potatoes, milk, fruits and vegetables
Folate (part of B vitamin group)	Water-soluble	Growth, enzyme activity, prevents neural tube defects	Liver, lima and kidney beans, dark green leafy vegetables, beef, potatoes, whole wheat bread

Vitamin/ mineral	Type	Assists in	Sources
Vitamin B$_{12}$	Water-soluble	Metabolism of nutrients, prevents anemia	Liver, kidneys, meat, fish, dairy products, eggs
Biotin (part of B vitamin group)	Water-soluble	Enzyme activity; deficiency can lead to a type of dermatitis	Liver, milk, meat, egg yolk, vegetables, fruit, peanuts, brewer's yeast
Vitamin C	Water-soluble	Many cellular functions, promotes healthy teeth, skin and tissue repair	Citrus fruits such as oranges and grapefruit, leafy vegetables, tomatoes, strawberries
Vitamin D	Fat-soluble	Essential for normal growth, development, bones and teeth; helps protect against auto-immune diseases	Liver, butter, fortified milk, fatty fish (fish liver oils), exposure to sunlight
Vitamin E	Fat-soluble	Antioxidant function protects cells; assists neurological function, prevents anemia	Vegetable and fish oils, nuts, seeds, egg yolk, whole grains
Vitamin K	Fat-soluble	Blood clotting	Green leafy vegetables, liver, wheat bran, tomatoes, cheese, egg yolk
Iron	Mineral	Formation of hundreds of proteins and enzymes; it is part of the protein hemoglobin, which carries oxygen from the lungs to the rest of the body's tissues, by way of blood circulation	Liver, meat, chicken, fish, tofu, infant cereal, spinach, lentils, beans, raisins, apricots, nuts
Calcium	Mineral	Signaling within nerves, muscle tissue, and blood vessels; it is the main structural component of bones and teeth	Milk, cheese, yogurt, tofu, broccoli, spinach, chickpeas, beans, nuts, seaweed, sunflower seeds, sesame seeds
Zinc	Mineral	Growth and development, immune, reproductive, and neurological system function; almost 100 enzymes require zinc to function; it is an important part of proteins and cell membranes	Meat, poultry, eggs, dairy products

Adapted by permission from Daina Kalnins and Joanne Saab, *Better Baby Food*, 2nd ed. (Toronto: Robert Rose, 2008).

Calcium

Calcium is the basic building block for bones and teeth. While adequate calcium intake is important at all ages for long-term bone health, the critical periods are during early childhood and during adolescence.

Calcium requirements

For children of 1 to 3 years, the recommended amount of calcium in the diet is 500 mg per day, and in children of 4 to 8 years, it is 800 mg per day. In both cases, this intake of calcium can be met with 2 to 3 servings daily of milk or milk products (such as yogurt and cheese) or other calcium-rich foods (such as calcium-enriched orange juice, rice, and soy beverages). There is no need to take supplements unless recommended by your health-care provider.

Food Sources of Calcium

The following foods contain at least 300 mg of calcium per serving.

Food	Serving
Milk and milk products	
Milk: skim, 1%, 2%, whole (homogenized), lactose-reduced, chocolate	1 cup (250 mL)
Milk: evaporated	½ cup (125 mL)
Milk: powdered	6 tbsp (90 mL)
Ice milk	1 cup (250 mL)
Yogurt: plain or flavored	¾ cup (175 mL)
Yogurt: frozen	1 cup (250 mL)
Cheese: firm (brick, Cheddar, Colby, etc.)	1½ oz (45 g)
Cheese: grated Parmesan	4 tbsp (60 mL)
Cheese: ricotta, regular or light	½ cup (125 mL)
Milk puddings (rice pudding, custard, instant)	1 cup (250 mL)
Non-dairy beverages	
Soy beverage, calcium-fortified	1 cup (250 mL)
Rice beverage, calcium-fortified	1 cup (250 mL)
Orange juice, calcium-fortified	1 cup (250 mL)
Canned fish	
Salmon, with bones	½ can (7½ oz/213 g)
Sardines, with bones	7 medium
Soy-based foods	
Tofu: firm or extra-firm, set with calcium	½ cup (125 mL)
Tofu: silken or regular, set with calcium	1 cup (250 mL)
Soybeans: cooked	2 cups (500 mL)
Soybeans: roasted	1 cup (250 mL)
Vegetables	
Bok choy: cooked	1 cup (250 mL)
Turnip greens: cooked	1 cup (250 mL)
Kale or mustard greens: cooked	1½ cups (375 mL)
Dried seaweed (hijiki, arame, wakame)	1 oz (30 g)

Adapted by permission from Daina Kalnins and Joanne Saab, *Better Food for Kids* (Toronto: Robert Rose, 2002).

Vitamin D

No discussion of calcium is complete without mentioning vitamin D. Vitamin D enables the body to absorb calcium from the diet and allows the absorbed calcium to be used in the formation of bones and teeth. Vitamin D has recently been recognized as playing other roles in the body, potentially preventing many health disorders ranging from some types of cancer to cardiovascular problems and multiple sclerosis.

Vitamin D is unique because it can be ingested in the diet, as well as manufactured as the result of exposing the skin to the sun. (You may have noticed that the definition of "vitamin" states that it must be ingested and not made by the body. In this light, it has been argued that vitamin D is in fact a hormone.) Dietary intake of vitamin D is critical, especially in the far north and far south of the planet, where for much of the year the sun's rays are not strong enough to cause adequate vitamin D to be manufactured. This is also true for individuals who for religious or cultural reasons do not expose much of their skin to the sun and for those who are meticulous about applying sunscreen.

Food Sources of Vitamin D

Here is an analysis of the vitamin D content of foods containing this key nutrient.

Food	Serving	Vitamin D (IU)
Fortified foods		
Milk	1 cup (250 mL)	100
Fortified rice or soy beverage	1 cup (250 mL)	80
Fortified margarine	2 tsp (10 mL)	51
Fortified orange juice	½ cup (125 mL)	45
Eggs		
Egg yolk	1	25
Fish		
Tuna, bluefin: cooked	2½ oz (75 g)	690
Salmon: canned or cooked	2½ oz (75 g)	608
Tuna, skipjack: cooked	2½ oz (75 g)	381
Sardines, Pacific: canned	2½ oz (75 g)	360
Salmon, Atlantic: cooked	2½ oz (75 g)	225
Herring or trout: cooked	2½ oz (75 g)	156
Mackerel: cooked	2½ oz (75 g)	80
Sardines, Atlantic: canned	2½ oz (75 g)	70
Tuna: canned, light or white	2½ oz (75 g)	41

Vitamin D requirements

For children over 1 year of age, the recommended daily requirement of vitamin D is 400 IU, although some authorities feel this may be an underestimate. There are not many foods that naturally contain vitamin D, only fish, liver, and egg yolk. Some beverages, including milk, soy, and orange juice, are vitamin D–fortified, but these may not be easy to find. There's no need to take supplements unless recommended by your health-care provider.

Iron

Iron is an essential component of hemoglobin, the part of the red blood cell that carries oxygen to the important parts of the body. An abnormally low hemoglobin level is called anemia.

Because all body tissues and organs require oxygen to perform their tasks, adequate iron is crucial, especially for children, who are still growing and developing. An anemic child may appear pale and fatigued, and may suffer from behavior and developmental problems. There is evidence to suggest that iron deficiency during the important years of brain development can lead to permanent loss of points in the child's intelligence quotient (IQ) score.

Getting enough iron

For most children who eat a balanced diet, there is no concern about meeting the nutritional requirement for iron. Even the pickiest eaters are able to extract enough iron from their diets. Nevertheless, you may want to take some steps to prevent a deficiency of this mineral. A health-care provider who suspects iron deficiency or

Food Sources of Iron

This analysis of the iron content of common foods provides the total iron in the foods listed, but the availability of the iron will depend on its absorption.

Food	Serving	Iron (mg)
Infant cereal	½ cup (125 mL)	9
Cream of wheat	¾ cup (175 mL)	8
Liver	1½ oz (45 g)	6
Beef, lean: broiled	3½ oz (100 g)	3
Spinach: cooked	½ cup (125 mL)	3
Potato: baked, skin on	6½ oz (190 g)	2
Beans, navy: canned	½ cup (125 mL)	2
Raisins	⅓ cup (75 mL)	1
Avocado	½ medium	1
Chicken, light or dark, no skin	3½ oz (100 g)	1
Halibut	2½ oz (75 g)	1
Whole wheat bread	1 slice	0.7
Strained infant meat	4 tbsp (60 mL)	0.6
Apricots: raw	3 medium	0.6
Broccoli: chopped, cooked	½ cup (125 mL)	0.5
Rice, wild: cooked	½ cup (125 mL)	0.5

Adapted by permission from Daina Kalnins and Joanne Saab, *Better Food for Kids* (Toronto: Robert Rose, 2002).

anemia will likely require blood tests to confirm the diagnosis. Treatment involves dietary counseling for parents, in addition to iron supplementation. Parents of children requiring iron supplements should not be alarmed when they darken the color of their child's stools, which may even look black.

Iron requirements

Children between 1 and 3 years require about 7 mg per day of iron; the requirement increases to 10 mg per day for children 4 to 8 years old. These requirements can be met by eating iron-rich foods. Foods that are rich in iron include meats (beef, lamb, pork, veal, liver, chicken, turkey), fish, eggs, grains and cereals (iron-fortified cereals, whole-grain breads), legumes (chickpeas, lentils, beans, peas), and vegetables (broccoli, spinach, Brussels sprouts). There is no need to take supplements unless recommended by your health-care provider.

Guide to

Preventing iron deficiency and anemia

- Exclusively breast-feed for the first 6 months of life. If you decide to stop breast-feeding, you should use an iron-fortified formula until 12 months of age.
- Introduce iron-rich foods, including fortified cereal and puréed meats, after 6 months.
- Offer a wide variety of foods, because some dietary components (e.g., vitamin C) help with iron absorption.
- Limit juice intake. The American Academy of Pediatrics recommends no more than 6 ounces (175 mL) of juice daily to help encourage the intake of a wider variety of foods.

- After the age of 1 year, offer milk in a cup, not in a bottle.
- In children between 1 and 5 years of age, limit the intake of cow's milk to no more than 20 ounces (625 mL) per day. Cow's milk is a poor source of iron.

This last factor may be the most important. While milk provides an excellent source of protein, calcium, and vitamins, larger volumes of daily milk intake are associated with iron deficiency. And children who drink milk from infant bottles tend to drink more; therefore, an earlier transition from bottle to cup may decrease total milk intake for those toddlers who are reluctant to limit consumption.

Organic foods

"I want only the best for my child." This statement is clearly very close to any parent's heart. Given the knowledge that diet and nutrition play such a key role in a child's health and development, combined with well-publicized concerns about the state of our environment, it is not surprising that organic foods have become far more popular and available in recent years. Between 1990 and 2005, the area of land devoted to organic farming in the United States more than doubled, from one million to more than two million acres. Businesses, both large and small, have jumped on the organic food bandwagon.

Conventionally grown versus organic foods

While the majority of parents perceive organic foods as safer and more nutritious than conventionally grown foods, the term "organically grown" refers to how a food item, such as a fruit, vegetable, or dairy product, is grown and/or processed. It does not necessarily relate to the nutritional content, quality, or safety of the food.

Organic farmers grow and process their food without using synthetic fertilizers or pesticides. In addition, antibiotics and hormones are not used in the production

Guide to

Buying and preparing safe and nutritious food

Regardless of what type of food you ultimately choose, play a proactive role in keeping your children's food as safe as possible. Here are a few tips:

- Buy the freshest foods available. This often means locally grown foods, which do not require lengthy and expensive transportation.
- Check the "best before" dates on all products and avoid dented or bulging cans of food.
- Always wash fruits and vegetables. Use a brush to gently scrub off potential dirt, bacteria, and chemical residues.
- If possible, peel fruits and vegetables and remove the outermost layers of leafy vegetables.
- Offer a variety of fresh fruits and vegetables whenever possible. Most authorities recommend 5 to 9 servings every day.
- Be sure to thoroughly cook foods from animals, such as beef, chicken, and eggs.
- Don't mix uncooked meat with cooked food.
- Wash hands and cooking surfaces thoroughly before preparing any food and between the preparation of various foods.
- Store foods at the correct temperature. Bacteria thrive in warm environments.

of organic meats, poultry, and dairy products. Conventional farming has employed some of the techniques and substances banned from organic methods in an effort to maximize production and improve efficiency. This has generally led to higher crop yields and lower food prices.

Potential toxins

While it may appear obvious that food free of potential toxins is healthier than conventionally grown foods, there are no good studies to prove that children fed organic foods are healthier in the short or long term than children who consume non-organically grown foods. There is also no convincing proof that organic foods are more nutritious than conventional foods.

Despite the lack of clear evidence, many parents, not surprisingly, take comfort in the fact that they are avoiding these chemicals and drugs. The main drawback of organic foods is the cost: they are typically more expensive than conventionally grown foods because of the higher production costs.

Rather than being dismayed by the difficult decision they may face between conventional and organic, parents should feel heartened by the fact that their children can be completely healthy with either choice.

Vegetarian diets

In some parts of the world, vegetarian diets are standard. People are also increasingly adopting vegetarian diets for health, ethical, and environmental reasons. There are several varieties, or levels, of vegetarian diets: semi-vegetarians, lacto-ovo vegetarians, lacto vegetarians, and vegans.

Alternative nutrient sources

While there are some challenges to ensuring adequate nutrition for children on vegetarian diets, these can be overcome with education and careful dietary planning. A consultation with a registered dietitian may be helpful to assess a child's specific diet and ensure that all the caloric and nutritional needs are met.

Iron sources

Iron content can be low in a vegetarian diet that eliminates or restricts meat, especially red meats, which are an excellent source of this mineral. However, many non-meat foods contain iron, including tofu, legumes, dried fruit (prunes, raisins, apricots), cereals, and dark green leafy vegetables. Be sure your vegetarian toddler eats plenty of these foods.

Kinds of Vegetarians

Semi-vegetarians	Tend to avoid red meats but generally eat fish and poultry such as turkey and chicken
Lacto-ovo vegetarians	Eat no meat but do consume eggs and dairy products (this is the most common practice in North America)
Lacto vegetarians	Eat no meat and no eggs but do consume dairy products
Vegans	Eat no animal products (no meat, no fish, no eggs, no dairy products) and consume only plant-derived foods

Did You Know?

Vitamin B_{12} deficiency

Vitamin B_{12} is essential for normal red blood cell production, as well as for the normal functioning of nerve cells. Since vitamin B_{12} is only found in animal products, children receiving vegan diets are particularly at risk of vitamin B_{12} deficiency. Non-meat sources of vitamin B_{12} include cow's milk, eggs, fortified cereals and beverages (including soy beverages), and multivitamin supplements.

Protein sources

Proteins are the building blocks from which many of the body's important tissues are formed. While meats provide an excellent source of protein, a vegetarian diet can meet the protein needs of a growing child. Grains (such as wheat, oats, and quinoa), legumes (such as peas, peanuts, soy products, beans, and lentils) and nuts and seeds are all excellent sources of protein.

Calcium and vitamin D supplements

Calcium intake is not a problem for lacto-vegetarians who drink enough milk. Many plant foods also contain some calcium, but it is poorly absorbed and often very low in quantity. Vegetarian toddlers may need to have calcium-fortified foods or supplements added to their diet. If the child has regular exposure to sunlight, then vitamin D will be produced in the skin. If this is not the case, a vitamin D supplement may be required.

Did You Know?

Vegetarian advantages

There may be some health advantages in adult life as a result of a vegetarian diet. The rates of high blood pressure, heart disease, certain types of cancer, obesity, and adult-onset, or type 2, diabetes are somewhat lowered in vegetarians. Whether these benefits extend to toddler vegetarians is not known but deserves further study.

Food allergies and intolerances

The term "allergy" is often incorrectly used to describe any negative reaction to foods, such as bloating, abdominal cramps, changes in behavior, diarrhea, and some types of skin rashes. Most health-care providers call these symptoms food intolerances, not allergies. Food allergies can cause these same reactions, but also cause other, more serious symptoms.

Allergies

Allergic reactions to food can be mild or serious.

Mild reactions

Mild allergic reactions are typically limited to the skin and usually result in hives. These are quite often itchy and uncomfortable, but on their own they do not represent a danger to the child. Creams and lotions are ineffective, but hives can usually be treated with over-the-counter oral antihistamines.

Anaphylaxis

During a serious allergic reaction, a child may experience swelling of the lips, tongue, or face. This alone can lead to breathing difficulties. In addition, serious allergic reactions can also cause trouble breathing — medically, this is called respiratory distress — resulting from spasm of the bronchial tubes in the lungs, as seen in an asthma attack, which may or may not be accompanied by wheezing, a musical whistling noise heard when trying to exhale. These symptoms are the result of the child's immune system "overreacting" to a protein contained in the food.

The medical term for severe reactions is "anaphylaxis," which is defined as "a serious allergic reaction that is rapid in onset and may cause death." A reaction of this nature demands immediate medical attention.

Diagnosing food allergies

When a food allergy is suspected, a child should be seen by a physician who is specifically trained to diagnose and treat allergies. The diagnosis involves a

Did You Know?

Prevalence

While up to one-third of parents report — or believe — that their child is allergic to certain foods, food allergy actually affects only 6% to 8% of children, often beginning in their second year. Fortunately, most children outgrow food allergies, so the number of adults with food allergies is around 3% to 4%.

Food Allergy Symptoms

The symptoms of food allergies typically occur within minutes of eating and include the following:

Condition	Description
Hives	A blotchy, raised, red, itchy rash, which appears and disappears in random places all over the body
Swelling	Often occurs around the mouth and face
Breathing	Difficult, labored, or noisy breathing
Vomiting	Can occur shortly after ingestion of the allergenic food (but vomiting alone, without the hives and swelling, is not likely to be caused by an allergy)

Adapted by permission from Daina Kalnins and Joanne Saab, *Better Food for Kids* (Toronto: Robert Rose, 2002).

combination of an accurate and detailed history and physical examination, as well as specific skin tests called prick tests, and sometimes blood tests.

MedicAlert

If your child has a serious food allergy, he should wear a MedicAlert bracelet to help identify the problem in case it occurs when he is not accompanied by a family member. Your child's doctor might suggest that he have injectable epinephrine and an antihistamine close at hand at all times. His caregivers at daycare or preschool should be advised of the problem and what is required in the event of an allergic reaction.

COMMON ALLERGENIC FOODS

The most allergenic foods include:
- Cow's milk
- Eggs
- Legumes (especially peanuts and soybeans)
- Tree nuts (almonds, cashews, pecans, pine nuts, pistachios, and walnuts)
- Fish
- Shellfish
- Wheat flour and wheat products

Children with allergies to milk and eggs tend to outgrow them over time, while peanut, tree nut, and shellfish allergies tend to be lifelong. Food additives and food coloring agents are not a common cause of allergies.

Prevention

Can you prevent your child from developing a food allergy? The short answer to this important question is probably not. This is a topic that generates a great deal of medical research and media headlines. The results from different researchers around the world are, unfortunately, contradictory and confusing.

THINGS WE DO KNOW
- Genetics plays a role. A family history of allergies increases a child's risk.
- Children who have specific health conditions, such as eczema and asthma, are more likely to have

allergies in general, including food allergies.

- Breast-feeding may protect against the development of food allergies.

THINGS WE'RE NOT SURE OF

Does avoiding certain foods during pregnancy and breast-feeding help prevent allergies in the child? This is still a bit controversial. To date, there is no conclusive proof that maternal diet changes the risk of food allergy. A mother who eats peanuts while pregnant or breast-feeding probably doesn't increase or decrease the chance that her child will have an allergy to peanuts (or any other food).

Does waiting to introduce certain foods into a child's diet — for example, waiting until 2 or 3 years of age before introducing peanut butter — change the risk of developing a peanut allergy? Probably not. The current feeling is that if you're going to get it, you're going to get it! The American Academy of Pediatrics has recommended that if you have exclusively breast-fed your child for the first 4 months, and he is not otherwise at risk for allergy,

you don't need to wait beyond a year to introduce any food. In children at risk for allergy, avoiding foods for a period may delay the onset of the allergy, but it doesn't prevent it.

Lactose intolerance

Lactose is the main source of sugar found in most dairy products, including human breast milk, cow's milk, cheeses, and yogurts. From a biological point of view, the fact that lactose is found in the milk of all mammals tells us that it is an important nutrient for the young. However, some people have a problem digesting lactose.

The term "lactose intolerance" refers to a condition where an individual has difficulty digesting lactose. This condition leads to a variety of symptoms, including abdominal pain, nausea, bloating, flatulence (gas), and sometimes diarrhea. But intolerance to a food or a food component is not the same as a food allergy. Intolerances are much more common and fortunately much less potentially dangerous than real allergies.

Did You Know?

Lactase levels

Lactase levels are highest at birth, which is why lactose intolerance is extremely uncommon in newborns and infants. After the age of 4 to 5 years, lactase levels drop until adulthood. As a result, lactose intolerance is more common in later childhood and increases toward adulthood. This also explains why, for some people, smaller amounts of dairy products containing lactose can be tolerated but larger amounts overwhelm their ability to digest lactose. Another factor playing a role in lactase levels is racial background. Most people of European descent maintain higher lactase throughout their lives. In contrast, the majority of people of Asian, African, and Hispanic backgrounds have a degree of lactose intolerance later in life.

Lactase enzyme

For the body to properly digest lactose, the wall of the intestine (the small bowel) contains a specific enzyme (or chemical) called lactase, whose role it is to break down the lactose so it can be absorbed through the bowel wall. If a person has low levels of lactase, the undigested lactose passes down to the large bowel (also called the colon), where it creates gastrointestinal symptoms.

During and after an episode of acute gastroenteritis, or stomach flu, a child's lactase levels may be briefly lowered and he may become temporarily lactose intolerant. This explains why, in the past, many health-care providers recommended no dairy after a bout of diarrhea. Today, most authorities feel that this risk was overstated and children can generally resume consuming milk and dairy products as soon as they feel well enough.

Guide to

Managing lactose intolerance in toddlers

Fortunately, there are many options for families with lactose-intolerant children or adults:

- Many lactose-free dairy products, which contain all the important nutrients but substitute other sugars for lactose, are widely available.
- Many adults and older children are able to take lactase enzyme supplements to replace or boost their lower lactase levels, which enables them to enjoy regular dairy products symptom-free.
- Avoiding dairy foods completely may solve a lactose intolerance problem, but it can increase the risk of calcium and vitamin D deficiency. If you go this route, appropriate supplements can be helpful but should be taken in consultation with a qualified nutritionist.

Eating issues

There are a number of other important food issues that pertain to toddlers and preschoolers. Obesity and high cholesterol and triglycerides can have a major impact on your child's future health. The eating and exercise habits that can lead to these problems are often set early in life. Underweight, or "failure to thrive," may be a sign of an underlying chronic disease and is always a source of significant anxiety for parents and extended family members. As your child broadens his repertoire of foods, you also need to be proactive in minimizing his risk of choking on something while eating.

Overweight and obesity

Weight gain during childhood is healthy and desirable. Chubby rolls in the arms or legs of a 1-year-old are not a cause for concern. Children tend to thin and stretch between 2 and 5 years of age, and again, this should not be a cause for concern. However, toddlers can become overweight or obese.

Twenty years ago, not many people could have imagined that an important section in a chapter about childhood nutrition would be devoted to childhood obesity. The World Health Organization has called obesity "a global epidemic" for children and adults. The figures are sobering. Childhood obesity will have a profound effect on health outcomes in the coming decades. Consider the following:

- In preschool-age children (2 to 5 years) in the United States, the prevalence of obesity has tripled, from 5% to almost 14%, between 1980 and 2004.
- The prevalence of obesity among school-age children in the United States increased from 6.5% to almost 19% between 1980 and 2004.
- In the United States in 2004, 26% of children between 2 and 5 years of age were considered overweight or obese, and that number rises to 34% of older children and adolescents.
- Having an obese parent doubles a child's chances of obesity.

Did You Know?

Predicting adult obesity

It is very difficult to predict which overweight toddlers will become overweight adults. Obese preschoolers have an increased risk of obesity in adulthood. This risk increases significantly for obese school-age children and adolescents. Parental obesity is a strong predictor of a child's risk of being overweight or obese as an adult. Promoting healthy eating habits and physical activity when children are young can have a lasting impact.

Guide to

Preventing overweight and obesity

At present, the outcome of obesity treatment is dismally poor. Preventing this condition is preferable, but requires a family-centered lifestyle change.

- Model healthy eating habits. Parents with better habits tend to pass them on to their children. Minimizing high-calorie junk food and fast food in the family diet, as well as sitting down for meals as a family, are a couple of ways — among many more — to teach healthy eating habits. Serve homemade meals rather than prepared or convenience foods whenever possible.
- Focus on improving health rather than on losing weight when educating children about eating and dietary habits. There are a number of developmentally appropriate children's books your toddler will enjoy that highlight these principles very effectively.
- Be physically active. Active play on a daily basis is important for the healthy growth and development of all children. While organized activities and sports are excellent tools for weight management, especially as your children get older, regular unstructured outdoor playtime is an effective and simple route to fitness. Once again, family role modeling is crucial. In the toddler years, family walks or hikes can be fun, and as the kids get older, family bicycling outings are a healthy way to spend time together.
- Limit screen time. Devices with screens, such as televisions, computers, and video games, are playing an increasing role in children's lives. These sedentary activities have unfortunately replaced many forms of physical activity. Both the American Academy of Pediatrics and the Canadian Paediatric Society have advised limiting screen time to 1 to 2 hours per day.

Body mass index

The body mass index (BMI) is the accepted measure of overweight and obesity for children 2 years of age and older. A diagnosis of a child as overweight or obese must take into account the child's height and age.

The BMI is a measure of weight for height. It can be derived from standardized tables or calculated by dividing the body weight in kilograms by the height in meters squared, or the equation BMI = weight (kg) ÷ height (m)^2. Just like the growth charts for weight and height, there are standardized

Did You Know?

Cholesterol testing

The American Academy of Pediatrics recommends that cholesterol levels should be checked only in selected groups of children between the age of 2 and 10 years. These selected groups include children who have a family history of high cholesterol or a family history of premature cardiac disease. Premature cardiac disease is defined as a heart attack prior to age 55 in males and 65 in females. Children who are considered overweight or obese should also have their cholesterol levels checked.

curves for BMI. A child whose BMI falls above the 95th percentile for age and gender would be considered obese. Between the 85th and 95th percentile would be considered overweight and at risk for obesity.

For more information on calculating BMI and the standardized curves, see pages 236–237.

Cholesterol and triglycerides

Cholesterol is the agent that, along with triglycerides, carries fat in the bloodstream. Together, they are called lipids, and they provide building blocks needed for many cells in the body. They are crucial for the health and normal function of the body. However, excessive levels of cholesterol and triglycerides are associated with poor health.

Adult risk factors

Research studies among adults have shown that higher levels of cholesterol form a very important risk factor in the development of atherosclerotic heart disease, a blocking of the coronary arteries that supply blood and oxygen to the heart muscle, which can lead to heart attacks. In the developed world, cardiovascular diseases remain the single most frequent cause of death in adults.

Toddler risk factors

While a child's diet plays an important part in determining the level of lipids and fat in the bloodstream, there are several other factors. The most important of these factors is genetics, or family history. Some individuals have inherited "good genes" that help them maintain healthy body weight and cholesterol levels regardless of good or poor eating and lifestyle habits, whereas others with "bad genes" will struggle to maintain healthy weight and cholesterol levels. This does not minimize the importance of healthy diet and activity, because "good" or "bad" genetics can be altered to variable degrees.

The treatment for high cholesterol levels in children should be guided by a health-care practitioner. As in adults, it may involve diet and lifestyle changes, as well as various medications.

Underweight and failure to thrive

"Failure to thrive" refers to a child's failure to gain weight at an appropriate rate. Failure to thrive is not an actual diagnosis but a symptom, which may be caused by a multitude of medical problems (such as heart conditions and gastrointestinal problems) and non-medical conditions (such as inadequate nutrition). The complex part of assessing a child's weight gain is not the act of weighing, which should be routinely done at each checkup throughout childhood, but rather the determination of what is "appropriate weight gain."

Growth charts

Failure to thrive will be detected by your health-care provider as weight and height are plotted on growth curves during regular checkups. For more information on growth charts, see page 14.

Children who seem to be falling well below their curve or whose weight seems to have reached a plateau with no increase would be considered as failing to thrive. At that point, a complete history and thorough examination by their health-care provider would be required to determine a further investigation or course of action.

Choking

The peak age for choking is between 1 and 2 years of age, with 80% of choking episodes occurring in children under 3 years. While toddlers are highly mobile and curious and have the fine-motor skills to pick up small objects, they still don't have a complete set of molars to chew their food adequately.

Choking can result in "aspiration." Aspiration occurs when something put in the mouth, usually a piece of food, ends up in the respiratory tract instead of in the stomach. The respiratory tract includes the trachea (windpipe), the larynx (voice box), and the lungs. Blockage of the body's airways is a potentially life-threatening risk.

In the year 2000 in the United States, choking and aspiration caused 160 deaths and accounted for more than 17,000 visits to hospital emergency departments.

Food items are the most commonly aspirated objects in toddlers, while non-food items, such as coins, paper clips, pen caps, and small toy pieces, are the most commonly aspirated objects in slightly older children. In the past, toy balloons were the object most commonly involved in fatal foreign-body aspiration.

FOODS MOST LIKELY TO BE ASPIRATED
- Peanuts (account for one-third to one-half of all choking episodes!)
- Nuts
- Seeds
- Popcorn
- Hard candies
- Raisins
- Whole baby carrots
- Chewing gum
- Whole grapes
- Fish with bones

HOW TO
Prevent choking

1. Completely avoid the highest-risk foods, such as peanuts, nuts, popcorn, and chewing gum, until your child is 4 years of age.

2. Modify some foods by chopping them into small pieces; for example, grapes can be quartered.

3. Always feed children while they are seated and supervised. They should not be fed while lying down, walking, or running around.

4. Never force-feed!

5. Learn cardiopulmonary resuscitation (CPR) and the appropriate techniques required in the event of a choking episode. For more first aid information, see Part 8.

Frequently asked questions

As family doctors, pediatricians, and nurse practitioners, we answer many questions from parents. Here are some of the most frequently asked questions. Be sure to ask your health-care providers any other questions that may arise. If they don't have the answers, they will refer you to a colleague who does.

Q: Should I be concerned about my child eating fast foods?

A: Fast-food restaurants have become a way of life in North America during the past 40 years. The average American eats out an average of three to four times a week, and the National Restaurant Association estimates that 47 cents of every food dollar is spent on meals away from home. A number of explanations are put forth — busier lifestyles, convenience, and successful marketing, among others. Of the estimated $157 billion dollars spent on fast foods each year, children between 4 and 12 years old spend up to $8 billion of their own money and exert a large influence on their parents' spending habits!

From a nutritional point of view, the general concern about fast foods is that they are very high in calories, fats (including those that raise cholesterol and triglyceride levels), and sodium (salt). While they are not considered highly nutritious, there is no real concern about nutrient deficiencies — it is all about excess. This is an obvious problem for overweight and obese children, and it can become a health issue for all children if fast foods are consumed to an excessive degree. Since there is no consensus on what "excessive" means, it is up to each family to decide for themselves.

Parents need to model healthy eating behavior. Parents can also, to a large degree, control the choice of meal for their toddlers and younger children. Good habits need to be taught early. Once children reach adolescence, they are far more independent in their food and restaurant choices.

Q: I never know what to pack for my preschooler's lunch. Any tips?

A: There is no point in packing it unless your child is going to like it and eat it. Now the challenge is to keep it healthy and easy.

- Involve them. Let them help you compile a list of their favorite lunch options, take them grocery shopping, let them help with preparation.
- Make small servings that are easy to eat. Peel and cut up vegetables and fruit.
- Avoid strong-smelling or messy foods.
- Keep the contents separate.
- Pack a frozen juice or ice box to keep the lunch cool.
- Be creative. Some popular items include a thermos of soup or macaroni and cheese; veggies and dip; yogurt tubes; lunch meat wrapped around a pickle, celery or carrot sticks; and cold pizza.

Q: Does my toddler need to take vitamins?

A: In general, medical studies do not support the routine use of multivitamins. The majority of healthy children, even those who are very picky eaters, will extract the needed vitamins and minerals from their diets. There is no proof that taking extra vitamins will improve a child's appetite or decrease the frequency or severity of common childhood infections. Children with specific medical problems or chronic health conditions may require added vitamin or mineral supplementation as directed by your health-care provider.

Q: How can I tell if my child is lactose intolerant?

A: A test called the hydrogen breath test can be done in older children, usually above

5 years of age, who are suspected to have lactose intolerance. Sometimes, attempting to minimize the lactose in a child's diet and observing the symptom response can be helpful. Remember that dairy products are a key component of a child's healthy diet, so if you are going to try a period of excluding dairy, it shouldn't continue for more than a week if no improvement in symptoms is seen before then.

Q: Should my toddler's cholesterol level be checked routinely?
A: This seemingly simple question does not have a simple answer. The medical experts have not reached a consensus on when cholesterol levels should be measured in children. However, there is no need to routinely test children less than 2 years of age, who require more fat in their diet for normal growth and development than older children do. Cholesterol levels in children under 2 normally fluctuate and are not very predictive of future levels. In children more than 2 years of age, screening is recommended sometime before the age of 10 years if there is a family history of cholesterol problems or premature heart disease (<55 years in men, <65 years in women) or if the child is overweight or has diabetes or high blood pressure.

Q: What about trans fats and omega 3 fats? It's all pretty confusing.
A: In brief, trans fats bad, omega 3s good! Trans fats are used to give products a longer shelf life and make them solid at room temperature and are found in hydrogenated foods (e.g., hard margarine and shortening). If one of the main ingredients is listed as containing partially hydrogenated or hydrogenated fat, then the product likely has saturated and trans fats, both of which increase the risk of heart and blood vessel disease. Try to use vegetable oils and soft, non-hydrogenated margarines instead.

Omega 3 fats are polyunsaturated fats with many health benefits. The best source is fish, such as salmon, mackerel, trout, tuna, sardines, anchovies, halibut, and haddock. Other good sources are soybeans, flaxseeds, and nuts. Many food items, such as infant formula, eggs, yogurt, and breads, are now fortified with omega 3 fats.

Q: How tall will my toddler be as an adult? Does this depend on her diet?
A: Adult height and weight are most frequently determined by genetics. Taller and heavier parents tend to have taller and heavier children. This fact is often overlooked by parents who wish their children to be at the "top of the curve" on the weight and height growth charts. There is a widely held misconception that doubling a child's height at the age of 2 years is an accurate predictor of adult height. A far more accurate *prediction* (at best, an educated guess) can be found in this formula:

- For males, add 5 inches (13 cm) to the mother's height, add this figure to the father's height, then divide by 2.
- For females, subtract 5 inches (13 cm) from the father's height, add this figure to the mother's height, then divide by 2.
- *Note:* Diet is not a variable in either equation.

Sam's Diary

May 20 (15 months old)

You are at an amazing stage, Sam — it's wonderful to spend time with you these days — you're such fun, much less frustrated, more able to entertain yourself, and just so aware and alert. You're a very affectionate, loving little boy, often giving Mom and Dad kisses and hugs. You blow kisses to the animals at the zoo and the farm. You like to "talk" to the birds. You wave goodbye to everyone. You have these words now: up, Pooh, moon, nana (banana), geese, donkey, no.

You're going through a "Daddy" phase lately and don't enjoy it when he has to go to work on the weekends. During the week, you've started to sleep till 7:30, by which time Dad has already left for work. He's been working every weekend lately, and you really miss him.

When we put you to bed at night now, we read you a story and then you put your little head on one of our shoulders and we sing to you for a bit, then we put you down with Pooh bear and cover you with a blanket. We chat for a little while, give you a kiss, you call out Mama or Dad, then you talk to yourself for a little while or you switch on your musical toys and then go off to sleep. You're really growing up so quickly. Sweet dreams, baby.

June 24 (16 months old)

We spent over an hour in your little pool today. Your fingers and toes looked like raisins when you came out — but you loved it! You learned to pour water from one container into another. You had a great time with the bubbles and listening to and watching all the planes flying overhead — you love airplanes. On the weekend, we went down to the fire station, and you had a ball looking at all the fire trucks and watching the firemen washing windows using the fire truck's ladder. You made quite an impression on the guys down there.

June 26 (16 months old)

Hi again, my angel. Mom and Dad have just learned that you're going to have a brother or sister in March next year — you'll be about 25 months old when the baby comes along. You're going to be a wonderful, loving big brother.

We've had a great month. You're talking so much now, with so many new words — money, monkey, birdie, help, bath, and lots more. You're really so grown up.

We spent a wonderful three days at a cottage in the countryside. You went in the boat to the beach, swam for ages in the lake, which you absolutely loved (you're a real water baby!), had baths with your friend Maya, and went to Santa's Village, where you fed the reindeer and went on a pony. You were delighted by the animals. We think you're going be a vet!

August 4 (18 months old)

You went for your 18-month checkup today with Dr Murphy and had your immunization — you're so good with these. You cried a lot when she looked in your ears but didn't even seem to feel the injection. We gave you some Tylenol before and a patch on your arm to numb the area. You were a real trooper. One other thing — you now tell us when you have a poop in your diaper.

Your Older Toddler

(Age 2 to 3 years)

Thriving during the terrible twos 138

Visiting the doctor again 143

Temper, temper 145

Disciplining your toddler 150

Teaching your child to share 155

Talking with your child 157

Private parts 159

Television time 161

Welcoming a new sibling 165

Traveling with your toddler 169

Dental care 179

Right to play 182

Dad's role 190

Frequently asked questions 193

Thriving during the terrible twos

Many parents approach their child's second birthday with an air of trepidation — after all, the phrase "the terrible twos" does not exactly fill one with confidence. In fact, the twos need not be terrible at all. Your child is entering her late toddler years, an incredibly rewarding stage when she is learning at a rapid pace and is increasingly developing into a self-possessed, unique individual.

Physical growth: Age 2 to 3

At your toddler's checkups, your health-care provider will again measure her weight and height and plot these measurements on the standard weight and height growth curves. For information on plotting and reading growth curves, see page 14. Your health-care provider will determine if there are any growth problems and ensure that there are no nutritional or medical concerns.

Normal

"Normal" on the growth curves is a wide measurement, ranging from those whose weight or height plot below average (3rd to 50th percentiles) to those whose growth is above average (50th to 97th percentiles). Few children are, in fact, average or grow exactly alike. Looking at a crowd of people waiting for the bus, some will be taller, others shorter, some slim, others heavier. If you and your partner are both shorter than average, there is a good chance that your toddler will be too.

Growth over time

More important than determining if your child is above or below average on the growth curves is making note of her growth over time. If she is, for example, on the 25th percentile for height, she should — generally speaking — track along the same

---

Did You Know?

Physical growth facts

The average 2-year-old will increase from $26\frac{1}{2}$ pounds (12 kg) for girls and 28 pounds (12.7 kg) for boys on the second birthday to $30\frac{1}{2}$ pounds (13.8 kg) for girls and 32 pounds (14.5 kg) for boys by the third birthday. In height, toddler girls grow on average from 34 inches (86.4 cm) to 37 inches (94 cm), while toddler boys grow from $34\frac{1}{2}$ inches (87.6 cm) at 2 years to $37\frac{1}{2}$ inches (95.3 cm) at 3 years. Remember that these are just averages. There is a wide range of normal. Regardless of his growth parameters, if your toddler is healthy, energetic, and developing appropriately, he is unlikely to have a problem.

Did You Know?

Imaginary friends

Three years is the age at which the imagination starts to take flight, as your toddler floats on the border between reality and fantasy. Fantasy allows your child to experiment with strong feelings and new sensations. At this stage, many toddlers begin to identify imaginary friends. Your toddler may use imaginary characters to create a more ideal parent, a playmate, or someone to provide comfort at times of distress. Rest assured that this process is entirely normal. It is not that he doesn't have enough real friends or lacks the social skills to make them! In fact, it may be that those who have gone through a stage of having imaginary friends have more friends in school and become more socially advanced in general. In time, children will outgrow their pretend friends.

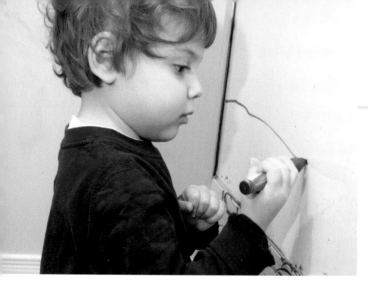

percentile from one medical checkup to the next. Of course, there are times when children drop to a lower-percentile curve or jump up to a higher one. This may well be normal, because growth patterns may vary or your child may be moving toward her "genetic destiny."

Development

The third year of life is a busy period of development for your toddler. This year is marked by great changes in motor development as your child becomes more proficient at walking, running, and climbing. She may learn to ride a tricycle. She will learn to draw lines and circles, her language skills will flourish, and she will strive for independence. Your toddler will begin to work through negative feelings, as well as interactive difficulties with siblings, playmates, parents, and caregivers. At this time, your toddler will progress from independent parallel play and learn to play with her peers cooperatively. Understanding the normal developmental stages is crucial to helping you as parents navigate through the behavioral challenges that can be expected at this age.

Milestones

While certain attitudes, behaviors, and physical milestones tend to occur at certain ages, a wide spectrum of growth and behavior for each age is normal. Milestones offer a way of showing a general progression through the developmental stages, rather than fixed requirements for normal development at specific ages. Keep in mind that your child will likely attain some milestones earlier and other milestones later than the general trend. If you have questions or concerns about your toddler's development, speak to her health-care provider.

Red flags

While some developmental variation is normal, it is important to identify any warning signs early so problems can be addressed and appropriate therapy implemented. Consult your health-care provider for a complete assessment if your child meets any of the following criteria by the end of her third year:

- Frequent falling or difficulty with stairs
- Persistent drooling or very unclear speech
- Inability to build a tower of more than four blocks
- Difficulty manipulating small objects
- Inability to copy a circle
- Inability to communicate in short phrases
- No involvement in pretending while playing
- Failure to understand simple instructions
- Little interest in other children
- Extreme difficulty separating from her mother

Adapted by permission of the American Academy of Pediatrics, *Your Baby and Young Child: Birth to Age 5* (New York: Bantam, 1998).

Developmental Milestones: 24 to 36 months
Motor, Language, and Problem-Solving Skills

Months	Gross Motor	Fine Motor	Language	Problem-Solving
24	• Throws and kicks ball • Walks down stairs one at a time, holding rail • Climbs on furniture	• Imitates a straight line with crayon • Makes a train out of blocks	• Speaks 50+ words and two- to three-word sentences • Refers to self by name • Is understood by others 50% of the time • Follows two-step commands • Can put toy "in," "on," "under"	• Sorts objects, matches objects to pictures • Does three- to four-piece puzzles
30	• Jumps • Runs easily	• Builds tower of eight blocks • Imitates circular drawing stroke	• Refers to self by pronoun "I" • Speaks 350+ words • Uses action words (e.g., "run," "fall")	• Continues to exhibit trial-and-error behavior in solving problems
36	• Throws ball overhand; catches with straight arms • Walks up stairs, one at a time • Rides tricycle • Stands on one foot	• Builds a bridge with three blocks • Copies a cross and circle with an awkward, high pencil grip • Uses scissors	• Speaks 1,000+ words • Knows age and sex • Counts three objects correctly • Is understood by others 75% of time • Identifies seven body parts • Knows two colors by name • Stuttering is common	• Increasingly uses reasoning to solve problems • Does nine-piece puzzles

Developmental Milestones: 24 to 36 Months
Psychosocial Development

Months	Emotional	Social	Adaptive
24	• Begins to change reaction to events and emotions based on the influence of others	• Imitates others to please them • Engages in parallel play • Begins to tolerate separation	• Removes clothes without buttons • Opens door by turning knob • Unzips zippers
30	• Continues to cry and hit at times • May be shy around strangers • May show fear of unfamiliar objects or activities	• Pretends while playing • Dresses and undresses dolls	• Helps put things away • Can begin toilet training • Drinks from a cup with minimal spilling
36	• Becomes more flexible and adaptable • Begins to talk about dreams	• Learns how to share • Negotiates conflicts • Begins cooperative play with peers	• Unbuttons clothing, puts on shoes • Washes hands • Pours liquids

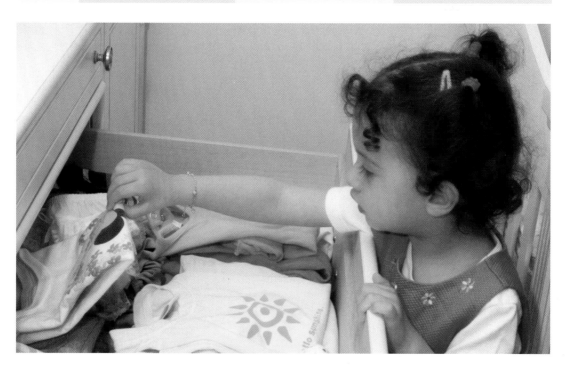

Visiting the doctor again

Your toddler's checkups with her health-care provider will now decrease in frequency to an annual basis. It is recommended that your toddler see a health-care provider for a routine checkup around her second birthday and again around her third birthday. Your doctor will ask you questions to learn about your child's development. This is a good opportunity to discuss any concerns you may have about your youngster's learning and growth.

Routine well-child checkup

Your toddler is now at an age where you can certainly discuss with her ahead of time what to expect at the doctor's office. Be honest, which is of course much easier if no needles are required! There are many excellent educational books specifically written to help prepare toddlers for visits to the doctor or dentist, and these can be fun and helpful to read ahead of an appointment. If your child seems particularly nervous in the doctor's office, it may even be worth investing in a toy doctor's kit, which will allow her to become familiar with the various instruments in a relaxed and playful way.

Physical examination

The physical examination will likely include a review from top to toe, including eyes (vision), ears (hearing), teeth, chest, heart, blood pressure, and abdomen. If you have any concern about vision or hearing, it is critical to point it out to the doctor because the problem may not be obvious during the checkup. Early recognition of hearing or vision problems makes a big difference in treatment outcomes.

At the same time, your doctor will be checking to make sure that your toddler is meeting her developmental milestones. As in previous checkups, your toddler's height, weight, and head circumference will be measured and plotted on the appropriate growth charts to monitor the rate of her growth. Remember, the key is progress over time. For example, a child who has always plotted on the 10th percentile is fine, but if your child was growing on the 75th

Did You Know?

Vaccinations

And now for the best news: no routine shots are required at the second- and third-year visits, provided that your toddler is up to date with his immunizations. Otherwise, some catch-up may be indicated. The one possible exception is the influenza immunization, which the American Academy of Pediatrics recommends be given routinely in the fall every year to children over 6 months of age. You may want to discuss this particular recommendation with your doctor — opinions about the necessity of this shot certainly vary.

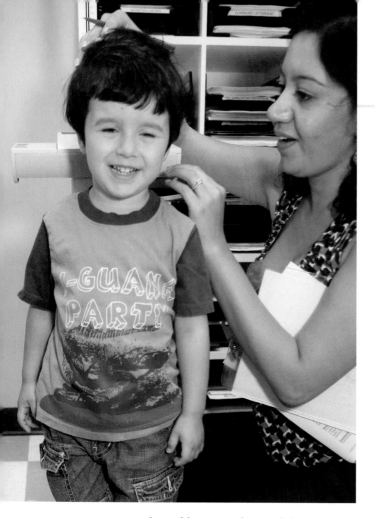

percentile and has now dropped down to the 10th percentile, a bit of investigation will likely be required to find out why this has happened.

Discussion

You will have an opportunity to share any concerns or issues that have come up since the last routine checkup. Sit down with your partner ahead of time and make a list of items for discussion to help ensure that you don't forget something important. It is easy to get distracted while you're keeping your little one entertained and preventing her from tearing the place apart.

Education

Your doctor will likely want to give you a bit of anticipatory guidance and advice about a number of issues.

NUTRITION
- Changing from full-fat milk to 2% or less and continuing to limit total milk intake to a maximum of 16 to 20 ounces (500 to 625 mL) a day (see page 107)
- Reviewing the USDA MyPyramid food guide or Canada's Food Guide for age-appropriate servings (see pages 96–98)
- Decreasing the proportion of fat in the diet
- Preventing picky eating habits (see page 100)

SAFETY
- Using age-appropriate car seats (see page 314)
- Practicing water safety (see page 322)
- Locking up medications and toxic substances (see page 310)
- Keeping the hot water tank temperature turned down to avoid scald burns from hot tap water (see page 309)
- Avoiding secondhand smoke

GENERAL
- Continuing good tooth-brushing techniques at least twice a day; starting routine visits to the dentist (see page 179)
- Learning to manage temper tantrums (see page 146)
- Setting limits and using effective discipline strategies (see page 150)
- Beginning toilet training (see page 200)
- Reading to your toddler (see page 189)
- Monitoring child-care arrangements (see page 66)
- Noting how your toddler is getting along with siblings and peers (see page 155)
- Watching for any sleep problems (see page 284)

Temper, temper

There is no denying that this stage is a challenging one that will at times test you to your limits and beyond. Rather than view it negatively, however, place it in the context of your child's normal growth and development. In the end, you will come to understand your toddler better and be able to provide appropriate discipline and guidance through the year ahead. At this stage, your child will benefit from continued supervision, limits, and routines. Of course, these ideas are easier to discuss in theory than they are to apply when you are confronted head-on with a willful toddler! What follows are some disciplinary principles and specific strategies to help you and your toddler thrive. When you get frustrated and are pushed to your limits, seek help from your support network — your partner, family, or friends. Your health-care provider is also trained to support parents frustrated by their toddler's behavior.

Independence

Between your child's second and third birthdays, you will more than likely notice that she is striving for independence in every aspect of her life, be it feeding, dressing, or toileting, and generally resisting help at every turn. The extent of this independent behavior is variable, depending both on the child and the particular task at hand.

Your toddler is asserting herself and takes pride in each successful task that is mastered. Hand in hand with these achievements, however, comes frustration when goals cannot be reached and needs are not immediately met, leading to the much-talked-about temper tantrums and other behavioral manifestations.

Keep in mind that your child's acts of defiance are not necessarily directed at you. They are part of becoming an independent human being.

Temper tantrums

Temper tantrums are probably first on the list of behavioral challenges associated with the third year of life. While tantrums may occur as early as the first year and continue for some past age 4, they tend to peak in the toddler years. Striving for greater independence, mastering skills, and gaining control are dominant developmental characteristics at this age, but if a child encounters difficulty in achieving these goals, frustration can result, often manifesting as a temper tantrum. Compounding the frustration may be a lack of expressive language, which makes it difficult for the toddler to express her feelings. Many parents find that as their child's language skills improve, her temper tantrums diminish.

Just remember that tantrums are a normal — albeit unpleasant — part of your toddler's development. And they can be managed quite successfully.

Guide to

Managing temper tantrums

The principles behind dealing with temper tantrums are simple, though admittedly often easier said than done:
- Stay calm.
- Avoid inadvertently reinforcing the behavior.
- Provide reassurance and guidance once the tantrum is over.

MANAGEMENT STRATEGIES AT HOME
While no one will be able to completely prevent tantrums, here are a few strategies to try to minimize their effect on your toddler and you:
- Many tantrums are precipitated by hunger, boredom, fatigue, and overstimulation. By recognizing your child's pattern of reaction to various situations, you can try to intervene before the tantrum begins. For example, provide a snack, suggest a quiet activity, or settle him down for a nap before he gets to the beyond-help stage.
- Since frustration underlies many tantrums, avoid setting your toddler up for failure. While challenges are

important to some degree, toys much beyond your child's level of ability will only serve to frustrate him and erode self-esteem.

- To dampen rising feelings of frustration, anger, or other emotions that lead to tantrums, find an outlet for your toddler to expend his energy. Ensure that he has plenty of free time and space to play or run around outside.

- Provide your child with some control in his life by allowing him to make manageable choices. Asking your toddler if he would like to use the red or the blue cup is an appropriate question that he will be able to handle while feeling good about both having control and seeing you respect his decision. Try to avoid open-ended questions that may serve to increase frustration.

- Help your toddler express his feelings. "I know that makes you really angry" acknowledges his feelings and may prevent the anger from manifesting as a tantrum. Follow it up with comfort and reassurance, then try to redirect him to a different activity.

- Children often react to their parents' negativity, so it is best to keep the number of times you say no in check. Choose your battles, ensuring that "no" is reserved for things that are truly important. In many situations, you may be able to negotiate or redirect your child in a way that he finds acceptable. "Why don't you try

hammering on the rubber mat?" may be a solution both parties can accept when your toddler wants to hammer away at your new wooden furniture.

- While your toddler is having a tantrum, he is not being rational, making it an unsuitable time to provide a rational explanation or even reassurance. During the tantrum itself, it is best to ignore your child. Remain calm and quiet (if your emotions escalate, so will your child's), don't move your child (but do ensure that he is safe), and don't confront him or make eye contact.

- After he has calmed down, speak to him quietly, help him find words to describe his feelings ("I know that was frustrating for you"), and provide guidance about how to handle his emotions ("We all get frustrated sometimes. Tell Mommy when you're frustrated and we can talk about how to make it better"). As always, reassure your toddler that you love him and redirect him to a different activity.

- At the same time, it is important not to give in to your toddler's demands in the midst of a tantrum. Keep in mind what his tantrum is allowing him to achieve. If he screams and kicks his legs until he gets what he wants, he will know exactly how to proceed the next time around. Similarly, resist the temptation to laugh at your child. This serves as positive reinforcement and shows disrespect for your child's genuine feelings.

MANAGEMENT STRATEGIES IN PUBLIC

It is one thing to ignore your toddler and let him cry it out in the privacy of your own home, but what do you do when he acts up in the middle of the grocery store?

- First, rest assured that you're not alone and you're not a bad parent.
- While it may be embarrassing for your toddler to be kicking and screaming in public, do your best to ignore those around you. It's likely that many of them are parents themselves and understand the position you're in.
- Unlike tantrums that happen at home, this is a situation where it is appropriate to move your child. Pick him up (rather than dragging him by the hand) and bring him to a relatively private place, perhaps your car, the bathroom, or a park bench. Hold him gently until he regains control, and provide reassurance and guidance as you would at home.
- Resist the temptation to give in to your toddler's wishes. Children quickly realize that they are more likely to get their way when they act up in public, and a repeat performance will be almost guaranteed.
- Depending on the severity of your child's tantrum and his emotional state once it is over, you may be able to continue with your errands, or it may be in both of your best interests to head home early.
- As always, consider whether there were any precipitating factors, such as hunger or fatigue, that could be avoided the next time around.

Anger and aggression

Just as we all feel angry at times, so too does your toddler. This normal emotion is exacerbated in this age group because young children are egocentric and believe that the world revolves around them. Your toddler will want you to do things her way, and now, if not sooner! Don't worry — this is a normal developmental stage that will not last forever.

While it is normal for toddlers to feel and express anger, they must learn that it is not okay to manifest it in an aggressive manner. Aggression, be it biting, hitting, kicking, hair pulling, or pinching, often occurs because language skills aren't yet developed enough to allow toddlers to articulate their feelings.

No matter how hard we try to help our children express their anger without being aggressive, most toddlers will manifest their emotions in a physical manner at some point. Following are some tips to manage biting and hitting, two of the most common forms of aggression. If your child is resorting to different but equally unacceptable physical behaviors, the same principles apply. If you are really concerned that your toddler is unable to control her anger or is particularly aggressive, seek advice from her health-care provider.

Guide to

Managing toddler anger

- As parents and caregivers, it is our job to help our children acknowledge and express their feelings verbally. Use appropriate phrases, such as:
  - "I know you wanted to stay outside and play longer, and you're angry with me because I asked you to come inside."
  - "It's okay to feel angry."
  - "Tell me what's making you angry."
- Try to stay calm when your child is angry — whether he is expressing his feelings verbally or aggressively —

in order to act as a role model. The last thing you want to do is to act out the very behavior you are finding unacceptable in him. His actions are likely to escalate as he reacts to your emotional response by ramping up his anger and aggression even further!

- As part of your daily routine, try to model empathy and kindness toward others and talk about feelings so it will be easier for your toddler to do so when the time comes.
- Provide constructive outlets for your child's energy, such as opportunities for running around and active play.

Biting

Finding out that your child has been bitten or — perhaps even worse — that your child has bitten someone else can be horrifying. While the action is indeed inappropriate and requires discipline, remember that it is simply another outlet for your toddler's frustration and was probably done with no different intention than any other form of aggression.

Biting may occur between children, or a child may bite her caregiver. In child-care settings, children often imitate one another, resulting in clusters of biting incidents.

As with all forms of aggressive behavior, remain calm and refrain from resorting to aggression yourself. The injured child needs to be comforted and appropriate first aid, if needed, administered. The biter

needs to be disciplined. Be firm, making her aware that this is serious, but try not to scare her, as the intended message will then get lost. A definitive "No biting" is appropriate, as is pointing out that biting hurts people. This is a good time to use the effective time-out form of discipline (see page 152).

Hitting

As with biting or other common forms of aggression, remain calm, serious, and firm when reacting to a hitting incident. Brief explanations — "No hitting" or "Hitting hurts people" — are appropriate, as is a time out. Remember to help your toddler find words to express her emotions, and provide her with strategies for dealing with her anger and frustration. Never hit toddlers to "show them how it feels."

Disciplining your toddler

Too often, the word "discipline" is equated with punishment. In fact, the theme of the *Oxford English Dictionary*'s definition of the word is training aimed at both controlling others' behavior and self-control. By teaching and guiding our children, we can provide them with a structure whereby they can function throughout the rest of their lives and can use self-discipline to control their behavior so that it is appropriate to a given social context.

Principles of discipline

With this overriding goal in mind, there are a few principles to consider when applying discipline in practice:

- **Respect:** As parents, we all hope our children will grow up with a healthy respect for their environment and the people around them. There's no better place to start than by demonstrating respect within your own family. Just as

you should insist that you be shown respect as a parent, so too is your toddler never too young to be respected in a similar fashion.

- **Trust:** Trust will closely follow respect and should always be maintained between you and your toddler. Shaming or abandoning your child will result in a loss of trust and a step away from the goal of effective discipline.

- **Consistency:** Consistent messages from parents and other regular caregivers are fundamental to your toddler's ability to understand her limits, avoid confusion, and learn to respect your authority. You can imagine how confusing it is for a young toddler to find that certain behaviors are acceptable on days you're not stressed or exhausted but not on other days, or that they are acceptable to one parent but not to the other.

- **Developmental appropriateness:** A behavior's consequences must be appropriate and applied in a fair and timely manner. These principles should fall into place, provided that you keep your child's developmental stage, as well as her individual temperament, in mind.

HOW TO
Provide appropriate discipline

Toddlers between 2 and 3 years of age continue to require consistent supervision and need their caregivers to set limits. The temperament of every child, and indeed every family, is different, necessitating flexibility in how limits are set. Generally speaking, children thrive in an environment where some structure is provided.

1. Praise and reward. You don't need to wait for a negative behavior to occur before applying discipline. We all enjoy praise, and a toddler is no exception! When your child does something desirable — whether it is cleaning up his toys or using polite manners — show him that his good behavior is recognized. This does not mean you need to dole out rewards every time your toddler does something positive. Rather, provide verbal praise and a hug. Telling him how proud you are will go a long way in building respect and love, and you might even be rewarded with a repeat performance!

2. Choose your battles. Depending on the day, you may be tempted to reprimand your toddler for countless behaviors, but it is important to prioritize and choose your battles, so to speak. Appropriate discipline about safety (e.g., keeping away from a hot oven) should always come first. Some behaviors (e.g., repetitive banging on the table) may be annoying to you but of no harm to anybody else, in which case they can be safely ignored.

3. Keep your expectations realistic. A toddler of this age may spill some milk out of his cereal bowl when eating independently. This is developmentally normal and should not be punished. In fact, seeing you lose your temper over such an insignificant event may even confuse your child, as his attempt at independence and mastery of a skill was met with negativity rather than with positive direction and teaching.

4. Model appropriate behavior. This is fundamental to the principle of respect. Teaching your child to ask for things politely or to use a utensil properly will be ineffective if he sees that you don't follow your own rules. Of course, some rules are inconsistently applied on the grounds of safety; for example, using a pair of scissors or eating whole nuts. In these instances, explain to your toddler that you are an adult and this behavior is safe for you but not for a 2-year-old. While he may not grasp the concept immediately, he will at least see that you recognize the inconsistency.

5. Demonstrate love and trust. No matter how you treat a behavior, all forms of discipline should always be followed by a demonstration of love and trust. Applying discipline to "bad behavior," as opposed to a "bad boy," will help your toddler understand that it is his behavior, not his person, that is being disciplined. While the distinction may seem subtle, it forms the foundation for respect as a principle for effective discipline.

Forms of discipline

It is all very well to understand the principles behind good discipline, but how on earth do you implement these concepts when you just want to scream and pull your hair out? Fortunately, much work has been done in this field from which we can learn.

Time out

Many authorities endorse "time out" as one of the most effective forms of discipline. In brief, when your child is doing something unacceptable, she is calmly told to go to her time-out place — one that is safe but not interesting to the child — for a set length of time, after which the child is comforted and you both move on. Time out is based on the premise that the child is being disciplined while not receiving attention or positive reinforcement that may encourage the undesirable behavior. If time out is used unemotionally and consistently, the technique will work.

1-2-3 Magic

Dr. Thomas W. Phelan's book *1-2-3 Magic: Effective Discipline for Children 2–12* is a bestselling manual popular with parents, teachers, and physicians. Dr. Phelan, a clinical psychologist and expert on child discipline, describes a "counting" method to stop unwanted behaviors, such as whining, yelling, or tantrums.

COUNTING

At the onset of the unwanted behavior, the parent or caregiver is to look at the child and calmly say, "That's 1." After 5 seconds, say, "That's 2," and if the behavior continues after yet another 5 seconds, "That's 3, take 5." "Take 5" means that the child gets a time out, or what Phelan calls a "time-out alternative," such as the loss of a privilege for a specified period.

Essential to the program's effectiveness are what Phelan calls the "No-talking and no-emotion rules." As with time-out discipline, the caregiver is to remain calm

Did You Know?

Physical punishment

Based on research demonstrating that spanking and other forms of physical punishment are associated with negative outcomes in children, the Canadian Paediatric Society and the American Academy of Pediatrics take a strong stand against these forms of discipline. By directing violence toward our children, we are not only teaching them that aggression is an appropriate way to manage conflict, but we are eroding any trust built between caregiver and child. In effect, spanking teaches our children that hitting is okay, as they follow our example. Clearly, spanking and other forms of physical punishment are inconsistent with effective discipline and are strongly discouraged.

HOW TO
Use time-out discipline effectively

Who?
Time out should be introduced by 2 years of age and is effective until approximately 12 years of age.

When?
As with all forms of discipline, time out is best reserved for behaviors that are important for your child to curb — anything compromising their safety and aggressive actions, such as hitting and biting.

How long?
The length of time that your child stays in time out should be 1 minute per year of his age (e.g., 2 minutes for a 2-year-old), to a maximum of 5 minutes, though this is just a guide and should be adjusted as appropriate for each child. If your child leaves the time-out spot, quietly and quickly put him back and reset your clock.

Where?
It is important that the time-out spot — for example, a chair or a hallway — be free from built-in rewards that would seem desirable to the child. For example, the television should not be on, and he should not be allowed to interact with anyone, including you, during this time. It is also suggested that time outs not occur in the child's bedroom, to avoid creating a negative association with being in the bedroom.

How?
When you initiate time out, help the child connect his behavior with the discipline by briefly and calmly telling him what he has done. Try not to lecture or give a long explanation: "No biting," for example, is sufficient. During time out, your child should be ignored completely. When you declare that the time out is over, briefly comfort your child and move on to another activity. It is best not to discuss the negative behavior once the time out is over.

throughout and is not to talk to the toddler or child while counting or during the time out. This not only prevents the child's emotional level from rising to meet that of the caregiver, but it also encourages the child to think and begin to take responsibility for her own behavior.

After some time using the counting technique, children begin to respond and curb the unwanted behavior at counts 1 or 2, thus avoiding a time out altogether. Of course, some unacceptable actions, such as hitting or biting, do not deserve a warning. For these, a time out should be applied immediately.

START BEHAVIORS

Counting and time outs are not appropriate for what Phelan calls "start" behaviors. Things that you want your toddler to *do*, such as getting ready for bed, take more motivation to start and see through to completion than things that you want him to *stop doing* and thus warrant strategies more complex than simple counting.

Verbal punishment

Verbal punishment, while not physical, is humiliating and emotionally traumatic and also works against trust and respect. Parents are human beings too, and quite often our toddlers will push the wrong button just once too often, making us feel like we want to explode. Resist that urge! If you find yourself losing control as a parent or caregiver, take a time out for yourself, separate yourself from your child — first ensuring that the child remains safe — and draw upon your resources and supports to help manage your challenging toddler.

Disciplining peers

It is one thing to understand how to approach disciplining your own toddler, but you may feel quite differently when it's other people's kids who are acting out. Remember that you're not the other child's parent and are therefore not responsible for the child's discipline. If you are in a supervisory role, however, you are entitled to set your own rules. If the toddler under your care is kicking, for example, remember to always first provide comfort to the child on the receiving end of the discipline. Then tell her firmly that nobody kicks in this house and that she won't be able to play here anymore if she continues to kick.

Distraction

Distraction remains a frequent and effective strategy to try to diffuse situations. Try breaking for a snack or moving play out of doors. If none of your strategies are working and your guest continues to be outwardly aggressive, it may be time to call her parents and put an end to the visit. If you are going to be involved with the aggressive child regularly, discuss ground rules and disciplinary strategies with the parents so consistent messages and actions are relayed.

Prevention

In the spirit of prevention, think about what may be at the bottom of the child's aggression. Some children will act out if they are uncomfortable in a new environment, so help put them at ease by providing close supervision and ensuring that your guest is receiving equal attention and opportunity as she plays with your child.

Teaching your child to share

Sharing is a concept we all want our children to understand and demonstrate when they play with their peers. As parents and caregivers, though, our expectations must be realistic and account for their developmental stage.

Ownership

Before they are ready to share, toddlers must first master the notion of ownership. This concept — frequently expressed emphatically as "Mine!" — is usually developed by the age of 2 years. Rather than indicating selfishness, ownership represents the toddler gaining autonomy and establishing her sense of self. It is also a fundamental step on the road to sharing, a concept that is learned over a few years. Between these two developmental milestones of owning and sharing, toddlers will become comfortable with showing their toys to others without actually parting with them. This behavior should be recognized and encouraged. Sharing will follow shortly thereafter.

Play dates and sharing

A play date with other children is the ideal time for your toddler to either demonstrate her willingness to share or absolutely refuse to perform this particular social grace.

If the get-together is at your house, help prepare your child for sharing. Give her the option of putting a few of her special toys away — for the moment, these do not need to be shared with others. Encourage her to understand that the toys still left out are to be shared with guests. If your toddler is really not ready to share her belongings, try engaging the kids in activities that don't involve toys or things over which she claims ownership. Art projects may work well, particularly if each child is given an individual supply of paper and crayons.

You may notice a difference in your toddler's willingness to share in a child-care environment. On someone else's turf, she may be less likely to be possessive about her belongings. Keep this in mind when planning a play date. If sharing is an issue, try choosing a location outside of your home — the park, for example — to increase the chance of success.

HOW TO
Encourage cooperative play

While children may not be completely comfortable with cooperative play until approximately 4 years of age, most toddlers between the age of 2 and 3 can learn to become comfortable with the concept and practice, at least to some degree. Here are a few tips to encourage sharing at a younger age.

1. Role modeling: Use the word "share" as you demonstrate sharing with those around you. Involve your toddler directly by offering to share a piece of fruit or the Play-Doh.

2. Lending and borrowing: For toddlers, the concepts of lending and borrowing are new. Understanding that when they lend a toy they will get it back is a key stage in being able to share their belongings. Model this concept in your daily routine by asking to borrow or offering to lend a toy to your toddler, ensuring that the borrowed toy is returned to the lender after a few minutes.

3. Taking turns: Watch kids take turns, for example, on the swings at the park. Encourage your toddler to do the same.

4. Expressing feelings: Incorporate sharing into your discussions about feelings, helping your child put words to his emotions. "That made Anna happy when you shared your crayons," or "It makes Mommy sad that you won't share your cookie," are both appropriate examples.

5. Praising: When your toddler begins to share his belongings, be sure to praise his efforts. Positive reinforcement will encourage further sharing in the future.

Talking with your child

The third year of your child's life is a time of rapid language development. As your toddler's ability to speak increases, you may note disfluencies, or difficulty speaking smoothly or freely, particularly at the beginning of her sentences. In fact, everyone exhibits some degree of disfluent speech from time to time, but it is some particularly prominent in young children as their speech is developing.

Stuttering symptoms

Stuttering refers not just to these disfluencies in speech, but also to the reactions to the speech difficulties. For example, a child who stutters may occasionally have tremors, visible in the muscles around the mouth or jaw, when she is having difficulty with a word. You may also find that both her pitch and volume increase, and she may exhibit tension in her lips, tongue, throat, or chest as she struggles to speak. Emotional reactions can include fear or frustration, and ultimately the child may avoid talking, or at least avoid saying specific words she finds troublesome.

Causes

The reasons why children stutter are many, and unfortunately they're not very clear cut. What is known is that people who stutter are no less intelligent than those who don't. Additionally, stuttering is not the fault of parents or, for that matter, anyone else.

Given that stuttering is aggravated by stress and anxiety, many suggestions for caregivers are aimed at decreasing these factors. However, old methods that you may have heard about, such as asking your child to talk slowly or relax, are based on the false belief that stuttering is simply a bad habit. In short, these methods do not work and may even make the behavior worse.

Risk factors

To help determine whether your child is likely to outgrow her stuttering without the need for intervention, it is useful to consider these key risk factors:

- Family history of stuttering
- Onset of stuttering after $3\frac{1}{2}$ years of age
- Stuttering that has already been present for 6 to 12 months
- Stuttering in boys
- Stuttering accompanied by other language concerns (e.g., difficulty being understood or in following instructions)

Did You Know?

Prevalence of stuttering in toddlers

Stuttering occurs in approximately 1% of the population, though the numbers of youngsters who transiently stutter are much higher. In fact, 75% to 80% of children who begin to stutter stop within 1 to 2 years with no therapy.

If your child has any of these risk factors, or even if you are just worried, it is wise to obtain a consultation with a speech-language pathologist. Your child will be assessed, and the professional therapist will judge whether ongoing speech therapy is warranted.

Guide to

Talking with your toddler

The following seven tips for talking with your child are offered by the Stuttering Foundation of America. These tips are appropriate to use with any child, whether he stutters or not.

- Speak with your child in an unhurried way, pausing frequently.
- Reduce the number of questions you ask your child. Children speak more freely if they are expressing their own ideas, rather than answering an adult's questions.
- Use your facial expressions and other body language to convey to your child that you are listening to the content of his message and not to how he is talking.
- Set aside a few minutes at a regular time each day when you can give your undivided attention to your child. Use slow, calm, and relaxed speech. This quiet time can be a confidence builder for younger children, letting them know you enjoy their company.
- Help all members of the family learn to take turns talking and listening.
- Observe the way you interact with your child. Try to increase those times that leave your child with the message that you are listening to him and he has plenty of time to talk. Try to decrease criticisms, rapid speech patterns, interruptions, and questions.
- Above all, convey that you accept your child as he is.

Adapted by permission from B. Guitar and E.G. Conture, *7 Tips for Talking with Your Child: A Guide for Parents*, 7th ed. (Stuttering Foundation of America, 2006).

Private parts

Sometime between the ages of 2 and 3, most children become involved in the process of toilet training. If they haven't already begun to discover their private parts, the interest is sure to emerge now that their diaper is off and more attention is being paid to their bodily functions. And during this time, some toddlers take great delight in being nude. Both behaviors are normal, if not always socially appropriate.

Genital exploration

When boys and girls first notice their penis or vagina, their interest is no different from when they were infants and first explored their fingers and toes. They soon discover that touching their genital area is pleasurable and may return their hands to the area again and again. A little boy may begin to notice erections — a normal, non-sexual occurrence at this age — and ask why his penis is getting big.

At this age, your toddler's actions are not sexual. This exploration is normal. These youngsters are simply discovering their bodies.

Toddler nudity

A related concern is nudity. Toddlers in this age group are learning to dress and undress themselves. Many youngsters prefer the undressing half of this equation and enjoy running around in the buff! Fear not — your child is not destined to become an exhibitionist.

If the environment is socially appropriate (i.e., in the privacy of your own home), let your toddler be comfortable with her body and enjoy being nude. As with most things, if you make a big deal out of this habit, your willful toddler is likely to strengthen her resolve to keep her clothes off. Take this opportunity to teach what is acceptable in a public versus a private environment, setting limits by not allowing nudity in a public space or while guests are visiting. Of course, the stage of toilet training your toddler is at may also influence how tolerant you can be! Regardless, handle your toddler's nudity with composure, take pride in her comfort, and wait for the stage to pass.

Did You Know?

Parental discretion

There is no magic age when nudity in front of your children goes from being okay to being inappropriate. Parents of the same gender as the child may well feel comfortable for much longer — if not always — than an opposite-gender caregiver. As a general rule, if you are beginning to feel uncomfortable, if you sense that your child is uncomfortable, or if your child is displaying increasing interest in your private areas, it is probably time to become more discreet around your little one.

Guide to

Managing genital exploration

If your toddler's exploration of his genitals is excessive or inappropriate in the social context, these guidelines might help:

- Try not to be embarrassed and take care not to act shocked or scold your child for this behavior. This will only teach him that embarrassment and shame are what he should feel in response to a natural curiosity. Rather, this behavior should be ignored, provided that the exploration is taking place in the privacy of your home.
- Take the opportunity to teach your toddler the names for the relevant anatomical parts. Proper terms are to be encouraged, though your family may use different names with which you are more comfortable.
- Teach your child that his genitals are private. They shouldn't be shown to or touched by anybody, with the exception of a parent when the area is being cleaned or a doctor when being examined.
- If your youngster touches himself in a public area or around guests in your home, take his hand and distract or redirect him, again emphasizing that these body parts are private.
- It is not unusual for children of this age to take an interest in each other's genital area while playing doctor or similar pretend play. If you see your child involved in such an interaction, tell the pair that those areas are private and are not to be shown to other people. Redirect the activity, once again avoiding scolding and inducing shame.
- If you are worried that your toddler's interest in his or others' genitals is excessive and out of keeping with what you think is normal, consult your child's physician. While it's certainly not usually the case, this interest can occasionally be a sign of sexual abuse.

Family nudity

At some point, your toddler may comment on or ask about the anatomy of a parent of the opposite gender, and this may make you wonder whether it is okay for her to be exposed to your nudity.

Being comfortable with your own body is likely to influence your toddler positively. Indirectly, you are teaching her to be comfortable with, not ashamed of, her own body, and you are creating an environment that is conducive to discussion and questions that may be important both now and in the future.

At this young age, answer her questions simply and truthfully: "Boys have penises and girls have vaginas," or "When boys and girls grow up, hair grows in these areas."

Television time

Chances are you have at least one television in your home, and you may well turn it on and off without much thought. But have you considered how the TV is affecting your toddler? Is she privy to the shows that you watch? Is she beginning to take an interest in children's television? Is she accustomed to having the TV on in the background or at mealtimes?

Television viewing can have both positive and negative effects on children and adults alike. As parents, it is our job to take responsibility for our children's television habits. The information that follows aims to empower you with information and tips to tackle this task.

Developmental considerations

The effect that television will have on your child will depend in part on her developmental stage.

Reality versus fantasy

Keep in mind that toddlers cannot yet distinguish between reality and fantasy. It is not uncommon to hear about toddlers having nightmares after having watched the news with Mommy or Daddy. Global news can at times be traumatizing enough for adults, let alone young children who don't understand that what they are witnessing is, generally speaking, far removed from their own micro-universe. Likewise, many children's classics demonstrate violence — both Bambi's and Babar's mothers are killed, for example — which your toddler will not yet be able to recognize as fantasy and which can feel very frightening.

Programming versus advertising

Just as they cannot yet distinguish between reality and fantasy, toddlers are not able to differentiate between regular programming and commercials. Children of this age believe what they are told, which renders them particularly susceptible to the influence of advertising.

Depending on the message being conveyed, this influence may be positive, but young children are often the target market for unhealthy snack foods, toys based on TV characters, and the like. You may find your willful toddler demanding these products, falling prey to but too young to understand the power of television marketing.

Benefits

When used wisely and responsibly, TV can provide your toddler with both entertainment and education. Excellent educational programming that aims to teach everything from social skills (sharing, kindness, and manners) to early literacy and math is available. Television can also expose young children to far-off places and people different from themselves, providing opportunities for learning that they might not otherwise have. While not a replacement for active learning, moderate TV viewing with appropriate content can be a positive thing.

Risks

The negative side of TV comes from two factors. The first is the content of the television programming itself, while the second is the time taken away from other, more constructive activities. Studies show that the average North American child spends approximately 3 hours per day in front of the TV.

Violence

Caution must be exercised to monitor violent images your toddler may be exposed to. Apart from the fact that it may be traumatizing for her to see, violence on TV is often glamorized, with little depiction of punishment for or consequences deriving from the violent acts. What's more, there is evidence that viewing violence on TV is associated with an increase in violent behavior, especially in boys.

Did You Know?

TV and obesity

Nutrition is an issue much discussed in relation to TV watching, particularly in light of the increasingly recognized and studied epidemic of obesity among children. Several factors related to television and other screen-based media are thought to have a negative effect on children's nutritional status.

Time spent sitting in front of the television or computer screen is time spent away from active playing and physical activity, both of which promote physical well-being and healthy habits.

Compounding the problem is that studies show that children who are less fit are more likely to consume snack foods that are higher in fat. They are influenced by TV commercials promoting sugared cereals, fast food, and other unhealthy food choices. Children who are allowed to eat in front of the TV may also be consuming unhealthy snacks. Evidence suggests that when mesmerized by the screen, youth and adults alike lose their ability to regulate their intake and eat more than their body requires.

HOW TO
Monitor television viewing by toddlers

Both the American Academy of Pediatrics and the Canadian Paediatric Society endorse the following guidelines to help you take responsibility and guide your children toward healthy viewing habits.

1. Set ground rules for television viewing in your home, helping to form the basis for a lifetime of healthy habits. The American Academy of Pediatrics specifically states that TV should be discouraged completely before the age of 2. Instead, encourage other activities that promote proper brain development, such as talking, playing, and reading. After the age of 2, time spent in front of the television or other screens, such as computers, should be limited to less than 1 to 2 hours a day.

2. Carefully monitor and control your toddler's television viewing. Program ratings are available to guide you, as are electronic devices that allow you to control when the television is turned on and what stations can be viewed. Neither of these, however, are a substitute for personally previewing the programs that you will allow your kids to watch and ensuring that you are comfortable with their content and the values portrayed.

3. Choose educational programming appropriate to your child's developmental stage whenever possible. Ensure that the content is not violent and pay attention to references to sexuality, alcohol, and smoking. Make use of a PVR or VCR to record appropriate programming that can be viewed with your children at a convenient time. Rented DVDs provide similar flexibility.

4. Watch television with your toddler, rather than using it as a babysitter. Take the opportunity to discuss what you are viewing — both the programming and the advertising.

5. Ensure that caregivers, including parents who live in separate households, have consistent rules.

6. Do not have a television set in your child's bedroom. A central location will allow for supervision and increased family interaction.

7. Make a habit of turning the television off during mealtime. This is an ideal time to sit together and talk with your children. Similarly, avoid keeping the television on when you're not watching it, contributing to unnecessary background sound.

Did You Know?

Computer time

Generally speaking, the same guidelines for responsible television viewing can be applied to computer and Internet use. After the age of 2, a maximum of 1 to 2 hours of total screen time (TV, computer, video games) is way more than enough. From an Internet safety perspective, parental controls can be used so that certain sites are blocked or access is limited to a few sites that you choose. Share passwords within the family to keep tabs on your children's use. Care must be taken to avoid exposure to inappropriate content on the Internet, such as pornography.

Adult behaviors

Apart from violence, television may expose young children to adult behaviors, such as sexuality or alcohol and tobacco use, before they are old enough to understand their meaning and judge what they are seeing as good or bad. In this respect, caution should also be exercised with children's programming — some animated films deemed appropriate for youngsters show alcohol or tobacco use with no depiction of their potentially negative consequences.

Competition

Excessive television viewing not only takes time away from physical activity, but also competes with playing, reading, speaking, and generally interacting positively with family and peers. These activities are all part of active learning and social development, which are crucial to a child's development through her early years. Equally important is your toddler's ability to entertain herself for short periods of time. Television use may take away the opportunity for her to develop this skill.

Babysitting

We all need a break sometimes and may be tempted to resort to occasional use of the television as a babysitter, but doing this regularly will detract from important interactions between the caregiver and child. Additionally, when the TV is used as a pacifier when a toddler is acting up, the caregiver is avoiding an opportunity for effective discipline and its positive longer-term effects on the young child.

Welcoming a new sibling

Many parents of older toddlers are considering having a second child, if they haven't already taken the plunge. You have likely received lots of advice and many conflicting opinions about the best time to introduce a new family member. Some people prefer to have kids close together because they get through the baby stage sooner and feel that their kids will play together and be close. Others prefer to wait a little while. One baby on hand at a time is enough, and perhaps having kids at different stages will cut down on sibling rivalry. The fact is that there is no "right" time — just the time that works for you.

Preparing your toddler

There will be challenges to face no matter how far apart your children are spaced, and whether they will play together as kids, be rivals, or be close depends in the long run on many factors, most of which are beyond your control. Rather than worrying about these issues, you are better off to plan what is best for you and concentrate on achieving a happy transition into your expanding family.

Developmental stage

If you have a toddler at home and are expecting a new baby, consider your child's age and personality at this stage of development. Toddlers in the 2- to 3-year-old range are still firmly attached to their parents, and they may not yet understand that their caregivers can be shared with others. They might feel threatened at the thought of a new baby arriving, particularly if they are sensitive to change. Be aware of your toddler's needs and potential insecurities. As you begin to tell her about the new baby, always emphasize that your love for her will not change, reinforcing her sense of security within your family.

Timing

You don't need to begin the baby discussion with your toddler as soon as you become pregnant. Children in this age group have difficulty grasping the concept of time. The difference between 9 months and next week may only be the length of time required to anticipate something that is already difficult to understand. To avoid the confusing concept of time, try to relate the baby's arrival to a season or an event that she understands. "The baby will come in the wintertime, when there's snow on the ground," or "The baby will come around Halloween," are appropriate examples.

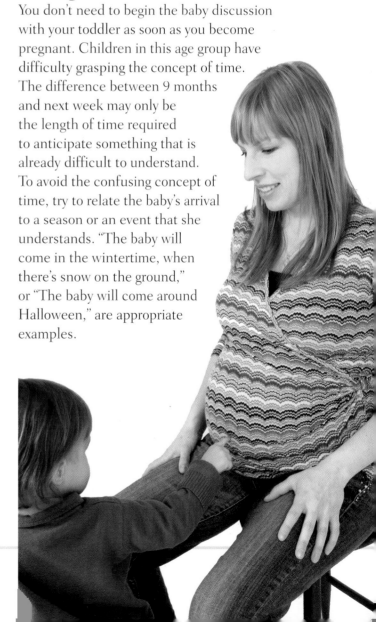

Did You Know?

Sibling rivalry

Rivalry at this early stage is usually limited to jealousy as the baby receives lots of attention from both the parents and the stream of visitors coming to the house. This can be addressed by ensuring that your toddler feels included, receives his share of attention — and perhaps some small gifts — and is assured of your love.

As you try to prevent sibling rivalry as your children grow, recognize that they will inevitably have different interests, strengths, and weaknesses and that you will need to respond to each as an individual. As your new baby develops, don't assume that he will do things in the same way as his older sibling. Be open to his emerging personality and interests, taking care to avoid judging him relative to his brother or sister. By the same token, try to avoid comparing the kids or commenting on their differences in their presence, focusing instead on each being special in his own way.

Chances are that a natural time will arise when it seems right to tell your child. She may notice that your belly is getting bigger, at which point you can let her know that a baby is growing inside. You may begin to shop for new baby items or set up the baby's room, in which case you can let your toddler know what you're doing. Allowing her to participate in these ventures can be positive in itself, making her feel included.

Life with a baby

Once your toddler knows that a baby is on its way, help your toddler imagine what life will be like with a sibling in the picture. Your toddler might envision an instant playmate, but be honest about what a newborn baby does — and does not — do. Explain, for example, that babies can't talk, so they cry a lot to try to tell us what they need. Suggest to your toddler that she will be able to help Mommy or Daddy figure out what the new baby is asking for. Several excellent "big brother (or sister)" books are on the market. Check out your local library or bookstore for suggestions, as both the words and pictures can be very helpful. Similarly, your toddler may be interested in pretending that her "doll" is a real baby and you can help her bathe, dress, and feed the doll so the abstract concept of a baby becomes more real.

Talking about the birth

Think ahead to what you have planned for the time of your new baby's birth. Tell your toddler that you and Dad will be going to the hospital when it's time to have the baby and that you and the baby will be there for a couple of nights before you will be home again. If grandparents or other family or friends will be caring for your toddler during this period, let her know this in advance and explain that she will have special time to spend alone with Grandpa and Grandma.

If appropriate, have your partner bring your toddler to the hospital to see you and to meet the baby — but be aware that the foreign environment of the hospital and seeing you in a hospital bed may frighten your toddler. Think about bringing a book or toy from home to read or to play with her. This will make her feel more comfortable, shifting the focus away from the baby and reminding her that her relationship with you remains unchanged. If everyone is buying gifts for the new baby, try to make sure that your toddler also receives some small gifts so as not to feel too left out.

Reactions

What you should expect from your toddler once the new baby has arrived is anybody's guess! Parents usually think they know how their firstborn will react, but they're proven wrong as often as not. Needless to say, reactions are extremely variable. Some toddlers ignore their new sibling; others are affectionate and want to play with the baby all the time; still others may be aggressive.

Be aware that the initial reaction may not last. This is a time of transition for the entire family, and your youngster's response to her new sibling is bound to change over time.

With this in mind, if her initial reaction is to ignore the baby, don't push the issue. With time, she will likely become more comfortable in her sibling's presence and confident that her relationship with you is not threatened, and she may well warm up to her younger brother or sister.

Acting out

Toddlers may act out or try to act like the baby in an effort to command attention. Mild regression in a new big brother or sister is entirely normal. After all, they are witnessing the shifting of much of the attention to the new baby in the house. Examples of typical behavior problems include potty accidents or a desire to wear diapers in a toilet-trained child and speaking baby talk in a toddler who usually speaks very clearly.

While this conduct certainly shouldn't be encouraged, avoid telling her to "act your age" or "stop being a baby." Depending on the behavior, you may be able to ignore it, knowing that it will pass in time. Find ways to give your toddler the attention that she is clearly seeking, and praise her at times when she is acting grown up.

Did You Know?

Aggressive reactions

Clearly, if your toddler is aggressive toward your new baby, this must be addressed. Teach toddlers to be gentle by demonstrating appropriate behavior. Providing a doll to practice with may be helpful. Be careful, though, not to alienate your toddler further in the disciplining process. Offer lots of praise for positive behaviors, whether related to the baby or not, remembering to give the toddler the love and security that he desires.

HOW TO
Help your toddler accept a new sibling

1. Maintain a routine. Toddlers thrive on routine, but a new baby at home can certainly change the daily schedule. Try as much as possible to maintain activities in which your toddler participates, giving him time to play or interact in a setting where nothing has changed. If you have help at home, or if your youngster is in daycare, this will clearly be easier than if you're on your own. Even taking advantage of your newborn baby's sleep times to take your toddler (and the sleeping baby) for a familiar play date can be advantageous. Changes in your toddler's routine should be minimized during this period of transition. This is not the time to change to a big-boy bed or to begin toilet training. Such major milestones should either be accomplished well before the baby is born or wait until your new routine is comfortably established.

2. Make your toddler feel included in the new changes surrounding him. Capitalize on the fact that children generally love to help by finding jobs that are manageable for your little one. For example, ask him to get the baby's towel and washcloth at bath time — you might even give him a cloth of his own and show him how to gently wash the baby's feet. Similarly, you might keep your supply of diapers in a spot accessible to your toddler and give him the job of keeping the diaper bin in the baby's room full. If he isn't interested in helping out, don't force the issue. That he sees you offering to include him is enough to show him that you're thinking about him, as well as the new baby.

3. Try to spend individual time with him too. This can be tricky for moms who are nursing because it is difficult to find time away from the newborn. Many women quickly become adept at reading to their toddler while nursing, or just inviting him to cuddle with them. If you can hand the baby off to your partner or another relative for a short time between feeds, you may be able to play one on one with your toddler, go for a walk, or do something else special with the two of you. This will inevitably become easier as the first few months pass, but even short periods at the beginning are worthwhile.

4. Ask for support. It is logistically easier and equally special to ensure that your toddler spends quality time with his dad, with grandparents, or with others to whom he is close. This is a hectic period in your household, and your little one will enjoy being taken out of the house on an outing or to the park. He will appreciate the love and attention, as well as a break from home life, where for the moment everything is revolving around his new sibling.

5. Be patient. The newborn period is both wonderful and a challenge — to you as a parent and to your toddler. Provide your child with love and with appropriate attention. Make him feel included. In time, the transitional period will pass and he will settle into his sibling role.

Traveling with your toddler

Toddlers between the age of 2 and 3 are active little people whose minds are like sponges, absorbing all they're exposed to. These traits make this age a great time to explore your surroundings with them. Don't be disappointed, however, to find that you may not be able to do all the things you had hoped. Traveling with a toddler is very different from taking an adults-only trip. Keep your expectations realistic, and you'll find that traveling with your little one can be rewarding in its own unique way.

Day trips

For tips on where to take your toddler around town, talk to other parents, explore your municipality's website, and look for kids' guides in your local library or bookstore. Many cities have museums, science centers, and galleries to explore. Some have areas designed specifically for young children. If your toddler seems to enjoy these activities, inquire about membership opportunities, which will make repeat visits much more economical.

Guide to

Safe and fun day trips

Whether you have planned a quick visit to a local site or a longer day trip, consider a few factors that will make carting your toddler around a more successful experience.

- Think about what time of day suits your child best. If he tends to nap in the afternoon, consider making an early start, reaching your destination soon after it opens. This way, you'll beat the crowds and be home — or back in the car — in time for your youngster's nap. Other toddlers peak later in the day. Whatever your child's temperament and routine, take it into consideration when making your plans.
- Make sure you pack a little bag with all the essentials. Healthy, portable snacks, such as soft granola bars or dry cereal, will no doubt be appreciated. Depending on your destination, a picnic meal may be toted along. Bring non-perishables or include a small ice pack to keep your lunch cool.
- Pack diapers or a change of underwear and pants. Diaper wipes are handy, as they can be used not just for wiping little bums but also to wipe dirty hands, spills, and the like.
- Keep in mind the strategies for preventing temper tantrums in public and applying effective discipline outside the home.
- Enjoy these outings as special family time or invite friends with children of the same age. You will no doubt find that having a toddler can open up the whole family's eyes to what your community has to offer.

mean a trip to the sugar bush to watch sap being tapped from the maple trees. Apple pies and pancakes with fresh maple syrup are guaranteed to please your toddler! Inquire around your neighborhood for other popular local options.

Longer trips

Where to travel? In short, anywhere! Travel with toddlers need not be restricted to child-focused destinations, though they are certainly popular options. Appropriate children's entertainment can be found in most cities, tropical destinations, and even places farther afield. Of course, where you choose to go depends on your own sense of adventure, your child's interests and temperament, and a little common sense. One thing you can be sure of after you have children is that your days of traveling light are over! Consider the following factors when planning your trip.

Planned activities

Before you choose your destination, make sure that your toddler will be happy with the activities on offer. This doesn't mean that an amusement park need be close by, unless this is what you are aiming for. Young toddlers can amuse themselves for hours in the sand — a great option, provided that you keep both sun and water safety in mind — and even if your vacation is not a sunny one, a hotel pool can be a lifesaver for a toddler who enjoys splashing around.

As a general rule to make sure that your toddler is happy and occupied, keep the time that you spend at each site to a reasonable length and make sure that food

Zoos are usually a big hit with this age group, as are water parks or open green spaces where youngsters can run around.

Unstructured play in your own home or local park is equally important. Strive for a healthy combination so that your toddler can take advantage of local opportunities for learning and play without being overprogrammed.

Farther afield

Day trips slightly farther afield can provide fun for the whole family and may be a special treat for your toddler. Conservation areas provide wonderful settings for toddlers to explore and are usually equipped with picnic areas and bathroom facilities. Depending on where you live, the fall season can offer apple picking and visits to the pumpkin patch, while the springtime may for snacks and meals, and a bed for naps, are available when needed.

LOCAL SITES

Local museums and galleries often include children's areas, and remember that curious little ones may enjoy looking around at the regular exhibits too. Use common sense and your knowledge of your child to determine how well this option will work for you and the adult visitors around you. Many families traveling together find it useful to get to know the local parks and playgrounds. These visits offer a reprieve from the tourist traps, allow your toddler a chance to let off steam, and may even provide insight into the local culture.

WALKING AND HIKING

If hiking is on your agenda, think about how your toddler will fare. While younger babies are usually happy to be carried in a backpack and older children may be able to walk long distances independently, toddlers are usually somewhere in between. Keep walks short and snacks on hand with a toddler in tow!

STAYING PUT

You may find that, rather than packing your bags every day to move on to a new area, your toddler will be more amenable to a trip where you stay put for the duration, perhaps with flexible day trips planned from your base.

Car travel

An important part of planning a long-distance trip with your toddler is choosing the most appropriate mode of travel.

Depending on your destination, you may have no option, but if the choice is yours, consider the pros and cons of traveling by car, bus, train, or airplane. What follows are some tips to make life easier with various modes of travel, starting with cars.

STARTING OUT

When planning a road trip, think ahead about what driving schedule will best suit your family. Will your toddler sleep in the car if you get an early start and stop for breakfast after you've got a couple of hours of driving behind you? Is she likely to nap in the car, or should you aim to reach your destination before a nap is required?

STOPPING

No matter what your schedule, be sure to make frequent stops. Toddlers need opportunities to stretch their legs and run around, even for just a short break. Stop for meals and snacks. Soft granola bars or precut fruit and vegetable pieces are healthy options that are unlikely to make a big mess. Remember to incorporate diaper changes into your pit stops and encourage your toilet-trained toddler to use the facilities.

ON THE ROAD

Think about car-friendly activities to keep your toddler occupied. Music and singing are sure to pass some of the time. Tell stories in the car or have your child participate in making up silly stories as you go. Take advantage of the scenes outside your window by playing games such as "I spy." If your child knows colors or shapes, see if she can find a brown cow or a round sign. Older preschoolers who are learning their letters and sounds may be able to find "something that starts with a B." Finally, many families find that a portable DVD player with one or two rented movies can make a long car ride much more bearable.

Buses and trains

While you can usually book bus and train tickets in advance, you often can't reserve seats ahead of time. Make sure that you arrive with plenty of time to find seats together.

Buses don't offer food, and depending on the route, food offered on trains is usually minimal and very costly, so bring enough snacks and meals to last the journey. Inquire ahead of time about bathroom facilities on the bus. Trains have bathrooms but may not be equipped with diaper changing facilities.

Finally, an advantage of trains is the comfort of looking out the windows and having room to roam. For both safety reasons and to be fair to your fellow passengers, watch your toddler closely and stay with her as she stretches her legs to explore.

Airplanes

Most airlines require that toddlers over 2 years of age occupy their own seat, and that means you have to pay for it. Unfortunately, discounted fares for children are uncommon nowadays, but it never hurts to inquire, just in case.

SEATING

Since airplane seats can be reserved in advance, give some thought to which type of seat would best suit your needs. The bulkhead has more leg room but serves as an emergency exit row on some aircraft, rendering it inappropriate for children. Window seats offer the advantage of a good view outside, while the aisle offers easy access to the bathrooms with the least disruption to other passengers.

STROLLERS AND CAR SEATS

For ease of travel through a large airport, bring a small umbrella-type stroller and then collapse and check it when you get to the gate. The flight crew will have it ready for you when you get off the plane.

The majority of toddlers in the 2- to 3-year-old range use a forward-facing car seat appropriate for children 20 to 40 lbs

HOW TO
Treat motion sickness

Even a short car trip can result in motion sickness for toddlers. Toddlers may not articulate that they're feeling sick until it's too late and they've already vomited, and some may express the vague sensation as "tummy" pain. If you know that your youngster is prone to motion sickness, here are some strategies:

1. Encourage your toddler to look straight ahead, out the window.

2. Let in some fresh air when possible.

3. Make sure he eats light snacks at regular intervals.

4. Use the power of distraction with funny stories or songs.

5. Try a "sea band," an elasticized bracelet that puts pressure on an acupressure point on the inner wrist. This safe, non-medicinal remedy is sometimes effective, but you may have to take it in with a few stitches to make it fit properly around your little one's wrist.

6. If motion sickness is still troubling your toddler, speak to your child's doctor about whether children's Gravol might be appropriate.

(10 to 18 kg) for car travel. While not a requirement on airplanes, most airlines will allow a car seat that meets safety standards to be used during the flight. This is the safest option, and will also ensure that you have a car seat to use throughout your vacation. Check the car seat's label to ensure that it is "certified for use in motor vehicles and aircraft," and remember that your toddler will need to be appropriately buckled in for the whole flight.

If you opt not to bring your car seat along, make sure that your toddler sits in her seat with her seatbelt fastened during takeoff, landing, and at times of turbulence. When in doubt, follow your flight attendant's direction.

DIAPERING

Use the bathroom or diaper changing facilities before boarding. Although most aircraft have a change table in at least one bathroom, you may not be able to use it until you're safely in the air and there's no significant turbulence.

EXTRA CLOTHES

Be sure to bring a change of clothes for your toddler.

Travel documents

Requirements for travel documents are subject to change and vary depending on your destination. It is best to check the requirements for both you and your toddler well before you are scheduled to leave.

Passport

In this age of increasing security, it is best to have a passport for both you and your child for travel outside of the country and, at the least, proper government-issued identification for trips within your national borders.

Guide to

Airplane activities and snacks

To keep your toddler happy, healthy, and busy on a flight, be prepared with some quiet activities and healthy snacks.

- Consider buying age-appropriate activity books, a fresh packet of crayons, a small toy, books, and the like and stowing them in a knapsack that your youngster can carry by himself. This will make him feel important and included, and the new loot inside will keep him both surprised and entertained.
- Avoid noisy toys or those with small pieces that may get lost.

- If you have more than one child, give them each their own bag. While sharing should always be encouraged, airplane rides are not the time to insist on it!
- Bring snacks and a meal packed from home to ensure not only that your toddler likes the food but that it can be eaten whenever he is hungry. Food offered on airplanes is variable, snacks may not be child-friendly — nuts, for example, may be a choking hazard and possibly an allergy risk — and the time it is served depends on a host of factors.

OFFICIAL DOCUMENTS

The following websites may be useful for up-to-date information, as well as applications for passports:

United States Bureau of Consular Affairs: http://travel.state.gov/passport
United States government information: www.usa.gov

Passport Canada
www.passportcanada.gc.ca
Canada Border Services Agency: www.cbsa.gc.ca

Visa

In addition to a passport, you may need a visa for entry, depending on what country you'll be visiting. Check with that country's local consulate or embassy for their visa requirements.

Letter of travel consent

If you are traveling on your own with your child, it is strongly suggested that you carry a letter of travel consent signed by the child's other parent or guardian with legal custody, if applicable. The letter should include the contact information of the parent or guardian granting consent, and it is strongly recommended that it be notarized. If the parent or guardian is divorced or deceased, a custody document or death certificate is required.

Insurance

Before you go, look into travel insurance — both travel cancellation and health. Plans can change out of necessity, or health issues may arise when you're away, even without children in the mix. Having a toddler along requires even greater flexibility!

Did You Know?

Immunization

Before traveling, always ensure that your child's routine immunizations are up to date, and for particular destinations, consider whether specific travel vaccines are indicated. In such cases, it is advisable to see your doctor or consult a travel clinic at least 2 months before your trip to allow time for any necessary vaccines to be administered.

For specific information on travel health and vaccines, the following agencies may be helpful:
- United States Centers for Disease Control and Prevention
- Public Health Agency of Canada

Itinerary

Be sure to leave all your contact information — your itinerary, with addresses, phone numbers, and fax numbers where applicable — with a trusted relative or friend. By the same token, bring along contact numbers for those you may want or need to be in touch with.

Healthy travel

Travel can result in various health issues, ranging from motion sickness to traveler's diarrhea and tropical diseases.

Traveler's diarrhea

When traveling to tropical destinations, care must be taken to avoid traveler's diarrhea. Stick to fruits and vegetables that can be peeled to ensure that the produce is not rinsed with contaminated water. Make sure that any meat, chicken, or seafood you eat is cooked through, and drink bottled water, ensuring that the cap is sealed before you open it. Similarly, avoid ice cubes in poured soft drinks.

It is wise to bring along packets of a children's oral rehydration solution, such as Pedialyte or Lytren. Reconstitute the powder according to the directions and seek medical attention if you are concerned that your toddler is becoming dehydrated.

International Association for Medical Assistance to Travelers

When far from home, your mind will be at ease if you know where to seek medical attention when needed. Take advantage of the International Association for Medical Assistance to Travelers (IAMAT) or other such organizations. IAMAT is a non-profit association that keeps a list of English-speaking doctors trained in either North America or Europe and now working in 125 different countries. Membership is free, though donations are encouraged, and entitles you to the up-to-date physician directory, among other benefits.

Travel safety

Your vigilance with respect to safety should be no less when you're traveling than when you're close to home. Use common sense in choosing destinations that are considered safe for visitors. If you're thinking about travel to an unstable region, purchase cancellation insurance and check for government-issued travel advisories before your departure.

Car seats

Think ahead about your need for car seats while you are away and decide whether you will bring your own or rent one once you have arrived. Look into car seat rentals either from baby equipment stores or from car rental agencies. Consider renting a car as opposed to using taxis so your car seat can stay in place for the duration of your trip.

Water safety

Travel with young children often involves swimming, whether at a hotel pool or the beach. Either way, don't rely on a lifeguard to ensure your child's safety. Maintain close supervision of your toddler at all times — most toddlers can't swim independently yet and need you right at their side. Even when you're both out of the water, do not stray from your little ones. They can quickly get lost on a crowded beach and wander into the water unattended.

Did You Know?

Jet lag

Should your destination take you across time zones, there's no easy solution to the unavoidable effects of jet lag. Strategies to prepare your child will depend on how far and for how long you're traveling. If you'll be away for just a few days, for example, and the time difference is only an hour or two, it may be worth keeping your toddler on your home clock, allowing him to go to bed and rise earlier or later than usual. If you can manage this schedule while you're away, the transition upon your return will be minimal. If your trip is longer and the time change more significant, expect the adjustment to be gradual and be as flexible as possible with your daily plans.

Hotel rooms

Your hotel room may not be as childproof as your own home. Take care to ensure that outlets are covered and that sharp objects and window cords are out of reach of your toddler's curious little hands.

Food away from home

Every toddler is different with respect to likes and dislikes, ability to sit still in a restaurant, and willingness to try new food. You know your child best, so to minimize everybody's frustration, consider these factors when planning a trip. Consider renting a condominium, for example, or ensuring that your hotel room has at minimum a small fridge and perhaps a kitchenette. Keep drinks and snacks in your room, and think about cooking some meals. Supper at home base is often best for a tired toddler at day's end and will go a long way toward making your evening and bedtime routine easier to follow.

Sleeping away from home

Sleeping in an unfamiliar environment is challenging at the best of times, so try to ease the transition by thinking ahead about what setup will best suit both you and your toddler. Renting a condominium might allow your toddler to have her own room, or perhaps she would be fine with — and may even prefer — a cot set up beside your bed. If she's still in a crib, call ahead to ensure that either a regular or portable crib is available for you to use. If not, look into local rental options.

Whatever the setup allows, try to maintain your home routine as much as possible. Traveling is not the right time to try out a new routine that you've been meaning to initiate, nor is it the time to break your toddler of her "bad habits."

Traveling *without* your toddler

While family vacations are special times, so are times for you and your partner to be on your own and reconnect without the children in tow. If planned appropriately, with arrangements for a responsible and loving caregiver to stay with your toddler, a trip on your own can be positive for everyone. After a little rest, you may even find you're a better parent upon your return!

Guide to

Traveling without your toddler

Regardless of your travel mode and destination, your primary consideration will be whom you will leave your toddler with.

- To care for your toddler while you are away, consider grandparents, a mature babysitter, a close friend, or another relative. Whoever you choose should be above all trustworthy and familiar to your young child.

- If possible, have the sitter move into your house while you are away, thus allowing your toddler to stay in his regular surroundings. Of course, if he is comfortable at Grandma's house, a change of setting might be a reasonable option.

- Because children of this age thrive on routine (e.g., daycare, activities, and bedtime), try to ensure that it will be maintained while you are away. This will involve leaving detailed instructions for the caregiver.

- Make sure to leave directions about any medications your toddler may take, as well as his health card and identification, the phone number of his physician, and emergency contact information.

- Leave your contact information, along with a detailed itinerary, so that you can be reached at any time.

- Keep the length of your trip reasonable. If you have never left your toddler before, begin with an evening out, allowing the caregiver to put him to bed, and progress to a short overnight trip away. With time, your toddler will become accustomed to saying goodbye to you and seeing you return home again, which will permit longer vacations.

- While you should never leave your toddler without saying goodbye, keep in mind that, from a developmental point of view, he sees little difference between "tomorrow" and "next month." Therefore, prepare your toddler for your departure, what to expect while you're away, and the fun things you may plan for your return, but do so only a few days before you leave. Any earlier will only increase anxiety as your toddler anticipates your vacation for what seems to him to be a drawn-out length of time.

- When you say goodbye, give your youngster a kiss and a hug, but don't force him to be affectionate if he isn't up for it. By the same token, by all means telephone to see how everyone is faring, but if your toddler doesn't want to talk to you on the phone, don't force the issue. You may find your little one to be either clingy or standoffish upon your return. Rest assured that this will be temporary — provide him with the same love, affection, and routine as you did before your vacation, and you'll find that before long, things will be back to normal.

Dental care

By the end of their third year, most toddlers' primary teeth, including two sets of molars, will all have erupted. These "baby" teeth have thinner outer enamel than permanent ones, making them more susceptible to decay. If not cared for properly, the pain that results will interfere with toddlers' sleeping, eating, speaking, and ability to concentrate and learn, which are all important at this stage of growth and development. Additionally, good habits formed now will be the basis for a lifetime of good dental care.

First visits to the dentist

The first dental visits are designed to catch problems early, to check if your home brushing routine is effective, and to make youngsters comfortable with the dentist.

Some dentists have specific pediatric training and specialize in tooth care for children. Many adult or family dentists are likewise comfortable seeing toddlers in their office and are well equipped to care for them, provided that there are no complicating issues. Ask your own dentist or pediatrician what she recommends for your toddler.

Consider bringing your toddler along on your regular visit before her own appointment is scheduled. This will give her the opportunity to see the office and equipment and will hopefully decrease any anxiety she may have. Several books about kids' trips to the dentist are also available, and it may help to read one of these.

Brushing and flossing

Toddlers should get in the habit of brushing their teeth twice a day for approximately 2 minutes each time, with particular attention paid to a good brushing immediately before going to bed. An age-appropriate toothbrush should be used — those designed for 2- to 3-year-olds generally have handles made for their little hands to grasp independently. The brushes should have soft, rounded bristles and will need to be replaced every 3 to 4 months or when the bristles appear flattened. Ensure that no more than a pea-sized amount of fluoridated toothpaste is used and teach your toddler to spit it out of her mouth

Did You Know?

Scheduling dental visits

The American and Canadian dental associations recommend that children visit the dentist after their first tooth erupts or by 1 year of age. If your toddler hasn't yet had his first dentist appointment, ensure that it takes place by his third birthday. It is recommended that dental visits take place every 6 months for routine care. Be sure to make an additional appointment if you notice any chalky white or brown spots on your toddler's teeth or gums or if you have specific questions or concerns.

Did You Know?

Fluoride facts

Fluoride is a naturally occurring element that has a topical effect on the teeth, helping to prevent dental caries, or cavities. It's added to most toothpaste, as well as to the drinking water in many communities. As with so many things, however, too much of a good thing can be harmful. If too much fluoride is ingested into the body, rather than simply exposed to the surface of the teeth, it can cause dental fluorosis in children under 7 years of age. This condition affects the enamel of the teeth. Most cases are mild, with changes apparent only to the dentist upon examination, while more severe cases can result in pitting or discoloration of the teeth.

To prevent fluorosis, children should use only a small (pea-sized) amount of fluoridated toothpaste. They should also be supervised closely when brushing their teeth and learn not to swallow excess toothpaste. If your local water source is fluoridated and otherwise safe, tap water should be encouraged over a bottled source. When such tap water is consumed, and fluoride is used appropriately for tooth brushing, you and your children are likely being exposed to the right amount — enough to prevent cavities but not enough to cause fluorosis.

Occasionally, fluoride supplements in the form of mouthwashes or lozenges are required. If your water comes from a well or a spring, you can have it tested to determine its natural fluoride concentration. If your local water source contains less than 0.3 ppm of fluoride, teeth are not being reliably brushed twice a day, and your toddler is at a high risk for dental caries — due, for example, to a family history of tooth decay — then speak to your dentist about whether a fluoride supplement is needed.

properly. Rinse the toothbrush after each use and allow it to air-dry.

At this stage of ever-increasing independence, your toddler may want to brush her own teeth. This certainly should be encouraged! Consider sharing the job. Your youngster may begin the process, so she takes responsibility and begins to learn the proper technique, and you may follow up, completing the job to ensure that all the surfaces are properly reached. You can also take the opportunity to role model, standing at the sink together and brushing your teeth. While it's not always easy, if your toddler will allow you to floss her teeth, it's never too early to practice this important habit.

Diet concerns

Apart from regular dental visits and proper brushing, youngsters' teeth and general health will benefit if you discourage sugary snacks, particularly sticky ones that get stuck on their teeth. Encourage consuming water over juice and be strict about no juice or milk, including breast milk, after teeth are brushed in the evening. The natural sugars in these drinks will sit on the teeth overnight, causing tooth decay.

Pacifiers and thumb sucking

There's no doubt that it's easier to break your toddler of her pacifier or thumb-sucking habit at a younger age than it is to tackle it now. By age 2 to 3, despite no longer having a "need" to suck, willful toddlers will be determined to hang on to the habit! But don't be too discouraged. You may not like them to continue the habit at this age, but it's not likely to affect their teeth.

To minimize harm, try to confine soother use to naps or bedtime and never put sugar, honey, or corn syrup on the soother. Of course, a thumb or fingers in the mouth are more difficult to control, but strongly encourage your toddler to give up both habits before the age of 5, prior to the eruption of her permanent teeth. For strategies on weaning toddlers from pacifiers and thumb sucking, see page 53 and 55.

Right to play

With a 2- to 3-year-old toddler at home, you are well aware that playing comes naturally to them. Left to their own devices, toddlers of this age are naturally curious, spontaneously exploring and learning from their environment. In fact, playing is so fundamentally important to children's optimal development that it is recognized by the United Nations Convention on the Rights of the Child as every child's right.

As parents, it is our job to provide our toddlers with a balance between structured and unstructured play, playing with other children and having time to play on their own. The appropriate balance for each child will be different, depending on her individual personality and interests. If your toddler is happy and thriving, you are likely providing the right mix.

Play dates

Play dates can be a wonderful, toddler-focused activity. Parents connect with one another, kids play together, and rotating hosts provide a change of scenery for all involved.

While all this is theoretically true, when the focus is on 2- to 3-year-old toddlers, your expectations need to be realistic. If you

Guide to

Play date success

WHEN?

Remember that play dates can be stressful for young toddlers, as they are exposed to a new environment and people and are asked to behave well and to share their toys. To ensure that your toddler looks forward to this social time, keep the frequency of play dates to once or twice a week, or even less frequently if they are regularly in a social child-care setting. Plan play dates around your little one's schedule, not vice versa, and limit them to 1 or 2 hours at the most. A tired or hungry toddler is sure to be a cranky one, resulting in your play date being miserable for all.

HOW MANY KIDS?

So as not to overwhelm your 2-year-old, keep the crowd down to one or a maximum of two other children. Sharing and playing together are skills that your toddler is just beginning to learn. A small group is most conducive to providing a comfortable and non-threatening environment.

WHERE?

Most likely you will rotate playing host with the other participating families. Keep in mind, however, that most toddlers find it more difficult when the play date is at their house. They are more likely to become territorial because they need to share their toys, their home, their food, and their caregiver.

Prepare your toddler appropriately, remembering to ask before his friends arrive if he'd like to put away special toys that he isn't yet ready to share. Also consider adult-directed activities that don't involve toys, such as singing songs or participating in a craft. As an alternative, host the play date at an outdoor location, such as a nearby park. Going with one other family to a favorite local spot, such as the zoo, provides an opportunity for the toddlers to get used to seeing one another in a neutral, comfortable, fun environment.

SNACKS?

A well-fed (and well-rested) toddler is a happy one. Make sure that your child has had a snack beforehand or plan to begin the play date with a snack. Provide toddler-friendly food that isn't too messy. Consider choking hazards in this age group, and keep the offerings nut-free unless you're confident that your guests are all allergy-free. Cheese and crackers or cut-up veggies — but not choking hazards, such as raw carrots — and dip are both good options.

ACTIVITIES?

Remember that in this age group, the toddlers are likely too young for you to expect participation in group activities or games, with the exception of some who are closer to 3 years of age and comfortable with one another. It's best to put out a few toys — be they trucks, blocks, dolls, or a tea set — that may pique the little ones' interests. Observe what they're playing with and adapt the selection on offer as you go. Offer them the opportunity of free play, changing to an adult-directed activity if and when redirecting is required.

envision the adults catching up in the kitchen while the little ones play games in the basement, you may well be disappointed. Read on for what to expect and how to plan an age-appropriate play date so that both you and your toddler will get the maximum benefit and the least pain from these experiences.

Group toddler behavior

Keep in mind where your toddler is at developmentally when planning a play date.

Most children in this age range are interested in one another's activities but will continue to play separately until they are closer to 3 or sometimes even 4 years old. At this point, they will be more likely to engage each other in interactive play and may even enjoy games with simple rules, such as hide-and-seek. You will likely witness toddlers in their third year participating in some imaginary play, such as talking on a pretend telephone, having a tea party, and so on.

As these youngsters are brought to another child's house, or as they play host to their guests, they may become shy or alternatively territorial and bossy, particularly if they are feeling threatened or insecure. Unless your toddler is very comfortable with her environment and playmate, she will need to see you periodically for reassurance. Staying close by and providing a lap, a hug, or simply verbal reassurance will go far toward building your toddler's security and ensuring the success of future play dates.

Toddlers of 2 to 3 years of age are prone to temper tantrums as they strive for independence and express their frustration. If a toddler in the play group chooses to act out, make sure she is safe from injury and use appropriate strategies to manage the tantrum.

Age-appropriate toys

Modern parents are often concerned about whether their very young children are learning enough, so we buy toys designed to teach, for example, early letter recognition and math skills. We anxiously regard their peers' toys and read the packaging of items on store shelves to see what potential benefits can be derived.

Did You Know?

Age recommendations

Every toy on the market is labeled with a recommended age. This is based on safety and on the developmental level for which it was designed, taking into account physical and cognitive readiness, as well as the usual needs and interests of children of the given age. The age recommendations are important to consider: a toy that's too simple may bore your child, whereas one that's too advanced may lead to frustration — and could even be unsafe if used inappropriately. Keep in mind that these recommendations are just guidelines. Take them into account when buying for your toddler, but recognize that each child is unique and that you are likely the best judge of your toddler's own abilities and interests.

Guide to

Encouraging creative play

- Encourage creativity by allowing your toddler to color, paint, build with blocks, and use clay, such as Play-Doh.
- While we would encourage you to take an interest in your child's project, try not to provide too much direction or criticize their creations. If colors don't match or lines aren't straight, so be it. If your toddler is praised and he knows how much you like his painting or the bridge he built, his confidence will grow and he'll be more likely to return

to such creative endeavors. He'll be especially pleased if you display some of his creations for others to see!

- Try not to stifle his creativity by insisting on a clean work space. Protect your furniture with plastic coverings, provide your little one with a smock, and expect that a mess will be made. As with all toys, encourage your toddler to help you clean up at the end of playtime. Make up a song or rhyme incorporating "Tidy up time, tidy up time, toys away" to help your toddler establish and participate in a cleanup routine.

Relax! Toddlers certainly do learn as they play, and this is to be encouraged, but keep in mind that learning extends far beyond literacy and numbers. Other skills, such as imaginative play, decision making, leadership, socialization, and physical coordination, will all be learned in good time when toddlers are provided with plenty of free play, age-appropriate toys, and direction where required. And these skills will stand our children in good stead as they move through their early years and carry the skills along with them.

Every child is bound to have different interests and will play with some toys more than others. Make time for plenty of free play, allowing your toddler to choose her own activities. By the same token, respect when she has lost interest and is ready to move on to a different activity.

Gross-motor play

Equipment to stimulate gross-motor, or large-muscle, development is easily found at your local playground. Providing your toddler with free play outside will encourage her to run and jump, taking

As your toddler approaches the age of 3, you may consider purchasing a tricycle or a small bicycle with training wheels. Children should get in the habit of wearing a helmet from the time of their first tricycle. Purchase a helmet that meets safety standards and is a good fit for your toddler — and make wearing it a rule from day one.

Fine-motor play

Not all children are natural artists, but providing them with simple construction paper and crayons will allow them the opportunity to express their creativity while refining their fine-motor coordination by drawing scribbles, lines, circles, and the like. Inexpensive easels are popular items that may include a roll of paper, an erasable white board, a chalkboard, or a combination of the three. Age-appropriate puzzles, stacking blocks, and toys with dials, buttons, and keys are all examples of items that encourage fine-motor skills.

Language and cognitive play

Language and cognitive skills develop rapidly in this age group as toddlers move

advantage of climbing structures and practicing her balance on low-to-the-ground balance beams found in many play areas. Plastic cars or trains that toddlers sit on and push with their feet may complement this equipment.

Did You Know?

Adapting games

To develop language and cognitive skills, try adapting games for older children to your young toddler's level. A deck of cards, for example, can be used to play "I spy" by asking your child to find a red diamond or even a card with the number 1 when he's a little bit older. Similarly, traditional memory games can be adapted to a matching game,

so that toddlers are shown one picture and asked to find a matching pair. If your toddler is ready for and interested in early letter recognition, blocks or puzzles with letters and corresponding pictures (e.g., D accompanied by a picture of a dog) are a good place to start. Don't push your toddler, though — these are still early years, and learning through play should be enjoyable.

Guide to

Toy safety

To ensure that toys are safe for your toddler, keep the following guidelines in mind:

- Read the toy's label and instructions for use so that it is used safely, in the manner for which it was intended.
- Avoid toys with small parts that could cause your young toddler to choke.
- Buy toys that are well made so small pieces don't fall off easily and become a choking hazard.
- Avoid toys with sharp edges or points. Soft plastic is generally preferred over metal.
- Always buy non-toxic forms of items such as paints, crayons, and markers.
- Nothing replaces adult supervision to keep your toddler safe!

from stringing together two words to speaking in phrases and even sentences by age 3. Their knowledge of colors and numbers increases, and some toddlers of this age begin to recognize letters, though this often doesn't occur until age 4 or 5. All of these skills are best encouraged by speaking with and reading to your toddler, which assists her in exploring her world. Toys that emphasize these areas are also plentiful.

Social play

Socially, children in the 2- to 3-year-old range enjoy imaginary or pretend play. This can be encouraged in so many ways! As with all areas, follow your toddler's interests. Many youngsters enjoy learning about and imitating what they see adults doing. Playing in a pretend kitchen or playing with real kitchen items — provided they are safe — can be lots of fun, as can allowing your toddler to help you while you cook or bake. Similarly, cleaning up, such as with toy vacuums or brooms, playing with dolls, having a tea party, or playing doctor are all popular themes for pretend play.

Reading

Repeated studies have shown that reading to children from a young age plays an important role in their brain's development. And not only will reading aloud to your toddler stimulate her cognitive growth, but it will also help form a close emotional relationship between the two of you. In addition, if reading time with your little one is made enjoyable, your toddler will begin to see learning as a positive experience — an important step toward succeeding in school in the years to come.

Reading readiness

Most children will begin to read independently sometime between the ages of 4 and 7. Toddlers in the 2- to 3-year-old range have a long way to go and will benefit most from being read to.

But if your toddler is beginning to pretend to read books on her own, encourage this behavior. She is beginning to think of herself as a reader. She will love to feel included in family reading times, and if she is receptive, offer her a section of the newspaper over the breakfast

Did You Know?

The ABCs

The ABC song is a good tool for introducing the alphabet to your toddler. If he's interested in learning more about letters, begin by showing him the letters in his name. Avoid sitting down with a pencil and paper to teach him the alphabet. Rather, keep it fun and integrate it into his play.

Blocks and puzzles with letters and corresponding pictures are another good place to start. Playing with refrigerator magnets and forming letters using brightly colored markers or an Etch-a-Sketch are also appropriate and less threatening than sitting at a desk. Remember, if he isn't interested in the alphabet at this early stage, he shouldn't be pushed. Continue reading for pleasure, and he'll let you know when he's ready for more.

table for her to "read." Finally, role model reading for your toddler so that she sees you enjoying books, newspapers, and magazines. Show her that reading is fun, not just for kids but for adults too!

Beyond reading

Language development extends beyond reading. Little ones benefit from listening to you talk about your daily routine and environment, using a grown-up voice and proper vocabulary. Take time to answer their questions, which in this age group can be plentiful! Make up stories or recount experiences for your toddler. She will love hearing what you have to say, and her listening and thinking skills will strengthen.

Similarly, singing songs and reciting rhymes will help your child develop an ear for language. Songs and poems with hand actions are especially fun. As the tunes become familiar to your toddler, encourage her to sing independently or to join in with you.

HOW TO
Read with your toddler

1. If you are not already in the habit, begin to read to your toddler at least once a day. Try to incorporate books into your child's routine before bedtime or naps or at another suitable time in your schedule.

2. Allow your toddler to participate in the choice of books. Don't worry if he repeatedly asks for the same book to be read — this is entirely normal and should not be discouraged. You might try having him pick one book and you choose a second.

3. Read from any type of book, as long as it piques your toddler's interest. Children of this age often enjoy books about experiences familiar to them.

4. Don't worry if you can't get through a whole book. Toddlers' attention spans are variable. If he's had enough, don't force him to sit through the remaining pages. It is better to end the reading time on a positive note.

5. Engage your toddler in the reading process. Begin with pointing to objects and asking him to name them, and progress to asking him open-ended questions, such as, "What do you think happens next?" Conversely, if your toddler asks you questions, stop reading and take time to answer them before moving ahead.

6. Make books accessible in your house. Have a bookshelf or a box where your toddler can keep his collection. And remember that books make wonderful gifts.

7. Take your toddler on a trip to your local library or bookstore. Help him to get his first library card and to borrow a book of his choice. Inquire about story hour times and take your little one to participate. Librarians and bookstore staff can be a wonderful resource to recommend age-appropriate books for your toddler.

8. Feel free to use funny voices, make animal noises, and so on. By all means have fun and your toddler will too!

Dad's role

There's no question that times are a-changin'. Many families now comprise two working parents, and fathers undoubtedly do more around the house and with their kids than in the past. Despite this, studies show that women continue to take a primary role in work around the house and child-care responsibilities. More important than whether this is right or wrong is that you communicate and be aware of how responsibilities are divided up in your household, respect and show appreciation for each other's roles, and remain flexible in taking on tasks that may be new to you.

Every family is different, and only you can decide what your role as a father really means. One thing is certain, though: being a dad is not just about wrestling with your kids, teaching them the latest bathroom humor, or watching cartoons together. Sometimes the best thing you can do as a dad is to help set boundaries, teach good manners, and enjoy family dinners.

Setting boundaries

To minimize the potential damage that can be wrought by your young rascals,

it is helpful to start by setting boundaries. It's okay to tell your kids that they can't eat on the couch or that they should sit on the chair and not the table. These boundaries will in no way hinder their fun and will, at least to the casual observer, make your child appear well behaved. When deciding on the limits your family will tolerate, make sure to consult with Mom. Boundaries don't work unless they are consistent among all caregivers.

Word and tone management

Ideally, the best way to impose these boundaries is to use a firm but calm voice. While raising your voice may make you feel better, it usually just results in escalating and prolonging a confrontation with your child. After a while, your loud voice becomes commonplace.

Not only is it important to set boundaries for your child's behavior, but you also need to set boundaries about how *they* speak. Word and tone management is critical. Polite words, such as "please" and "thank you," should be part of your child's everyday vocabulary. If your child asks for something, make sure she uses "please" and make sure she uses a non-aggressive tone without whining. There is nothing wrong with requiring your child to repeat

a request until she asks nicely. Given that toddlers are usually desperate for whatever they're seeking, they will toe the line and use the magic words.

Remember that you are your child's role model, so be sure to talk to others in the manner that you expect your child to follow.

Did You Know?

Family dinner

Don't underestimate the importance of sitting down as a family to eat dinner. It has been shown that children who eat around the table with their families have much better eating habits. It is also a time to catch up on the events of the day. Even if you work long hours, try your best to adjust your schedule so you're able to get home in time.

Frequently asked questions

As family doctors and pediatricians, we answer many questions from parents. Here are some of the most frequently asked questions. Be sure to ask your health-care providers any other questions that may arise. If they don't have the answers, they will refer you to a colleague who does.

Q: My son sits very close to the screen when he watches television. Will this hurt his eyes?

A: Despite what we were all told by our own parents, there is no evidence that sitting too close to the television screen is damaging to a child's eyes. If it is a persistent habit, however, it may be an indication that your child is nearsighted. A visit to an optometrist would be a good idea. And remember, television viewing should be limited to less than 1 to 2 hours a day for toddler and preschool-age children, no matter what distance they're at!

Q: What can I do if my 2-year-old daughter is constantly interrupting me when I'm on the telephone?

A: This common problem can be very frustrating for parents. It can be especially challenging and even embarrassing when you're fielding an important call with screaming and crying in the background. This can also be a difficult problem to tackle because toddlers don't have a sense of time and are used to communicating their needs and thoughts as soon as they arise.

Try to teach good manners and enforce clear general house rules through repetition of key words and concepts; for example, "Mommy is on the phone and can't hear what the other person is saying to me when you are talking to me at the same time, but I will be off soon," or "Please say, 'Excuse me,' if you are interrupting me." Whenever possible, you may want to limit extended conversations to times when someone else is around to supervise your child or when your daughter is napping or otherwise occupied with an activity that doesn't require your attention. Before you know it, your toddler will be a teen and the tables will be turned — you'll be desperate to get her off the phone!

Q: Music is important to me and I would like my daughter to appreciate it too. I'm anxious for her to take piano lessons. When can she start?

A: While there's no right age to begin piano lessons, very few 3-year-olds are ready for formal music training. Before beginning lessons, children should be able to recognize their numbers and letters, at least from A through G, and be able to sit still and focus on the piano for at least 10 to 15 minutes at a time. Rather than signing your toddler up for piano lessons, encourage her to gain an appreciation for music through singing and listening to a variety of music, whether it be children's songs, classical, jazz, or rock and roll. Consider a group music class where free play with various instruments is encouraged. Above all, follow your child's interests. Music is something you'd like her to enjoy. Avoid the risk of its becoming a chore by starting formal lessons too early.

Q: My son recently began picking his nose. I'm horrified! What should I do?
A: Most toddlers pick their nose at one point or another, often out of curiosity, boredom, or habit. While it's embarrassing for parents, try not to make it into too big of a deal. If you draw attention to this behavior and make a fuss, your toddler is likely to dig in his heels and his finger! Instead, try distracting him with an activity that involves his hands. Rest assured that he will curb his own habit, particularly when he quickly learns from his peers that it is socially unacceptable.

Take note, however, of particularly dry nasal passages. Placing a humidifier in the bedroom may cut down on the crusted mucus that may be encouraging your toddler to explore with his finger.

Finally, it isn't uncommon for nose picking to result in minor nosebleeds.

Q: We bought my son a tricycle, but he has no interest in riding it. How can we encourage him to become more athletic?
A: The toddler years are when little ones begin to express their own interests and demonstrate their abilities. As with adults, there will be wide variation in what they enjoy and are good at. Some will be natural athletes, others great storytellers, and yet others budding artists. The best thing you can do for your children at this stage is to expose them to a variety of activities that provide them with opportunities to build

on all areas of their development. Don't be concerned, however, if your youngster prefers one activity over another — this is entirely normal. While he may not want to ride his tricycle day in and day out, he may be interested in joining a family excursion to the park, where he can enjoy unstructured play while developing his motor skills. Don't pressure him to ride his tricycle, but keep the opportunity open. One day, he may even surprise you by wanting to give it a try.

Q: My toddler just won't share, even though his playmates do. What can we do?
A: If your toddler refuses to share at this age, he may simply not be ready from a developmental perspective. Establishing ownership over his things helps build security, and he may not yet want to let this go. Express your disappointment each time he doesn't share — "Daddy is sad that you won't share that toy" — but this isn't a reason for punishment or to force your toddler to share. Doing so may erode his sense of security and self-esteem. If you continue to encourage him to share, he will eventually become comfortable with letting go of his possessions, thus taking a step toward becoming a generous and thoughtful individual.

Q: What toys do I need for my 2- to 3-year-old toddler?
A: You don't need to buy your toddler a large number of toys. Toys and equipment enjoyed at the park, in a play group, or in a child-care center all count — and limit the number that you feel obligated to

purchase. To stimulate all spheres of his development, ensure that your toddler has the opportunity to play with a variety of items, which is much more important than quantity. Limit toys that discourage free imaginative play, such as coloring books that ask toddlers to stay within the lines. Also be wary of toys that are just for watching, such as battery-operated cars.

Similarly, remember that so-called educational television shows should take a back seat to learning based on more interactive play. Of course, there is nothing wrong with your toddler playing with such toys or just watching, as long as they are used in moderation and do not replace opportunities for imaginative and interactive play.

Sam's Diary

September 8 (19 months old)

Sam, you don't stop talking for one minute. You're like a sponge — there's nothing you don't copy or can't say. We are all having an absolute ball. You really enjoy communicating. You know some colors and shapes. You're putting two words together — tennis ball, Mommy's car, Sam's hand. You absolutely love trucks — "kuts," as you

call them. Garbage truck is "bija kut," ice cream truck is "ikeem kut," fire truck is "fijya kut," but we know exactly what you mean.

September 26 (19+ months old)

We started you in some community programs. You've had two sessions of kindergym and are very weary, to say the least. You're not that keen to go exploring on the equipment — ladders, tires, hoops — and really don't like the parachute. You're quick to say to Mom, "Out gym, out gym." We'll see how it goes with time.

On Friday morning we took a bus up to your playtime program. You loved the ride, giving the driver Mom's $2 fare (you went free), and at the end of the drive you said to the driver, "Thanks, bus driver."

October 4 (20 months old)

"Bija kut" is gone now, replaced with "garbage kut." You laughed like crazy when you realized that you could say "garbage." Now we say, "Bija kut is no more," it's "garbage" now — you're very proud of yourself. More firsts: you count perfectly to 10, know all your colors now, and identify things by their color (yellow car) when pointing out anything. "Strawberry" and "zebra" have replaced "tho" and "plo."

November 5 (21 months old)

You enjoyed your first proper Halloween. Although you wouldn't put on your lion outfit, you enjoyed watching the children come to our door, and you ran up and down the road commenting on all the pumpkins. You loved the one Dad carved for you and were very proud of it.

We have art class tomorrow, and it reminded me of the tantrum you had last week. You had woken up really early in the morning and had nearly fallen asleep in the car on the way down — so you were tired and had no tolerance. When Rachel took your project away before you were quite ready, you started to cry. We couldn't console you, so we left the class early. When I wanted to put your jacket on (you were in a T-shirt and it was freezing outside), you proceeded to have a tantrum. I had to battle to get you into your car seat, and you screamed all the way home! At home, you screamed some more and curled up on the couch, crying and sobbing until you'd nearly lost your breath. I couldn't console you at all — you were so distraught. I felt really sad for you, but I just had to let you be because you wouldn't really let me near you. Anyway, eventually you cried yourself to sleep and slept for ages. When you woke up, it was all gone and forgotten.

We're 21 weeks pregnant with your little brother or sister but haven't told you anything about it — at this stage it's too early and I don't think you'd really understand. You're amazing with babies, though, and are very gentle and loving when you play with your cousin Tali. It's as though you know she's smaller and more fragile than you are.

Toilet Training Your Toddler

Independence day 200
Toileting without tears 203
Children with special needs 208
Troubleshooting 211
Frequently asked questions 215

Independence day

Toilet training marks a significant milestone in your toddler's life, a huge step toward independence for him — and for you. Your baby is growing up — and your diaper bills are about to disappear! Despite rumors to the contrary, toilet training does not need to be a grueling experience. Look on it as a way of becoming more finely tuned to your child's developing personality and a way of finding out how he learns best. If you don't take it too seriously, toilet training can actually be a satisfying and enjoyable adventure for your toddler and for you.

Toilet training readiness

Toilet training is a complex task. Your child will need to achieve several other important developmental milestones — including physical, cognitive, social, and emotional skills — to master this one.

- He must be physically able to get to the toilet or potty and to sit unsupported.
- He must be able to undress himself — or at least to pull his pants up and down.
- He must recognize when he needs to use the potty.

- He must be able to control his bladder and bowel sphincters.
- He must have developed the necessary verbal or communicative skills to let you know when he needs to go to the toilet.
- He must be motivated to become independent and learn how to use the potty or toilet like other children and adults do.

Ready, set, pee

Several indicators suggest that your child is ready to learn how to use the toilet or potty.

Did You Know?

Toilet training timing

Like all other areas of child development, the range of what is considered the normal time for toilet training is very broad. In North America, most children learn to use the toilet or potty between 2 and 4 years of age, though it occasionally happens a little earlier or later. While some children show signs of readiness at 18 months, many others will not be ready to start training until 30 months or later. The average time from starting to train and achieving success also varies dramatically, but the process can take as long as 1 to 3 months.

In general, the longer you wait, the easier and quicker the process is likely to be. It is certainly possible to toilet train very young children. In societies where diapers are not readily available, toilet training is often initiated before 1 year of age, and a small but growing community in North America is toilet training their babies in infancy.

Guide to

Determining if your child is ready for toilet training

Your child does not need to show all of the following signs, but at least a few of them should be present to indicate that she's ready for toilet training:

- She can understand and follow simple instructions.
- Her diaper is consistently dry for 2 to 3 hours at a time or after naps.
- Her bowel movements start to become somewhat regular and predictable.
- She can walk to the bathroom and pull her pants up and down.
- She recognizes and tells or shows you that she needs to urinate or have a bowel movement.
- She seems uncomfortable with wet or soiled diapers and wants to be changed.
- She is interested and motivated to learn to use the potty or toilet.
- She shows interest in "big kid" underwear.

These include a desire to be independent, having a dry diaper for several hours at a time, and regular bowel movements. Once your child becomes aware of his bodily functions and indicates that he's had a bowel movement or urinated in his diaper, or that he needs to go, he is probably ready.

Physiological readiness

Some children will squat or hide when they need to have a bowel movement; others will wait until their diaper is off to urinate. This tells you that your toddler is aware of the need to go and has reached physiological readiness. The message needs to be transmitted to his brain, and his muscle control has to have reached the point where he is able to open and close the "taps." This ability usually begins around 18 months and gradually increases with time.

Emotional readiness

Emotional readiness may be more difficult to assess. Some children are obviously keen and excited to start using the potty. They can't wait to get into grown-up underwear. Others may demonstrate anger and resistance. Many will vary from day to day, particularly 2-year-olds, who try very hard to control their environments.

Parent readiness

Pick a time to start toilet training your toddler when you're not feeling particularly stressed. You certainly do not want to take this on when there are major changes happening at home, such as a new baby, a new child-care arrangement, a move to a new home, or a family issue.

Make sure that you're picking the time for the right reasons and not because of peer pressure, the comments of relatives or friends, or your experience with your other children. Don't rely on your child's age or what the other children in his play group are doing to guide you on when to start toilet training. Bear in mind that girls often train earlier than boys.

Be sure that your start time does not coincide with a particularly negative or resistant phase — you would probably be better off waiting for that to pass, unless you enjoy hitting your head against a hard object!

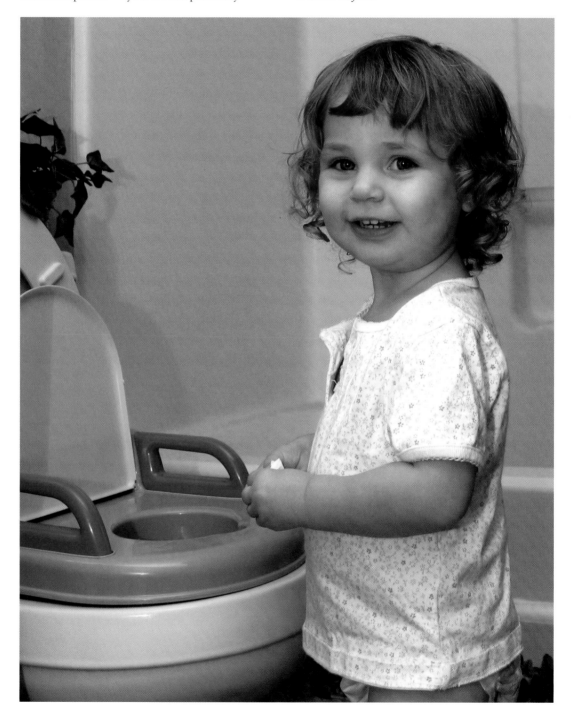

Toileting without tears

There are many different ways to go about toilet training. You need to find the techniques that best suit your child's personality and work best for your family. What follows are some well-tested strategies.

Toilet training games

To encourage their children, some people make toileting a game so the activity is fun. For example, you can pretend that your child is a favorite superhero and talk about how Superman, Spiderman, Cinderella, or Dora uses the toilet too. Your toddler may want to wear a special hat while sitting on the potty. Engage your child's active imagination by role-playing with a doll or stuffed toy, pretending that the toy is using the potty. Some children enjoy "aiming" at O-shaped breakfast cereal dropped into the potty or toilet, while others may respond well to the challenge of both of you sitting on the toilet and having a "race."

Did You Know?

Nighttime dryness

The majority of children will be trained to use the toilet or potty effectively during the day long before they stay dry through the night. Night wetting still occurs in about 20% of children by the age of 5 years. While about half of these children will stay dry at night by the age of 6, a considerable number — up to 5% of 10-year-olds and 2% of 16-year-olds — may continue to wet their beds. Girls tend to stay dry earlier than boys. When training pants are consistently dry in the morning for a period of several days, the child is ready to get rid of them.

Bedwetting that persists is called primary nocturnal enuresis. It occurs more commonly in boys, usually in children who are very deep sleepers, and there is commonly a family history of bedwetting. Nocturnal enuresis is a maturational phenomenon. Almost all children will eventually outgrow it, but it may persist for several years.

HOW TO
Toilet train your toddler

Set the stage

- Encourage your child to come into the washroom with you to observe how you use the toilet. Toddlers are often fascinated by others, especially other children, and learn by imitation, so exposure to siblings or peers is often an incentive to learn.

- Follow the lead of daycare centers that incorporate toilet training into their daily schedules. The combination of peer pressure and routine is very effective in facilitating training.

- Some children squat or strain before a bowel movement. If your child does this, explain to her that these signs mean a bowel movement is about to come and she should try to get to the potty in time.

- Read books and watch DVDs with your toddler on the topic of toilet training to familiarize her with the process.

Teach the language

- Teach your child age-appropriate words you feel comfortable using to equip her with the necessary language to communicate her needs. This includes words to describe body parts, such as penis, peepee, vagina, bum; words to describe body functions and excretions, such as pee, weewee, and poo; and labels for the equipment, such as potty and toilet. The words used by different families vary according to beliefs, culture, and first language. Studies that have looked at the words children use to describe their private body parts and functions have revealed that in multicultural cities, literally hundreds of different terms are used by different families.

- If your child is in daycare or preschool, try to be consistent with the language used there to avoid confusion and distress.

- Avoid words with negative connotations, like stinky or yukky, which may make your child think of toileting in a negative way. Remember that teachers, friends, and other caregivers will hear these words, so make sure that they will not confuse, offend, or embarrass your child or others.

Choose the right equipment

- Help your toddler to look and feel comfortable on the job. Potties are available in many sizes, colors, and designs. Some have arm-, foot-, or backrests. Armrests are useful for holding onto during bowel movements. A wide base will ensure that the potty doesn't tip over. Your child should be able to put her feet on the floor while using the potty.

- Make sure that the potty you choose will be easy and practical to clean after success is achieved. Most people dump the contents into the toilet, rinse the potty out each time with water, and use some form of cleaning solution or disinfectant at

least once every day. Many potties have splash guards so that little boys don't spray the floor when they urinate while sitting on the potty. Generally, boys initially learn to go in a sitting position but will later follow their dad's lead in urinating standing up (and likely leaving the toilet seat up as well!). Some potties have trays attached to the front so the child can read or color while sitting on the potty. Portable fold-up potties are useful for travel.

- If you are purchasing a new potty, take your child with you to buy it and allow her to choose the one she likes. Make a show of writing her name on it. Let her feel some pride in owning her very own potty. You can also give her some options about where to place it. Pick out some toys to store nearby.

- If you are using a toilet seat adapter, which fits onto the top of the toilet, be sure to adjust it to the appropriate size for small children. These adapters are quite practical if you have a particularly small bathroom or do a lot of traveling.

- If you are using an adapter, make it easier for your toddler by purchasing or using something to function as a footstool so her feet can rest on the stool, stabilizing her.

- At first, be careful using the flusher — some children are afraid of the noise.

Choose the right clothes

- Dress your child in comfortable clothes that are easy to pull up and down. Elastic waists and Velcro fasteners make it easy. Belts, buckles, snaps, zippers, and buttons will hinder the process and frustrate her.

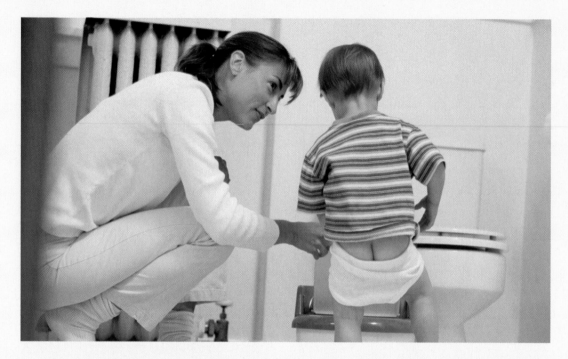

Overalls are especially difficult for a young child to manage. Some children are very motivated by the promise of trendy "big kid" underwear!

- Consider using training pants when your toddler starts toilet training. This makes the process easier because you and your child can pull them up and down much more readily than removing a diaper. If she has an accident, the training pants, unlike underwear, will contain it. Be aware, however, that some authorities argue that pull-ups delay toilet training because the child doesn't experience the discomfort of wet and soiled clothes.

- Once your child is interested and motivated, change from diapers to underwear. Take her shopping and allow her to choose her own underwear. Toddlers will usually choose a favorite character or color.

This tends to help motivate her and make her feel very grown up!

Establish a consistent routine

- When you initiate toilet training, you must show your child what to do. Show her how to pull down her pants and underwear, and gently seat her on the toilet or potty. You can show a boy how to urinate standing up, but initially most boys find it easier to sit. Keep the potty in the same place.

- Let your child sit for a few minutes. Running tap water in the sink or bathtub sometimes stimulates children to urinate. If she gets bored and wants to leave, let her go. If she resists, it may just mean that she isn't quite ready to start training. Success will depend on going at her pace.

- After she goes, wipe the genital and anal area gently with toilet paper. If you have a little girl, it is important to wipe front to back (the vaginal area before the anus) to avoid contamination of the vaginal and urinary tract with fecal material.

- If your toddler is using a potty, pour the contents into the toilet and flush. If she has gone on the toilet, flush the toilet. Some children enjoy flushing the toilet; others are afraid of the noise — use your judgment as to whether she should do the flushing.

- Wash and dry her hands. Teach your child how to clean herself up after going to the bathroom. Your toddler will need ongoing help with cleaning herself for a few years after she is trained. This is an important part of the process that needs to be practiced over and over again.

- Routines and expectations should be consistent among all caregivers, so be sure to discuss your preferred toilet training process with all others who may be involved.

Promote the right attitude

- Praise your toddler for trying — and even more for each success. Praise, patience, and positive reinforcement are crucial to the process. Also praise her for telling you if she's already gone and suggest that the next time she let you know in advance so you can help her make it to the potty.

- Consider giving a tangible reward, such as a small treat, a sticker, or a toy, when your child is successful. A sticker chart is an excellent way to provide positive reinforcement. It is also useful for you to keep a record of her progress. To keep her motivated, continue to praise your child every time she succeeds.

- Don't punish or discourage your child when accidents happen, but she should help to clean up in some way. Accidents are inevitable. Learning to use the toilet is not as instinctive as walking or talking!

Children with special needs

Toilet training is usually achieved later in children who are developmentally delayed or have neuromuscular disorders. However, the general principles for toilet training children with special needs are similar to those for toilet training all children: the child must be developmentally and emotionally ready, and parents and caregivers need to be patient and supportive. Indicators of readiness to toilet train are also similar: desiring to acquire this ability, remaining dry for prolonged periods, and being able to undress and access the toilet or potty. Although they often start later and take longer, many children with significant disabilities will ultimately become toilet trained. Some may not achieve complete independence but will become effectively toilet trained with the help of a caregiver.

Challenges

Toilet training a child with special needs may be challenging and time-consuming but will result in improvements to your child's self-esteem and confidence and increase his level of independence. It may also increase the opportunities available to him, such as day camp and other programs, many of which require children to be toilet trained.

To make appropriate accommodations, you will need to consider the type and severity of your child's disability. It is prudent to discuss your plan of action with your health-care provider, who will guide you in developing an individualized program for your child. There are also many websites and books that provide detailed advice on toilet training children with various special needs.

Hearing disabilities

For children with isolated hearing impairment, the extent of their communication skills will determine when to start and how long it will take to toilet train. Once he can understand your signals showing him how and when to use the potty, he should be ready. Use lots of visual cues to demonstrate and allow him to accompany you and other family members when you use the washroom. Make sure to teach him the signs that signify wet and dry, as well as, "I need to go." As with teaching other children, repetition and encouragement are key components of the program.

Visual disabilities

A child with visual disabilities cannot observe the process and equipment as other children can, so he will use his other highly developed senses: hearing, touch, and smell. You will have to explain what he should do and show him by sitting him on the potty, allowing him to feel his body parts and the potty. Once he is able to use the potty, make sure that it is always in the same place and that there are no obstacles interfering with access to the washroom.

Motor disabilities

Children with motor disabilities, such as cerebral palsy or neuromuscular disorders, who are cognitively normal will generally understand the process but find the physical element challenging. They often have difficulty with bladder and bowel control, and may need to wait until they are a little older to attempt toilet training. They may need help getting to the potty or toilet and may need assistance getting undressed, as well as maintaining stability while sitting. Back and side supports are very useful. Potties that resemble bedpans are useful for children who are unable to sit.

Spinal cord problems

Children with spina bifida or spinal cord injuries do not experience the sensation of needing to void because of an interruption of the sensory nerves, and many do not have the motor abilities to get to the toilet or potty. It is unlikely that these children will ever become fully toilet trained. As they get older, however, they can learn to use a catheter to empty their bladders regularly and can adopt a regular schedule for bowel movements. These children frequently suffer from chronic constipation and may require ongoing use of stool softeners or laxatives.

Developmental delay

Toilet training children who have cognitive delays, especially if they are associated with behavioral difficulties, can be extremely challenging. The timing must be based on each child's unique profile and temperament. Wait until your child seems ready, then introduce each stage of training slowly, one step at a time. Once he has conquered the first step of recognizing when he's wet or soiled, seat him on the potty at regular times. Praise him when he does urinate or have a bowel movement on the potty, and consider giving him a treat. Teaching him to take his pants on and off, wipe himself, and wash his hands can be taught a bit later, once he has mastered the act of using the potty successfully.

Behavioral challenges

It can be extremely trying to train children with behavioral challenges, such as autism, oppositional defiant disorder, and fetal alcohol syndrome. These children may be defiant, often do not learn by imitation, and may be very difficult to motivate. They may also have coexisting cognitive or speech delays. Autistic children in particular often have sensory difficulties and object to being dressed and undressed and to unfamiliar and new situations.

Did You Know?

Wheelchairs

If your child is in a wheelchair, you will have to ensure that your bathroom is wheelchair accessible. The child will need to transfer from the wheelchair to the toilet seat and back, so there must be enough space for the wheelchair to pull up next to the toilet. Some wheelchairs have a toilet seat with a removable pot under the cushion of the chair. These may be extremely useful when initiating toilet training.

HOW TO
Toilet train toddlers with behavioral disorders

Be aware that this process may take a long time and that regression and accidents may occur.

1. Wait until your child seems ready — that is, she can stay dry for 2 to 3 hours at a stretch, she is aware of the need to urinate or defecate, and she dislikes the sensation of being wet or soiled.

2. Try to determine when she usually urinates and has a bowel movement and then work around those times.

3. Observe your child closely to determine what motivates her and try to determine factors that may make it difficult for her. Then try to find ways to encourage her and avoid things that upset her. Small treats such as candy and stickers, for example, may help motivate her and reinforce behavior associated with toilet training.

4. If the sound of the toilet flushing upsets your child, use a potty that you can empty later or flush the toilet after she has left the room.

5. Progress very slowly, reinforcing each step toward training: going into the bathroom, taking her pants down, sitting on the toilet or potty, and, finally, using it.

6. Be encouraging but firm. Let her know in a gentle, non-punitive manner that having accidents is not acceptable.

Troubleshooting

Many toddlers will experience some "hiccups" in their journey to independent toileting. This is one time when accidents really do happen! It is also a process that can be sabotaged during a particularly defiant or controlling phase in a child's development. Urinary tract infections and constipation may occasionally complicate things. Here are some troubleshooting tips.

Accidents

They can be frustrating, messy, and annoying for all participants, but expect accidents to happen for several months after your child has been successfully toilet trained.

Many young children need to be reminded to go to the washroom regularly, especially when they become absorbed in play activities and forget that they need to go. For developmental reasons, toddlers are unlikely to be thinking ahead.

Accidents are more likely to happen when a child is out of his normal environment, during times of stress or change, and when you are in a hurry. Children who are very shy may not tell unfamiliar caregivers that they need to use the potty, so caregivers should be informed that they need to take the child to the washroom routinely or at least to remind him to go.

Accidents can also happen as part of your toddler's normal experimentation and testing of boundaries.

Urinary tract infections

If your child is having frequent accidents — especially if he was previously doing well — and seems unwell, complains of pain with urination, or seems to be urinating very frequently, he should be assessed by your doctor, who will probably ask for a urine sample for testing. It is extremely unusual, but a urinary tract infection or, even more rarely, a medical condition, such as diabetes, can cause more frequent and urgent urination. Both of these conditions can be quite easily ruled out by your health-care provider with a dipstick test of a clean, fresh urine sample.

Children with a urinary tract infection may have discomfort over the bladder area,

HOW TO
Avoid toilet accidents

Make an effort to anticipate and prevent accidents. They are often predictable.

1. When accidents do inevitably occur, remain calm and reassuring. Don't tell your child it's okay, but don't get angry and make her anxious and ashamed.

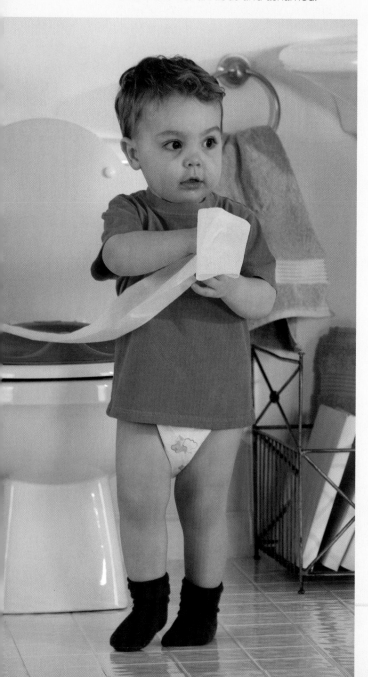

Your child needs to know that accidents shouldn't happen. While you help her clean up and change clothes, tell her gently that it is unfortunate that she did have an accident and discuss how it could have been avoided. You can gently remind her that "It doesn't feel good to be wet" and that "As soon as you feel like you may need to go, let me know, and I'll make sure that you get to the toilet in time."

2. Let your toddler help you clean up by passing you the tissue or putting the wet clothes into the laundry.

3. If you are traveling, encourage your child to use the washroom before you leave home, and ensure that you know where the washrooms are if you are in a strange place. Take a potty in the car on long trips. Always have at least one change of clothing and underwear with you. Waterproof mattress covers will protect the bed from being stained by nocturnal accidents.

4. Try to relax — and remind yourself that this stage will not last forever. It should taper off within 6 months of toilet training.

Stool withholding

Some young children develop a tremendous fear of having a bowel movement on a toilet or potty, and this may be a behavioral response or the result of painful bowel movements because of constipation. These children may start to withhold their stools for several days, which creates a cycle of infrequent, large, painful bowel movements and increasing reluctance to go. If the cycle isn't broken, long-term difficulties with withholding stool, constipation, and soiling may ensue.

back pain, foul-smelling urine, pain with urination, and the sensation of needing to go frequently and urgently. Sometimes they may just have a fever or not feel quite right without any specific symptoms. For more information on urinary tract infections, see page 400.

Constipation

Constipation is not an uncommon problem in toddlers and can result in both urinary accidents and stool soiling. If a child becomes very constipated, the large volume of stool in the bowel can press on the bladder, which reduces the bladder's capacity and makes the child feel as if he has to urinate frequently. Some children who are very constipated soil their underwear frequently because liquid stool leaks around a large mass of stool in the rectum.

These children usually do not even feel the need to have a bowel movement. The gradual but constant stretching of the bowel walls by the constipated stool will ultimately take away the sensation of needing to go. This message is usually provided by the nerves in the bowel wall, which pick up the fullness of the bowel by being stretched and then send the message to the brain.

Most mild cases can be managed by changing your toddler's diet to increase the amount of liquids and fiber. If your health-care providers feel that the constipation has reached the point where it is interfering with emptying the bladder or bowels, they will likely suggest some form of laxative or stool softener. Laxatives may be given orally or may be in the form of a suppository or enema given through the anus.

Regression

Some children regress when changes or disruptions occur in their lives; for example, when a younger sibling arrives on the scene, if the environment changes after a move, during a family holiday, or when child-care arrangements change. Your toddler may start to have accidents after a period of staying dry, withhold urine and stool, or simply refuse to go. Talk to your child about her fears or anxiety and try to help her cope with the stress. It is quite acceptable to use diapers again in these circumstances.

Preventing constipation

- Ensure that your toddler drinks adequate amounts of water or juice and ingests adequate fiber in his diet. This may be difficult in this age group, when children can be extremely picky eaters. See page 396 for information on increasing fiber in the diet.
- Encourage your child to sit on the potty more frequently, for no more than a few minutes at a time, after meals and at bedtime, rather than continuing to try for a prolonged period.
- Apply a small amount of petroleum jelly (Vaseline) around the opening of the anus if you see a small amount of fresh blood in the stool, which may indicate a small anal tear or fissure that can cause pain when your toddler is defecating.
- If withholding or constipation persists, don't wait too long before consulting your health-care provider. The earlier this problem is addressed, the more quickly it can be remedied.

Resistance

Toilet training is initiated at a stage of life when young children are trying to establish their independence. They are trying to gain control of their environment, and they may frequently enter into power struggles with the authorities — their caregivers! Not surprisingly, toilet training can become a focus of control and resistance for some toddlers. This is usually a phase, which resolves with time.

However, difficulties often arise when parents react negatively or punitively to a child's accidents. The more emotional a parent becomes, the more some children will resist, thereby creating a vicious cycle of anger, frustration, and resistance.

Guide to

Managing toddler resistance

- If you notice that your child is becoming increasingly resistant, try to identify what factors are making the process difficult. Are you annoying her by reminding her too frequently when she is in an independent phase, or is she forgetting to go because you are not reminding her enough? Is she easily distracted? Is she confused about what she should be doing? Is she very active and dislikes having to sit on the potty for too long, or is she particularly social and unwilling to be alone in the bathroom? Is she afraid of sitting on the toilet or flushing?
- Avoid changes in routine. For example, a new care provider may do things a little differently, or you may need to place your toddler in an unfamiliar daycare situation. If you can home in on the particular change that is bothering your child, you may be able to correct it.
- Back off for a few days — or a few weeks — and let your toddler take some control of the situation, then try again.
- If your child is verbal enough, talk to her about why she has become reluctant to use the potty and try to allay her concerns or fears.
- Try to remain calm, patient, and encouraging. This phase will pass.

Frequently asked questions

As family doctors and pediatricians, we answer many questions from parents. Here are some of the most frequently asked questions. Be sure to ask your health-care providers any other questions that may arise. If they don't have the answers, they will refer you to a colleague who does.

Q: How long will it take for my toddler to be toilet trained?

A: The average duration of toilet training is about 6 weeks, but this varies tremendously. Some children will be trained within a couple of days; some take much more time than the average. Obviously, there are many contributing factors, including the age, the maturity, and the individual characteristics of each child. It is important to remain involved and observe closely, as your toddler's needs and behaviors are constantly changing. This process should not be rushed.

Q: Will it be easier to train my child in the summer?

A: Toilet training is more difficult in the winter months because of the multiple layers of clothing. So it is optimal to toilet train in the warmer months, but it can certainly be accomplished in the winter. It is always wise to have a change of clothing available.

Q: How can I tell if my child has a bladder infection?

A: The most common symptoms in children who are of "toilet training age" are pain or burning with urination and very frequent urination. Children who have stayed dry for a while may start to have frequent accidents. They may complain of abdominal or back pain. Your child may have a fever. You may notice that the urine smells bad or looks different. If you suspect that your child has a urinary tract infection, you should consult your doctor.

Q: How can I tell if my child is constipated?

A: If your child has infrequent, hard, large, and dry stools, he is constipated. These bowel movements are often very painful, and the stools may cause tears in the anal area (anal fissures), which can bleed. Children with long-standing constipation may have small hard stools, or sometimes only watery material that leaks around the impacted stool into their underwear.

Sam's Diary

January 10 (23 months old)

You recently started daycare for three days a week. Mom was very sad to change our home arrangement with Bambi and your buddy Evan, but we felt that the change would be beneficial. Before starting, Mom took you "to school" on two occasions, and we stayed for just an hour so you could get used to the environment and your new friends and teachers. On your first day, you stayed alone from 10 to 12, and on the next few days Mom picked you up after lunch. You settled in incredibly well in a very short

time. You cry a little when Mom leaves but settle down very quickly, and then your teachers — Josie, Amir, and Joanna — report that you're having a great time.

January 25 (23+ months old)

You are one amazing, gorgeous little boy. You've had a rough few weeks with a cold and interrupted sleeps, and on Friday you stayed home from school with a fever. Your teachers absolutely love you — they are such warm, caring people — and were sad that you wouldn't be there on Friday. You've made quite an impression on them.

Sam, Mom and Dad have mentioned that you're going to be getting a brother or sister, but we haven't made a fuss of it as it's still a little way off. Anyway, today, without any prompting at all, you lifted Mom's top and said, "Baby in Mommy's tummy." You've been stroking Mom's tummy, kissing the baby and singing to it. You are just so amazing! "Open up, see baby nicer," was your response to Mom's pulling down her top to go to the kitchen. You're an incredibly gentle, loving little boy. You often talk to our baby. You've also lifted your top and said, "Sam's baby in his tummy."

School is going really well — you've been so amazing with this gigantic change to your routine. You're too sweet when you arrive. You've stopped saying, "Don't want to go to school, Mom," when we drive in and replaced it with, "Mom stay with Ham (Sam) a little bit," which is what I usually say to you. You walk in now on your own, take your jacket off at the front door, and run down the hall. You're just delicious! And everyone there thinks so too.

Another milestone happened over this weekend — you moved into your "big boy bed." You've handled it like a star — you really are good with

change. You've been very excited by your bed. This is the third night now that you've been in it, and so far so good. It's quite funny, because you haven't realized that you can actually get out of bed by yourself, and when you wake up, you always call for Mom or Dad to come and get you.

You're still very determined, and you give Mom a much harder time than Dad — you listen to him much better, will brush your teeth and change diapers very easily with him, but are much more testy with me.

February 9 (2 years old)

Happy second birthday — you are growing up so quickly! We had such fun at your birthday party on the weekend. Now you say, "I'm 2, Mom, I'm 2," holding up your index and middle fingers. We are looking forward to our new baby's arrival next month. We know that it's going to be hard to share Mom and Dad's attention and have someone in your space, but we know that with time you'll get used to the idea and that you'll be a wonderful, caring big brother.

Your
Preschooler
(Age 4 and 5 years)

Big enough to go to school 220
Routine visits to the doctor 234
Preschooler behavior 240
Disciplining your preschooler 244
Helping your child cope with loss 248
Parenting an adopted toddler 251
School readiness 253
Recreation options 259
Dad's role 262
Frequently asked questions 265

Big enough to go to school

During the fourth and fifth years, your child will mature from a toddler to a young child ready to attend school. The active — sometimes very active — exploration of the new-to-her world you observed in your young and older toddler will slowly evolve into more organized and interactive communication, activity, and play in these two preschool years. As your child's world expands through her developing motor and social skills, she will need some time outside your home in playgrounds, parks, and public indoor play spaces. Enjoy and promote this evolving independence — it's a wonderful time!

Physical growth: Age 4 and 5

At your well-child checkups, your health-care provider will once again measure your child's weight and height and plot them on standard growth curves to see if your

child is growing appropriately for her age, "genetic destiny," and ethnic background. Remember that determining *growth over time* is more important as an indication of healthy growth than determining if your child is above or below average on the growth curves. She should track along the same percentile for weight and height from one medical checkup to the next. Any significant deviation from this pattern will be investigated by your health-care provider. For information on plotting and reading growth curves, see page 14, and for the growth curves for ages 2 to 20 years, see pages 222–227.

Development: Age 4 and 5

As you will have realized by now, children develop at different rates within a range of normal. The following information about developmental milestones provides a general progression of the average ages for developmental gains, but individual children may develop these skills slightly earlier or later. If you have questions or concerns about your child's development, please speak to your child's health-care provider.

CDC Growth Charts

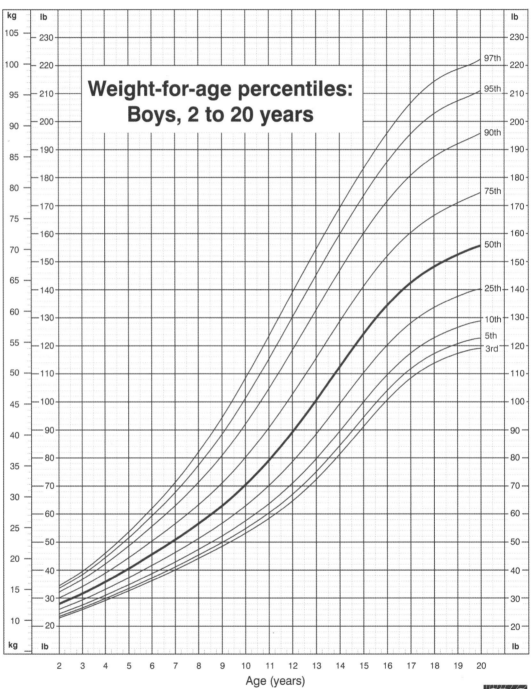

Weight-for-age percentiles: Boys, 2 to 20 years

Published May 30, 2000.
SOURCE: Developed by the National Center for Health Statistics in collaboration with
the National Center for Chronic Disease Prevention and Health Promotion (2000).

CDC Growth Charts

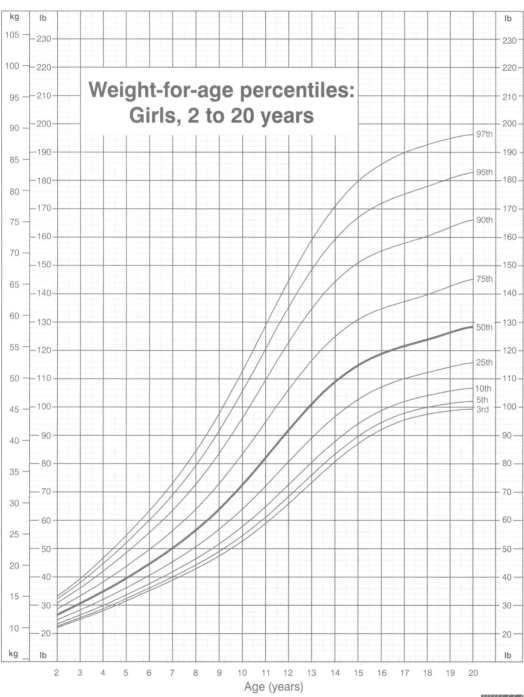

**Weight-for-age percentiles:
Girls, 2 to 20 years**

Age (years)

Published May 30, 2000.
SOURCE: Developed by the National Center for Health Statistics in collaboration with
the National Center for Chronic Disease Prevention and Health Promotion (2000).

SAFER · HEALTHIER · PEOPLE™

CDC Growth Charts

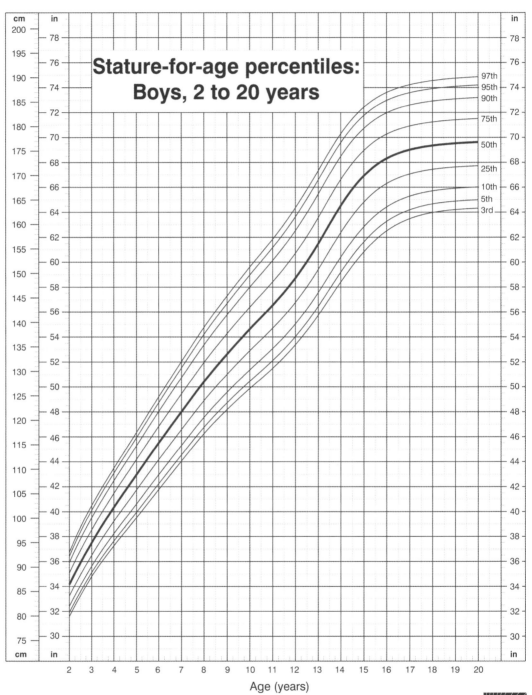

Stature-for-age percentiles:
Boys, 2 to 20 years

Age (years)

Published May 30, 2000.
SOURCE: Developed by the National Center for Health Statistics in collaboration with
the National Center for Chronic Disease Prevention and Health Promotion (2000).

SAFER·HEALTHIER·PEOPLE™

CDC Growth Charts

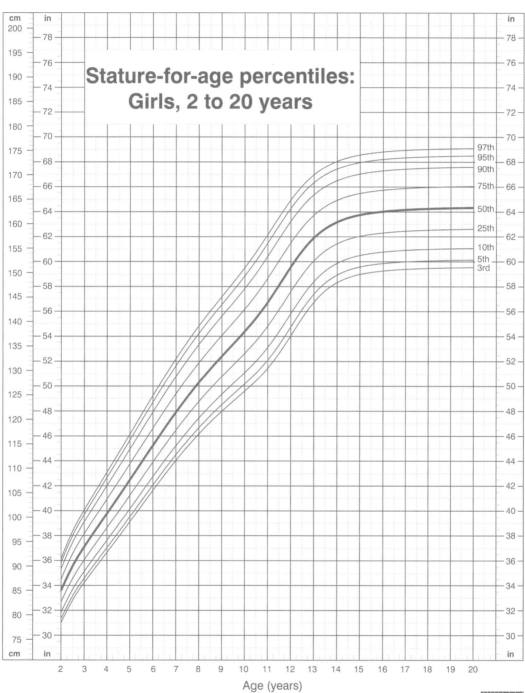

**Stature-for-age percentiles:
Girls, 2 to 20 years**

Age (years)

Published May 30, 2000.
SOURCE: Developed by the National Center for Health Statistics in collaboration with
the National Center for Chronic Disease Prevention and Health Promotion (2000).

SAFER · HEALTHIER · PEOPLE™

CDC Growth Charts

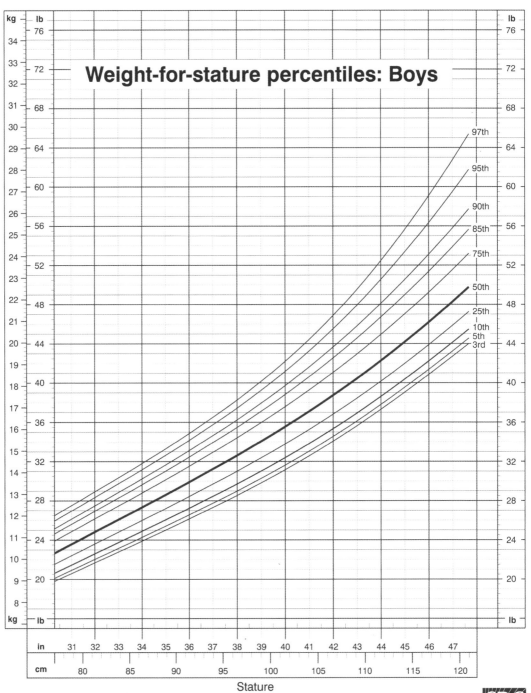

Weight-for-stature percentiles: Boys

Stature

Published May 30, 2000 (modified 11/21/00).
SOURCE: Developed by the National Center for Health Statistics in collaboration with
the National Center for Chronic Disease Prevention and Health Promotion (2000).

SAFER·HEALTHIER·PEOPLE™

CDC Growth Charts

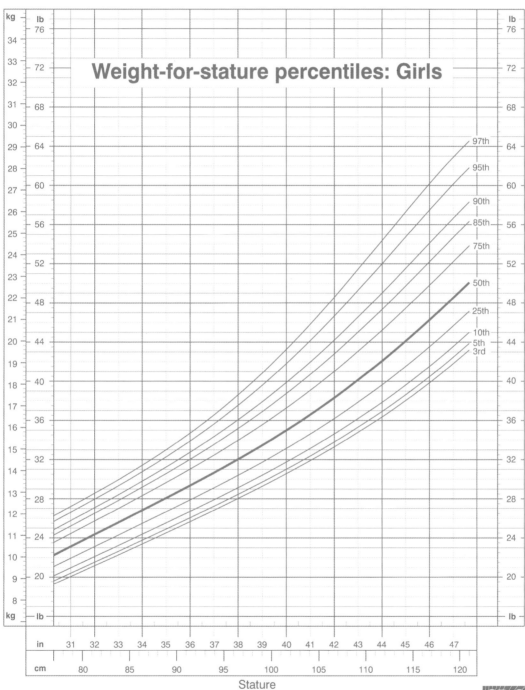

Weight-for-stature percentiles: Girls

Published May 30, 2000 (modified 11/21/00).
SOURCE: Developed by the National Center for Health Statistics in collaboration with
the National Center for Chronic Disease Prevention and Health Promotion (2000).

SAFER·HEALTHIER·PEOPLE™

Did You Know?

Evolving skills

Your child's evolving coordination and social skills may lead to an interest in participating in noncompetitive games for young children, such as soccer, T-ball, or basketball. If your child expresses interest, encourage him, as long as participants are of a similar age and size. Close supervision is appropriate. At this age, your child will be interested in relatively informal play without necessarily being able to follow all the formal rules and regulations.

Gross-motor development

During the fourth and fifth years, your child will become both increasingly mobile and progressively more coordinated. A trip to the park now involves independent climbing, sliding, and swinging. Getting there no longer involves being pushed in a stroller but is a run, skip, or bike ride (with training wheels, of course). At this age, children are able to throw, catch, and kick with some competence. Physical activity is important for children and helps them develop healthy active interests for the rest of their lives, so encourage it!

Fine-motor and adaptive skills

In addition to her more coordinated gross-motor skills, you will also notice that your preschooler is becoming increasingly proficient with her hands. During the fourth year, children generally develop the ability to dress independently. At first, they may need some help to get a shirt the right way around or their shoes on the correct foot. By the end of the fifth year, most children are able to dress themselves fully, including fastening buttons and zippers.

This increasing independence is also evident at the kitchen table, as your child is now able to pour cereal and milk — although probably at risk of spilling it! — eat competently with a spoon and fork, and spread with a knife. A child is also now able to clear the table, including breakable items, and even to help with setting it.

Pre-academic skills

Most 4- and 5-year-olds attend preschool programs or kindergarten. During this time, children acquire academic and social skills required to prepare them for the first grade.

SEPARATION COMFORT

Major milestones include the ability to separate from parents without experiencing separation anxiety. For some children who have previously attended preschools or daycare centers, this may be an easy process. For other children, there may be an initial period of crying when they are dropped off. Don't worry — it will pass as your child progressively develops comfort with her new environment and becomes more independent.

DRAWING SHAPES

You will notice your child developing an increasing ability to create forms and shapes on paper during the fourth and

Did You Know?

Writing and reading

As children develop control over a pencil and interest in words on paper, they start to print letters. By the end of the fifth year, most children are able to identify and print the letters of the alphabet and print their first name. Many children will be able to identify the sounds corresponding to letters, and some may be starting to read. Learning and printing letters is an important foundation to develop during these years. If you are concerned about your child's progress in this area during the fifth year, speak to his teacher or a health-care professional.

fifth years. Initially, faces will look Halloweenish, with large grimacing mouths and eyes only. Gradually, features will be added and, as your child gains more pencil control, will become increasingly refined in size and shape. Four-year-olds often make their first attempts to draw people, initially consisting of a face with two sausage-like legs protruding from the bottom. By the end of the fifth year, she will be drawing a body with arms and legs, although not always hands and feet.

COUNTING NUMBERS

As your child acquires increasing competence with letters, you will also notice her ability to manipulate numbers increasing. As your child progresses through the third to fifth years, she will learn to count up to 10 objects and identify numbers.

Social and emotional development

During the third to fifth years, important gains in social and emotional development occur as a new world of more independent, interactive play opens up for your child.

IDENTITY

In her fourth year, your child will develop the concept of herself as an individual beyond just the immediate family. She will start to define herself; for example, "I am 4 years old. I play soccer. I am Jess's friend. I like *Power Rangers*." She will also explore her place and role in life by observing her role models, trying on different personas in looks and actions, and experimenting with social roles in the family, at preschool, in the neighborhood, and with peers. Four-year-olds are generally capable of understanding gender, and they start to differentiate their specific play activities and toy preferences by the time they reach 5 years of age.

INTERACTIVE PLAY

As your child develops an individual identity, she is also developing increasing interest in interactive play with other children. During the third and fourth years, children start to develop a preference for some children over others and may have a preferred friend of either gender. During the fifth year, children develop a more specific group of friends, increasingly of the same gender. You will notice your child becoming increasingly able to approach others and initiate play. Her play will become progressively more interactive, imaginative, and complex over this period.

Although children are typically interested in interacting with others of a similar age during this stage of development, they often require some support with choosing activities and negotiating differences of opinion. It is recommended that parents keep play dates short and relatively structured at first, with increasingly independent play as your child continues to develop.

Red flags

Some red flags apply to development at these ages. Consult a physician or a professional with experience in the area of child development if your child exhibits any of the following:

- Has problems seeing or hearing
- Gets stuck on words or sounds (stuttering)
- Gets frustrated when trying to talk
- Seems unable to use toys appropriately
- Is not interested in playing with other children
- Rarely uses fantasy or imitation in play
- Consistently has difficulty using one side of the body or uses one hand all the time
- Cannot build a tower of six to eight blocks
- Has trouble taking off clothing

Developmental Milestones: 4 and 5 years
Motor and Language Skills

Age	Gross Motor	Fine Motor	Receptive Language	Expressive Language
4 years	• Runs • Goes up and down stairs without support • Climbs on high play structures • Can balance briefly on each foot • Catches a large ball • Can throw overhand • Rides a bicycle with training wheels	• Copies a plus sign (+), then a square • Cuts out a square with scissors • Draws a face with eyes and a mouth • Draws a person with two to four parts	• Understands three-step commands (e.g., "Go upstairs, look in the cupboard, and bring me your sweater") • Knows gender of self and others • Understands opposites	• Speaks 50 to 1,500 words • Can speak in four- to five- word sentences • 100% intelligible to strangers • Uses past tense, present tense, and plurals • Sings songs, nursery rhymes • States first and last names • Counts to 4 • Names four colors
5 years	• Walks backwards • Hops • Skips • Throws, catches, and kicks well • May be starting to ride a bicycle without training wheels	• Copies a triangle • Draws a person with a body • Identifies and prints letters • Prints first name • Can build elaborate structures	• Counts up to 10 objects • Understands four-step commands • Links past and present events • Recognizes all letters of alphabet	• Has a 2,700-word vocabulary • Understands definitions • Uses future tense • Uses mature conversation with "how" and "why" questions • Knows telephone number and address

Developmental Milestones: 4 and 5 Years
Psychosocial Development

Age	Emotional	Social	Adaptive
4 years	• Enjoys being silly • May show new fears • Is becoming aware of new dangers	• Plays interactive games • May visit friends to play • Prefers peer play to solitary play • Gets involved in elaborate fantasy play, tells fanciful tales, has imaginary friends • Sings songs, dances, acts, listens to stories • Follows rules in simple games	• Helps set the table • Dresses independently • Goes to the toilet independently
5 years	• Begins to express more feelings in words • Embarrasses easily • Cannot yet laugh at self • Has feelings about death • Shows guilt over misbehavior • Likes independence	• Has a group of friends • Likes make-believe and dress-up play • May have imaginary friends but keeps them private • Follows rules of games and community rules	• Helps prepare food • Dresses independently • Goes to the toilet independently

Delayed Development

Your child may have a delay in development if he is not able to do one or two of the following:

Development	Age 3 years	Age 4 years	Age 5 years
Language development	• Speak in short sentences • Say most words right • Respond to simple questions	• Speak in long sentences, talk about an event • Be understood easily by an adult when speaking • Pay attention to a story and answer simple questions about it	• Tell detailed stories • Understand long instructions • Associate letters with the sounds they make
Fine-motor development	• Turn pages of a book • Hold a crayon and copy vertical or circular strokes	• Hold a crayon correctly and copy a circle	• Draw simple shapes, copy a cross • Dress and undress without help except for small buttons and snaps
Gross-motor development	• Run well, changing direction smoothly • Walk up stairs without support	• Ride a tricycle using the peddles	• Kick, throw, and catch a ball successfully most of the time • Hop on one foot
Social and emotional development	• Come to a parent for comfort when hurt or sad	• Take turns • Look for adult approval	• Play make-believe games with other children • Respond verbally to "Hi" and "How are you?" • Control aggression (hitting, kicking, or biting other children)

Routine visits to the doctor

An annual visit to the doctor is usually recommended in this age group. Well-child visits are a lot like your own annual checkup. As with your toddler's previous checkups, you can expect that you will be given an opportunity to share any concerns you may have encountered since the last checkup. Don't hold back — this is your chance to ask all those questions that every parent has. Remember, there are no stupid questions!

Well-child checkups

These visits will usually last between 10 and 20 minutes, depending on how much there is to discuss.

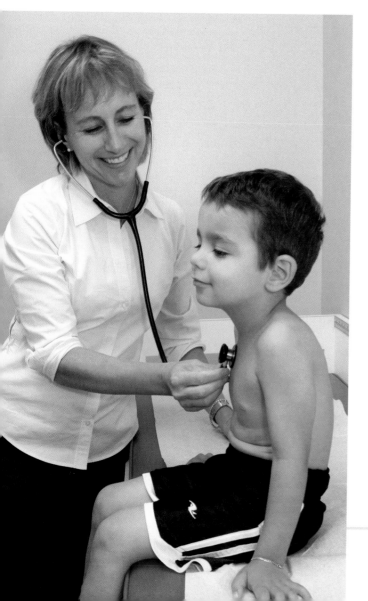

History

First on the agenda will be an opportunity to share any concerns that have arisen since your last visit. This is usually followed by some specific questions from the doctor about your toddler's diet, sleeping habits, and developmental milestones. Once again, this will provide an opportunity to find out if your child's patterns are within the normal anticipated spectrum. If not, you can ask for strategies to help with, for example, toilet training, picky eating, and those dreaded middle-of-the-night awakenings.

Physical examination

The physical examination part of the visit will usually start off with measurement of height and weight and the plotting of these values on the growth curves, and perhaps on a body-mass index (BMI) chart, to ensure that your child is following her particular growth trajectory and maintaining an appropriate weight. A top-to-toe physical examination will include checking vision and inquiring about hearing. The doctor will listen to and examine the chest (lungs) and heart and check the pulse and blood pressure, as well as the tummy and genital area. If there are birthmarks, skin lesions, or other things that concern you, point them out to the doctor.

Body mass index

Your health-care provider may now begin to calculate your child's body mass index (BMI), often used to determine if your child's weight is appropriate for her height and if she is at risk of being overweight or underweight. The BMI is a measurement of the level of body fat, and it takes a person's height and weight into account in one calculation. You can measure BMI by using a mathematical calculation, precalculated BMI tables, or an Internet calculator at the Center for Disease Control and Prevention (CDC) website.

BMI curves

BMI curve charts are made by calculating the BMI for a large group of healthy children and then plotting these measurements separately on graphs for boys and girls according to their age. Since all children of exactly the same age do not have exactly the same height or weight and BMI, these charts have ranges of lines that show the typical measurement and variation on the typical measurement.

The BMI curve charts can give your child's percentile for body fatness. Percentiles tell you how many in the group of children at the same age as your child were higher or lower than your child in body fatness. For example, if your child's BMI is at the 95th percentile, her body fatness is higher than 95 out of 100 children who are the same age and sex as your child, and 5 of those children would have higher body fatness. It would also mean that your child's body fatness is farther from the average, or the 50th percentile.

Red flags

The BMI percentile is accepted by most health-care providers as an accurate indicator of the risk of health problems, such as diabetes and stroke, associated with being overweight. Your health-care provider will discuss with you strategies for reducing or increasing your child's weight if these conditions emerge on the BMI curves:

- **Overweight:** Children are considered at risk of being overweight if they are above the 85th percentile and are considered overweight if they are above the 95th percentile for BMI.
- **Underweight:** Children are considered at risk of being underweight if they are below the 15th percentile and are considered underweight if they are below the 5th percentile for BMI.

Education

Your doctor may give you some advice and guidance, and perhaps some written information, on a number of issues.

SAFETY
- Correct use of car seats (see page 314)
- Importance of bike helmets (see page 321)
- Carbon monoxide and smoke detectors (see page 310)
- Water safety (see page 322)

BEHAVIOR
- Strategies for dealing with discipline, limit setting, and coping with conflicts and stress (see pages 150 and 244)

HOW TO
Determine BMI

Calculation formulas

You can use a calculator to find out your child's BMI by using her height and weight measurements. The formulas to use are as follows:

For pounds and inches:

1. Take your child's height measured in inches and multiply it by itself (square it).

2. Take your child's weight in pounds and divide it by the number you just calculated. Then multiply that number by 703. The answer is your child's BMI.

Formula: weight in pounds ÷ (height in inches x height in inches) x 703 = BMI

For kilograms and centimeters:

1. Take your child's height measured in centimeters and divide it by 100 to get height in meters. Multiply this number by itself (square it).

2. Take your child's weight in kilograms and divide it by the number you just calculated. The answer is your child's BMI.

Formula: weight in kilograms ÷ (height in meters x height in meters) = BMI

BMI tables

Another way to find out your child's BMI is to use precalculated tables provided by the United States National Center for Health Statistics and the Center for Disease Control and Prevention (CDC) at www.cdc.gov/growthcharts/.

HOW TO
Plot BMI curves

1. Select the correct chart for BMI-for-age percentiles for your child's sex.
2. Fill in the table in the upper left-hand corner with the information you used in calculating your child's BMI.
3. Find your child's age along the scale at the bottom of the chart.

4. From that point, move straight up until you find the level of the BMI scale on the left side of the chart that matches your child's BMI.
5. Each of the curves represents a different percentile. Note which percentile line your child's BMI is at or between. The middle curve represents the 50th percentile.

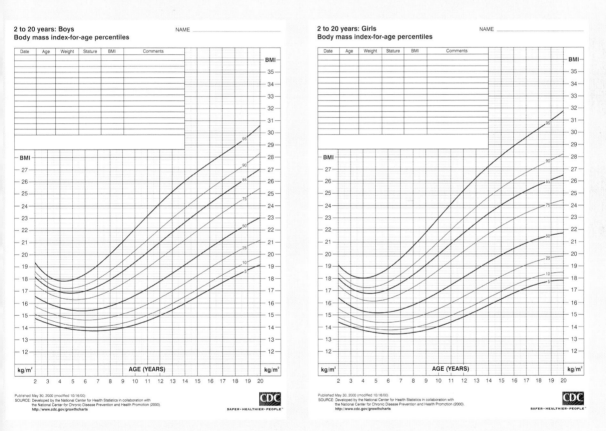

Adapted by permission from Brian W. McCrindle and James G. Wengle, *Get a Healthy Weight for Your Child* (Toronto: Robert Rose, 2005).

- Value of healthy, active living and setting a good example by being active (walking and bicycling, for example)
- Importance of limiting screen time and encouraging reading
- Need to prevent exposure to secondhand smoke (if you must smoke, don't do it in the house or car or anywhere in the vicinity of your toddler)

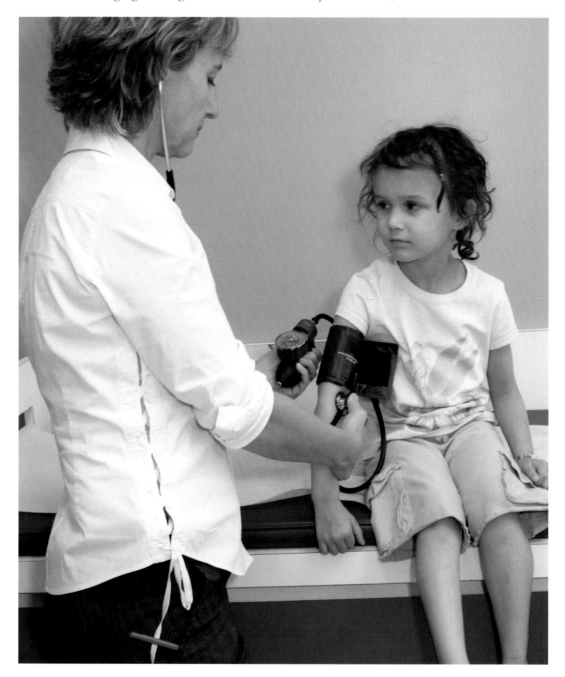

Vaccinations

Fortunately, the number of immunizations required at this age is much less than in the first few years, but some are still required. For more information on vaccinations, see pages 33–39.

- **DTaP-IPV booster:** This shot is required prior to school, sometime between 4 and 6 years of age.
- **MMR booster:** If it hasn't already been given earlier, this vaccination is also required at this time.

- **Influenza, or flu, shots:** The American Academy of Pediatrics has recommended that these vaccinations be given annually in the fall up to 18 years of age. Unfortunately, the flu shot, if given, needs to be repeated every fall because the virus changes from year to year and protection isn't long-lasting. Opinions on the necessity of this vaccination vary, so if in doubt, discuss it with your health-care provider.

Guide to

Easing the discomfort of vaccination needles

As your toddler is older now, you will need a strategy to get him through the discomfort of needles. There is no right or wrong approach. You will need to be flexible depending on the personality of your child, but some basic principles apply in most cases.

- Be honest. If he is scheduled for a booster shot that visit, don't say he won't be getting a needle, and don't say it won't hurt, because it probably will. Rather, try to highlight how brief the discomfort will be and compare it with an uncomfortable sensation that he can relate to, such as a pinch or a bug bite.
- Give some warning. For most children, it is probably better to have some time to mentally prepare. That said, do not warn them days ahead of time, which will only prolong the torture!
- Create incentives. You can also balance out the impending discomfort with a positive incentive; for example, an activity that he really enjoys or even a special food treat.
- Use pain relievers. It has been scientifically proven that a dose of acetaminophen (e.g., Tylenol or Tempra) or ibuprofen (e.g., Advil or Motrin) given about 1 hour before the needle, as well as 4 to 8 hours thereafter (as per directions on the bottle), decreases the amount of discomfort. In addition, there are creams that you can apply to the skin that will freeze the area and decrease the pain felt when the needle breaks the skin. Discuss this with someone at your doctor's office ahead of time, because you will need to know where to apply the cream (usually the "badge" area on the upper outer part of the arm that he doesn't use for writing). You will need to purchase the cream from the drugstore and apply it 30 to 60 minutes before the needle is given.

Preschooler behavior

The toddler years are over and many challenging behaviors are behind you. You may be surprised, however, when you continue to encounter some difficult conduct in your preschooler. This is to be expected, not only in these years but also throughout childhood and adolescence, although the form and type of behavioral challenges change with time. Some of the following advice may sound familiar from previous chapters, because basic principles of effective behavior management are similar for all ages.

Whining, complaining, and crying

In preschool children, these are common behaviors that can be quite annoying to parents and other caregivers. Whining in particular is common in preschool-age children, typically when they're tired or hungry. Whining may progress to crying and temper tantrums. It isn't uncommon to see a hot and tired 4- or 5-year-old child at a family outing progress from complaining to whining to crying and eventually to a full meltdown.

Aggressive behavior

Your preschooler is still in the process of learning to control and channel the feelings of frustration and anger that result in aggressive behavior, such as hitting, kicking, pinching, and yelling. This is part of normal childhood development and does not necessarily predict long-term difficulties. Your job is to help your child develop strategies to contain and redirect these feelings in a more socially acceptable way.

Time out

Time out is the most popular strategy to deal with angry, aggressive behavior, but it isn't always easy to implement successfully. Time out is based on the premise that children would prefer any attention to no attention and that withdrawal of attention is experienced as an undesirable outcome of negative behaviors. The child needs to understand why a time out has been called; for example, "No hitting."

Did You Know?

Support network

If you are struggling with your child's behavior, you are not alone. Speak to your physician, daycare provider, or school staff. There are support programs available to parents in most communities. Your local early years or parenting center or children's mental health agency are there to help all parents, not only those of children with identified medical problems or disorders. They can direct you to other specialized resources. It is best to get help early and not to wait until you're at the end of your rope.

HOW TO
Manage whining and complaining

1. Take a short break from activities and offer a cool drink and a snack. This may turn things around before they get out of control.

2. Keep activities developmentally appropriate and know when to call it a day. If the activity is beyond your child's development level, he will quickly become frustrated, and if the activity is tiring — well, he'll become overtired soon enough.

3. Try using a simple, calm statement, such as, "I can't hear whining. Please use your big-boy voice." If this is followed up by ignoring the whining until it stops but immediately responding to appropriate requests from your child, you should be able to reduce whining and complaining.

4. Offer choices. A brief, calm, face-to-face discussion of options, such as "We can choose one more activity or we can go home now" or "You can play nicely together or you can each go play quietly in your rooms," may help if you take the time to allow your child to listen and make a decision — and if you follow through consistently. Don't rush the decision. Where possible, keep your tone calm and neutral when offering alternatives.

5. Do not resort to bribing, cajoling, or threatening. These responses do not help your child develop inner motivation for desirable behavior.

6. Do not mock your child by imitating his whining and complaining. This will only belittle your child, not solve the problem.

in demonstrating a time out technique and troubleshooting common difficulties parents encounter in delivering it. For more information on this program and instructions on using the time-out strategy, see pages 152–154. Books and DVDs illustrating the program are also available.

TIME IN

Time out only works if it is used intermittently and for the minority of parent–child interactions. When it is used too frequently, there is not enough pleasurable "time in" interaction for time out to be perceived as an undesirable experience.

TIME LIMITS

Time outs should be timed. A general rule of thumb is no more than 1 minute per year of age. Following the time out, redirect your child to another activity and do not discuss the negative behavior further.

Time outs provide a means for the child to calm down in an uninteresting location.

The most difficult situation in which to use time out is when a child is in the midst of a temper tantrum and is unable to sit quietly in the time-out location. In these situations, ensure the safety of your child and others and ignore the tantrum.

For parents who are interested, the 1-2-3 Magic program is particularly helpful

Sexual behavior

During the preschool years, children become increasingly aware of and curious about gender differences, body parts, and body functions. It is normal for children in this age group to explore their own body

---

Did You Know?

Bathroom talk

It is common for children around the age of 5 years, particularly boys, to joke about body parts and body functions. Silly wordplay involving the words "poo" and "pee" is quite common. For the most part, when it occurs between same-aged children during play, this can be ignored by adults. If such talk creeps into discussion at the family meal table or around other adults, children should be calmly directed to "talk nicely" or "no bathroom talk" without drawing too much attention to the behavior.

Did You Know?

Uncommon sexual behaviors

There are some uncommon sexual behaviors in this age group that should be discussed with a physician or mental health–care professional. Between children of differing ages, sizes, or temperaments, for example, interactions that are coercive or secretive in nature may require further evaluation. Similarly, sexual talk that includes language or content unusual for a young child may require exploration by a professional with experience in this area. Self-insertion of objects into a young girl's vagina may be part of childhood body exploration, just like putting a small object into her nose or ear, or it may signal inappropriate sexual experiences.

Engagement in these behaviors may indicate that a child has been exposed to adult sexual material through magazines, computer, television, or movies; has witnessed sexual activity or experienced sexual abuse; or has developed a behavioral or developmental problem. Determining the cause and providing an appropriate response to these behaviors requires the assistance of professionals with experience in this area.

parts by touching and manipulating them. Boys of this age frequently play with their genitals in the bathtub and often have erections. Girls may rub their genitals against the furniture or some other convenient object. Some parents find this behavior disturbing and wonder how to curb it.

You should not overreact to this normal developmental behavior. Do not shame or punish your child. Instead, calmly help your child learn what is socially acceptable by advising that these behaviors should be done in private. Some 4- to 5-year-olds seem to have their hands down their pants all the time. A calm, quiet reminder, such as, "Hands up," that does not overemphasize or draw too much attention to the behavior will generally be helpful. By the time your child is 3 years old and has developed the ability to talk in sentences, it is helpful to teach words that refer to the genital area. Some parents prefer to use anatomically correct words, such as "penis" or "vagina," while others use words and expressions that their family is comfortable with or that are common in their culture. For more information on how to manage these behaviors, see page 160.

Playing doctor

At this age, children may engage in curiosity-based activity with same-aged peers, such as undressing and showing their body parts or "playing doctor." This is part of normal development as children become more aware of gender and anatomic differences. This behavior need not be a cause for alarm. Again, a calm adult response with a brief explanation of what is appropriate will help your child learn social boundaries without causing shame or embarrassment.

Disciplining your preschooler

Our children's behavior is often frustrating and exhausting and at times embarrassing. This makes it difficult to remember that challenging behaviors are a normal part of development and an opportunity for us to help our children recognize appropriate boundaries and interactions. Granted that these challenges are a part of parenting, it is helpful to plan a response ahead of time. It is much more difficult to think clearly in the heat of the moment. Thinking ahead, controlling our own emotions, and focusing on the goals of discipline are some of the cornerstones of effective parenting.

Disciplining preschooler behavior

The purpose of discipline is to teach, not to punish.

Prevention

An ounce of prevention can make all the difference! All undesirable behaviors are worse when children are hungry or tired. This is probably true when you're hungry or tired as well!

- Watch for signs of fatigue and keep in mind when your child's last meal or snack was.
- Plan ahead when you can. Take a stroller or wagon when you anticipate more walking than your child will find comfortable, even for your older preschooler, and always try to keep a snack and drink handy.
- Don't forget about yourself. You can't be effective when you're stressed, hungry, or overtired. It is often tempting to try to fit in that last errand, but remember, if you all dissolve in tears, it probably won't get done anyway.

Anticipation

You know your child and what tends to trigger her problem behaviors. For some, it may be anxiety surrounding change or transition; for others, frustration related to not getting what they see and want — the dreaded candy at the grocery store checkout, for example.

- Anticipate these behaviors. A few words of preparation laying out the ground rules may not prevent all problems but are often successful in preventing a meltdown.
- Keep such preparatory work brief and positive. Avoid lengthy discussions about the last time things went wrong.
- Focus instead on a simple positive discussion of the expected behavior; for example, "We're going to the toy store to buy a present for the birthday party. We're not buying toys for

ourselves today." At this age, your child isn't old enough to remember this advice for long, so the preparation should occur just before the transition or outing.

Positive family environment

It is all too easy to forget to notice when our children are behaving well — difficult behavior seems much more effective at generating a reaction. To promote good behavior, children need to know what is desirable and feel good about it. Rewarding good behavior does not always have to mean offering a treat, toy, or bribe when your child cooperates.

- Praise good behavior. Eye contact, a smile, a stroke of your child's hair, or a quiet word or two of praise are very effective forms of reward. In the whirlwind of being a parent, it is sometimes difficult to remember to save some time to focus on positive interactions with your child.

- Try to save some time each day to do something together where he is the only focus of the activity. This could be time to throw a ball or play a game together, tell stories about your day, snuggle up and read together, or sing a song together. Remember to take time during quieter moments to really listen to your child. There are lots of brief opportunities during even the busiest of days — the car ride home, the moments before bed, at the breakfast or dinner table. Taking these moments to engage positively with your child can make all the difference

to the atmosphere in your home and will go a long way toward promoting desired behaviors and preventing negative interactions.

- Plan family time. Many parents choose a weekly family evening for discussion, movies, or games. This is a wonderful habit to develop while your children are still young and can be continued throughout adolescence. Another great habit is to try to sit down together as a family for at least one meal a day where there are no distractions — make sure the television is off — and just spend some time discussing daily activities. Actually, it doesn't really matter what the activity is, as long as the focus is on a positive and pleasurable interaction.

Battle tactics

All of us have had times when we realize that the majority of our interactions with our child have turned into telling her what to do — or more often what *not* to do. Remember that the goal of discipline is to teach children how to respond positively and interact effectively.

- To maintain this positive, educational focus, target the most troublesome behaviors for disciplinary attention and ignore less important undesirable behaviors. By focusing on the most troublesome behaviors, you will avoid spending all your time on behavior management and will have more time to interact positively with your child.
- Focus on behaviors that involve physical aggression or present danger to your child or others. Many of these

may have been dealt with during the toddler years, but you may still find that your preschooler will hit, kick, or yell when frustrated or angry. These physical behaviors will become increasingly problematic as your child enters the school environment.

- Once the more serious problem behaviors have been resolved, you can turn to less troublesome behaviors. Squirming in her seat at the dinner table or picking her nose, for example, could be managed with simple, calm reminders, such as "Sit on your bottom," or by quietly offering a tissue.

Intervention

Thinking ahead, preparing your child for anticipated difficulties, preventing fatigue and hunger, and picking your battles go a long way toward promoting positive behavior, but there will be moments of negative or undesirable behavior when you need to intervene. When these moments occur, keep the following tips in mind to make disciplinary interventions as effective as possible:

- Deliver discipline in a calm manner. One of the most challenging tasks a parent faces is to try to suppress the emotional response we have to our child's behavior and to respond in a measured and thoughtful way. Much of difficult child behavior is attention-seeking. This doesn't mean that your child is consciously trying to drive you crazy but simply that any reaction from a parent, positive or negative, is desired and at this stage is developmentally preferred over no reaction at all. As much as possible, avoid reinforcing negative behavior by reacting angrily or emotionally to it. Remember, the focus is on teaching positive interactions and social boundaries. Imagine a schoolteacher trying to teach a child to read by yelling, berating, or crying — these strategies would clearly not be effective. When you intervene in your child's problem behaviors, you are role modeling effective methods of dispute resolution, which your child will repeat in the future. For this reason, physical punishment is not recommended — it is virtually impossible to deliver in a calm manner and is not permissible behavior between children or adults.

- To be effective at modulating behavior, disciplinary interventions must be consistent. Having a consistent approach to managing problematic behavior not only provides parents with a means of remaining calm but reinforces to the child that you mean what you say. Inconsistent parenting leads to prolonged behavioral challenges in children. It is helpful, although not essential, if all caregivers respond in a similar manner to problem behaviors, particularly for very difficult situations. However, children can and do understand that adults in their lives respond in different ways, and it isn't a problem if different management strategies are used by a parent, teacher, and babysitter. What is most important is that each caregiver responds in an individually consistent way to negative behaviors and that particularly problematic behaviors are not routinely overlooked in one caregiving environment.

Communication

Your child needs to understand why her behavior is problematic and what is expected of her. During the preschool years, as was true in the toddler years, your child will not listen to or understand lengthy, detailed discussion of the merits of good behavior and the drawbacks of the targeted behavior.

- Provide a brief warning before intervening, such as, "No hitting, please."
- Keep any explanations of the rationale for the desired behavior concise and simple. Remember that if your child is frustrated, angry, or in the middle of a temper tantrum, she won't be able to hear and incorporate your well-intended explanation.
- Plan ahead so you will have the words at the ready to deliver when needed.

Helping your child cope with loss

Life can be full of unexpected twists and turns, some good and some bad. Sadly, young children may be required to deal with losing a parent or other loved ones through divorce or permanently through death. These are very traumatic events for a young child to cope with.

Dealing with separation and divorce

Unfortunately, more than one-third of marriages in North America end in divorce. Couples are most likely to divorce or separate after four or five years, often with very young children becoming innocent victims. Children of different ages react to and cope with divorce in a variety of ways. Young children may display anxiety, oppositional or regressive behaviors, and depression.

Guide to

Coping with separation and divorce

- Reassure your children that they are in no way responsible for the separation and that they will always be loved by both parents. They should not be burdened by their parents' problems and should not be involved in any conflicts between their parents.
- Avoid discussing details of the divorce in the presence of your children.
- Maintain ongoing relationships with both parents, except in cases of severe abuse.
- Consider the options for custodial arrangements:
  - Joint physical custody occurs when the child spends approximately 50% of the time with each parent. This arrangement is common.
  - Joint legal custody means that both parents share parenting decisions, although the child may live primarily with one parent.
  - Sole legal custody means that one parent has the right to make all decisions regarding the child.
- Stay in touch with the other parent. Good communication between the parents is key to maintaining consistency. Some parents have difficulty communicating with each other verbally, so email or a communication book may be a preferable option. It is often helpful to plan ahead for special occasions such as birthdays. But even the best parenting plans require flexibility because parents' circumstances may change and children's needs will certainly differ as they get older.

Ongoing conflict between parents can cause ongoing harm to the children. It is critical that the parents establish a cooperative and cordial relationship with each other, as well as clear and consistent rules and routines for their children. This may be very challenging, especially since the parents are frequently struggling to cope with their own pain, anger, and loss. It is important to seek out available support systems, including family and friends, religious leaders, counselors, mediators, and health-care professionals.

The transition to becoming a divorced or separated family is always a difficult one. However, children demonstrate tremendous resilience. With time and effort to avoid conflict and tension, most families reach a new state of equilibrium in which it is possible for children to thrive.

Understanding death

Coming to terms with death is a complex process that takes years. Many adults continue to struggle with questions about death and dying. For young children, death is a confusing concept.

Guide to

Coping with death

- Talk to your child about death in an open and honest fashion, in simple language that he will understand. Don't tell him that the person who has died has "gone to sleep forever." This may make him afraid to go to bed at night.
- Make sure the child knows that the death wasn't his fault.
- Be supportive and comforting, and encourage him to ask questions, which should be answered in a sensitive and age-appropriate fashion. If you have religious beliefs about death and afterlife (e.g., going to heaven), these should be communicated to your child, who may find them comforting.
- If a loved one has died, ensure that you share your memories of that person with your child in an ongoing way so that he will have lasting and wonderful memories of the person.
- Use the life cycle around you as an opportunity to introduce your child to the idea of death. The changing of the seasons, the passing of time, and the process of growing up and aging provide a good background for the concept.
- Read books written to help children understand and cope with death. Some are written in child-friendly language and convey stories and simple explanations about death and dying; others provide advice to parents about coping with their own grief, as well as how to support their children.
- Seek support from agencies that deal specifically with bereaved families and palliative care programs that can provide support, advice, and counseling to families and children who have lost a loved one. Religious groups and leaders are good resources to provide comfort and support.

Loss and grief

Toddlers and preschool children cannot comprehend the permanent and irreversible nature of death, but they certainly experience loss and grief when a family member or pet dies. They are at an age when magical and imaginative thinking is very prominent, and it may be difficult for them to separate fantasy from reality. As a result, young children's reactions to death are often very different from the grief and mourning experienced by older children and adults. Young children may repeatedly ask when the person who has died is coming back or want to go and visit them. Some children blame themselves for the deceased person's "going away," thinking that he or she died because the child misbehaved.

Behavioral changes

It is difficult for young children, who have limited language, to verbalize their sadness, so behavioral changes are common manifestations of loss. Grief may be expressed as changes in appetite or sleep routine, regression, aggression, anger, withdrawal, and difficulty with separation. These changes may last for months and reappear intermittently. Children who have been exposed to the death of a loved one require long-lasting, ongoing support and understanding from their caregivers.

Parenting an adopted toddler

The difference between being born into and being adopted into a family is hard for children to grasp at this developmental stage. There is no "right" age to start talking with a child about being adopted, and the experts don't always agree. Although many parents think there's no point in talking about adoption until their child is older and can grasp the concept, starting to talk about adoption with your toddler gives everyone time to become comfortable with key terms, such as "birth mother," and gives you time to compile your child's personal adoption "story."

Talking about adoption

At this age, the goal is for your toddler to become familiar with adoption terms, not necessarily to understand the concept. Be positive and comfortable when discussing your child's adoption with her. Set the right tone. When parents are relaxed, their children will feel comfortable enough to come to them when doubts, fears, and questions arise. At best, this dialog about being adopted will continue for a lifetime as you watch your child at different development stages and listen to her talk about her adoption experience. At worst, if parents are unable to discuss adoption issues or tighten up when the subject comes up, the child will get the message that being adopted is something "bad."

Conversations

Work the issue of adoption into normal conversation rather than having "the adoption talk" once and never revisiting the issue. These conversations can occur formally or informally. Take opportunities between activities to raise questions. This might be in the car, on a walk, in the bath, at bedtime, during imaginative play, or on a vacation. But try not to place too much emphasis on the topic. Your child does not need to be reminded on a daily basis that she is adopted. Encourage conversations with other children who are adopted. Openly acknowledge the differences between any children born into the family and your adopted child without focusing on them too closely. Talking with other families who have adopted a child is also helpful.

Life story

Some families create a life story book that describes their child's adoption process, including relevant photographs and documents. This can include not only a record of the child's journey to the family but also the family's journey to the child. There is no prescribed time to share the book with your child, but it is not something you should keep for a

Multicultural families

Many families who adopt internationally find ways to include their child's culture in their family life. This may be done by attending festivals, learning the native language, decorating the child's bedroom with items from the region, or reading books about the country. Many adoption agencies also organize events throughout the year to allow for families and children in the same situation to meet with one another and celebrate special occasions.

Adopting internationally can lead to some awkward questions that may disturb your child. Be prepared for strangers to ask "Is she adopted?" or "Where did she come from?" or "Do you know who her real parents are?" — sometimes in the company of your adopted child. At this age, you will need to decide how much of your child's story you want to share. It is up to you to respond to questions with grace and tact. Your child will soon learn to follow your example.

"better" time. The life story told can evolve as the child grows older. The toddler version can be small and easy to hold, with laminated pages that won't damage easily. As your child grows, a more comprehensive book can be created.

Instructional books have been written for adoptive parents suggesting how best to share their child's story. These books often include a glossary of terms to help you find the words that are most comforting to your adopted child. Books have also been written telling a child's adoption story. Read these with your child, but be sure to have a wide variety of books in your child's library, not just those that refer to adoption.

Did You Know?

Birth story

Later in their third or fourth year, adopted children typically begin to ask questions about their birth. Mothers should be prepared to answer the question "Was I in your tummy?" This may be the first time your adopted child experiences a loss associated with adoption. Your child may have a strong desire to have been in the tummy of the person he identifies with most closely and loves intensely. The adoptive mother may also feel sad, and the mutual longing can be expressed by both mother and child, bringing closure to the issue.

School readiness

A major goal of the preschool years is to prepare our children for full-time school attendance in the first grade. There are several factors that predict a child's success in school at age 6, and you can help promote the development of these factors and address concerns early to maximize your child's chances of settling into school successfully.

The role of these kindergarten years is to help establish and evaluate your child's readiness to attend the first grade and begin the school curriculum. If you are concerned about your child's school readiness, speak with your health-care provider or kindergarten teacher to determine how best to address the area of concern.

Physical well-being

To be successful in school, children need to have the energy to stay awake and be attentive for the full school day. Key to this is good nutrition and adequate sleep. A nutritious breakfast has been shown over and over again to be of critical importance. In most households, this can be a busy and somewhat chaotic part of the day. Getting everyone awake and prepared for school and work can be stressful.

Fine-motor skills

In addition to the physical stamina required to be attentive in school, there are some specific physical skills required for success in the first grade.

Reading and printing are an essential part of the school curriculum in the first grade and will continue to be throughout the school years. By the time children are 6 years old, they need to have acquired the fine-motor skills required to turn the pages of a book and to hold and control a pencil. Pencil games, drawing, and coloring are activities that will help establish the pencil control essential for printing. Make sure that you have a steady and easily accessible supply of paper and pencils for your preschooler.

Guide to

Good mornings

- Plan ahead. Try to do as much as you can the night before. You may want to get your child to pick out his clothes and lay them out, as well as help you prepare lunches to keep in the fridge overnight.
- Allow enough time. You don't want to start the day by having to nag and rush, so make sure you set the alarm early enough to give your preschooler a fair chance to wake up and move at his own pace without causing you stress about being late for school or work.
- Role model. It is up to you to set a good example by eating a healthy breakfast and having your own stuff organized ahead of time so you're not hunting around for your keys or the dry cleaning when you should be walking out the door.
- Ensure adequate sleep. As the end of summer approaches and you are preparing for the school year in September, it may be helpful to start getting children and families back into a regular routine and normal bedtimes. Children aged 4 to 6 generally require at least 10 hours of sleep a night.
- Set up a routine. Establishing these habits now, while your child is a preschooler, will assist with the transition to full days in school.

Emotional health

During the toddler and preschool years, your child is developing skills that will allow her to learn in an environment outside the home as she develops curiosity about the world and an interest in trying new things.

Curiosity

You can foster these characteristics by spending some time each day playing with your child, allowing her to explore her interests and praising her discoveries with a smile, a hug, or a word or two of encouragement. As long as you know she is safe, allow her more freedom and independence to experiment and to learn from her own experiences. This will also help your child develop self-confidence and the ability to persevere as she tries out new things.

Patience

During the toddler years, your child is learning to control aggression and how to wait for something he wants. These will be critical skills when he enters the classroom and needs to interact with a group of peers. You can help him develop these skills by responding in a comforting way when he's hurt or frightened and by teaching appropriate responses when he's angry or frustrated, rather than yelling at or punishing him.

Social skills

During the infant, toddler, and preschool years, children acquire social skills that are essential to functioning in school and other social environments.

Respect

To be able to receive instruction and guidance from teachers, children must have developed a sense of respect for adult authority and an understanding of what is considered acceptable behavior in a public place. During the preschool years, you are fostering these skills by teaching your child basic rules, such as to walk, not run, in indoor public spaces, to line up and wait when required, to stay seated while eating meals, and to keep the volume of her voice low indoors. Taking your child to the library, church, a concert, or any other public place that requires such behavior will help her learn and will reinforce these skills.

Interaction

Your child needs opportunities to interact with other children of the same age and developmental level. During the toddler and early preschool years, these playtimes will need to be supervised by an adult who can help teach taking turns, sharing, how to approach other children to engage in play, and how to use negotiation rather than aggression during peer interactions. Children who develop the ability to

Developing conversational skills

- Talk to your child about your day and your own experiences and encourage him to do the same.
- Go for a walk or sit outside and talk about all the different things in the environment, describing their colors and shapes and making comparisons.
- Ask him questions about his day, a birthday party, or something he's interested in, and encourage his answers by paying attention and commenting back.
- Rather than correcting his grammatical errors, repeat his sentence back appropriately with your additional comment attached. As you talk to your child, you are helping to expand his vocabulary and teaching him grammar without him even being aware of it!

comfortably interact with one another by the age of 5 tend to be successful in their friendships throughout school, while those who do not develop these skills are at risk of being neglected or rejected by their peers. As your child becomes more independent and requires less adult support and supervision during play interactions, you can start to drop her off for play dates and activities, which will promote her ability to separate from caregivers, as will be required for school.

Language skills

Language skills are essential for learning. The ability to understand adults and other children and to communicate effectively using spoken language should be well established during these years. If you are concerned about your child's language development, discuss this with your child's physician and teacher to ensure appropriate and early intervention.

Conversation

You can help encourage your child's language development by taking time to talk and read to her. Everyday conversation is one of the most important ways that children are exposed to language. During the preschool years, this becomes increasingly relevant, as your child is now speaking in full sentences and is able to participate more fully in conversation.

Phonetics

During the preschool years, your child will be learning specific skills that will help support reading in the first grade. By age 4, most children can name the letters of the alphabet. There are many games (e.g., magnetic letters or puzzles) that will make this learning a fun activity. During the next year, children learn the sounds that correspond to letters — initially, consonant sounds, followed by vowel sounds.

By the age of 4, children are usually speaking in full sentences with good pronunciation. However, your child may still have some difficulty with some sounds, such as "r" (e.g., saying "wabbit" instead of "rabbit"). This is normal and will improve over the next year or so.

As your child learns to print, don't worry if she gets some letters backwards. This is normal until a child is 6 or 7 years old. It is also very common to mix up the letters "b" and "d."

Did You Know?

Phonological awareness
A fundamental skill required for reading is "phonological awareness." This refers to recognition of the component sounds of words; for example, the first, middle, and last sounds — not letters, but the sounds those letters make — in the word "c-a-t."

You can help your child develop this skill by playing games that encourage separation of the sounds in short words. The initial sounds are the easiest to learn, followed by the last sound, then the middle sound. Make this a fun activity that you do together when you think your child is ready.

Literacy

In addition to learning how to communicate through language and how to use letters, your child is also acquiring other basic knowledge during these years that forms the basis for learning in school. By age 6, for example, children develop an understanding that stories have a beginning, middle, and end, and that language can be used to describe remote and imaginary events.

Now that language is more established, children begin to learn how to remember what they have heard and repeat it back. In fact, children at this stage are like little sponges, so you can be sure that if they hear something inappropriate, it may be repeated at the most inopportune time! It cannot be emphasized enough how important it is to converse and read with your child during the preschool years to develop these skills.

Numeracy

By age 4, most children can count to 10 and can compare groups of objects in terms of amount (more or less, a little or a lot). At this age, most children can sort objects by color or shape. During the next year, children learn to integrate these so that they can sort by two characteristics (e.g., shape and color: red circles, blue squares) and determine which of two numbers is

bigger (4 or 5). These are the fundamentals required for learning arithmetic.

You can help reinforce these skills by playing games that use numbers, colors, and shapes with your child. Some of the many examples of such games include the board games Snakes and Ladders and Candy Land and the card game Go Fish. Paper picture games that require recognizing similarities and differences also help children develop these skills. If your child likes to work on a computer, there are a number of programs available for the preschool age group that focus on developing and practicing these skills.

Guide to

Easing school separation anxiety

- If you are the parent of a 3-year-old, consider enrolling your child in a part-time preschool program or other activity that occurs regularly and requires the child to leave caregivers briefly to attend with other children. This practice separation may ease the transition to school.
- Attend the school's open house the spring before your child will be going to school to introduce your child to the classroom environment. Meeting the teacher and describing the typical classroom activities may be helpful.
- Encourage interaction with other children in the community who will be attending the same school. This may provide some support and reassurance.
- When you drop him off, make sure your child knows that you will be there to pick him up.

School separation difficulties

During the third to fifth years, many parents struggle with their child's difficulty in separating from them to attend school for the first time. How your child manages separation depends on many factors, including temperament, previous experiences, her degree of anxiety or worrying, and caregiver responses.

Just as with other behavior, children experience a range of difficulty in separating from their caregivers. Some children leave without even a wave goodbye, others may have brief expressions of sadness, and others have prolonged periods of crying that may continue for weeks. If you anticipate that your child will have difficulty transitioning to school, some early preparation may help.

Developmental delays

For some children, difficulty separating from parents may be extreme or prolonged and require further evaluation. In some cases, extreme difficulty settling into school may be related to developmental delays or immaturity. Remember that there is a wide range of emotional development at the time of school entry, with some children entering kindergarten before they are 4 and others when they are almost 5. For some children, a smaller preschool program with more adults per child may be more appropriate.

Family issues

Issues within the family environment may contribute to difficulty separating. Children who live in homes where parents are in frequent conflict, arguing, shouting, or threatening physical violence, may worry about what could happen while they are away from their home and parents.

Similarly, children whose parents experience depression, alcohol or drug addictions, or other mental health problems may develop separation difficulties and other behavior problems.

Recreation options

As your child leaves the toddler years, the variety of recreational programs offered these days is mind-boggling! Which activities are best? How many can she handle? There is no right or wrong answer, although it is better to be guided by your child's specific personality and needs than by what your friends and neighbors are doing with their preschoolers. Probably most important is the example that you as parents set toward physical activity. Many couch potato parents will end up with little couch potatoes. Even if you are not sporty, you can participate in family walks, bike rides, or swimming. Remember, you are instilling lifelong habits, so be a good role model!

Sports

Organized sports programs are not essential for providing physical activity, but for those who opt to enroll their children, these activities do provide opportunities for skill development, socialization, and instruction on simple rules. They also provide a break for caregivers. Factors to consider in deciding which types of sports programs might suit your child include her interests and preferences and her needs and aptitude. Children who love to run and engage in highly active ball play may be interested in soccer, while others may be interested in karate.

Many parents enroll their children in swimming lessons around this age. Children typically develop the strength and coordination to begin to swim unassisted at around 5 to 6 years of age, but introducing children to water with the aid of flotation devices, adult support, and careful supervision prior to age 5 may help them develop a level of comfort in the water that will aid with later swim instruction. Similarly, children are generally ready for ice skating and skiing around 5 to

6 years of age. All sports programs should include a focus on safety, supervision, and appropriate protective equipment.

Unstructured play

Physical activity does not need to be focused on organized sports programs in this age group. Unstructured playtime is very important and encourages social development, creativity, and problem-solving. Unstructured activity might include playing in the park or playground, kicking or throwing a ball with friends or caregivers, building a snowman, playing tag, swimming in a backyard or community pool, or sliding down hills on a snowy winter day.

Art and music programs

For many children, informal physical activity is sufficient at this age, and some parents may be interested in enrolling their children in other types of activities. Again, at this age, any organized activity should be developmentally appropriate and safe, with the emphasis on fun. Art and music programs are very popular. Generally, programs directed at the preschool age group are more fun than instructional, although some music programs provide early instruction in playing musical instruments.

Did You Know?

Competitive sports and overprogramming

At this age, your child is not ready for competitive sports activities and should not be overprogrammed. If your child is routinely tired and whiny before or after such programs, he may not yet be ready for the program, the timing may not be appropriate (evening programs for children this age are frequently not well tolerated), or he may have too much going on. During the transition to going to school for the first time, it may be helpful to wait to see how much energy your child has at the end of the day before enrolling him in after-school activities — or choose weekend programs.

Did You Know?

Resources

Programs for preschoolers should be coordinated by adults so that the activities are developmentally appropriate, safe, nurturing, inclusive, and fun. Programs are available in most communities at community centers, local YMCA and YWCA chapters, or private facilities. Local libraries typically have flyers and information for municipally supported activities, while local parenting magazines usually advertise private programming. Internet searches may help parents find local noncompetitive sports leagues, which generally include children age 5 and up.

Dad's role

"Healthy eating, active living." While not all fathers participate in the "healthy eating" component of this popular recipe for good health, most are involved in their children's "active living" programs. One of the great things about the 4- to 5-year-old age group is that they still love doing things with their dad.

Sports fan

You don't have to push your child to be the next Michael Jordan, Wayne Gretzky, Derek Jeter, Maria Sharapova, or Kristi Yamaguchi, but it is good to expose your children to different sports to see if they have an interest. While baseball may be your favorite sport, it doesn't have to be your child's. Don't try to make your child the supersportsman you could or should have been.

Especially at this age, sports are all about the fun. Most children will enjoy the basic elements involved in most sports, such as running wild. You start with the running, add a ball, and, presto, you have soccer, baseball, football, or basketball. Add a stick and you could have hockey, baseball, golf, or lacrosse. There's nothing wrong with teaching your child the fundamentals of each sport, but if you hear yourself saying things to your child like "Get your head in the game" or "Quitting is for losers," you may want to change activities.

Splash coach

Splashing, jumping, and swimming in the water is a classic father–child activity.

Ideally, your child has been gradually acclimatized to water from an early age. When your child is 3 or 4 years old, you can start teaching her the basics of swimming. Swimming indoors in the winter is a great way to rid yourself of the stir-crazy blues and will help prepare you for the next summer.

Biker dad

Tricycles and bicycles, with training wheels or without, are a great way for kids to get good exercise. Let them pick out a bell. Helmets and clear safety tips are a must for any biking adventure. If you start them young, these rules of the road will become second nature to your children. As your

Did You Know?

Model behavior

Kids learn by watching, so set a good example by exercising. Let your children see you sweat. While you don't need to tell your children that you're exercising because of a direct command from their mother to lose the spare tire around your waist, it's okay to tell them that you're exercising to keep healthy. If you play a sport, have your children come watch you. Remember to set a good example by observing the rules of safety and good sportsmanship.

children get older, you can enjoy longer trips together. Biking is great for family bonding, as is the ice cream or popsicle that is sure to follow. Don't forget to wear your helmet too.

Free play

Taking your kids to the park and letting them run free can become a fun-filled morning or afternoon. Kids need a little bit of their own space to run around and discover things, and the park allows them to do just that. Aside from the almost never-ending pushing on the swings, the park allows you as dad to watch your children have fun and interact with the kids in the neighborhood. And it's a good deal — it doesn't cost anything.

Frequently asked questions

As family doctors and pediatricians, we answer many questions from parents. Here are some of the most frequently asked questions. Be sure to ask your health-care providers any other questions that may arise. If they don't have the answers, they will refer you to a colleague who does.

Q: My son has suddenly developed a fear of the dark. What should I do?
A: Children between the ages of 3 and 5 commonly develop new fears. This is normal. The most common are fears of the dark, monsters, being away from parents or being alone, dogs, fire trucks, and death. At this age, children frequently have difficulty separating fantasy from reality. As their development progresses, they become able to imagine dangers they have not been exposed to. Fears may worsen during major life changes, such as moving or a divorce or death in the family. Exposure to frightening material in books, radio news, TV shows, or movies may create or worsen fears.

It is important to pay attention to your child's fears because they are very real to them. Don't ignore them, tell your child that he's silly, or get angry about his fears. Ask your child questions to better understand what he is afraid of and how to help him cope with his fears. Providing support, comfort, and explanation is generally helpful. Fear of the dark is best addressed by utilizing a night light, leaving on a hallway light at night, or moving objects that create scary shadows. If fears become excessive or these recommendations don't help, discuss your concerns with your child's physician.

Q: Do you have any tips for dealing with car seat wars? My two children are constantly provoking and bothering each other in the back seat. I can barely concentrate on driving.
A: Short of walking or purchasing earplugs or a minivan with an extra row of seating, here are some practical tips for surviving car journeys:

- Bring duplicate snacks and toys to keep your children occupied — better yet, keep these items stocked in the car.
- Try a distraction, such as music or a game like I Spy or counting all the yellow cars that pass by. Don't despair if there are arguments about what CD to play or who goes first. Implement turn taking.
- Pull over to the side of the road, safely, until the outbursts subside.
- Create car rules with specific consequences and enforce these consistently.
- Ignore them. Try not to get riled up by the back-seat shenanigans and keep your eyes on the road.
- Catch them being good! Don't forget to reinforce good behavior. For longer trips, start a reward system for every hour of peace.

Q: My preschooler seems overly active. Does he have ADHD?

A: Many preschool-age children seem to have boundless energy. They tend to be very physically active, have trouble sitting still, and talk frequently and loudly. These are normal developmental features in this age group and don't necessarily indicate that a child has attention deficit hyperactivity disorder (ADHD).

ADHD is characterized by difficulty paying attention, particularly when there

are distractions, increased activity level, and impulsivity. The diagnosis cannot be made until school age. It requires that a particular set of symptoms be present that are not caused by any other developmental problem. The symptoms must be noticed in more than one environment, usually at home and at school.

If you are concerned about your child's ability to focus and pay attention, discuss this with your physician and your child's teacher. Keep an eye on things as he progresses into the first grade, when a diagnosis can be made more reliably. Effective treatments are available for this disorder.

Q: My son came home from preschool last week talking about guns and shooting. My partner and I have never talked about weapons in his presence and were taken aback. What should we do?
A: Children learn all sorts of things in preschool — both good and bad. In addition to being influenced by you, they are also beginning to be influenced by their peers. When older toddlers express ideas that run contrary to your household's values, confront the topic head on. They may not know that their new interest is a negative one, making discipline at first inappropriate. Rather, talk about the subject, ensuring that your little one has a clear understanding of your views. "Mommy and Daddy don't like guns. They hurt people. We don't play with guns in our house" are examples of age-appropriate statements to make. It is important that your preschooler sees that you are open to discussing the subject so he doesn't hide

newly gathered information in the future. By maintaining an open dialog, you will teach your little one correct information, instill your own values, and set the stage for a future of healthy communication.

Q: Should my child attend the funeral if a close family member has died?
A: This is a decision that should be made on an individual basis, and you need to take several factors into account. It is likely that others attending the funeral will become very emotional. How will this affect your child? Will he be more anxious and afraid if he attends the funeral or if he is left at home without his close family? Do you think your child will be traumatized by the funeral ceremony? If you do decide to take him to the funeral, ensure that a familiar caregiver stays with him, explains the process, and comforts him. And if not, make sure that he stays with somebody he knows well and you can trust to be sensitive and supportive of his needs.

Q: My spouse died suddenly. Should I send my 3-year-old to stay with my parents for a while until I feel better?
A: Most experts believe that if the surviving parent can cope, it is preferable for the child to remain within the comfort and familiarity of the family home, with the people he is closest to. Sending your child away may result in fear and insecurity and the belief that he's done something wrong. However, be sure to draw on friends and family who are available to provide support, to be with your child at home, or to take him on outings.

Sam's Diary

April 5 (26 months old)

Your sister, Dani, arrived a month ago yesterday — 5 days earlier than expected. You have been absolutely wonderful with her. You are incredibly gentle when you touch her and give her kisses. You've automatically included her into our family whenever you talk about us. When we walk her in the stroller, you hold on to the handle (you did this on your own without prompting).

On a few isolated occasions, you've been more rough, but nothing too bad at all. The change in routine with so many visitors around and your grandparents staying with us had upset you a little. You became quite loud and boisterous when they were around, but since they've left and things have settled down, you're back to your normal self.

May 9 (27 months old)

You've recently learned to say "s" and "f," so instead of "Ham" you can say "Sam" properly now. You caught a ball for the first time today —

you're so pleased with yourself, it's wonderful. You're mad about basketball now and love to watch our next-door neighbors playing.

You continue to be amazing with Dani. You share your toys with her. You love to put your yellow school bus beside her to play with. Today, while she was sleeping, you quietly put a toy down next to her for when she woke up.

Sam, you're having a bit of a rough time, partly because you're 2, but also because of Dani's arrival, we think. Although you're amazing with her, you're giving Mom and Dad a hard time — not listening, shouting a lot, doing just the opposite of everything we ask. We know this time will pass, but we feel bad for you — and for us when you don't give us a break!

A big first! For three nights in a row now you've made your "bath time wee" in the potty. You're so proud of yourself! Well done, my angel.

The other day you asked for a ladder so that you "can climb up and touch the sky." You bumped your head on Dad's belt the other day and said, "Sorry, Dad, I bumped into your seat belt."

June 4 (28 months old)

It was your cousin Tali's first birthday party today, and you had a ball. There was a lady who came to entertain you all with singing and a guitar. When she handed out instruments, you took a tiny guitar and were dancing and playing beautifully to the music. At the end, she came over to tell you to keep the guitar, as she saw what a "talented" musician you are. You slept with the guitar in your hand for your afternoon nap!

July 17 (29 months old)

You have been having quite a tough time lately and have now started pulling hair and spitting! Yikes, Sambo, we wish you could tell us what's bothering you. Anyway, we know this is normal 2-year-old behavior. Your teachers at daycare never see any of it! They say you're a smart, wonderful little guy who follows routines and listens beautifully. Well, they're right — I guess it's easier for you to be that way at school than at home, where Dani has invaded your space. Anyway, this too shall pass, we know.

You're having swimming at school today, which you absolutely love. You're like a real fish in the water. You talk non-stop at school, always telling your teachers stories. They're amazed at your memory and your train of thought — which reminds me: you're besotted with Thomas the Tank Engine. You devour the books and videos and know all the names of the trains and their coaches.

Helping Your Toddler Sleep

Understanding sleep 272

How much sleep does my child need? 275

Secrets to a good night's sleep 280

Problematic sleep behaviors 284

Solving sleep problems 287

Frequently asked questions 300

Understanding sleep

Sleep deprivation is an age-old form of torture inflicted on parents by their young children. Toddlers and preschoolers are champs at finding ways to avoid napping, to delay bedtime, and to sneak into their parents' bed in the middle of the night. And parenting a toddler is a tough enough job without adding the further challenge of doing so in a sleep-deprived state!

But where did your children learn these behaviors? In fact, many of these bad sleeping habits are inadvertently taught to them and reinforced by their parents. Sleep habits are not only innate — they are also learned. Fortunately, there are many things you can do to avoid bad sleep habits and promote healthy habits that will help your child — and you — sleep well.

Functions of sleep

Sleep is essential for your child's optimal growth and development. Without sleep, our bodies cannot function properly. A basic understanding of sleep can help you teach your toddler to be a good sleeper.

Sleep experts at the Hospital for Sick Children and elsewhere have identified several possible functions of sleep that promote good health:

- Restoration and regeneration of body systems
- Protection and recovery from infections
- Consolidation of memory
- Optimum daytime function of learning, memory, mood, attention, and concentration
- Growth and development of body and brain

Adapted by permission from Shelly K. Weiss, *Better Sleep for Your Baby & Child* (Toronto: Robert Rose, 2006).

Types of sleep

There are two main kinds of sleep: REM (rapid eye movement) and NREM (non–rapid eye movement). Toddlers typically spend 75% of their sleep in REM and 25% in NREM states.

REM sleep

REM sleep is commonly referred to as dreaming sleep. In REM sleep, your brain is in an active state even though you are asleep. Your eyes continue to move rapidly under your eyelids, and your heart rate and breathing rate may also fluctuate. While your brain is very active, your body remains very still, apart from some small muscle twitches. In this state, it may be easier for someone to wake you up than if you were in NREM sleep.

In children, REM sleep is thought to help with the development of memory and contribute to learning.

NREM sleep

NREM sleep is a deeper, more restorative kind of sleep. There are different degrees of NREM sleep, from light to deep sleep. If you are in deep NREM sleep, you may feel confused or disoriented if someone wakes you up. In fact, it may be very difficult to wake you if you are in deep NREM sleep. This is the stage of sleep that allows you to carry your sleeping child from the car to the crib without waking him. In this stage, your heart rate and breathing rate stay fairly consistent, and you don't dream as much as you do in REM sleep because your brain is not as active. In children, the purpose of this sleep is to restore body systems.

Sleep cycles

During an average night, your child will go through several cycles of REM and NREM sleep:

- Children typically fall asleep quickly, in less than 30 minutes, but may wake up soon after because this transitional sleep phase is easily reversed.
- Children cycle from dreaming (REM) to restorative sleep (NREM) throughout the night. A toddler's sleep cycles last 50 to 60 minutes. These cycles lengthen with development, and by the time they reach adulthood, sleep cycles will have lengthened considerably, to 90 to 120 minutes.
- Children typically have their first episode of deep sleep in the first third of the night. Your child may have a briefer episode of deep restorative sleep in the early morning hours before waking.
- Children have their first episode of dreaming sleep about 90 minutes after falling asleep. The dreaming episodes become longer throughout the night, with most dreaming happening in the last third of the night.

Did You Know?

Similar cycles

Toddlers have sleep cycles that are more like adult cycles than infant cycles. This is important to know when you're determining sleep expectations for your child. A toddler is physiologically able to sleep through the night in her own bed without getting up for any reason, including feeding. It is not unreasonable for you to expect to be able to sleep through the night yourself, most of the time!

- Children may experience periods of brief arousal during the night. When your child ends one sleep cycle and starts the next, he may awaken briefly, but this awakening is usually short-lived. These arousals occur as he comes out of REM or the lighter stages of NREM sleep.
- Children who have slept well typically wake up by themselves in the morning.

Circadian rhythms

Circadian (24-hour) rhythms also play a part in regulating our sleeping and waking. Light and dark, eating patterns, physical activities, and hormones all affect a toddler's biological sleep rhythms, regulating when he will feel sleepy and when he will be wide awake and ready for action.

How much sleep does my child need?

Your toddler requires a significant amount of good-quality sleep for optimal growth and development. Unfortunately, for many children, this is not always happening. There is an increasing tendency for children to be overprogrammed and underslept. Life just seems to get in the way of a good night's sleep.

Sleep needs
Young toddler (12 to 18 months)

Toddlers require an average of 12 to 14 hours of sleep a day. Younger toddlers (12 to 18 months of age) usually still need two naps a day, one in the morning and one in the afternoon. This is often complemented by a relatively early bedtime and an early waking time.

This is not true for all families, because bedtimes and waking times may be shifted by family schedules. If this is the case, just keep in mind that a child who stays up late should also be able to sleep later in the morning. Children require more sleep than adults, and many times their schedules will not be compatible with their parents.

Average Sleep Needs

Bear in mind that these are just averages and certainly may not apply to every child. Nevertheless, you may want to record your child's sleep duration and compare it with the average amount of time other children of a similar age spend sleeping.

Age	Average Hours of Sleep	Your Child's Hours of Sleep
0 to 2 months	16 to 18	
2 to 6 months	14 to 16	
6 to 12 months	13 to 15	
1 to 3 years	12 to 14	
3 to 5 years	11 to 13	
5 to 12 years	10 to 11	
12 to 18 years	8.5 to 9.5	

Adapted by permission from Shelly K. Weiss, *Better Sleep for Your Baby & Child* (Toronto: Robert Rose, 2006).

Young Toddler (12 to 18 months) Sleep Schedule

	Early wake/bedtime	Average wake/bedtime	Late wake/bedtime
Wake time	5:30 a.m.	7:00 a.m.	9:00 a.m.
1st nap (1 hour)	8:00 a.m.	9:30 a.m.	11:00 a.m.
2nd nap (1–2 hours)	12:00 noon	1:00 p.m.	2:00 p.m.
Bedtime	6:30 p.m.	8:00 p.m.	10:00 p.m.

Toddler (18 months to 3 Years) Sleep Schedule

	Early wake/bedtime	Average wake/bedtime	Late wake/bedtime
Wake time	5:30 a.m.	7:00 a.m.	9:00 a.m.
Nap (2 hours)	12:00 noon	1:00 p.m.	2:00 p.m.
Bedtime	6:30 p.m.	8:00 p.m.	10:00 p.m.

Preschooler (3 to 5 Years) Sleep Schedule with Nap

	Early wake/bedtime	Average wake/bedtime	Late wake/bedtime
Wake time	5:30 a.m.	7:00 a.m.	9:00 a.m.
Nap (1 hour)	12:00 noon	1:00 p.m.	2:00 p.m.
Bedtime	6:30 p.m.	8:00 p.m.	10:00 a.m.

Preschooler (3 to 5 Years) Sleep Schedule *without* Nap

	Early wake/bedtime	Average wake/bedtime	Late wake/bedtime
Wake time	5:30 a.m.	7:00 a.m.	9:00 a.m.
Bedtime	6:30 p.m.	8:00 p.m.	10:00 p.m.

Older toddler (18 months to 3 years)

By 18 months of age, most toddlers will have weaned themselves off their morning nap. You should evaluate the cues your child provides to see if he is ready to drop this morning nap. For example, your toddler may not seem tired anymore when you try to put him down in the morning and may not sleep, or his nap may become very brief. Furthermore, if you remove the morning nap, you may notice that your child is happy all morning long and just sleeps longer during his afternoon nap.

Preschooler (3 to 5 years)

Your preschool-age child will need less sleep than a toddler. Preschoolers typically need 11 to 13 hours of sleep a day. Some preschoolers still require a daily nap, while others outgrow it. Each child is different. The decision regarding a nap may also be related to other schedules, at daycare or at school, for example.

Be flexible with these changes. Your child might still take a nap, but it may shorten in duration. You may also notice signs that your child does not need a nap at all. Evaluate these cues. If your child is having difficulty falling asleep at night after a long afternoon nap, then he may not need as much daytime sleep. If he continues to nap, ensure that it happens in the early part of the afternoon.

Consistent schedules

Other factors affect waking and napping schedules, requiring you and your child to be somewhat flexible. When other schedules conflict with your standard schedule, adapt — but be consistent in your new schedule. Try not to change the schedule too often.

Daycare schedule

Many children have to rise early in the morning to get to daycare before their

---

Did You Know?

Sleeping through the night

By the time your child becomes a toddler at 1 year of age, she should be very good at sleeping through the night. At this age, children are physiologically able to sleep through the night for 10 to 12 hours (or more in some cases). They do not need to feed at night, so it is appropriate to wean them off nighttime feeds if you haven't already done so. However, incorrect sleep associations and improper parental reinforcement may hinder a child's ability to sleep through the night.

parents go to work. At daycare, there are often set time schedules for naps and meals. When planning your child's schedule, keep these factors in mind. If your child has to get up early for daycare, he should be going to bed early. If the family dinner occurs later in the evening, adjust your child's schedule to accommodate his sleep requirements and feed him before the rest of the family, or adjust the family's dinnertime.

Weekends

The family's schedule is likely to change on the weekend. At times, it may seem impossible to match your child's schedule with that of the rest of the family. In these cases, you need to be flexible and use common sense. Try to maintain consistency, which means sticking with the same wake time, nap time, and bedtime whenever possible.

Quiet time

The day that your child stops napping may be met with mixed feelings by the members of your household. Many parents look forward to nap time with anticipation so they can complete other tasks they can't do when their child is awake. Parents may also need to catch up on some much-needed shut-eye.

To retain these advantages after nap time is no longer needed, some families introduce a period of quiet time into their schedules. Children retire to their room as they would if they were napping, but instead of napping, they play alone quietly. This allows you and your child some downtime to rest and regroup. About 45 minutes to 1 hour would be a typical quiet time. Besides the rest, empowering toddlers or preschoolers with the ability to entertain themselves is invaluable.

Mealtime

Just as a consistent nap time, wake time, and bedtime are important for promoting good sleep, so too are consistent mealtimes. Children should be fed dinner before going to bed at night, but not right before bedtime. After dinner, they should have some time to unwind and then a bedtime routine should start.

Children between the ages of 1 and 5 years do not need to eat during the night, although many still do. For most, this is a habit that can be changed. Nighttime feedings interrupt precious sleep time. If your child is still feeding through the night, he can certainly be weaned if you want to improve his (and your) chances of sleeping through the night.

Secrets to a good night's sleep

A child who sleeps well is a happier, better-behaved child, which is clearly in everyone's best interests. Establishing a bedtime routine, sleeping in a comfortable environment, and developing positive sleep associations are all good sleep habits.

Bedtime routines

What your child does just before bed, what time he takes a nap, and who he falls asleep with all affect how your child falls — and remains — asleep. Common bedtime routines include a bath, putting on pajamas, brushing teeth, reading a book, turning out the lights, and leaving your child's bedroom. Aim to leave your toddler's room while he's still awake. This way, he can learn to fall asleep on his own.

Sleep environment

Where your child falls asleep should also be consistent. Your child should fall asleep in the same place where he will wake up — ideally, alone in his bed in his room. This is very important because your child has several sleep cycles throughout the night, each with the potential for him to wake up. If the environment your child falls asleep in is not the one he wakes up in, then he is much more likely to need that first environment recreated to fall asleep again, which may involve his being with you in your bed or your being with him in his bed. This leads to disrupted sleep for both you and your child, and ultimately puts you both at risk for inadequate sleep.

Nighttime environment

For nighttime sleep, the room should be dark. If your child is afraid of the dark, use a small nightlight or keep the door open to let in some light. If you do choose to use a nightlight, make sure it is safe and tamperproof. Whatever light is present when your child falls asleep should remain on all night long. If the door is ajar, it should remain open throughout the night.

HOW TO
Establish a good bedtime routine

1. Make the bedtime routine consistent and repeatable. It should be the same every night so your child knows what to expect. It should start at the same time (e.g., 30 minutes before bedtime) and last for the same amount of time.

2. Make the routine relaxing, not stimulating. Have a relaxing bath, not a stimulating shower. Play quietly and avoid loud music. Your child should fall asleep without sleep "props," such as television or music.

3. Provide a drink from a sippy cup before your child goes to sleep if it doesn't interfere with potty training. If you're giving anything other than water, make sure to brush your child's teeth afterward. For both sleep and dental health reasons, don't provide a bottle in bed to help your child fall asleep.

4. Leave the room while your child is still awake so she can fall asleep by herself in her own bed.

Did You Know?

Caffeine

Caffeine is found in many foods in our diet, from soft drinks to chocolate. Children do not need caffeine — although they will inevitably ingest some along the way. If your child does take in caffeine from chocolate, soft drinks, or other sources, evaluate what time of the day she commonly eats or drinks these foods. Caffeine is a stimulant that can affect sleep and should be avoided in the late afternoon or evening.

Nap time environment

If your child is napping at home, it is best if he naps in his bedroom, as opposed to the car seat or a stroller, for example. The room should not be dark — window coverings that block out sunlight are not needed. Natural light is appropriate for daytime sleep because your child is sleeping for only a short period of time. If your child is in daycare, this daytime sleep will likely happen in the same place on a daily basis.

Bedrooms, beds, and cribs

Your child's bedroom should be a haven he can retreat to when he's tired. To ensure the best possible chance of a good night's sleep, he needs to feels safe and secure in his bedroom and comfortable in his crib or bed. A favorite comfort object — a special blanket, pillow, or stuffed animal — can reassure him that all is well as he falls asleep. Commonly, young toddlers sleep in a crib until they grow into a bed, but there are no hard and fast rules about this transition. For more information on the transition from crib to bed, see pages 60–62.

Sleep associations

Sleep associations are things and activities that your child associates with going to

Examples of Sleep Associations

Positive	Negative
Predictable bedtime routine	No bedtime routine
Consistent bedtime	Variable bedtime
Child falls asleep in her own bedroom	Child falls asleep in another room
Dark environment	Bright light
Quiet environment	TV or music playing
Parent leaves room while child is still awake	Parent stays in child's room until she is soundly asleep
Child falls asleep without bottle	Child falls asleep drinking from bottle or breast-feeding; drinks off and on through the night
Child falls asleep in her own bed	Child falls asleep in parent's arms

sleep; for example, a specific routine or a bedtime story, a specific toy or a favorite blanket. As with most things, there are good and bad sleep associations.

Good sleep associations remind your child that it's bedtime, help him relax, and help him fall asleep on his own. Good sleep associations are replicable — meaning your child can re-create them in the middle of the night should he wake up. Bad sleep associations are things that help your toddler fall asleep but not necessarily on his own, and they are often not reproducible in the middle of the night without your presence.

Co-sleeping

Co-sleeping in the same bed or same room with a toddler is the norm throughout most of the world, although it is unusual in North America. There are no conclusive studies that prove a position for or against co-sleeping, so if everyone is happy with the arrangement, then it makes sense not to rock the bed, so to speak. If you are co-sleeping because it's the path of least resistance or because you're avoiding another problem, however, you may need to consider implementing strategies to teach your child how to fall asleep on his own in his own bed.

Reasons for co-sleeping with your toddler
GOOD REASONS

- Your cultural beliefs lead you to think that a child shouldn't sleep alone at night.
- Your child or family has undergone a recent stressful event — a move, an illness, or a burglary, for example — and this is a temporary family choice.
- You don't have enough rooms or beds in your home for everyone to have a separate space at night.

POOR REASONS

- You're too tired at night to try any other sleeping arrangement to get your child to sleep independently, although this is what you'd really like.
- This is the only way you can get your child to fall asleep and sleep through the night.
- You or your partner are working late and you just want more time in the presence of your child, regardless of whether you're awake or asleep.
- You fall asleep at night in your child's bed or with him in your bed and then you're too tired to either move or move him.
- This is the only way you and the rest of the family get some sleep at night.
- You or your partner prefer keeping your child in bed to avoid marital communication and intimacy.

Problematic sleep behaviors

Poor sleep is a common problem in childhood that can lead to broader problems with growth and development. Most directly, poor sleep habits can negatively affect a child's daytime behavior and learning. In addition, parents need their sleep to care for their children safely and function adequately during the day.

Symptoms of a sleep problem

Identifying a sleep problem is the first step in treating it. If you think your toddler has a sleep problem, try to characterize its most common symptoms. The majority of sleep problems in young children are behavioral in nature and may be solved by changes in parental behavior, although this may involve some short-term pain.

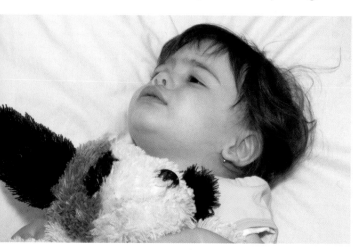

Kinds of sleep problems

Health-care providers divide sleep problems into three technical groups: dyssomnias, parasomnias, and medical conditions leading to sleep problems.

- **Dyssomnias** include sleep-onset association disorders and limit-setting disorders.
- **Parasomnias** are defined as unusual behaviors while sleeping, including rhythmic movements, such as head banging, as well as nightmares and night terrors.
- **Medical problems,** such as obstructive sleep apnea, can cause difficulty with breathing at night and result in secondary sleep disturbances.

Did You Know?

Sleep expectations

For a variety of social or cultural reasons, families may have different expectations of what is appropriate in terms of their toddler's sleep habits. In addition, individual parents may have differing levels of tolerance for disrupted sleep at this stage of parenthood. Depending on the family's expectations and perspective, the exact same sleep habits may be seen as a problem by one family and completely normal by another. What you consider normal may be unacceptable to your neighbors and vice versa.

Common Sleep Problems

Symptoms	Problem	Treatment
• Child wakes up several times during the night • Child requires rocking or holding to fall asleep initially and during the night • Child requires parental presence or the presence of another object (e.g., TV) to fall asleep	Sleep-onset association disorder	• Teach your child appropriate sleep associations and to fall asleep alone, using graduated extinction techniques (see page 291)
• Child uses various tactics to avoid going to bed at night (e.g., wants a glass of water, wants another story)	Limit-setting disorder	• Set consistent limits and follow through with consequences
• Child wakes up screaming or confused in first third of the night or in the early morning • It is difficult to comfort child • May be talking to you, but it feels like she doesn't appreciate your presence • Has no recollection of this event the following morning	Night terrors	• Do not disturb the child or try to wake her up • Make sure she can't hurt herself
• Child wakes up scared in the middle of the night • Can recount to you a scary dream she just had • May feel that this dream was real	Nightmares	• Reassure your child that she's safe • Discuss the event during daylight hours • Avoid scary images (e.g., stories about monsters)
• Child rocks herself to sleep • Bangs her head on the wall, crib, or headboard to fall asleep	Rhythmic movements	• Most of these movements tend to be normal and will disappear on their own
• Snoring, with periods of no breathing between snores • Tired during the day • Restless or hyperactive during the day	Sleep apnea	• See your health-care provider for further evaluation

HOW TO
Evaluate your toddler's sleep behavior

Children who are not sleeping well generally tend to be tired, although this may not be the first symptom you see. More commonly, a lack of attentiveness or even hyperactivity may be the first behavior you notice.

When evaluating the quality of your child's sleep, ask yourself:

1. Does she have a consistent sleep schedule with regular wake, nap, and bedtimes? Children who lack a consistent sleep schedule often have fragmented sleep and demonstrate poor sleep behavior. Parents will often describe these children as "bad sleepers."

2. Does she take a long time to fall asleep? If she's taking more than 30 minutes to fall asleep, she may not be tired, or if she's falling asleep wherever she may be (e.g., in a stroller or car seat), then she needs more sleep.

3. Does she wake up spontaneously in the morning or does she need to be woken up? If you constantly have to wake your child up in the morning, then she is not getting enough sleep at night. She is either not going to bed early enough or she is having broken or fragmented sleep at night.

4. Does she appear tired during the day? Children who are tired (often called overtired) look tired. They may have dark circles under their eyes. They will fall asleep quickly in places other than their bed. When they're playing, they may appear to have more energy than the other kids or their behavior may be out of control.

5. Does she fall asleep easily in the car or stroller? Children who don't get enough sleep at night tend to make up for it in other ways. They may fall asleep quickly in a moving vehicle, whereas a well-slept child will be alert and interactive.

6. Is she hyperactive? Children who don't get enough sleep may demonstrate their lack of sleep through increased activity, as opposed to adults, who may just want to rest.

7. Does she wake up several times during the night? By 6 months of age, children should be able to sleep through the night on their own without your intervention. If your toddler or preschooler is waking up throughout the night, she has not learned to put herself back to sleep.

Solving sleep problems

The following treatments are not cookie-cutter solutions — what may come as a godsend to some families may not conform to parenting beliefs in others. We believe that these tried and tested strategies have a good chance of success, but they may not appeal to all.

Sleep-onset association disorder

This is probably one of the most common complaints among sleep-deprived parents of young toddlers. These disorders are most easily explained as inappropriate sleep associations, the conditions we associate with falling asleep.

For example, we will usually sleep in our own bed, with our own pillow, in a quiet, dark room. These associations help us fall asleep every night, but without them our sleep is disturbed. We all have cycles of deep and light sleep throughout the night. Every time we enter a lighter kind of sleep (every 60 to 90 minutes), we are at risk of partial or full arousal — meaning we might wake up.

If nothing changes in the night and our environment is consistent, we will likely sleep through the night and have no recollection of these arousals. If, however, we are in a new or different environment (e.g., sleeping in a different location with different bedding and changes in light or noise levels), we are more likely to have a full arousal and, consequently, a very interrupted sleep. This will leave us tired and often a little grumpy in the morning. We may also find it difficult to wake up at the required time.

Toddler disassociations

Toddlers have the same problem. If a child is accustomed to falling asleep stroking his mother's face or being rocked by his father and this activity or condition is not present all night long — once your child is asleep, you leave their room — every time he moves into a lighter sleep, he will likely wake up. Then you may need to recreate the environment that the child fell asleep in (i.e., you will need to lie down with or rock him) for him to fall asleep again — perhaps all night long.

Behavioral treatments

Inappropriate sleep associations, and their associated frequent night awakenings, are unlikely to disappear on their own. Before embarking on a specific treatment plan, you and your partner will first need to agree that this sleep problem is something that you need to address. Next, you and your partner will need to agree on what sort of treatment approach you are comfortable with. Making changes to your toddler's behavior requires commitment, consistency, and fortitude. You and your partner and all other caregivers will need each other's unqualified support during the process — there isn't much room for ambivalence.

HOW TO
Treat inappropriate sleep associations

The key treatment goal is to teach your child to fall asleep on her own by teaching appropriate sleep associations. Once your child knows how to fall asleep on her own, her awakenings during the night will not become full awakenings. She will learn how to soothe herself back to sleep independently or to stay asleep throughout the night. However, this is easier said than done!

1. Begin slowly. Baby steps are often more tolerable than big steps. Avoid changing too many things at once — this may increase the risk of failure.

2. Before removing any inappropriate sleep associations, first create a consistent sleep schedule and routine. Evaluate your child's schedule — wake time, nap time, bedtime, and mealtimes. Readjust as needed to ensure that your child is eating and sleeping an appropriate amount for her age. If she's still feeding at night, wean her off these feeds. If your child initially spends a lot of the night awake crying, she should still be woken at her regular time and be kept awake until her regular nap times. This prevents your child from shifting her sleep schedule (i.e., sleeping much longer during the day because she was awake all night). Do your best, bearing in mind that this is sometimes pretty difficult.

3. Assess your child's sleep-onset associations. What does your child's bedtime routine look like, where does she fall asleep, and what is happening while she's falling asleep? Is she in her room or your room when falling asleep? Are you present? Are you holding her, rocking her, singing to her? Do you carry her to her room once she is asleep? Often, parents are present when their child is falling asleep.

4. Write out a list of these sleep associations. This will be your working list for change.

5. Choose an appropriate start time. Some sleep experts suggest starting this process during a daytime nap or on the weekend, if you're not the caregiver on weekdays. The rationale is that you may have more energy and determination at this time of day. Other parents prefer to start this approach when they feel it's most important, during the night. This is a personal decision.

6. Remove incorrect sleep associations. If your child has multiple sleep associations, remove these associations gradually, one at a time. For example, if your sleep routine is to walk your child up and down the stairs, then sing and rock her to sleep, you should eliminate each association individually over the course of 2 to 3 days. For the first 2 to 3 days, stop walking up and down the stairs; for the next 2 to 3 days, stop rocking her to sleep; and for the last 2 to 3 days, stop singing at sleep time. You can certainly still rock her and sing as part of your bedtime routine — just ensure that your toddler isn't falling asleep while you do so. Ultimately, you will be putting your child to bed sleepy but awake.

7. Be consistent. All caregivers should use the same approaches during the day and night. There is nothing more confusing for your toddler than getting different responses to the same behaviors at different times. And don't start any technique unless you have the time, energy, and family support to see it through. Starting and stopping a method prior to completion will only confuse your child and worsen her sleep habits.

SLEEP-ONSET ASSOCIATION DISORDER CHARACTERISTICS

- Your child is unable to fall asleep at nap time or bedtime unless a certain object or set of circumstances is present.
- When these conditions are present, your child has a normal sleep pattern. When the conditions are not present, however, transitions to sleep at bedtime and after nighttime awakenings are delayed.
- Although it may seem like the number of times that your child wakens at night is excessive, it is probably part of a normal sleep pattern. This becomes a problem when your child cannot settle himself back to sleep on his own.
- When you recreate the required conditions (e.g., rocking, cuddling, singing, or nursing), your child falls back to sleep quickly.
- The sleep-onset association conditions usually require participation by you, your partner, or your child's caregiver.
- This problem is mainly a childhood sleep problem.

Adapted by permission from Shelly K. Weiss, *Better Sleep for Your Baby & Child,* (Toronto: Robert Rose, 2006), based on American Academy of Sleep Medicine, *The International Classification of Sleep Disorders, Revised,* 2001.

Falling asleep on their own

To help children fall asleep on their own, most sleep experts recommend a process of graduated extinction, which is a more gradual approach than the extinction, or "cold turkey," method.

Extinction

Using the extinction method to modify sleep behavior, you would, for example, simply decide that you are not going to respond to your child's frequent requests at bedtime and during the night, close the bedroom door, and let your child "cry it out" or scream until he learns to fall asleep on his own. However, many families prefer not to use this method because it may result in their child's becoming very distressed, making it difficult to carry through in a consistent manner. They opt instead for more gradual methods of changing sleep behavior.

Graduated extinction

"Timed waiting" and "chair sitting" are methods of graduated extinction that have been successfully used by parents to teach their children to fall asleep on their own. In both methods, you leave your child alone in his room for increasing periods of time until he falls asleep on his own.

The timed-waiting approach is more successful with younger toddlers who are in a crib or toddlers who are in a bed but have difficulty staying in bed. The chair-sitting approach works better with older toddlers or preschoolers, to whom you can explain the logic of the process.

This can be a tricky process. You may find that when you begin to implement these strategies, your child's behavior and sleeping gets worse before it gets better. This is completely normal. Like all other behaviors in children, these approaches to graduated extinction require practice.

Timed-waiting method

This routine, outlined on page 292, should be repeated for all naps, bedtimes, and awakenings during the night. Each and every time your child wakes up during the

Graduated schedule for timed-waiting and intermittent door-closing strategies (in minutes)

Night	First Wait	Second Wait	Third Wait	Fourth Wait	Subsequent Wait
Night 1	2 minutes	4 minutes	6 minutes	8 minutes	8 minutes
Night 2	4 minutes	6 minutes	8 minutes	10 minutes	10 minutes
Night 3	6 minutes	8 minutes	10 minutes	12 minutes	12 minutes
Night 4	8 minutes	10 minutes	12 minutes	14 minutes	14 minutes
Night 5	10 minutes	12 minutes	14 minutes	16 minutes	16 minutes
Night 6	12 minutes	14 minutes	16 minutes	18 minutes	18 minutes
Night 7	14 minutes	16 minutes	18 minutes	20 minutes	20 minutes

Adapted by permission from Shelly K. Weiss, *Better Sleep for Your Baby & Child* (Toronto: Robert Rose, 2006).

night, you need to follow the exact same routine as you did when you put him to bed.

The timed-waiting process can last from a few minutes to a few hours, which will test the most determined parent. It may take a few days before your child stops complaining before going to bed and before returning to sleep in the middle of the night.

Follow the time progression in the chart on page 291 when using timed-waiting strategies at bedtime and during the night. If your child wakes up more than four times, continue each time thereafter with the same time as for the fourth wait.

Guide to
Using the timed-waiting method

- Ensure that your child's bedroom is safe. Because she may get out of her bed when you're not in the room, there shouldn't be anything that she can pull down or climb onto that could injure her.
- Put your child down in her crib or bed following your normal bedtime routine (bath, brush teeth, read a book, give her a hug and kiss, etc.). Explain to her that you will leave her door open and will be outside her room. Explain that if she tries to leave her bed or her room, you will close her door.
- Leave the room. This may evoke many responses from your child, including protests and crying.
- Leave the door open, if this is your normal routine, as long as your child doesn't leave her room. If she tries to get out of bed and leave her room, you will need to use the door-closing technique.
- If your child is in a bed and keeps getting up and tries to leave her room, implement the following door-closing technique: First, escort her back to her bed and remind her that if she tries to leave her room, you will have to close her door. Tell her that if she returns to her bed, you will open it. Next, if she leaves her bed, close her door. You may open it once she returns to her bed. If your toddler tries to open the door, you may actually even need to hold it shut. This may upset your toddler, who does not want to sleep alone in her room. Remind her that you will open her door if she returns to her bed. In the beginning, she may actually fall asleep on her floor rather than in her bed. This is okay. It may continue for a few nights until she learns to fall asleep alone.
- Continue to return to your child's room at timed intervals (see chart on page 291) until she is calm or asleep. When you return to her room, if she's still awake, remind her that you are still there, that it is her bedtime, that she should be sleeping, and that you love her. You can escort her back to bed if she'll go, but this isn't essential. Then leave the room.
- Do not pick her up or cuddle her, because this will serve as positive reinforcement of inappropriate behavior. This should be a businesslike interaction, reassuring but not particularly desirable. When you check in on your child, do not introduce any new sleep associations.

Chair-sitting method

This method, outlined below, works best with an older toddler, and especially preschool and school-age children. It also works well for parents who do not feel comfortable with the timed-waiting approach.

The chair-sitting approach also involves a gradual weaning of your presence from your child's room at night. As with the timed-waiting approach, you need to use this method during nap time, bedtime, and any nighttime awakenings. The approach usually takes about 3 weeks to implement. If you try this method and you are not able to keep your child in bed, the timed-waiting approach is recommended. You may also decide to use a combination of the two approaches.

Guide to

Using the chair-sitting method

- Ensure that your child's bedroom is safe. Because she may get out of her bed when you're not in the room, there shouldn't be anything that she can pull down or climb onto that could injure her.
- Place a chair that can be easily moved, such as a dining-room chair, beside your child's bed. Inform your child that you are going to sit in this chair while she falls asleep and then leave when she is asleep.
- During the first week of the process, place the chair beside the bed, and if you usually touch your child when she's falling asleep, you can do this initially, but don't lie on the bed with her. Discourage talking and eye contact — it is now time for sleep.
- Let her know that you will always be around and that if she wakes up, she can call you and you will return to the chair and sit there until she falls asleep. (If this is in the middle of the night, chances are that you will fall asleep before she does!)
- Every couple of nights, move the chair gradually closer to the bedroom door. Once you start to do this, you should discontinue physical contact with your child while she's falling asleep. You should also stop having conversations. You can turn the chair so that you're not looking directly at your child but she can still see you and know that you're there. By the end of the first week, your chair should be at your child's door.
- At the start of the second week, position the chair outside your child's door so that she can see you (but not necessarily your face). For the next week, sit in the chair while your child falls asleep, day or night.
- At the start of the third week, inform her that you will no longer be sitting in the chair while she falls asleep but that you will be close by, and if she calls out to you, you will come to her doorway. Find a quiet activity (e.g., reading a book) that you can do near her room so she knows you're close by. By the end of the three weeks, your child should be able to fall asleep without you. She will have progressed from falling asleep with you to doing it all by herself.

HOW TO
Set sleep behavior limits

The best way to deter limit-setting disorders is for you to establish and maintain a bedtime schedule and routine.

1. Make sure your child has consistent bedtimes, wake times, and nap times and stays on schedule. If your child stays up later with frequent curtain calls, she should still get up at the regular time the next morning. If you let her sleep in, she will get used to staying up later and adjust her routine accordingly. Be firm.

2. Make sure that you also have a routine you follow at bedtime. This routine can include strategies to avoid callbacks. For example, your child can have a small drink of water before going to bed. She should also try to use the potty or toilet before going to bed.

3. Once your child is in bed, leave the room.

4. If the issue is keeping your child in her room, you may need to assess her sleep-onset associations. Does your child always fall asleep with you and need to learn how to fall asleep on her own?

5. If the issue is callbacks, make a plan and share it with your child. For example, tell your child that it's bedtime, that she should be sleeping, and that you won't be talking to her. Stick to this plan — do not answer her callbacks (unless they are valid). If you do, plan on being called back many times!

6. Create a method to reward your child for a job well done (e.g., a sticker calendar or special toy) and let her know what she needs to accomplish to receive her reward. Praise good behavior to reinforce it.

Routine changes

After you have taught your child how to soothe himself to sleep, he may have nights when he still needs you from time to time; for example, if he's not feeling well. Attend to his needs so he knows you are there, then resume the process.

It is very common for children to forget their good sleep habits as soon as their schedule is altered. Vacations are a common time for children to relapse. Try your best to keep a consistent routine, even on vacation. If this is not practical — if you are all sleeping in the same room, for example — resume the process to remove any new but inappropriate sleep associations and reinstitute graduated extinction on returning home. Once children learn this approach the first time, they are usually pretty quick to pick up where they left off.

Limit-setting disorder

Children are incredibly intuitive and are often very good at sensing their parent's weaknesses. In a limit-setting disorder, the child, not the parents, makes the rules or sets the limits surrounding bedtime.

A common example is the child who's been put to bed and immediately starts calling to you, asking for a multitude of things. First, it may be a glass of water; next, it may be to pee; third, he may want to tell you something; and on it goes. Some

people refer to these attention-seeking behaviors as "callbacks" or "curtain calls." This behavior may result in children who "just can't sleep" in their own bed — and prefer yours.

These behaviors are very common in children in the toddler and preschool age group. Remember that your toddler ultimately wants your attention and is willing to work really hard to get it. Turn this around by giving him lots of positive reinforcement for appropriate behavior and minimal attention for inappropriate callbacks.

Nightmares, night terrors, and sleepwalking

Parasomnias are characterized by events (nightmares) or actions (night terrors and sleepwalking) during sleep time. The underlying cause may be related to stressful situations for your child or a lack of good sleep. It isn't unusual for children who have night terrors or who sleepwalk to have parents who had similar issues in childhood. These behaviors usually resolve in childhood and do not continue into adulthood. Being able to

Nightmares versus Night Terrors

	Nightmares	Night terrors
Presentation	• Dreams • Wakes up scared in the middle of the night • May feel the dream was real • Experiences partial arousal	• May sit up in bed • May be screaming • Seems to "look through" parents, not comforted by their presence • Thrashes around, kicks • May be sweaty, breathing quickly with a fast heart rate and wide pupils
Time of night	• Second half of night	• First 2 to 3 hours of sleep or early morning • May occur during naps
Sleep stage	• REM	• NREM
Typical age	• 3 to 6 years	• 2 to 4 years
State of wakefulness	• Awakens after dream • May be scared • Able to interact with parent and describe nightmare	• Appears awake but isn't really awake • Not able to interact with parents
Return to sleep	• Delayed — especially if scared	• Rapid
Recall of event	• Vivid	• None
Treatment	• Comfort • Eliminate triggers	• No intervention • Ensure a safe environment and adequate rest

Guide to

Managing nightmares

- Go to your child and reassure her as quickly as possible.
- To help a child overcome this fear, evaluate the situation and see if you can identify a cause. Has your child suffered a traumatic event? Does your child watch scary TV shows or programs that are not age-appropriate? Does she look at books with scary pictures? All of these factors should be eliminated, especially before bed.

- Discuss your child's dream with her, but make sure to do this during the daytime so as not to increase her anxiety.
- Help your child work through her fears; for example, explain to her that monsters aren't real.
- Try to find ways that your child can feel safe and comfortable in her bed at night. Ask her what would make her feel safe; for example, leaving the bedroom light on for a short period or leaving the bedroom door open.

differentiate between nightmares and night terrors is important if parents are to understand how to respond, because the treatment of nightmares and night terrors differs.

Nightmares

Nightmares can cause anxiety and fear in your child. As adults, when we wake up from a nightmare, we are able to recognize that it wasn't a real event. Young children, however, are not able to make this distinction. Nightmares are very scary for them.

Night terrors

Night terrors are partial arousals, which the child cannot recall or remember. They are not uncommon, occurring in as many as 6% of children. Night terrors are usually more frightening for the parent than for the child. These episodes usually last for only a few minutes. They are not a sign that your child has an emotional or psychological problem but can sometimes occur after a stressful event or experience. They may be triggered by sleep deprivation or after some late nights. And it's usually a phase that children will grow out of in time.

Guide to

Managing night terrors

- Ensure that your child is in a safe environment and that there is no way she can hurt herself during an episode.
- Do not try to pick her up or wake her up. This will not stop or shorten the

episode and may lengthen it. In fact, it may even scare your child if she wakes fully to find you holding her for no reason. As a parent, the best response to these events is no response at all, however difficult that may be.

Sleepwalking

Sleepwalking is more common between the ages of 4 and 6 years. As with night terrors, your child will not be aware of what he is doing and will not remember the incident in the morning. The most important intervention for sleepwalking is ensuring safety. Don't let him sleep in the top bunk, and remove potential obstacles that he could trip over. Baby gates on the stairs need to be carefully locked, and there should be no way your child can open doors (or windows) and try to exit the house. In some extreme instances, parents may need to install alarm systems to ensure the safety of their sleepwalking child.

Rhythmic movements

When your child is falling asleep, you may see him developing a soothing repetitive motion, such as rocking his body or banging his head. These movements are most commonly seen when the child is first falling asleep at night and during normal arousals during the night. This behavior is usually developed as an infant. It generally lasts for less than 10 minutes and will cause no harm.

Although these movements may look strange or disturbing to parents, they are soothing and pleasurable to children. They do not interfere with sleep or development. And they usually resolve during the toddler years.

Obstructive sleep apnea

Obstructive sleep apnea is usually caused by another problem, such as obesity, enlarged tonsils and adenoids, or various neurological problems. It results in brief pauses in your child's breathing pattern when asleep. Typically, a child who is snoring (lots of noise) will suddenly stop breathing for a few seconds (no sounds), then will act as if he is gasping for air. If severe enough, it can start to affect many aspects of your child's well-being, including his growth and development.

If you are concerned about obstructive sleep apnea, you should seek help from your health-care practitioner. You can help by either audio- or videotaping your child during an episode. If your health-care provider is concerned, she may send your child for a sleep study, also called a polysomnograph.

Guide to

Managing rhythmic movements

- Make sure your child is in a safe environment and is unlikely to harm herself during a rocking or head-banging event.
- Don't make a big fuss about it. If your child sees you reacting, she is likely to increase the movements.

- If your child has an underlying chronic medical problem, such as seizures, autism, or developmental delay, discuss this behavior with your health-care provider.
- If your child is displaying rhythmic movements during the day while awake and this is interfering with her ability to play, see your health-care provider.

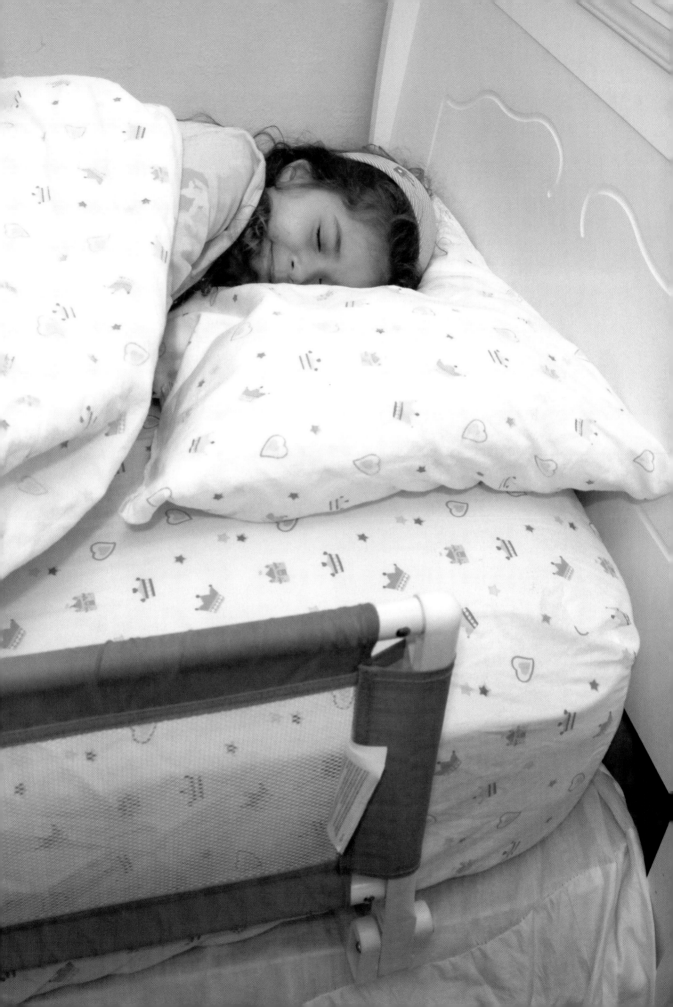

Frequently asked questions

As family doctors, pediatricians, and pediatric nurse practitioners, we answer many questions from parents. Here are some of the most frequently asked questions. Be sure to ask your health-care providers any other questions that may arise. If they don't have the answers, they will refer you to a colleague who does.

Q: My 18-month-old still needs to be breast-fed twice during the night. I'm not sure that she's hungry, but I don't want to starve her. What should I do?

A: In most cases, physiologically speaking, a healthy 18-month-old child will not need to be fed at night. You can confirm this with your health-care provider. In fact, the majority of children do not need to feed at night after 6 months of age and can take in all their caloric needs during the day and sleep for long stretches at night. Most likely these feedings are not needed for nutrition but more for their soothing value. Moreover, it is important for your daughter's growth and development that she sleep through the night so she can benefit fully from the restorative aspects of sleep. If you feel like it's time for both of you to start sleeping through the night, you can gradually wean her off nighttime feedings.

Q: My 4-year-old is waking up in the middle of the night telling me stories about monsters. I have been bringing him into my bed to comfort him, but then I can't sleep. How should I handle this? I want to address his needs, but at the same time I have to get up early for work.

A: A child's fear and anxiety following a nightmare is very real. Unlike us, they have difficulty recognizing that it was "just a dream." You need to come up with some creative ways to comfort your son without bringing him into your bed. For some kids, it's as simple as a night light. Discuss his dream with him during the day. Determine if there are any triggers for this dream (e.g., scary movies or books) and eliminate these.

Q: My husband and I have very different ideas about my 3-year-old's sleep needs. My husband works late, so he wants our daughter to go to bed later (9 or 10 p.m.) so he can see her. My daughter has to get up at 6 a.m. to get ready to go to daycare. I always have to wake her up, and I'm worried that she is exhausted, which in turn affects her behavior. My husband says she will just nap longer during the day if she needs the sleep.

A: Your concerns are valid. If you're having trouble waking your daughter up in the morning, it is likely because she is not getting enough sleep and is tired. Furthermore, this lack of sleep can affect her behavior, as well as her ability to learn. Although it is wonderful that your husband wants to spend more time with your daughter, sometimes our adult schedules are not good for our children. Your daughter likely needs to be in bed and asleep by

7:00 or 7:30 p.m. if she has to wake at 6 a.m. At this age, she may also need to nap for 2 hours a day, but it is not reasonable for her to nap for 4 to 5 hours to make up for sleep lost at night.

Q: We are going away on a family vacation with another family this week, and our 2-year-old daughter still needs us to lie down with her to fall asleep and stay asleep. What method should we use to get her to go to sleep so we can spend time with our friends at night?

A: It sounds like it's almost time to implement some strategies to teach your daughter how to fall asleep and stay asleep alone. Unfortunately, starting new sleep behavior training techniques a few days before a vacation isn't worthwhile or fair to your daughter. Once you are home from vacation and your schedule is back to normal, you can start teaching her how to sleep alone.

Sam's Diary

August 28 (30+ months old)

Sambo, we think your terrible twos are a thing of the past now — thank goodness. You really gave Mom and Dad a hard time. One evening we walked wearily up the stairs saying that we felt like battered parents! You're back to your loving, humorous, delicious earlier days. You are just such fun to be with. Today we were buying new shoes, and you walked around in one pair and said, "Mmm — these are very comfy. I guess we'll take these." You're too funny.

You still enjoy your naps and going to sleep at night and will often say, "It's time for bed." You love your stories and always have a big kiss and a hug for Dani before you go to sleep.

Your tricky thing at the moment is sharing and being gentle with your friends, although you're much better than you used to be. You're quite quick to push or hit and are only now learning to let your friends play with your toys. We know this is a 2-year-old thing, but it's quite stressful when you're being nasty to a friend who has come to play! We'll laugh when we look back and read this, I'm sure.

September 29 (31+ months old)

You're undressing yourself all on your own before your bath at night —

what an independent young man you are! You're going through a phase of holding Dad's hand when we go for walks. He loves it, and I love to walk behind you and watch the two of you together.

When Granny was visiting, you were standing outside when she was coming up the steps. You put out your hand to her and said, "Let me help you up the steps, my dear!" What an interesting character you are.

October 14 (32 months old)

What a big day today. You woke up and announced that you wanted to wear underwear. So you did! Only one accident and the most amazing first day out of diapers. What a star you are!

November 9 (33 months old)

You're doing brilliantly with your toilet training. You now tell us when you need to go to the washroom and go independently at school as well.

We've been having issues with you pushing your friends at school. We had to meet with your teachers — they all say you're a wonderful little boy, you just need to learn that we use "gentle hands" and that there's NO HITTING! It doesn't seem to have sunk in yet, but then we've just learned (at a parenting workshop held at your school tonight) that at your age it takes about 3 months for a behavior to disappear. Mom has been getting frustrated by the fact that all the repetition seems to be making no difference, so it's reassuring to know that you are developmentally on track.

December 1 (34 months old)

We predict you'll be good at music, as you absolutely love your toy guitar and piano. You sing amazingly well, considering that Dad and I can't hold a tune, and will often burst into song while you play. You also really love drawing. You're learning the alphabet at preschool now and are very interested in letters, pointing out what they stand for.

Tonight you fed Dani her bottle. You are so sweet with her. You asked for Mom to put her on your lap and then you helped her hold her bottle. She adores you and gets so excited to see you in the mornings and when you play peek-a-boo or clapping hands. You chat to her so beautifully when she's fussing in her seat. It's not all roses, though. You take the occasional swipe at her and get very annoyed when she gets into your toys — and who wouldn't get annoyed?

Protecting Your Toddler

Accidents don't just happen 306

Safety at home 307

Safety on the road 314

Water safety 322

Playground safety 324

Winter sports safety for colder climates 327

Frequently asked questions 328

Accidents don't just happen

Accidents — motor vehicle and pedestrian collisions, drowning and falls, choking and burns — are the most common cause of disability and death in children 1 to 14 years of age. Many accidents, both outside and inside the home, are preventable. In fact, to make the point that these events can often be predicted and prevented, experts in the field of child safety do not refer to these injuries as "accidents." Accidents don't just happen.

Principles of toddler safety

Being the parent of a toddler or preschooler means you will never look at the world the same way again. Parents of young children spend much of their time worrying about their child's safety and well-being. Toddlers and preschoolers develop independence by exploring their environment, and with these developmental stages comes risk of injury. Many injuries can be prevented by:

- Understanding your child's developmental stage and abilities
- Ensuring that your environment is safe
- Using appropriate safety equipment
- Providing adequate supervision

By following these principles of safety, you can protect your child and allow her to develop independence and enjoy her environment while keeping her safe inside the home, on the road, and in the playground.

Safety at home

Your child's home should be a safe place for her to grow, develop, explore, and have fun. However, many injuries in toddlers and preschoolers occur in the home, including falls, drownings, poisonings, burns and scalds, and choking. Fortunately, a few simple measures will prevent many of these serious injuries.

Falls

Falls are the most common cause of hospitalization in young children. Children fall at home from chairs, beds, and stairs. Falls can also occur at daycare centers and in the playground. And young children have on occasion tragically fallen from windows.

Reducing the risk of falls

- Supervise children closely and use proven safety products, keeping developmental stages in mind. While a stair safety gate is useful in preventing falls for young toddlers, once they can climb over the gate, it places them at higher risk of falls. Don't use the older accordion style of gate or any that don't meet current safety standards. Your toddler could get her head stuck trying to get through and suffocate.
- Use a non-slip mat or decals on the bottom of the bathtub and a non-slip

Did You Know?

Ban on baby walkers

Baby walkers can cause severe injury and even death. Walkers increase the risk of serious injury if the child falls down the stairs. They also allow the baby to move quickly, making it tricky for parents to respond in time. The American Academy of Pediatrics has called for their ban in the United States, and they are already banned in Canada.

Did You Know?

Window safety devices

Screens on windows and balcony doors are not designed to prevent falls and can easily give way under the weight of a small child. Always place cribs, beds, and other furniture away from windows to prevent a child from easily accessing the window. Also, make sure that doors to balconies are kept locked. Furniture or other objects on balconies should be arranged away from railings that children could climb over and fall from.

When used correctly, window guards or stops can greatly reduce the risk of falls. Window guards act like a gate in front of the window, and window stops are small devices that prevent a window from opening more than 4 inches (10 cm). They can be found at local hardware stores. When using these devices, make sure you follow the instructions provided. If you're planning to install new windows, make sure to use windows designed to reduce the risk of falls.

bath mat on the floor. Make sure that your child doesn't place her wet feet on slippery tile when she's getting out of the bath.

- Place protective covers on the tub water spouts and other pointed fixtures, such as soap dispensers.
- Fasten the safety straps in the high chair.
- Place a non-slip lining underneath your mats and carpets.

Choking and suffocation

Choking, suffocation, strangulation, and entrapment are the fourth-leading cause of death in children. These events can also result in severe brain damage in the children who survive. Major concerns include choking on foods, small objects, and latex balloons; strangulating on the cords of blinds; and suffocating in cribs or beds.

Reducing the risk of choking and suffocation

- Keep choking hazards away from children under 4 years of age. Nuts, carrots and other hard fruit or vegetables, and large pieces of hot dogs are examples of the types of food that cause choking among children. Coins, batteries, and small pieces of toys are the most common non-food-related choking risks.
- Ensure that your crib, baby gates, playpen, and bunk bed meet safety

standards. Young children can get their heads caught between the slats. Crib bars should be no more than $2\frac{3}{8}$ inches (6 cm) apart. Don't use cribs made before 1986 or baby gates made before 1990.

- Ensure that your child's furniture is away from windows and that the cords of blinds are either cut or tied up well out of reach. Children have been strangled with blind or window cords or when drawstrings on clothing or scarves become caught on things. Choose clothing without drawstrings or cut them off.

Scalds, burns, and smoke inhalation

Many children are hospitalized with burns or smoke inhalation every year. Children under 5 years of age are at the highest risk for all types of burns. The two most common causes of serious burns are scalding-hot liquids and house fires.

Reducing the risk of scalds, burns, and smoke inhalation

- Lower the water temperature in your home to 120°F (49°C). The typical water temperature in new North American homes is 140°F (60°C), which can severely burn a young child in just 1 second. By dropping the maximum temperature, you will increase the exposure time to more than 2 minutes before severe burning results, giving you valuable time to get your child to safety.
- As an extra precaution, install a single tap for both hot and cold water: If you

don't, always switch the cold tap on first and off last.

- Keep hot drinks away from your child. Put a lid on hot drinks. Do not pick up your child at the same time as you have a hot substance in the other hand.
- Keep your child safely out of the way when you are cooking or making hot drinks. Put a baby or toddler in a high chair with the safety straps on or in a playpen. Make sure a preschooler stays seated at the kitchen table. Or use a safety gate to keep young children out of the kitchen.
- Cook on the back burners of the stove whenever you can. Turn pot handles to the back of the stove so the pots won't get pulled over. Make sure that cords from your kettle and other appliances don't hang over the edge of the counter. If your child pulls on a hanging cord, she could pull a kettle of hot water down on herself. If you have hot serving dishes on the table, keep them where your child cannot reach them.

- Put a smoke alarm on every level of your home. Most house-fire deaths happen in homes without a working smoke alarm. Make sure there is an alarm right outside the bedrooms. Test each smoke alarm every month by pressing the battery test button. Put in fresh batteries at least once a year.
- Plan how you will get out of your house or apartment in the event of a fire and where you will meet outside.
- Avoid using space heaters.
- Keep lighters and matches out of sight and reach.
- Install a fire extinguisher in your home — this is essential.
- Ensure that the glass fronts of fireplaces and oven doors are insulated or that you have a protective barrier so your toddler does not burn her hands. These glass surfaces can reach very hot temperatures. They are particularly attractive to toddlers as they cruise around the living room or kitchen.

Poisoning

Toddlers are naturally inquisitive and love to explore their environment by putting everything they can get their hands on into their mouths, including poisons and medications. Medications are the leading cause of poisoning in children. Even small amounts of some adult medications can be fatal to a child. Household cleaners and other everyday products, such as nail polish, are other common causes of poisoning.

Preventing and dealing with poisoning

- Keep all household poisons, such as toilet bowl cleaners, in their original containers and locked out of reach. Ensure that poisonous products stored in the garage or basement, such as antifreeze, pesticides, and paints, are kept in their original containers and locked out of reach. Even perfumes and deodorants should be kept well out of reach.
- Keep all medications in their original child-resistant packaging. But don't rely on the safety caps alone; medications still need to be locked away out of reach. Be especially careful when around relatives and friends who might carry their pills in their handbags or leave them within easy reach on a bedside table.
- Don't refer to your child's vitamins or other medications as "candy" — it sends the wrong message.
- Install a carbon monoxide detector near sleeping areas to detect this poisonous gas emitted by heaters and furnaces that burn oil or gas.

- Post poison control information and the telephone number for your local poison control center in a convenient place — such as the kitchen bulletin board, the refrigerator door, or the telephone stand — and program the number into your telephone.

Home hazards

Toddlers have an uncanny ability to find hazards around the house, even after you have looked up and down and all around in an effort to anticipate problems. You might want to get down on your hands and knees to see your home from a toddler's perspective. Toddler temptations are bound to emerge that you will need to remove or repair.

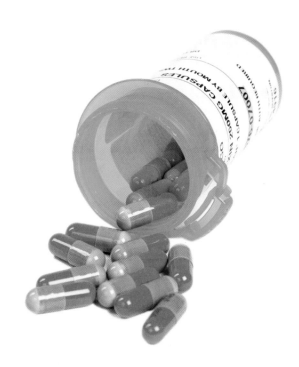

Toy boxes and chests

Children have been hurt when the lids of toy boxes fell on their heads and necks, and they have also been trapped inside toy chests. Most commonly, little fingers can get caught when the lid closes. Use toy boxes with lightweight lids and hinges that prevent them from slamming down, or use a box that does not have a lid. If it is a big box with a lid, ensure that there are holes for air circulation.

Guide to

Childproofing your home

- Use table mats rather than tablecloths. The edges of tablecloths present an irresistible temptation for your toddler to yank down on, which risks bringing whatever is on the table down on top of him.
- Place plastic covers in all electrical sockets. Unused appliances should be unplugged and the cords kept well out of reach.
- Use lids on your trash cans.

- Place decals on your glass doors to prevent your toddler from running into them, and ensure that all doors and screens have child-resistant locks.
- Do not leave plastic bags where your toddler can reach them and put them over his head.
- Install child-guard locks on drawers and cabinets that contain dangerous items. Consider setting aside one drawer or cabinet for safe items that your toddler can explore and play with.

Did You Know?

Bunk bed hazard

There are more than 35,000 bunk bed–related injuries annually in the United States. Bunk beds can be dangerous if children's heads get caught between the parts, and children can be injured from falls from the top bunk. It is best not to use bunk beds, but if you must, take these precautions:

- Check your bunk bed for a label that says it meets safety standards.
- Do not allow children less than 6 years of age to sleep or play on the top bunk.
- Be sure the top bunk has guardrails on all four sides.
- Check the space between the guardrails on the top bunk to ensure they are no more than $3\frac{1}{2}$ inches (9 cm) apart.
- Never place bunk beds within reach of ceiling fans or lights.
- Keep the area around the bunk bed carpeted and free of furniture.

Twinproofing your home

If you have twin toddlers, you may want to take some extra safety precautions since you may not always be capable of keeping both children under your careful watch. A sturdy bookshelf may hold the weight of one toddler climbing onto it, but it may easily collapse with the weight of two! One toddler may not have the strength to move a chair or coffee table over to a high shelf or counter, but the strength of two together may just do the trick.

Consider gating off rooms in the house when you cannot keep a watchful eye on both children. Building a fence around your backyard or lawn to keep both children in sight will reduce risks. Be sure to fasten freestanding bookshelves or stands to the wall to prevent the possibility of them toppling over when twins climb. Designate an area on each floor of the home as a play area — one that is free of dangers and where twin toddlers can have easy access to a few toys or books. This way, if you're busy with one, you can keep an eye on the other one in the near distance. Keep extra clothes, diapers, and wipes, or even a spare change table, on every floor of your home so you don't need to leave one or both children unsupervised as you run up the steps.

Safety on farms

Children who live on farms face unique risks of being injured at home because of farm machinery, heavy equipment, large animals, and ponds. In children under 6, most deaths are caused by being run over by tractors or pickups, falling off vehicles, or drowning. In addition, their parents often face unpredictable work demands, making supervision difficult at times.

Preventing farm accidents

- Prohibit children from access to farm work sites.
- Don't allow children to ride on farm vehicles.
- Install physical barriers, such as fencing, around haylofts, silos, machinery, and water hazards.

- Create safe play spaces away from farm activities.
- Ensure that tools and sharp objects are stored safely.
- Organize child-care alternatives during busy seasons.

- Keep children off all-terrain vehicles (ATVs) and snowmobiles. ATVs and snowmobiles are not safe for children under 16 to operate because these vehicles require adult skill and judgment.

Safety on the road

The road is a dangerous place for your child. Car crashes and pedestrian injuries are the leading cause of death and disability in children. You can greatly reduce this risk by choosing and installing the right car seat or booster seat, teaching your child how to cross the road safely, and ensuring that your child wears appropriate safety equipment while cycling.

Child passenger safety

Although car crashes kill more children than any other injury, most of us need to transport our children in automobiles. We can reduce the risk of injury by driving safely and choosing the right car seat or booster seat and using it correctly on every ride. You can't always control whether you will be involved in an accident, but you can certainly ensure that your child is appropriately restrained and protected!

Safe driving

Drive with as few distractions as possible and use common sense. Avoid multitasking while driving. Be sure you are well rested, follow the speed limits, turn off your cellphone, and avoid driving in hazardous conditions.

Car seats

There are many different kinds of car seats — rear-facing, forward-facing, convertible, and booster seats — for use in automobiles and on airplanes.

Choosing the correct car seat can be very confusing. There is no "best car seat" on the market — the best seat is one that fits your child's height and weight, and your car. All car seats sold in the United States and Canada must be tested to meet government safety standards. Each state, province, and territory may have its own specific legislation for the use of car seats and booster seats. Familiarize yourself with your local regulations.

It may seem like a pain in the neck, but always fill in and mail back the registration card that comes with your seat. The car

Did You Know?

Seat safety

Car safety seats have been shown to be highly effective in reducing death and injury in motor vehicle crashes. According to the National Highway Traffic Safety Administration (NHTSA) in the United States, car safety seats are 71% effective in reducing deaths for infants and 54% effective in reducing deaths for children age 1 to 4 years, while belt-positioning booster seats reduce the risk of injury by 59% for children age 4 through 7. Clearly, restraining infants and children in the proper car safety seat does help keep them safe.

Infant seat with base
(rear-facing)

3-in-1 seat (infant/child/booster)

Combination seat (child/booster/
2-to-1 forward-facing to booster seat
in child mode with harness)

High-back booster seat

No back booster seat

Combination seat (child/booster/
2-to-1 forward-facing to booster seat
in belt position, booster seat mode)

seat manufacturer will use this information to contact you if there are product recalls or problems with the seat, which do happen from time to time.

REAR-FACING CAR SEATS

Rear-facing car seats are recommended for children until they are at least 1 year old and weigh at least 22 pounds (10 kg). Babies have proportionally heavier, larger heads and smaller, weaker necks than older children. A rear-facing car seat protects the head, neck, and spine.

If your baby outgrows his infant car seat before age 1, purchase a convertible car seat and use it in the rear-facing position until he reaches the height limit or weight limit for rear-facing use. Follow the installation and operation instructions provided by the car seat manufacturer. For more on convertible car seats, see page 316.

Did You Know?

Seat belt syndrome

Seat belts are meant to fit people who are at least 4 feet, 9 inches (1.4 m) tall. A 5-year-old weighing more than 40 pounds (22 kg), for example, is not safe to graduate directly from a forward-facing car seat to an adult seat belt. "Seat belt syndrome" is how doctors describe injuries to the spine and internal organs (such as the spleen, intestines, and liver) incurred by children who are in a crash and are too small to be supported adequately by the regular seat belt.

All rear-facing car seats must be secured to the vehicle with the vehicle seat belt or universal anchorage system (UAS), also known as the LATCH (lower anchors and tethers for children) system.

FORWARD-FACING CAR SEATS

Forward-facing car seats are recommended for children who are more than 1 year of age and weigh at least 22 pounds (10 kg). They may be used up to a weight of 40 to 65 pounds (22 to 29 kg) and a height of 48 inches (1.2 m), depending on the manufacturer's specifications. For forward-facing seats, the harness should be snug, not allowing more than one finger to be inserted between the collar bone and the harness, and the chest clip should be placed at the level of the child's armpit.

CONVERTIBLE CAR SEATS

Also called infant/child seats or 2-in-1 rear-facing to forward-facing seats, these seats can be used rear-facing and then forward-facing. Do not move your child to a forward-facing position until she is at least 1 year of age and weighs at least 22 pounds (10 kg). You can keep her in the rear-facing position until she has reached the height or weight limit specified in your car seat instruction booklet.

COMBINATION CAR SEATS

Also known as child/booster seats or 2-in-1 forward-facing to booster seats, these seats can be used as a forward-facing car seat and then as a booster seat.

Did You Know?

Tether strap

Forward-facing seats use a tether strap to hold the top in place. It helps secure the seat and keeps a child's head from moving too much in a crash or sudden stop. The strap hooks into a tether anchor in your car. Read your car owner's manual to find where the anchors are located. In addition, you must use the vehicle seat belt or the UAS/LATCH system to secure the seat in place. Do not use the tether strap for a rear-facing car seat or booster seat unless your car seat instruction booklet says you should. The safest position for a child seat is in the middle rear seat position.

Did You Know?

Most common car seat mistakes

- Recalled or otherwise unsafe seats used
- Seat not tightly secured to vehicle (can move more than 1 inch/2.5 cm in any direction)
- Harness not snug (more than one finger's width between the harness strap and the child)
- Chest clip not at armpit level
- Tether strap not anchored for forward-facing car seats
- Rear-facing seat placed in front of an air bag
- Infant seats not at correct angle (head and neck should be at 45-degree angle for maximum support)
- No locking clip on the vehicle seat belt when recommended in the vehicle manual
- Seat belt routed through an incorrect path of the infant or child restraint
- Harness straps routed through the incorrect slots
- Failure to restrain the child

Adapted by permission from the Canadian Paediatric Society, Injury Prevention Committee Statement, 2008.

3-IN-1 SEATS

This infant/child/booster seat combination can be used first as a rear-facing car seat, next as a forward-facing car seat, and then as a booster seat.

BOOSTER SEATS

Using a booster seat instead of a seat belt alone reduces the risk of injury by about 60%.

Once your child has outgrown the height or weight requirements for the forward-facing car seat, she is ready for a booster seat. Refer to the manual of your booster seat for exact height and weight limits.

Some states and provinces have laws that specify age, height, or weight standards for how long a child should continue to use a booster seat. Weight standards vary between 80 and 100 pounds (36 and 45 kg), while the height standard is usually 4 feet, 9 inches (1.4 m). Children usually hit these weights and height when they are between 8 and 9 years old. Learn the specific regulations in your state or province.

The purpose of the booster seat is to help ensure that the seat belt fits properly on your child by lifting her up so she sits at the level of an older child or adult. When a child is in a booster seat, the shoulder portion of the vehicle's seat belt should not come into contact with her neck but should go over the middle of her collar bone and chest, with the lap belt over the pelvis and below the abdomen.

Stores also sell some devices that can be used to adjust the fit of a seat belt. These seat belt adjusters may not have been tested for safety, however, and should not be used unless you are sure they have been formally tested.

There are several different types of boosters: 3-in-1 or 2-in-1 (combination) car seats, high-back booster seats, no-back

Guide to

Using a booster seat
- If you are using a combination car seat (3-in-1 or 2-in-1 seat) as a booster seat, remove the harness straps and do not use the tether strap.
- If your car has adjustable head restraints, use a no-back booster seat.
- If your car does not have adjustable head restraints or high seat backs, use a high-back booster seat to protect your child's head and neck. The back of your child's head needs to be properly supported.
- Even when you're not using the booster, buckle it into the car's seat so it won't hit anyone inside the car in a crash.

booster seats, and even a booster seat that attaches to the car with the UAS/ LATCH system. Again, there is no best booster seat. The one that fits your child and can be installed in your car is the best seat for you. Further information is available from the American Academy of Pediatrics and Safe Kids Canada.

Used car seats

If you are considering buying a used car seat, the rule of thumb is to refer to the instruction booklet or manual that came with the car seat to determine if it is still safe to use.

First, make sure the seat meets national standards and fits your child's height, weight, and age. Before using it, make sure that the car seat or booster seat has all of its parts and an instruction booklet.

Check to be sure the seat hasn't been recalled and check the date when was made. Some may include an expiry date. In general, a car seat has a lifespan of five to six years, and some even extend to 10 years. Once a seat has reached its expiry date, the plastic begins to break down and will not protect your child in a crash.

Do not use a car seat that was involved in a crash.

Pedestrian safety

In children, most pedestrian deaths and severe pedestrian injuries occur where there is no clear form of traffic control. A child might be hit by an automobile while trying to cross the road from between parked cars, while entering the road from a driveway, or while playing behind a reversing car in the driveway itself.

Start teaching your child the rules of the road when she's young, and keep talking about road safety as you walk and play with her in your neighborhood. As she grows, talk about different traffic situations and encourage her to practice the safety rules under your guidance.

Stroller safety

Many children are injured when they fall out of strollers because the safety straps haven't been used or the brakes haven't been set to stop the stroller from rolling away. A child can also slide down and get her head caught in the leg opening if she's not wearing the safety straps. To reduce

HOW TO
Cross the road safely

Crossing the street involves a complex set of skills. When crossing the street, children less than 9 years of age should always be accompanied by an adult or responsible older child. Teach your toddler to:

- Cross a street at a pedestrian crosswalk, stop sign, or stop light, not from between parked cars.
- Stop, look left, right, and left again, listen for traffic, wait until the street is clear, and keep looking until he reaches the other side of the street.

- Recognize the meaning of traffic stop and go signals, but always be sure traffic has stopped before crossing.
- Never run into the street for any reason.
- Stop before crossing driveways and alleys.
- Listen to the crossing guard's rules.
- Walk on the sidewalks, not the road.
- Never play at railway tracks or around trains.

Did You Know?

Shopping cart safety

Children can be injured when they fall from the child seat of a shopping cart or the cart tips over. Unfortunately, such events are not uncommon and can result in severe injury to the head and neck.

Because the stability of shopping carts varies and the safety of the seats is not regulated, parents should be aware of the potential risk of injury before transporting their child in a shopping cart. Parents are strongly encouraged to seek alternatives to this mode of transport, such as a stroller or baby carrier. Older children can be encouraged to walk along close by the cart. If a parent chooses to transport a child in a shopping cart, an effective safety restraint should be worn by the child at all times. Children should not be left unattended in a shopping cart and should not be allowed to stand up in a cart, be transported in the basket, or ride on the outside of a cart.

the risk of these hazards, purchase a stroller that is sturdy and appropriate for your child's weight — and use it safely.

- Always use the safety straps when your child is in the stroller. Choose a stroller that includes a strap for the waist and a crotch strap that fits between the legs.
- Use the stroller brakes every time you stop your stroller.
- Make sure the stroller has locks to stop it from folding when your child is sitting in it.
- Do not leave your child unattended in a stroller.
- Do not hang heavy purses or other bags on strollers — they may cause the stroller to tip over.

School bus safety

School buses are generally very safe. They are designed to protect passengers by using compartments where children are confined in a padded area in the event of a crash. The seats have high backs and are anchored to the vehicle. However, children are at the greatest risk for school bus–related injuries when they are outside, not inside, the bus. Teach your children to stay away from the front, back, and sides of the bus, where they may not be seen by the driver, and to be careful not to run or jump while entering and exiting the bus. Don't dress your child in clothing with drawstrings or scarves that could get caught in the bus doorway.

Cycling and skating safety

Bicycling, in-line skating, and riding a scooter are great fun and provide healthy exercise. These activities are not without risk of injury, however, the most serious being head injuries. Children can also get cuts and bruises and, less commonly, broken bones. Their risks of getting hurt are much higher if they ride or skate near cars and traffic, don't use the correct safety gear, are beginners, or go too fast and try stunts. Children under 10 years of age should not ride near traffic.

Guide to

Cycling and skating safely

- Children should always wear the appropriate helmet for the activity. Different helmets are designed for different sports because the type and location of a potential injury are different. A bicycle helmet should be used for bike riding, in-line skating, and riding a scooter. Skateboarding and ice skating require different helmets that protect the back of the head.
- Make sure the helmet has a sticker in it that shows that it meets safety standards.
- Make sure the helmet fits. Try the different foam pads sold with the helmet until it fits snugly. The helmet should cover the top of the forehead and rest about two fingers' width above the eyebrows. The side straps should be adjusted around the ears in a V shape. The chin strap should be tightened until only one finger can fit between the strap and the chin. Have your child shake his head from side to side to see that the helmet doesn't move.
- Use protective gear: elbow pads for scooters; wrist guards, elbow, and kneepads for skateboarders and in-line skaters.

- Take the helmet off when your child is playing at a playground, because the straps could get caught in the equipment, possibly causing strangulation.
- Set rules for the whole family, including parents. For example, stay away from cars and traffic and always use safety equipment. Keep young children on wheels off the road by using the sidewalks.
- Parents are role models — make sure that you wear your own helmet and safety gear to encourage your children to protect themselves.

Water safety

Drowning is the second-most-common cause of injury-related death in children under 4 years of age. Drowning most often occurs in swimming pools, followed by open bodies of water, such as lakes or streams, and finally bathtubs.

Developmental stages are important to consider in preventing drowning. Children under 5 are attracted to water but do not understand the danger. In addition, their upper bodies and heads are heavy, and it is very easy for them to fall in.

Young children can drown in very small amounts of water — drowning has occurred in as little as 1½ inches (4 cm) of bathwater. Most drownings occur in the few minutes when a toddler was unsupervised. Adult supervision is vital.

Guide to

Preventing drowning injuries

BACKYARD POOL PRECAUTIONS

In children under 5 years of age, appropriate fencing could prevent 7 out of 10 drowning incidents in private pools. Install four-sided fencing — fencing that goes around all four sides of the pool and separates the pool from the house — with a self-closing, self-latching gate around home swimming pools. Fencing should be designed to prevent climbing by young children. The fencing should be at least 5 feet (1.5 m) high, with openings no larger than 4 inches (10 cm) wide.

SWIMMING LESSONS

Teach your children how to swim, but remember that swimming lessons will not drownproof a child.

LIFEJACKETS

Be sure everyone on a boat wears a properly fitting, age- and weight-appropriate lifejacket. You can also put your young child or a weak swimmer in a lifejacket whenever he is in or close to the water.

SUPERVISION

Adults should be within an arm's-length reach of any child under 5 or any child who is a weak swimmer whenever he is in or near the water, including the water in the bathtub. If the telephone or doorbell rings while your child's in the bath, you can either ignore it or wrap your child in a towel and take him with you. Do not leave an older sibling to supervise bath time.

BABY BATH SEATS AND BATH RINGS

Do not use these devices, because they can be mistakenly seen as a safe substitute for supervision. Babies have drowned while using baby bath seats and rings. Babies can tip them over, climb out of the seat, or slip through the leg opening. If you do plan to use one, make sure it has met the safety standards and remain within arm's reach at all times!

Playground safety

Most playground injuries occur in children under 14 and are caused by falls that result in scratches, bruises, and broken bones. Head injuries are the most common serious injury associated with playgrounds, and these injuries can occur on any playground, including those in parks, at schools, and at home.

Children 5 to 9 years of age are at highest risk for injuries, likely because they spend the most time on playgrounds and enjoy testing their limits on playground structures. Children 1 to 4 years of age are the second-most-common group of children injured on playgrounds, usually because they are still developing their balancing and climbing skills.

Public and home playgrounds

In the United States and Canada, there are safety standards for playground equipment in public areas. In Canada, these standards are voluntary, meaning there is no national body that enforces them and it is up to the playground owner or operator to follow them.

When building a home playground for your own children and the many friends and guests who will share this equipment, keep safety uppermost in your mind. Many playground injuries occur in the backyard. Don't let your child or her playmates be injured during your watch at home.

Public playground safety

Before you go to the playground, check your child for anything that could cause strangling. Take off drawstrings on clothing, use a neck warmer instead of a scarf, and remove bike helmets. Children should not take skipping ropes onto the playground.

Survey the playground. Choose a playground with a deep, soft surface (sand, pea gravel, wood chips, rubber mats) and make sure the equipment has good handrails and barriers to prevent falling from a height. Check for broken glass.

Look for the sign that identifies the age group the playground equipment is designed for. Keep your child off equipment that is higher than 5 feet (1.5 m). If she is under 5 years of age, stand beside her when she's climbing or swinging.

Teach your child rules for playground safety, which include:
- Wait your turn
- Slide down feet first
- Hold on to railings
- Sit down on swings and slides
- Stay away from moving swings and the bottom of slides

Actively supervise children. Stay close to them while they're climbing and swinging, especially with children under 5 years. Always supervise children at water play.

Building a home playground

- Choose playground equipment that is appropriate for your children's ages.
- Use a deep, soft surface to cushion the impact of falls. Loose-fill surfacing, such as sand, wood chips, and pea gravel, should be laid at a depth of at least 6 to 12 inches (15 to 30 cm) under and around swings, climbers, and slides.
- Keep equipment height under 5 feet (1.5 m).
- Make sure you have guardrails or barriers to prevent falls. If a piece of equipment is too high for your toddler, you can remove the lowest rung of the ladder to keep her from climbing up.
- Construct or buy swing seats made of a soft material, such as rubber or canvas, to limit injuries from being hit with the swing.
- Make sure there is at least 6 feet (1.8 m) of space between play equipment and fencing or other structures.
- Make sure there are no sharp points that could catch children's clothing.
- Inspect your backyard regularly for broken equipment and surfacing.

Winter sports safety for colder climates

Participating in winter sports will help keep the whole family healthy. However, all winter activities require safe clothing and some weather precautions.

Children should not play outdoors at all under the following weather conditions:
- Temperature is –25°C (–13°F) or below
- Wind chill factor (the temperature felt by the skin in windy conditions) is –28°C (–15°F) or below

To prevent sunburn, use sunscreen, even on cloudy days.

To prevent drowning, keep children away from the banks of ponds, lakes, streams, and rivers, especially during the spring thaw.

Playing outdoors in cold weather

To prevent frostbite, children should wear a warm, close-fitting hat covering the earlobes, water-resistant mittens, a single pair of socks, either wool or a wool blend, and dry boots that are not too tight. They should wear loose layers of clothing with an absorbent synthetic fabric next to the skin, a warmer middle layer, and a water-resistant or -repellent outer layer. Jackets should be zipped up. Children should get out of wet clothes and boots as quickly as possible, because these are the biggest factors in frostbite.

To avoid strangulation during play, use tube-shaped neck warmers instead of scarves. Remove drawstrings on hoods and jackets, because they are also a safety hazard.

Frequently asked questions

As family practitioners, pediatricians, and nurse practitioners, we answer many questions from parents. Here are some of the most frequently asked questions. Be sure to ask your health-care providers any other questions that may arise. If they don't have the answers, they will refer you to a colleague who does.

Q: I want to make sure my child is safe in the water. Should I start swimming lessons?

A: Swimming lessons for young children are designed to introduce them to water, build water confidence, teach water safety to parents and guardians, and promote enjoyment in the water. They will not ensure that children under age 5 are "water-safe." Aquatic programs for infants and toddlers should not be promoted as a way to decrease the risk of drowning. Children are generally not developmentally ready for formal swimming lessons until after their fourth birthday. Studies have shown that the earliest mastery of basic water skills happens around 4 years of age, regardless of when the toddler began swimming lessons. Swimming instruction should be carried out by trained instructors in pools that comply with current standards for design, maintenance, operation, and infection control.

Q: How can I encourage my toddler to develop independence if I'm trying to protect him from injuries?

A: Promoting the development of independence in a safe environment is an important goal for parents of toddlers. Toddlers must be given opportunities to explore their environment and be physically active. Each developmental stage allows for increased independence and different approaches to supervision. Ensuring a child's safety includes strategies to improve his environment and effective child supervision. For children under age 5, for example, inspecting the playground for safe surfaces and standing close by while the child is climbing or swinging is recommended. For cycling, safety and supervision strategies include keeping children on the sidewalks and away from traffic, using helmets and other appropriate protective gear, and riding or walking close to your child.

Q: Are organized sports safe for my child?

A: Physical activity is very important for children of all ages. For children 1 to 5 years of age, this may include free play, playing in the park, riding tricycles or bicycles, and participating in organized sports. Many children find participating in organized sports, such as playing on a soccer team or taking gymnastics lessons, a fun way to keep active.

To benefit most from a sport, children need certain skills; otherwise, they may get frustrated and not want to play at all. Learning basic skills, such as throwing, running, and jumping, is a normal developmental process. They learn each skill in small steps, and some children learn faster than others. To play organized sports, children need to learn how to put these skills together (e.g., how to run and throw at the same time). And that doesn't usually happen for most children until they're about 6 years old.

From 3 to 5 years of age, participating in fun activities and trying different things is more important than competing. Suggested activities for this age group include running, tumbling, throwing, catching, and riding a tricycle or bicycle.

If your children are participating in organized sports, such as soccer, skating, or gymnastics, ensure that they are wearing properly fitting protective gear and that their activity is supervised by trained instructors in facilities that comply with current standards for design, maintenance, and operation for their age group.

Q: Home trampolines are popular, but are they safe?
A: Even with close supervision at all times, this activity is somewhat dangerous. Even if you do everything possible to prevent it, the potential for serious injury, including fractures, head injuries, and neck injuries, remains. The American Academy of Pediatrics and the Canadian Paediatric Society recommend that trampolines should *not* be used at home, inside or outside. If you are determined to let your children use a home trampoline, ensure that all the safety precautions, especially the safety net, are in place.

Sam's Diary

January 6 (35 months old)

Today you went skating for the first time, and you loved it. You walked around in your helmet all afternoon and had to be persuaded to take your bob skates off after coming home. Dad says you did really well! You were dying to skate like the other kids, and that will come in time. Just before you went to bed, you said to Mom, "I have one last thing to tell you. Dad wasn't very good and I wasn't very good on my skates today." I reassured you that, with a little practice, we'll all be skating better.

    On Friday, a new little girl joined your class, and they call you the new couple because you held her hand and showed her all around. The other day, when Mom came to fetch you, you took me to the window and told me that during the day you'd "waited patiently" for me to come.

April 5 (38 months old)

You'll laugh about this one day, I'm sure, but today you made your first poop on the toilet! A breakthrough. You've been out of diapers for a while for peeing but wouldn't go to the toilet for poos. Now you've done it — yeah! — so soon no more stinky diapers to change!

You're crazy about Toy Story (remember that?). We bought you a Buzz Lightyear outfit (until now, you wouldn't go near dress-up clothes) and you ran around the shopping center bringing smiles to everyone's face. Then you went to school in it for three days running, refusing to wear anything else.

    Just wanted to tell you about a conversation we had today. Quite a while ago, we were talking about something (can't recall exactly what), and you came up with, "Mom — I don't want to grow up." I didn't press you for why but was quite intrigued. Anyway, tonight we were reading about Peter Pan, who didn't want to grow up, and you remembered our conversation. Only now you said you wouldn't mind growing up, because then "I can wear big-boy clothes like Dad, I can watch adult movies" — your exact words — "and I won't be scared." Last night Dad read "Little Red Riding Hood," which frightened you a bit, and you slept with your door open. You're also afraid of the dark and have had some bad dreams. You do come up with the most amazing insights. It's fun to listen to you and to hear your thinking and reasoning — quite amazing for a 3-year-old!

May 2 (39 months old)

You had your first real play date over the weekend with one of your little friends from school. There were one or two moments of crying when you had a hard time sharing — but you played so beautifully. You took him up to show him your room and helped him go to the toilet — so sweet. It was quite a success.

We're going to the dentist for the first time next week. When Mom was talking to you about this, you mentioned that you didn't want to go. When asked why, you answered that you were afraid. On further probing, you told Mom that you were afraid of getting "silver paper" on your teeth like Dad (fillings!).

You've learned to whistle this week. Mom and Dad bought you your first real bike (with training wheels) two weekends ago — a shiny red bike with a fancy bell.

And . . . you're still wearing your Buzz outfit.

June 29 (40+ months old)

You've been to your first proper movie with Dad. You sat on a booster, had treats, and absolutely loved the whole experience — you've been talking about it all the time.

First Aid for Toddlers

Basic life support 334

Choking, drowning, and poisoning 335

Cardiopulmonary resuscitation 342

First aid for major injuries 346

First aid for minor injuries 350

Creating a first aid kit 357

Frequently asked questions 358

Basic life support

By preventing critical injuries, poisoning, and drowning, we can help protect the lives of our children, but knowing how to use basic life support (BLS) strategies is an important insurance policy. Being able to provide basic life support can mean the difference between life and death for one of your own children or someone else's child. And in the event of sudden unexpected suffocation, drowning, poisoning, or choking, it has been shown that rapid and effective cardiopulmonary resuscitation (CPR) or use of the Heimlich maneuver can improve potentially tragic outcomes.

BLS training

BLS courses are offered at many different venues in your community by various agencies, such as the Red Cross or St. John Ambulance, but if you're having trouble locating a convenient course, ask your child's health-care provider for information. For toddlers, the course needs to deal specifically with BLS child (1 to 8 years old) guidelines, not adult courses, which differ significantly. You will be able to practice on a mannequin and get comfortable with the necessary techniques — and you can't achieve that just by reading through these pages. Once you've learned the basic principles and techniques, you will need to refresh your memory from time to time with refresher courses.

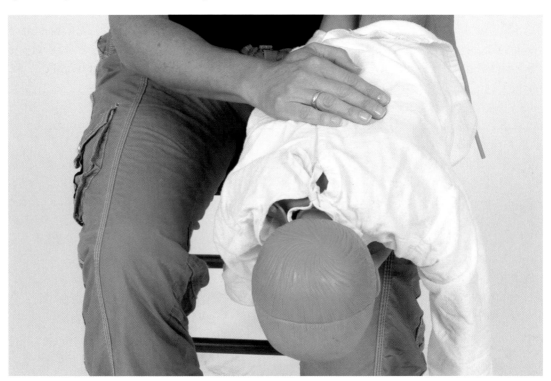

Choking, drowning, and poisoning

BLS training has direct application to life-threatening situations. Beyond prevention, the best policy is to be prepared to treat a child in distress.

Choking

The best treatment for choking is preventing your child from swallowing common hazards, such as hot dogs, hard or sticky candy, nuts, popcorn, whole grapes, balloons, marbles, coins, pen or marker caps, small button-type batteries, and other small toys. Don't feed your toddler any round, firm food unless it is chopped completely, and keep children away from toys or household items with small parts that may come off. Children should sit at the table while eating, because running or playing with food in their mouth will increase their choking risk. And watch what their older brothers or sisters are giving them!

Symptoms of choking

If a child aspirates a foreign body — that is, it goes down "the wrong way" — he will usually have a sudden increase in his work at breathing. This may be accompanied by coughing, gagging, and stridor (a high-pitched, noisy sound heard when breathing in) or wheezing (a whistle-like sound heard when breathing out). Some infections, such as croup, can look and sound very similar, but choking due to aspiration of a foreign body can usually be distinguished because its onset is sudden without any preceding cold symptoms or fever.

Drowning

Tragically, drowning is not uncommon in the toddler age group, particularly among little boys. Many of these events happen in the bathtub or swimming pool at home, and often occur when the caregiver is distracted for only a brief period. Clearly, prevention is imperative (see Part 7 for helpful safety tips).

The ultimate outcome will depend on the time spent underwater, the temperature of the water, and how promptly CPR was started. In icy water, a good outcome is still possible even after the child has been underwater for a while.

Symptoms of drowning

On removing the child from the water, his appearance may vary from almost normal to no sign of life. He may feel cold to the touch, especially if the drowning episode happens in water other than in a bath or heated swimming pool. His color could be pale or even a shade of blue, especially around the lips. He may be showing signs of breathing difficulties, such as labored, rapid, or noisy breathing — or he may not be breathing at all. He may cough or even vomit. Level of alertness varies from relatively normal to comatose.

Guide to

Treating emergency choking

If the obstruction to the airway is mild, the child will still be able to cough and make some sounds. If this is the case, allow her to continue to clear her airway by coughing and intervene only if the obstruction is severe. Stay with her, and if the cough is not settling, call or visit your local emergency services for immediate help.

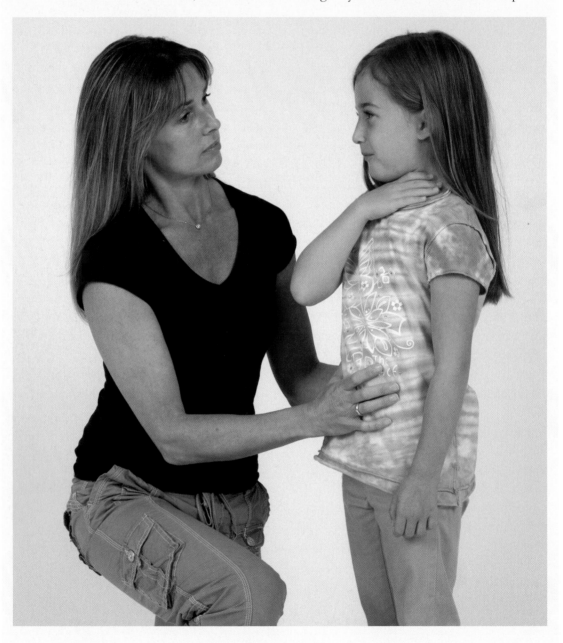

If the obstruction is severe, the child will not cough or make any sound at all. She will likely be making strong efforts to breathe, and she may start to turn blue, initially around the lips but then spreading to the rest of the face. If this occurs, perform abdominal thrusts below the diaphragm using the Heimlich maneuver.

THE HEIMLICH MANEUVER

Kneel or stand behind the child, depending on her height, and wrap your arms around her waist (see picture 1).

Make a flat-sided fist with the thumb side pointing against the child's tummy (see picture 2). Place it just above her belly button but below the rib cage.

Cup your other hand over the fist (see picture 3). Move both hands quickly and forcefully inward and upward. The amount of force will depend on the size of the child. This maneuver should imitate what would happen to her if she coughed forcefully, which she isn't able to do at this point: it should empty the lungs of air, and the foreign body should be expelled out of the lungs with the air.

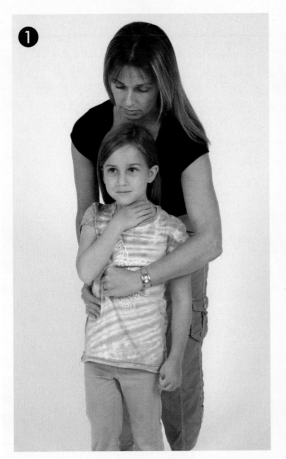

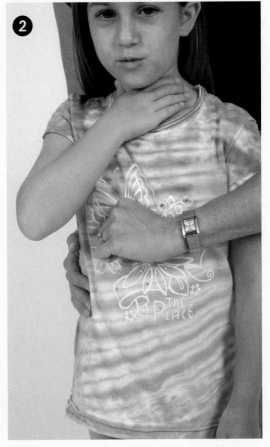

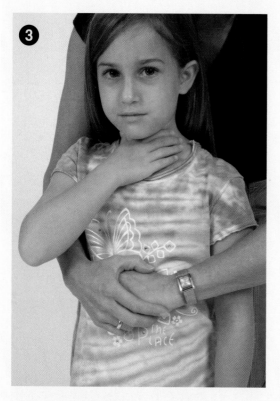

STRADDLE METHOD

If the child is less than 1 year of age or too small to stand up for the Heimlich maneuver, straddle her over your forearm, face down, using your hand to stabilize her head and neck (see picture 4).

Rest your forearm on your lap or thigh and take care to avoid putting pressure on her throat. Her head should be slightly lower than her body (see picture 5).

With the heel of your hand, give five firm blows between the shoulder blades to try to push the foreign object out of the airway (see picture 6).

If this doesn't work, roll her over onto her back while supporting her head and neck, so that she is resting on your forearm on your lap with her head slightly lower than her body (see picture 7).

Use two fingers positioned over the middle of the breastbone, one finger-width below the nipples, and rapidly push straight down five times (see picture 8). The breastbone should move about ¾ inch (2 cm) with each thrust.

Repeat the sequence of five back slaps and five chest thrusts, with increasing force, until the object is expelled or the child becomes unconscious or entirely unresponsive.

If the child is unresponsive, you will need to lay her gently on her back on a flat surface. Look into her mouth, and if you see a foreign body, remove it. Then commence CPR (see directions on page 343).

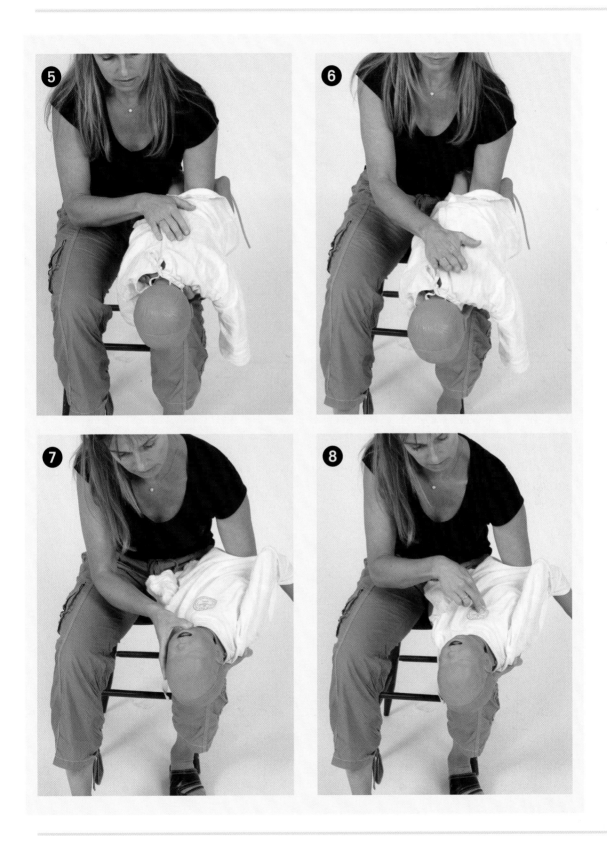

Guide to

Treating drowning

The challenge is to rescue the child safely from the water and then begin first aid immediately if necessary.

- Contact emergency medical services immediately.
- If the child is not breathing or if her breathing is ineffective, begin mouth-to-mouth rescue breathing immediately (see directions on page 345). Assess her for a heartbeat or pulse, and if this sign is absent or uncertain, initiate chest compressions. A toddler has a much better chance of survival if CPR is instituted immediately, while you're waiting for the paramedics to arrive.
- If it's possible that the child has a neck injury from diving into a swimming pool or other trauma, be very careful to stabilize her neck when moving her.
- If the child starts to breathe or cough, and provided there is no concern about injury to the spine, roll her onto her side, in the "recovery" position.
- Remove her wet clothing and cover her with warm blankets.
- Wait for the emergency medical personnel to arrive.

Poisoning and other toxic ingestions

Our homes contain a wide range of potentially toxic products, including household cleaners, pesticides, fertilizer, gasoline, cosmetics, alcohol, medications,

and vitamins. Toddlers are inquisitive little explorers and often like to taste their discoveries. Once again, prevention is of the utmost importance (see Part 7 for advice on childproofing your home against these hazards).

Keep the telephone number of your local poison information center readily accessible (e.g., on the refrigerator door) and be alert to common symptoms of poisoning.

Common poisoning symptoms
- Tummy pain, with or without vomiting
- Drowsiness
- Jerking (convulsions)
- Labored, rapid, or noisy breathing
- Redness or burns in and around the mouth
- Drooling

Guide to

Treating poisoning

Even if your child appears okay after ingesting a toxic substance, call your local poison information center. The more detail you have, the better — have the label of the substance available, if possible, so that you can tell them the name of the product and the list of ingredients, if printed on the label.

- If there is anything left in her mouth, take it out. Don't discard it, as it may be helpful in identifying the poison.
- If a chemical has been spilled on your child's clothes, remove them immediately and rinse her skin with lukewarm water for 10 minutes.
- If a poisonous substance has splashed

into her eye, rinse it out with lukewarm water for 15 minutes.
- Don't try to make your child vomit it up, unless specifically advised to do so by the poison control center. Syrup of ipecac, which used to be given to induce vomiting, is no longer recommended. If you have some around the house, get rid of it.
- Don't apply any other home remedies.
- If your child is having trouble breathing, is jerking (having convulsions), cannot be easily aroused, or is unconscious, place her on her side, in case she vomits. Immediately call emergency services.
- If she is unconscious or not breathing, start CPR (see directions on page 343).

Cardiopulmonary resuscitation

Cardiopulmonary resuscitation (CPR) has saved the lives of many children when administered by caregivers and bystanders trained in this basic life support technique. Take the time to learn CPR — you never know when a child may need your lifesaving skills.

HOW TO
Administer CPR

First response

1. If you come across a child who isn't moving and isn't responsive, immediately shout for help. If someone responds, send that person to contact your local emergency response system.

2. If you are alone, provide about five cycles of CPR (each cycle is made up of 30 compressions and two breaths)

before going to activate the emergency response system yourself.

3. If the child is small and you're not worried about trauma or injury to the neck, carry the child with you to the telephone. The dispatcher may even be able to guide you through the steps of CPR.

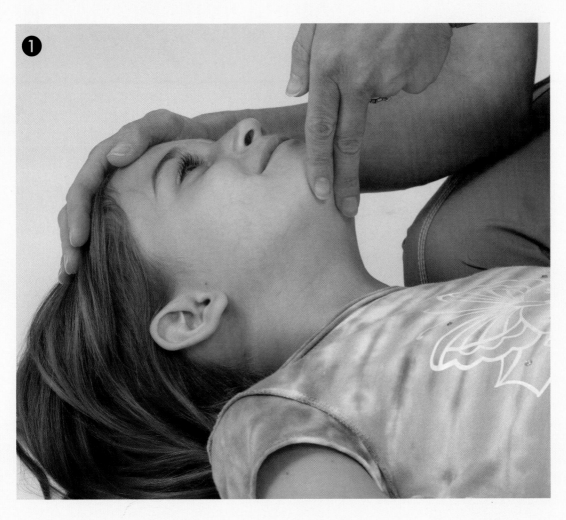

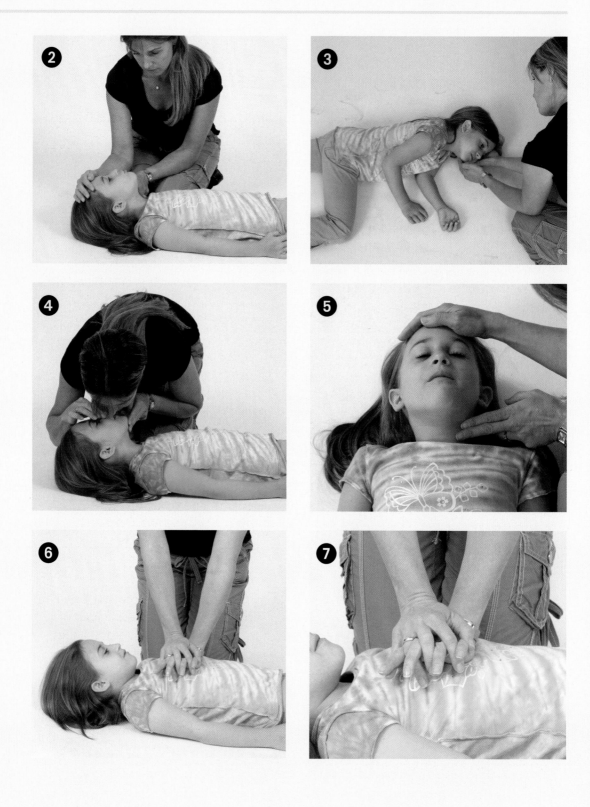

Resuscitation

1. Open the child's airway by placing one hand on her forehead to tilt her head back slightly. Place the fingers of the other hand under the bony part of the lower jaw near the chin to bring it forward (see picture 1). This is called the head tilt–chin lift position.

2. *Look* for chest and tummy movement, *listen* for sounds of breathing, and *feel* for exhaled air with your cheek for 5 to 10 seconds (see picture 2).

3. If she is breathing, turn her on her side to decrease the risk of vomiting and choking and wait for help to arrive (see picture 3).

4. If she is not breathing, give her two breaths. In small children and infants, this will be mouth-to-mouth-and-nose. With the head tilt–chin lift position maintained, place your mouth over her mouth and nose to create an airtight seal. If you cannot get your mouth over the child's nose and mouth, pinch her nose closed with your thumb and forefinger and make a mouth-to-mouth seal (see picture 4). Blow forcefully enough into her nose and mouth to make her chest rise with each breath. If her chest doesn't rise with each breath, reopen her airway by repeating the head tilt–chin lift (see step 1 above) and give two more breaths.

5. If you feel confident about feeling the pulse, check for her pulse in the neck (carotid artery; see picture 5) or groin (femoral artery) for 5 to 10 seconds. To find the carotid artery, place two fingers between the windpipe and the muscles at the side of the neck. If there is no pulse, or if it is less than 60 beats per minute and her color is poor, you will need to start chest compressions immediately.

If you don't feel confident about feeling for a pulse — and most parents don't — proceed immediately to chest compressions.

6. For children 1 year or older, place the heel of your hand on the lower half of the child's chest, with your other hand on top (see picture 6 and 7). Compress about one-third to one-half of the chest depth — which takes a bit of effort — at a rate of 100 compressions per minute. Do not press near the bottom tip of the breastbone.

7. For smaller children, you may only require one hand — lift your fingers up to avoid pressing too hard on the ribs — and for infants, you can use two fingers placed over the breastbone just below the nipple level.

8. Push hard and fast, without interruption, if possible. Release the pressure completely between compressions to allow the chest to fully relax.

9. If you are alone, give cycles of 30 compressions followed by two breaths. If there are two rescuers, the ratio would be 15 compressions to two breaths.

Emergency Response System

After five cycles of CPR, you should call your local emergency response system if this hasn't already been done.

First aid for major injuries

As parents, even the possibility of a major injury to our child is very scary. We can give thanks that this is a rare occurrence, but when it happens, it is usually out of the blue, leaving us little time to plan what to do. Here are a few tips that may prove useful in an emergency.

Head injuries

Head injuries in children are common, the result of falls and collisions. Fortunately, most are minor, but major head injuries can be fatal. Prevention is most important (see Part 7 for tips on preventing head injuries, especially those resulting from automobile and cycling accidents).

Red flags

When your child suffers a blow to the head, you should be concerned if you observe any of the following symptoms. If you see any of these red flags, seek immediate care for your child. If the head injury occurs late in the day, you may need to wake your child up once or twice during that night to ensure that he awakens appropriately — that is, for someone being woken up in the middle of the night — and exhibits no other red-flag symptoms.

INFANTS AND TODDLERS

- Loss of consciousness
- Repeated vomiting
- Poor feeding
- Severe irritability; very difficult to console
- Lethargy, sleeping more than usual
- Weakness of an arm or leg
- Seizures or staring spells
- Bulging fontanelle (soft spot on top of the head)

OLDER CHILDREN

- Loss of consciousness
- Repeated vomiting
- Confusion or agitation
- Inappropriate drowsiness
- Severe headache that gets worse or won't go away
- Any difficulty with speaking, seeing, or walking
- Neck stiffness
- Seizures

Did You Know?

Toddler's fracture

There is a specific type of broken bone known as a toddler's fracture, which involves a fracture of one of the lower leg bones without an obvious injury or swelling, just a refusal to bear weight on that leg. Generally, an X-ray will need to be taken to see if the bone is broken or not.

Fractured bones

Toddlers' bones are less dense than those of older children and adults, but their ligaments are actually stronger relative to their bones. These factors mean that toddlers can fracture their bones after a less forceful injury, while adults may only end up with a sprain. Children can also bend the bone if the break goes only part of the way through the bone — this is known as a greenstick fracture. Most broken bones in this age group will need to be protected in a plaster cast.

Symptoms of a bone fracture

If a bone is broken after an injury or fall, you can usually expect to see some significant pain and swelling. In some toddlers, however, there may not be any swelling, only a refusal to walk, bear weight, or move the arm or leg.

Pulled elbow

Pulled elbow is a common injury in toddlers. It typically happens when the toddler is pulled up or swung around by the hands, but it can occur if you're holding your child's hand and he suddenly falls. The head of the radius (forearm) bone is pulled out of the elbow joint. And it doesn't take much force to do it.

Your toddler will immediately refuse to move his arm and will resist any attempt by you to bend or move that arm. Fortunately, a doctor is usually able to slip it back into the normal position, fairly painlessly, with a relatively simple maneuver.

This can be a recurring problem, so be careful not to swing your children or pull them up by the hands. A pulled elbow seldom recurs after 4 years of age.

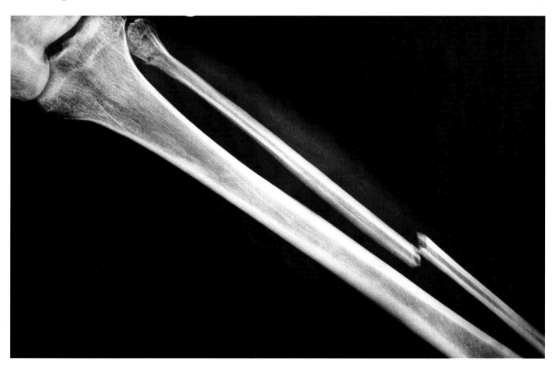

Teeth and mouth injuries

It is quite common for children to fall and injure their teeth, most commonly the incisors at the front of the mouth. If the tooth is loosened or chipped, you will need to see the dentist, even if it is a baby tooth, because it can interfere with the development and alignment of his permanent tooth underneath.

If a permanent tooth is knocked out, this is considered a dental emergency. Find the tooth, pick it up at the tooth, not root, end and rinse it off in water. You then have two options: you can place it back into the gum it came out of and hold it there with a piece of gauze, if practical, or you can immerse it in a container full of milk and place this on ice. Either way, you need to get to the dentist as soon as possible.

Burns

Burns and scalds are very common in the toddler age group. Every year, many children are admitted to burn units around the world with serious, extremely painful, and permanently disfiguring burns. These could often have been prevented (see Part 7 for tips on childproofing your home against burn and scald hazards).

Symptoms of burns

- **First-degree burns:** These burns involve only the most superficial layer of the skin, as in the case of a mild sunburn. They cause redness, with maybe a mild swelling and a little discomfort. These burns would only need to be seen by your doctor if there is enough swelling or pain to worry you. They should settle down within a couple of days.
- **Second-degree burns:** These burns are deeper and cause a lot of pain and blistering. These should be seen by a doctor. They will take 1 to 2 weeks to settle.
- **Third-degree burns:** These are the deepest kind of burn and involve the full thickness of the skin. They are often not immediately painful because the nerve ends may be damaged. The area may look white or charred. These are a medical emergency, and will often need skin grafting to heal.

Guide to

Treating burns

- Cool the area immediately. Place the burned area under cold running water or into a cool bath for 10 to 20 minutes. Cooling the area will limit the burn from extending further. Do not use ice — it can cause further damage to the skin.
- Cover with a cool clean wet cloth.
- Remove any clothing that may stick to the burn, but don't pull it off if it's already stuck to the skin.
- Don't use butter or greasy ointments or linty materials, such as a tissue, on a fresh burn.
- Don't break any blisters.
- Give your toddler something for the pain, such as acetaminophen or ibuprofen, if necessary.
- Seek emergency care if you suspect second- or third-degree burns.

First aid for minor injuries

Many minor injuries can be dealt with effectively at home. Here are a few practical tips.

Cuts and scrapes

When your toddler is just learning to walk, run, and climb, the world seems to be full of sharp pointed objects to run into or fall on. Most cuts and scrapes are fairly superficial, though occasionally a deeper cut may need stitches. You may simply need to clean up the wound and provide a big hug for the injured warrior. Sometimes, a clean ice pack or even a dose of acetaminophen may be helpful.

Red flags

Seek medical attention for any cuts and scrapes that

- Don't stop bleeding after 10 minutes of pressure
- Look deep
- Are on the face or over a joint
- Are caused by human or animal bites or are puncture wounds from a needle or nail
- Are dirty and you can't clean them out properly
- Look infected

Animal bites

In the United States, children are exposed to almost five million dog bites, half a million cat bites, and a quarter of a million human bites every year. Most of these bites occur at home, and the biter is usually known to the child. At least half of all dog bites seem to be unprovoked. Perhaps not surprisingly, little boys seem to get bitten more often than little girls. The most common offenders appear to be Rottweiler, pit bull, and German shepherd dogs, but despite a normally friendly nature, any animal that is teased or taken by surprise may bite. While animals are wonderful companions for your children, do not allow your toddler to play with them unless they are closely supervised. Animal scratches need to be treated in the same way as bites, because saliva and germs can often be found under the animal's claws.

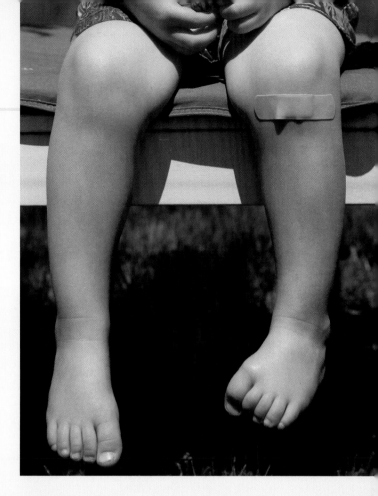

HOW TO
Treat cuts and scrapes

1. If the cut is still bleeding, work to stop the bleeding. Apply firm pressure with a clean cloth or paper tissue. Elevate the bleeding part, if practical; for example, if a finger is bleeding, compress it firmly while holding it above the level of the heart. Ongoing bleeding is not uncommon if the injury involves the scalp, face, or mouth. These parts of the body have a very strong blood supply, which is actually good news, as this is why they heal so quickly and nicely.

2. Clean the wound with soap and water. Try to flush it under the faucet for 5 to 10 minutes. If there's a lot of gravel or stones that you can't clean out from the scrape, you may need to visit your health-care provider.

3. Determine whether the cut needs to be closed. Cuts and scrapes do not necessarily need to be covered with a bandage or dressing unless they are likely to get dirty or rub against something. Leaving the wound uncovered, even for short periods, allows it to dry out, which helps prevent the growth of bacteria. Facial cuts will often need to be closed. Any cut that is gaping, does not easily stop bleeding, or is in an area that is constantly moving, such as over a joint, may require closing by your health-care provider or at your local emergency room. If it does need to be closed, the earlier the better. It is preferable to stitch it within about 6 hours of the cut. Sometimes, if it is very clean and not too deep, the doctor may be able to close it using special sticky strips or glue.

4. Until it heals, keep an eye on the cut on a daily basis for any signs of infection. Infection usually causes increasing and spreading redness or swelling, or a creamy whitish discharge (pus), as well as increased complaints of pain from your little one. Any suggestion of infection needs to be discussed with your health-care provider.

5. Some physicians recommend using a topical antibiotic cream, applied two to three times a day. This generally depends on the size of the cut or scrape and how clean it is after you've washed it.

To help prevent scarring, cover the healed wound with sunblock when the child is in the sun.

6. Check that your toddler's immunizations, specifically her tetanus shots, are up to date.

HOW TO
Treat animal bites and scratches

1. Wash bites and scratches very carefully. The best way to do this is to place the bitten area under a running faucet for 5 to 10 minutes. Alternatively, fill a pitcher with water and flush the area repeatedly with a syringe or turkey baster.

2. If the bite is superficial and the skin is not punctured, you should not need to consult your health-care provider. If it is a deep bite, especially from a dog or cat, with puncturing of the skin, it is advisable to at least discuss this with your physician.

3. In the case of a bite or possible bite from a raccoon, fox, or bat, you should always consult your physician because there is a risk of rabies and treatment may be required. Bites from small pets, such as hamsters, gerbils, and rats, pose no risk of rabies and are generally very superficial. Small wild rodents, such as mice and squirrels, are also free of rabies.

4. Observe the wound for any signs of infection. About 5% of dog bites and more than 20% of cat bites become infected. If this is going to happen, it will usually be in the first three days. You may see increasing redness or swelling of the area, hear increasing complaints of pain, and sometimes even notice a creamy whitish discharge (pus). If you see any of these signs, consult your physician immediately.

Some physicians recommend using a topical antibiotic ointment, available without a prescription from the drugstore. Covering the bite with a bandage is usually not necessary unless there is a risk that it may get dirty or the child feels more comfortable with having it covered. If she seems to be uncomfortable, an anti-inflammatory pain reliever, such as ibuprofen, can be given as needed.

Red flags

Call your doctor if the bite is deep and shows any signs of infection (increasing redness, swelling, pain, or pussy discharge). Also seek medical attention if your child is bitten by a raccoon, fox or bat, or an unknown animal, because of the risk of rabies.

Insect stings

Most "bee" stings are from yellow jackets rather than bumblebees or honey bees and typically occur on the hands and feet of toddlers who have unwittingly disturbed the insect. Bee stings cause an immediately painful, swollen red bump that can be itchy. Most bee stings will improve after several hours, but multiple

stings — usually more than 10 to 20 when a hive is disturbed — can lead to vomiting, headache, and fever.

Rarely, children can have a generalized, or anaphylactic, allergic response, which can cause swelling of the lips or tongue, a tingling sensation around the mouth, and

Guide to

Preventing and treating stings

PREVENTION

- Don't let your toddler walk around in bare feet when you think stinging insects may be around.
- Keep children away from insect nests.
- Don't let your child drink from an open sweet-drink container when eating outdoors — bees and yellow jackets occasionally fly in unnoticed.
- Avoid open food and strong perfumes or hairsprays that can attract stinging insects.

TREATMENT

- If your child shows any sign of an allergic reaction to the sting, such as trouble breathing or swallowing and

swelling around the mouth, seek emergency care.
- With honey bee stings, remove the stinger, which might still be present and usually appears as a small black dot in the middle of a sting, by gently rubbing it away.
- Gently massage the area with ice for several minutes to soothe the sting.
- Rub the area gently with baking soda, an aluminum-based deodorant stick, or meat tenderizer to neutralize the insect's venom.
- Use acetaminophen or ibuprofen for pain relief. A liquid oral antihistamine can also help combat the allergic reaction.
- See a physician if persistent pain or swelling occurs after 24 hours.

difficulty breathing, with a tightness in the throat. This is a true medical emergency, and injectable adrenaline should be given if available. The child should be taken immediately to the nearest hospital. Relapses can occur, so he should be evaluated even if he's feeling better after experiencing any symptoms of an anaphylactic reaction.

Eye injuries

The most common eye problem toddlers suffer is getting something "in" it, typically grains of sand, dirt, or an eyelash. The toddler can be quite uncomfortable, with much rubbing of the eye. The eye then rapidly becomes red.

With all the inevitable tears, the foreign material often disappears by itself, but if the situation doesn't resolve itself quickly, the best solution is to try to flush the material out with lukewarm water. Meanwhile, encourage the toddler to stop rubbing. If this doesn't solve the problem, you will need to consult your health-care provider, who will be able to do a more detailed examination. If necessary, a drop of local anesthetic (freezing) can be used and the foreign material removed with a cotton-tipped applicator.

Nose injuries

The nose is well positioned to bear the brunt of a fall or a ball in the face, but the soft part of the nose (cartilage) is even softer in young children, making it more likely to bend than to crack. As a result, a broken nose at this age is very uncommon. If the nose is swollen, apply some gentle pressure with an ice pack or a pack of frozen vegetables, which may need to be wrapped in a towel if it is uncomfortable and too cold for your little one. Once the swelling has gone down, if the nose isn't straight after a few days, see your child's health-care provider for advice on procedures for realigning the nose.

Nosebleeds

Nosebleeds are not uncommon in toddlers and are mainly caused by nose picking. Children are especially prone to nosebleeds when they have a cold or allergies, which cause the tiny blood vessels in the wall between the two nostrils to become engorged with blood. At such times, a sneeze or a fingernail can easily start an impressive bleed! Occasionally, bleeding can be caused by a toddler experimenting with sticking a bead or other toy into his nose.

In general, while not very pretty and rather messy, nosebleeds are quite harmless. Very rarely, nosebleeds can be caused by an underlying tendency to bleed.

Slivers

Slivers or splinters are quite common in young children and are typically tiny pieces of wood or glass. In most cases, slivers should be removed to prevent discomfort and infection. If there are numerous tiny slivers of wood that are painless and very close to the surface, simply clean the area and let them come out as the skin cells are lost.

You will need some equipment if you're planning to remove the sliver: a good pair of tweezers and a sharp needle sterilized in alcohol. Start by cleaning the area with an antiseptic solution. If you can grasp one end of the sliver with the tweezers, try to pull it out along the angle of entry. If this isn't possible, superficial slivers can be removed by stroking the overlying skin softly with the needle to expose enough of the sliver to get hold of it with the tweezers or flick it out with the needle.

When the splinter is out, rewash the area with antiseptic and check on it daily for a couple of days to make sure that there is no sign of swelling, redness, creamy discharge, or pain, which may suggest infection.

HOW TO
Stop nosebleeds

1. Firmly squeeze together the two sides of the soft part of the nose just above the nostrils for at least 5 to 10 minutes.

2. Be sure the head is tilted slightly forward so your child will not gag on, swallow, and vomit blood.

3. Try to stop your child from picking, touching, blowing, and generally interfering with her nose for the next few hours. This is more easily said than done!

4. If nosebleeds are an ongoing problem, try using a humidifier in her bedroom and apply some lubricating cream to the inside lining of the wall separating the nostrils.

5. If the nosebleeds are frequent and severe, and especially if your child or another family member is prone to bruising or bleeding, take her to your doctor to test for an underlying problem.

Creating a first aid kit

A first aid kit is extremely convenient for treating emergency injuries. You can buy kits at your local drugstore or customize your own. You can take your kit to the sports field, on camping trips, and on vacation. Keep one in the house and one in the car.

Consider including the following components in your first aid kit. Include what seems most appropriate for your family and your individual comfort level.

- Scissors
- Tweezers
- Needle, for removing slivers
- Digital thermometer
- Syringe, for flushing or giving medications
- Bandages and Band-Aids of various sizes
- Gauze
- Adhesive tape
- Povidone-iodine solution (such as Betadine) as a disinfectant
- Alcohol pads, for cleaning
- Topical antibiotic ointment
- Cortisone cream, for bites or allergic reactions
- Sunscreen
- Insect repellant
- Antihistamine (e.g., Diphenhydramine or Benadryl)
- Ibuprofen (Advil or Motrin)

- Acetaminophen (Tylenol or Tempra)
- EpiPen, if any risk of anaphylaxis
- Bronchodilator inhaler, if any history of asthma
- Penlight
- Steri-Strips
- Instant cold pack
- First aid guide book

Frequently asked questions

As family doctors, pediatricians, and nurse practitioners, we answer many questions from parents. Here are some of the most frequently asked questions. Be sure to ask your health-care providers any other questions that may arise. If they don't have the answers, they will refer you to a colleague who does.

Q: My daughter has a peanut allergy, and now, as she's getting older and starting to go out for play dates and parties, I'm beginning to worry that she may be exposed to peanuts and go into shock. Is there anything I can do?

A: You need to let all her caregivers know about the symptoms of her allergy and what foods trigger it. An allergic reaction can cause tummy pain, nausea, vomiting, an itchy rash and eyes, and tingling tongue and lips, as well as coughing and wheezing. Anaphylaxis will result in difficulty breathing, with swelling of the mouth, lips and throat, dizziness, and loss of consciousness, usually within minutes of ingestion of peanuts. You need to carry an Epi-Pen with injectable adrenaline and some antihistamines with you at all times, and make sure that her caregivers have a supply at daycare or school. In the case of an anaphylactic reaction, give the adrenaline immediately and then transport her to the nearest hospital, because relapses may occur.

Bear in mind that there are many other names for peanuts, such as beer nuts, groundnuts, and nut meats. If your child is old enough to understand, she should be told not to eat anything without advising the caregiver of her allergy. This is one situation where sharing is not okay, so explain to her that she shouldn't take food from any of her friends because of the risk that it isn't nut-free. She should also wear a MedicAlert bracelet identifying this allergy.

Q: My 2-year-old has had croup a few times, and it always seems to be the middle of the night when he can't breathe. How do I know when to seek help?

A: Croup is a common viral infection that causes inflammation around the voice box (larynx), causing the classic hoarse or barky cough. And it does indeed seem to get worse in the middle of the night. Most authorities recommend using some form of humidity — for example, go into the bathroom and put the shower on hot to generate steam or, if practical, take the child into the cool night air outside. If he continues to have significant breathing difficulties — usually manifested by a fast breathing rate with sucking in between the ribs and flaring of the nostrils — even if he's not crying and upset, it is best to be safe and call for emergency medical services. Unlike with asthma, where a puffer may relieve the distress, no medication that you can use at home will be likely to help immediately.

Q: My 3-year-old has had a convulsion in the past, and I'm terrified it will happen again. I've heard that I should put a spoon in his mouth to make sure he doesn't swallow or bite his tongue. Is this correct?

A: For any parents, watching their child have a convulsion, or seizure, is extremely distressing. First, ensure that he is away from danger and not likely to roll off the bed. Then try to roll him onto his side — it doesn't matter which one — so that in case he vomits, nothing will go down his windpipe. But don't put anything in his mouth — this is likely to cause damage and doesn't help. Call emergency medical services if the seizure doesn't stop within a minute or two, or immediately if he's turning blue or having difficulty breathing. As terrifying as it may seem, if this is a febrile (fever) convulsion, it will usually be over in a few minutes, and by age 6, your child will likely outgrow the problem altogether, so hang in there!

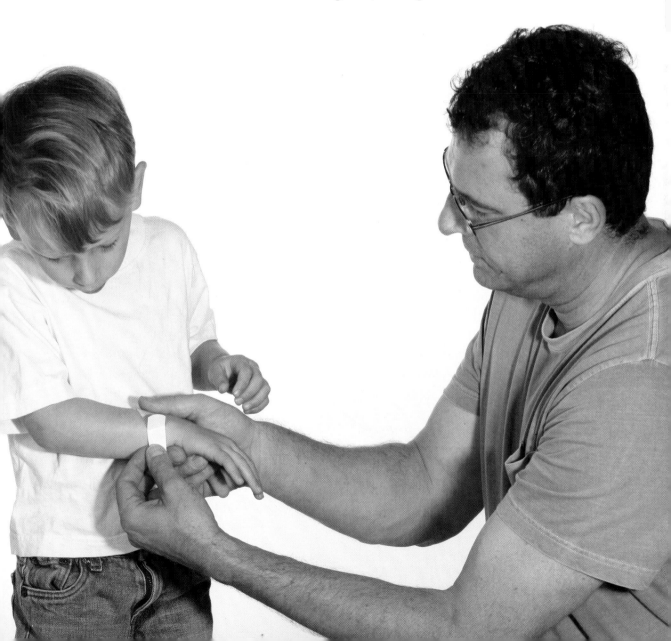

Sam's Diary

October 18 (44 months old)

It's been so long since I wrote to you last. Life is really very busy, and I feel like I'm not keeping up with this as well as I'd like to. You're developing a wonderful imagination, and you now play for short periods on your own with fantasy play.

We went to get you your first pair of proper skates this weekend in preparation for your skating lessons, which begin in the winter.

November 2 (45 months old)

Today you had your face painted for the very first time — like a lion. You sat so beautifully and still, with your eyes closed, while you were being painted. Previously, you'd never have done this. You enjoyed Halloween for the first time as well. Last year you didn't want to dress up. This year you had a ball greeting people at our door and giving out candy and money for UNICEF. Today you didn't want to kiss Mom, "because I don't want to get married."

December 30 (46+ months old)

Sambo, at this time in your young little life, you have some slightly disconcerting mannerisms — one is a great big scowl on your face when

you don't like something, and the other is a new thing, tapping your arms and legs quite frequently. This seems to be an anxiety-based thing, but I'm not really sure. We're hoping you grow out of this and it's not going to be the start of something, but I thought I'd tell you about it now. Time will tell, I suppose. Anyway, stay just the way you are — WE LOVE YOU!!

February 22 (4 years old)

It's been a long time since I've written, and there's lots to tell, so here goes. First, the mannerisms we mentioned earlier are gone! They were a bit worrying, so we're not sad to see them go. Yesterday you had your first real drop-off play date at a friend's place from school. You had your fourth birthday party on your actual birthday. Lofty the magician had you all enthralled for an hour. You loved being his trusty helper to do all the tricks — you just beamed from ear to ear!

You are doing the most amazingly intricate, mature drawings. You love "writing" and will spend a lot of time just writing letters down and asking us what they spell. You love playing school. Mom has to be your teacher. You sit at your desk and instruct me as to what to teach you. You are such a keen learner at this stage.

You had your first attempt at spelling the other day. You drew your elephant with "a twisted trunk," then asked Mom to spell "elephant" for you. Before I had a chance to write it down (you copy perfectly), you had spelled it out for yourself phonetically — that is quite a feat at just 4 years of age!

You are amazing with Dani and speak to her so beautifully. She continues to hit you on the head every now and then, and you get annoyed but never hit back. The other day you told me about "gentlemen and gentleladies."

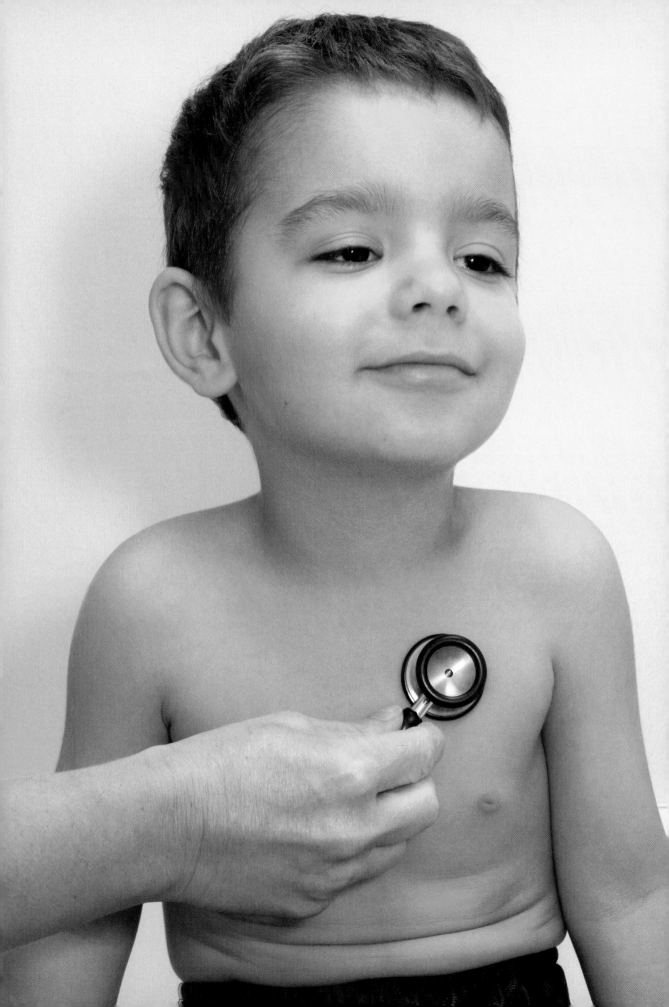

Caring for Your Sick Toddler

Recognizing illness 364

Managing a fever 365

Remedying a cold 369

Resolving skin problems 372

Treating eye problems 381

Dealing with ear, nose, and throat problems 383

Managing chest and breathing problems 390

Treating heart conditions 394

Taking care of stomach conditions 395

Addressing genitourinary problems 400

Managing neurological conditions 404

Recognizing musculoskeletal conditions 410

Giving medicine to your toddler 412

Preparing your child for surgery 414

Caring for a child with a chronic illness 415

Complementary and alternative medicine 421

Frequently asked questions 425

Recognizing illness

For a parent, there is nothing scarier than a sick child. No matter how relaxed you may be, seeing your little one uncomfortable or suffering is likely to bring on considerable anxiety and many questions. The million-dollar question remains, "When do I need to consult my health-care provider?" Recognizing the signs and symptoms of some of the more common illnesses your child may experience is the first step to answering this question. Luckily, most acute illnesses in this age group are caused by viral infections and tend to be benign and self-limited. Occasionally, however, certain red-flag signs and symptoms appear that indicate you should get things checked out by your health-care provider.

Acute and chronic illness

While acute illnesses tend to resolve in a matter of days or weeks, some toddlers will be born with or develop illnesses that will last for years, even a lifetime. Parenting a child with a chronic illness can be challenging and rewarding at the same time. Your life will be changed forever, and you may learn new things about yourself.

There are many things you can do to make this challenge a little less daunting. Take advantage of your resources and your organizational skills and embrace the support around you. See pages 415–420 for more advice on caring for a child with a chronic illness.

Red flags for urgent care

Seek urgent care for your toddler if she shows any one these signs or symptoms:

- Unresponsive; decreased level of consciousness (not interacting appropriately with you and the environment)
- Feverish, with a stiff neck
- Listless or hard to rouse
- Signs of significant respiratory distress, with very rapid breathing, increased work of breathing, or very noisy breathing
- Not eating or drinking and signs of dehydration, with decreased urination, dry tongue and eyes, and no energy
- Severe pain; inconsolable
- Uncontrollable jerking of the limbs suggestive of a seizure (convulsion)

Managing a fever

Every toddler experiences a fever from time to time, and fever is the most common reason for young children to be brought to emergency care. Fevers most commonly occur during self-limited and benign illnesses, usually viral infections, but most parents will at some point worry that a serious disease is causing the fever or that a fever will have serious effects on their child. Misconceptions about the causes and effects of a fever abound. Your anxiety will be reduced if you understand how fevers develop and know how to take your toddler's temperature.

Fever facts

What is a fever? Even this simple question is not as straightforward as it appears. A fever is an elevation in body temperature significantly above "normal." However, normal body temperature varies according to where and when it is measured. The surrounding environment and your child's clothing can also have minor effects on body temperature.

Fevers are diagnosed by taking a child's axillary (under the arm), oral (under the tongue), tympanic (ear), or rectal temperature and determining whether it is above "normal."

Causes of fever

Most fevers are caused by self-limited viral infections, such as an upper respiratory tract infection (common cold) or gastroenteritis (stomach flu). In fact, a fever is a normal and important part of the body's natural immune response to infection — it tells us that your toddler is fighting off the infection appropriately. Many parents are concerned about the potentially harmful effects of an elevated body temperature, but rest assured that a fever caused by uncomplicated infections does not cause brain damage, hearing loss, or blindness.

The severity of a fever does not indicate the severity of illness. In fact, some serious infections may be accompanied by a minimally elevated or even a lower than normal body temperature. Much more important than the degree of the fever is the behavior of your child. Most

Measuring a Fever

Method of Measurement	Fever
Axillary (under the arm)	> 99°F (37.2°C)
Oral (under the tongue)	> 99.5°F (37.5°C)
Tympanic (ear)	> 99.5°F (37.5°C)
Rectal	> 100.4°F (38.0°C)

Guide to

Taking your child's temperature

The type of thermometer and the method used to measure a child's temperature depend on his age, the circumstances, and the equipment available.

THERMOMETERS

Mercury: Old-style mercury thermometers are not recommended because of the potential for mercury exposure if the thermometer breaks.

Digital: Digital thermometers are safe, easy to use, inexpensive, and versatile and are suitable for use orally and rectally. In addition, they're ready to read in less than a minute.

Tympanic: Tympanic thermometers are convenient but less reliable in the child under 2 years of age because the device must fit easily inside the child's ear canal. They do give a reading in a few seconds but are more expensive than a simple plastic digital thermometer and are generally not necessary for use at home.

METHOD

Axillary (under the arm): Axillary temperature measurement may be convenient, but it is also the most unreliable route. You can use a digital oral or rectal thermometer, with the tip placed in the armpit and the arm held snugly against the chest.

Oral (under the tongue): This route is generally not practical for younger toddlers, but by the age of 4 to 5 years, children can generally cooperate for oral temperature measurement, which requires keeping the thermometer under the tongue.

Tympanic: Disposable tips are placed on the end of the thermometer, which is placed in the outer part of the ear until, after a few seconds, the machine beeps, indicating the temperature has been recorded. While these thermometers are often used in hospitals and doctors' offices, they are generally a bit expensive for home use.

Rectal: Nobody likes having things placed in their bottom end, and toddlers are no exception! This is not a practical method of temperature-taking in this age group.

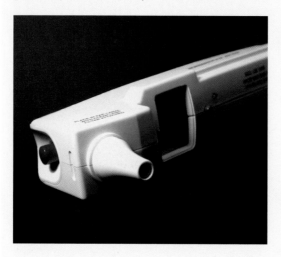

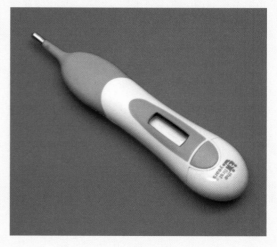

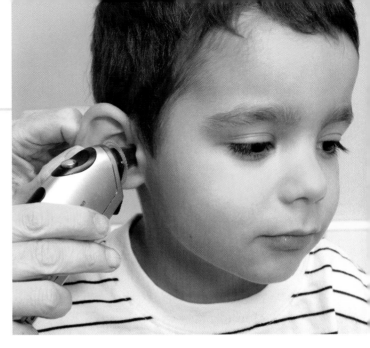

toddlers with a fever will be cranky and want to eat less, but the child who triggers concern doesn't show an interest in her surroundings, appears listless, or seems inconsolable to her caregivers.

Fever is like a burglar alarm warning you that your child is likely dealing with some sort of infection. Just as you wouldn't switch the burglar alarm off and roll over and go back to sleep, it isn't good enough to treat the fever without ensuring that there are no signs or symptoms that require attention from your health-care provider.

TEETHING MYTH

Many people believe teething causes fevers. While eruption of a tooth can cause irritability and discomfort, it does not cause a significant fever.

Febrile seizures

A febrile seizure, or convulsion, during the course of a fever is a common event in young children, occurring in about 1 in 30 children between 6 months and 5 years of age. Seizures with fever often run in families (your child's grandmother is often the person who best remembers them occurring in you or your partner when you were young). While extremely frightening for parents to observe, febrile seizures are usually a benign event for the child.

SEIZURE SYMPTOMS

These seizures are typically brief, 1 to 2 minutes, and do not cause brain injury or lead to a higher chance of epilepsy (recurrent seizures without fever). Febrile seizures usually appear as stiffening and jerking of the body and limbs. Seizures may also involve drooling and eye-turning, and the toilet-trained youngster may lose bladder control. Immediately after a seizure, many children are irritable and sleepier but recover after a short time.

RESPONSE TO A SEIZURE

If the seizure is brief, 1 to 2 minutes, you should call your health-care provider to

Did You Know?

Swallowing the tongue

It is a misconception that a child will "swallow" his tongue during a seizure and therefore needs to have something clamped to his tongue to prevent choking. In fact, caregivers should not attempt to open or put something in the mouth. Turning the child on his side in case vomiting occurs and making sure there are no hard or sharp objects around him are often the best actions to take. For first aid procedures on handling a seizure, see page 408.

determine whether your child needs to be seen to assess the cause of the fever and decide if any treatment is required for an associated condition — for example, an ear infection.

If the seizure is prolonged, lasting for more than a few minutes, call for emergency medical services.

Red flags

In all cases of fever, if your child shows any of the following signs and symptoms in addition to the fever, see a health-care provider immediately:

- Purple spots or bruises on the skin
- Difficult to rouse; poor eye contact
- Behaving as if her neck is stiff
- Not acting like herself
- Difficulty with breathing
- Dry tongue and eyes
- Fever that lasts more than 3 days

Treating fevers

Most fevers due to viral infections can be managed at home. If the fever is low grade and does not seem to be bothering your toddler, no treatment is indicated. If the fever is accompanied by chills, crankiness, and discomfort, most parents will resort to medications, such as acetaminophen or ibuprofen, which are available over the counter.

Beware of home remedies. Cold water baths and alcohol sponging are potentially dangerous and should not be used. Aspirin (ASA) should not be given to children because of the risk of Reye's syndrome, a serious condition that can cause liver and brain injury.

Medications

Medications such as acetaminophen (Tylenol, Tempra) and ibuprofen (Advil, Motrin) are safe and effective for fever management. There is little difference between acetaminophen and ibuprofen if used in the correct amounts. The concentrations, coloring, and flavoring vary, but there isn't much difference in the relative effectiveness of these products. Some people choose to alternate between the two types, but there is minimal evidence that this is particularly helpful to the outcome. These drugs are designed to provide for the toddler's comfort, rather than just eliminate the elevated body temperature.

DOSAGE

These medicines come in various forms: syrups, suppositories, and chewable tablets. The most important principle is to give adequate doses as per the instructions recommended on the box. A dosage guideline, often based on age or a range of weights, comes with the product, so knowing the individual dose for your child is important. The typical dosage for children at this age is 10 mg per kilogram of weight for ibuprofen and 15 mg per kilogram of weight for acetaminophen.

RESPONSE

Evaluate your child's appearance after medication for fever has been administered. Many children will feel and look miserable when they have a fever but will look better once the medication has had 30 minutes to 1 hour to work. In terms of their behavior and interaction with you, this response to medication can be reassuring.

Remedying a cold

Toddlers always seem to have a cold. In fact, the average toddler can be expected to have as many as eight to 10 colds a year, particularly if she attends daycare or has older siblings at home. Colds are caused by numerous viruses that are present throughout the year but are much more common during the fall and winter months. Nasal congestion and discharge, cough, fever, and mild sore throat are commonly seen. These symptoms tend to last for days, but it is not unusual to have a nagging cough for several weeks. If your child contracts several infections back to back, it may seem like she always has a cough or cold!

Preventing problems

It would seem logical that the cure for the common cold is preventing cold viruses from spreading, but preventing all colds is practically impossible. Careful washing of hands can help reduce infections, but viruses that cause colds are hardy. They can live on tabletops, toys, and other

objects for days before finding their way to your child's hands. It's only a short trip from there to the nose, mouth, and eyes — and the inevitable infection occurs.

Despite claims to the contrary by the manufacturers, no medications, vitamins, or nutritional supplements have been shown to prevent colds in toddlers. Many people are discouraged when they or their children catch colds despite getting an influenza vaccination, but this vaccine targets only a specific influenza virus — which generally causes more severe symptoms than a common cold — and not the many other viruses that cause colds.

Cold symptoms

Most colds will last from days to a week and resolve on their own. Colds affect the nose, sinuses, and throat, and while a nagging cough can persist for a few weeks, the most bothersome symptoms to your child — nasal congestion and discharge, discomfort, and fever — usually improve over days. Nasal congestion can make sleeping at night hard for your child — and for you! — but colds should not cause labored or difficult breathing.

Red flags

Signs that indicate that more than a cold might be present include the following. If you observe any of these red flags, you should see your doctor.

- Rapid breathing
- Visible use of the chest muscles to breathe
- Earache, suggesting a possible ear infection
- Persistent fever for more than 2 to 3 days
- Stridor (a harsh noise when breathing in)
- Wheezing (a whistling noise when breathing out)

Did You Know?

OTC remedies warning

Over-the-counter (OTC) decongestants, cough suppressants, and antihistamines should not be used to treat toddlers with a cold. They are not effective in improving the symptoms in toddlers, and they have the potential to cause serious side effects in young children. These drugs can also cause irritability, rapid heartbeat, and sleeping problems. Along with acetaminophen or ibuprofen, combination products that are marketed for a cold or sinus infection contain some extra ingredients, but these products have not been shown to be any better than acetaminophen or ibuprofen alone. For these reasons, many authorities have advised against using cough and cold products to treat young children.

HOW TO
Soothe a common cold

1. Make sure that your toddler is drinking enough fluids, because he likely won't have much of an appetite.

2. In younger toddlers, if their noses are really blocked and congested, you can try saline nose drops or spray, but most toddlers will not be too keen on them.

3. Try using acetaminophen (Tylenol, Tempra) or ibuprofen (Advil, Motrin) to treat discomfort, aches, and fever if they're causing the child to feel unwell. Do not use combination cough/cold products.

4. Be aware that antibiotics, which treat bacterial infections, have absolutely no role in treating a cold, so don't expect your health-care provider to provide a prescription.

5. Wash your child's and your own hands frequently to prevent spreading the virus to other family members.

6. Wait for the symptoms to settle, making sure they do not develop into something more serious.

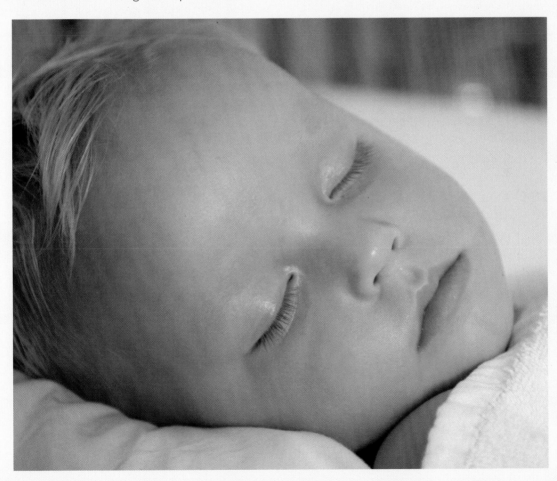

Resolving skin problems

Rashes and various types of skin lesions are very common in toddlers. Particularly when your toddler is suffering from a fever due to a viral infection, a non-specific, reddish, generalized rash will often be seen. These do not require any treatment and usually settle as the fever and viral infection resolve. Below are some examples of other common skin problems, how to recognize them, and what to do about them.

Warts

Warts are raised, round, rough-surfaced growths on the skin. They occur most commonly on the hands and feet, and can often be differentiated from a callus by the presence of brown-black dots in the middle of the wart. When warts occur on the bottom of the feet (plantar warts), they can be painful, but otherwise they don't generally cause discomfort.

Warts are extremely common in children. They are caused by viruses (papillomaviruses), and while not very contagious from person to person, warts can often spread from one location to another on the same child because of picking and thumb sucking.

Warts are harmless and generally disappear by themselves over the course of several years. Speak with your doctor

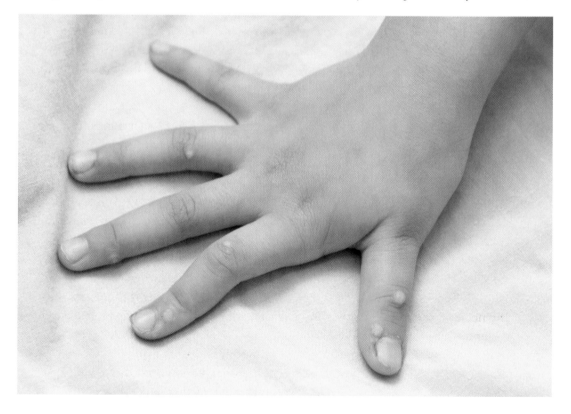

Guide to

Treating warts

While warts do disappear with time in most children, there are several treatments that can be effective in speeding up the process.

WART-REMOVING ACIDS

These preparations, which most commonly contain salicylic acid, are available without prescription. They come in liquid, patch, and ointment form. They are usually applied to the wart once or twice daily and covered with adhesive tape to promote drying. The acid dries the wart tissue, which then turns white. You can use a razor blade or emery board to shave

down the dead wart tissue once or twice per week.

DUCT TAPE

Warts can be covered with small pieces of duct tape, which are changed once or twice weekly. Covering the wart causes it to dry and the tissue to die. This process can take more than a few months to work.

LIQUID NITROGEN

An option available through a physician is freezing the wart with liquid nitrogen. This is effective but painful and usually requires multiple treatments. Because of the pain, it is seldom used for toddlers.

if warts are persistent or particularly bothersome or if they appear on the face or genital area.

Head lice

Infestations of head lice can cause a tremendous amount of anxiety in schools and in households.

Head lice are tiny ($\frac{1}{10}$-inch/2 to 3 mm) gray bugs that live in hair and feed off blood by biting the scalp. The signs of head lice include itching and irritation of the scalp. Sometimes you can see red bumps or scratch marks on the scalp. Live lice are difficult to see, often living close to the scalp, especially around the ears or at the nape of the neck. Lice eggs (nits) are usually easier to spot. They can be very numerous and look similar to dandruff, but differ in that they are stuck to the hair and cannot be shaken off.

Scalp and hair treatments

The most widely accepted treatments are chemical shampoo and rinses, such as Kwellada-P and Nix. These products are applied to the scalp and hair and left on for a number of minutes, followed by rinsing. A second application is required 7 to 10 days later. Follow the instructions on the bottle of the particular preparation you have chosen.

While the hair is being rinsed, nits can be combed away with a special comb. If there are lots of nits, some authorities recommend applying petroleum jelly or thick hair gel and leaving it on for 12 hours to suffocate the nits. It is not unusual to have transient scalp itching after the rinse is used, but this is not usually a sign of reinfection. See your physician if signs of infection persist after the second application of shampoo.

Did You Know?

Lice facts
Head lice are common in children and are thought to be most often acquired from direct head to head contact with another child. They may also be spread by sharing hats, combs, and brushes. Head lice live only on humans and are not spread by pets. They are not a sign of poor hygiene or infrequent hair washing. And head lice do not spread disease.

Housecleaning

Head lice require contact with the scalp to live and do not remain alive for long when away from the body. Extensive cleaning is not warranted. Combs, brushes, hats, and pillowcases should be cleaned in hot water and heat-dried. Alternatively, sealing the objects in an airtight plastic bag for about 2 weeks will kill any remaining lice.

Going back to school

Children can go back to school after the first application of medicated shampoo. The presence of nits is not a reliable sign of active infection, and there is no sound rationale for excluding children with nits from school.

Sunburn

Overexposure to the sun can cause visible injury to the skin. A minor sunburn will turn the skin pink-red, while a more significant burn can lead to blistering of the skin. Unfortunately, pain and other signs of sunburn develop after the damage has already occurred. Repeated sunburns can cause premature aging of the skin and increase the risk of skin cancer in adulthood. And a severe sunburn can easily turn a fun-filled family vacation into a miserable experience.

Red flags

Some sunburns may be particularly extensive or signs of heatstroke can occur after excessive sun exposure. See a physician if

- Fever, persistent chills, or vomiting occurs
- Signs of infection (pus, red streaking, or increasing pain) appear on blistered sunburns

Ringworm

Ringworm is caused by a fungus that is most commonly acquired from contact with a puppy or kitten, though human to human transmission is also possible. The infection appears as $1/4$- to $1/2$-inch

HOW TO
Care for sunburns

Avoiding sunburns

Fortunately, sunburns can usually be prevented with a common-sense approach.

- Avoid the sun during peak hours, 10 a.m. to 3 p.m.
- Keep in mind that the UV rays of the sun penetrate clouds and loose clothing.
- Apply sunscreen with an SPF (sun protection factor) of 15 or more to your child's skin. An SPF of 30 or more is appropriate for children who burn more easily, including children with previous sunburn experience, fair hair, or freckled skin. Frequent reapplication is necessary if the child is exposed to the sun for a long time or is swimming.
- When using sunscreen, pay attention to problematic areas, such as the rims of the ears, back of the neck, and tops of feet.
- Set a good example! Your child will be much more likely to have good sun protection habits if you do, so wear sunscreen and a hat.

Soothing sunburns

You can take several steps to help your child feel more comfortable if he has a sunburn:

- Apply cool compresses or dress him in damp clothes.
- Use pain relief medications, such as ibuprofen.
- Apply moisturizing mild anti-inflammatory creams (1% hydrocortisone) to unbroken skin.
- Avoid applying ointments and butter, which prevent perspiration and are difficult to remove.
- Avoid first aid creams or sprays containing benzocaine, which can lead to allergic reactions.
- Keep him out of the sun until the sunburn is completely healed.

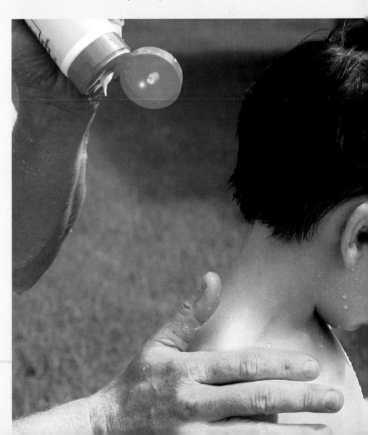

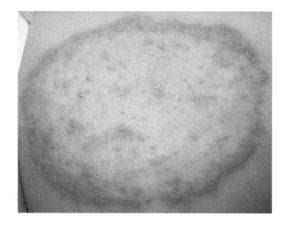

(0.5 to 1 cm) ring-shaped patches of skin that are slightly raised, pink in color with a clearer center, and often slightly itchy. These infections are usually not very bothersome to your child and do not cause serious disease.

Treatment

Ringworm infections are treated with antifungal creams, such as Lotrimin or Tinactin, available without prescription. The creams should usually be used for about 3 to 4 weeks in total and continued for about 1 week after the rash has disappeared. It is not necessary to take your child out of school. If you have a pet in your home, you may want to speak with your veterinarian. Young cats and dogs may not have signs of itching or hair loss and generally develop natural immunity to the fungus.

Hives

Hives, or urticaria, are raised, pink-red welts with a clear center that blanch when you put pressure on them, which differentiates them from a bruise. Hives can range in size from ½ inch (1 cm) to giant hives that can cover a whole extremity. They are often but not always itchy. Causes of hives include allergies, reactions to viral infections, and reactions to a host of physical stimuli, such as cold and sunlight. Most single episodes of hives, however, do not have a known cause.

Red flags

See a health-care provider immediately if
• Your child has difficulty breathing or swelling around the mouth or face
• Hives are present over the whole body
• Recurrent episodes of hives develop

Treatment

Most episodes of hives can be treated with an antihistamine, such as Benadryl, available without prescription. Drowsiness is the most common side effect of the medication. The best treatment for children who have a known cause for their hives, such as an allergy to a food, is avoidance of the trigger. Testing and treatment for allergies can be arranged through your physician. This may be

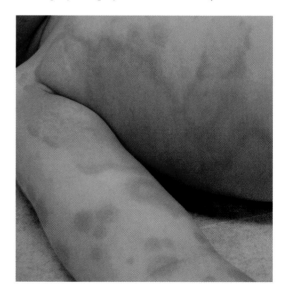

indicated for children who have recurrent hives or develop hives after being introduced to a new food, and especially if hives occur in association with other allergic symptoms, such as swelling of the mouth or difficulty breathing.

Rashes

Many children will at some time develop a pink- to red-colored, smooth or slightly raised rash that appears to come out of the blue. These rashes typically blanch when pressure is applied to the skin. Common causes for such rashes include viral infections (probably the most common cause), reactions to medications, allergies, and fever.

Often, rashes from viral infections appear after other symptoms, such as fever, have already resolved. This is very typical of roseola infections in young toddlers. When a rash occurs as a result of a viral infection, children are not typically bothered by itching or discomfort, and it usually disappears by itself within 24 to 48 hours. If a rash develops after starting a medication, this could signal an allergy, and the medication is usually stopped in consultation with your doctor.

Red flags

You should see a physician if
- The rash looks like bruises or blood spots that do not disappear with pressure (this can be a sign of a more serious infection or blood abnormality)
- Your child is acting unwell
- The rash persists for more than several days

Eczema

Eczema, also known as atopic dermatitis, is one of the most common rashes, affecting up to 15% of children. This rash consists of patches of red, raised, dry, scaly, and itchy skin.

Treatments

Eczema cannot be cured or prevented, but you can take effective measures to manage the symptoms. Irritants to the skin — harsh soaps, bleaches, fabric softener, bubble baths, wool clothing — should be avoided, while gentle soaps for infants, such as Baby Dove, and bath moisturizers, such as Aveeno, are helpful. After you pat your child dry, her skin can be kept lubricated with petroleum jelly or another moisturizer that helps trap

Did You Know?

Onset of eczema

Approximately 60% of people who have eczema develop signs of this condition in the first year of life. While eczema resolves by school age in about 50% of these cases, 25% of individuals continue to be affected into adulthood. It is more prevalent in individuals with a personal or family history of allergic conditions such as asthma, food allergies, and hay fever. In infants, the areas most commonly affected are the face, particularly the cheeks, and outer areas of the knees and elbows. As the child gets older, the insides of the elbows and backs of the knees are most commonly involved.

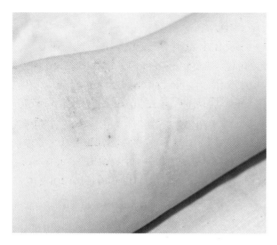

moisture and prevent dryness. Your physician will advise you on the use of topical steroid creams or ointments if there are inflamed areas, and the itchiness may sometimes need to be treated with an oral antihistamine.

Impetigo

Impetigo is a common bacterial infection of the skin, usually caused by bacteria (streptococcus or staphylococcus) that normally live on the skin. Impetigo typically develops when the skin is broken by insect bites and scrapes but can occur on normal skin as well. It is more common in the summertime.

The rash often starts out as a small (less than $\frac{1}{2}$- to $\frac{3}{4}$-inch/1 to 2 cm) bump that most commonly involves the areas around the mouth and nose. The bumps can be itchy and sore, leading to frequent picking and scratching. Impetigo is recognized by the location of the sores and the pus and scabs that develop over the bumps.

Treatment

To resolve, impetigo usually requires an oral antibiotic that is taken for 7 to 10 days. If the infection is mild (one or two small bumps), an antibiotic ointment may be sufficient. Because the sores are itchy, trimming your child's nails can help reduce irritation and local spread of the infection. Impetigo is quite contagious, so avoid sharing washcloths and towels. If the spots are extensive, children should not return to daycare or school for at least 24 hours after starting treatment with the antibiotic.

Chicken pox

This infection, caused by the varicella virus, used to be contracted by almost all children until the chicken pox vaccine was

---

Guide to

Treating chicken pox

The best treatment for chicken pox is immunization against the virus, but if your child develops this condition, the symptoms can be managed effectively.

- Use acetaminophen or ibuprofen for the fever and aches.
- Use an oral antihistamine, such as

Benadryl, and soothing oatmeal baths to relieve the itch.

- Try to keep your toddler's nails short to minimize trauma from scratching.
- Keep an eye on the blisters. If scratched, they can become infected. When infected, the skin around them tends to become red, hot, and swollen. If this occurs, see your health-care provider.

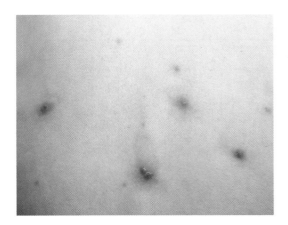

developed. Since immunization programs were introduced, the number of cases has dropped dramatically.

Immunized children can still get chicken pox, but it tends to be very mild, often causing only a few blisters in a relatively well child. In unimmunized children, the typical infection tends to start with a fever, headache, and muscular aches, followed by a very itchy rash. The small water blisters come out in crops over the course of a few days and usually dry up and form scabs within 4 to 5 days.

Chicken pox is very contagious: if one child in the home gets chicken pox, it will usually spread to all the others who live there. Most daycare centers require children to stay at home until the last blisters have scabbed. Children are usually contagious from about 2 days before until about 5 days after the rash has appeared.

Birthmarks

Approximately 20% to 40% of infants and young children have some form of birthmark. Most of these are normal and harmless and often fade over time, though a small number of birthmarks may be a sign of an important medical condition.

Salmon patch

One of the most common birthmarks in infancy is the salmon patch, a flat, pink-red area that is apparent in the newborn period. These typically appear on the neck ("stork bite") or eyelid ("angel's kiss"). The majority of eyelid marks disappear by themselves over the first year of life, while those on the neck often persist for longer.

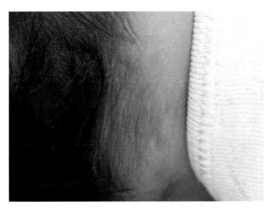

Mongolian spot

These marks are flat, blue-gray areas seen most often on the buttocks and back of darker-skinned babies. They may be mistaken for bruising because of their color. The markings fade and disappear in 95% of individuals by the time they reach school age.

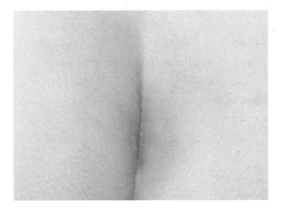

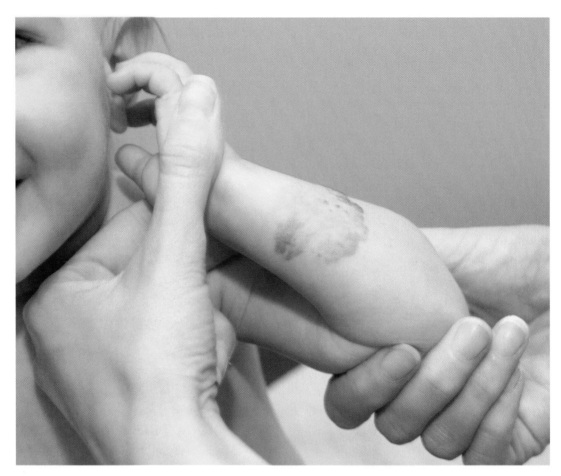

Hemangioma

Hemangiomas are growths of immature blood vessels that can appear as a raised, firm, red area ("strawberry") or a bluish lump that arises from the deeper skin and tissues. These growths are very common, arising most often on the face, scalp, and chest. They are seen more frequently in girls and in infants born prematurely.

Typically, hemangiomas are very small or absent at birth but have a rapid growth phase (out of proportion to that of the infant) during the first 6 months before shrinking over a period of years. About 60% of the growths will disappear by age 6 and 90% by age 9.

While most hemangiomas do not require any treatment, those that are in sensitive areas where they may obscure vision or are prone to bleeding may require some form of treatment, such as steroid medication.

Port wine stain

This mark is made up of mature blood vessels. Unlike hemangiomas, it is clearly present at birth and grows in proportion to the child. The areas are flat and usually red-purple in color, thus the name. The marks are often treated with laser therapy if they are extensive or in cosmetically important areas.

Treating eye problems

In this age group, the two most common problems affecting the eyes are conjunctivitis and squint.

Squint (strabismus)

Crossed eyes — a squint — occurs when both eyes don't look in the same direction. The medical term for this is "strabismus," and it occurs in about 1 in 20 children. One of the eyes may appear to be turning inward (the most common form), outward, up, or down. Newborn infants frequently appear to squint intermittently because babies' vision is immature and they have not developed the ability to coordinate their eye movements. This intermittent crossing of the eyes is normal and usually resolves by about 3 months of age. Squinting that is present after 3 months of age or is present continuously requires attention.

Causes

A squint may be congenital if it is apparent soon after birth; it may be because of a focusing problem in the lens of the eye; or, less commonly, it may be a sign of a more general brain or medical condition.

- A congenital squint runs in families and develops by 6 months of age. Usually, one of the eyes turns inward, which may be caused by an imbalance between the eye muscles.
- Squints due to focusing problems in the lens of the eye (near-sightedness, far-sightedness, and astigmatism) generally appear after 2 years of age.
- A squint that appears suddenly, out of the blue, can, rarely, be caused by a more general brain or medical condition — for example, there may be a growth behind the eye or in the brain that is putting pressure on one of the nerves responsible for moving the eye.

Treatment

If a squint is not treated, there is the potential to develop a "lazy eye" (amblyopia). The developing brain learns to suppress the faulty images coming from the eye that sees poorly and learns to ignore it. After about 7 years of age, the seeing pathways of the brain become fully formed and some visual loss in the involved eye can be permanent.

Treatment for a squint takes place under the direction of an eye doctor (ophthalmologist) and can involve several procedures:

- Prescribing glasses to correct a focusing problem, such as near-sightedness.
- Patching the good eye for periods of time throughout the day to encourage the weaker eye to catch up its visual development. Patching is often prescribed for weeks to months, and if started early in childhood, can prevent a lazy eye from developing.
- Surgery, which often involves changing where the eye muscles attach to the eyeball, may be considered to improve the appearance of the eyes and, in some cases, to improve vision.

Conjunctivitis

Conjunctivitis (pink eye) is an inflammation of the thin membrane that lines the eye and eyelids. It is extremely common in young children and spreads very readily in daycare and school settings. Conjunctivitis usually results from an infection by a virus (most often) or bacteria, and it may be a sign of an allergy. Pink eye typically resolves on its own if caused by a virus, and even in some cases of bacterial conjunctivitis.

Signs and symptoms of conjunctivitis

- Redness and swelling of the conjunctiva (mucous membrane lining the lid and eye)
- Itchiness or burning of the eyes
- Discharge from the eyes (typically yellow or green in bacterial infections, clearer with viruses and allergies)
- Irritation when looking into bright light

Treatment

- Proper handwashing is the best way of preventing these infections.
- Cool compresses can sometimes be soothing.

- Antibiotic eyedrops or ointment are an option if bacterial conjunctivitis is felt to be present (i.e., if there is lots of greenish yellow discharge or the eyelids are really stuck together).
- If an allergy is the cause of the inflammation, cool compresses, as well as an antihistamine (Benadryl, Atarax) and anti-allergy eyedrops, may be helpful.
- Allergic conjunctivitis caused by pollens or exposure to certain animals is best managed by avoiding the trigger, if possible.

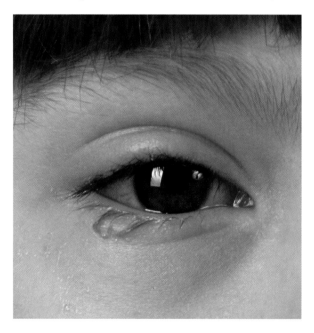

Did You Know?

Herpes eye infection

An eye infection caused by a herpes virus infection requires specific care. This kind of infection is usually signaled by small blisters on the eyelids and around the eye.

Unlike most other eye infections, herpes infection often involves one eye preferentially. If this infection is suspected, the eyes need to be examined by an ophthalmologist.

Dealing with ear, nose, and throat problems

Ear infections are often seen in toddlers and are probably one of the most common reasons for children in this age group to wake up in the middle of the night screaming in pain. You may be also wondering about a number of other problems that affect your toddler's ears, nose and throat.

Hearing loss
Newborn screening

Approximately two to three babies in a thousand will have significant hearing impairment that can be detected during infancy. The known causes include inherited genetic conditions (most common), infections that are acquired during pregnancy, and problems related to prematurity. Newborn screening programs have been established in most communities and have effectively reduced the average age when hearing loss is detected from about 24 months to 2 to 3 months.

While hearing loss is detected in many infants at birth using screening tests, some infants and children will have a delayed onset of hearing loss or develop conditions later in life that can lead to impaired hearing.

Conductive hearing loss

Hearing loss may also develop during childhood. Conductive hearing loss results from interference with sound waves traveling through the outer and middle parts of the ear, such as persistent fluid collection in the middle ear as the result of ear infections.

Sensorineural hearing loss

Sensorineural hearing loss results from a problem in the inner ear, or the nerve that transmits information from the ear to the brain. Meningitis can lead to this type of hearing loss. While many types of conductive hearing loss are temporary, sensorineural hearing loss is generally permanent.

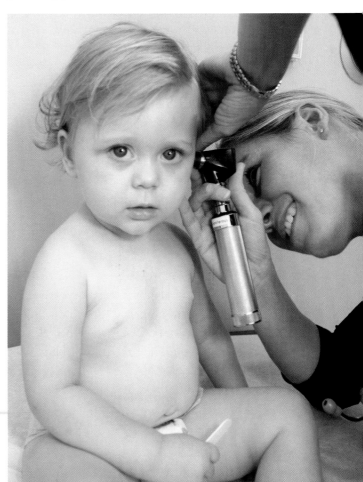

Risk factors

Some of the risk factors for hearing loss that may require further testing include

- Family history of childhood hearing loss
- Persistent fluid in the ear following ear infections
- Bacterial meningitis

Treatment

A child is never too young to have her hearing checked. Early identification of hearing impairment is crucial in allowing timely intervention that promotes normal language development. In general, any concern about hearing or language development should lead to a hearing test, which involves a referral to an ear, nose, and throat specialist and likely an audiologist.

The management of hearing loss depends on the underlying cause and the part of the hearing system that is affected. For example, hearing loss caused by persistent fluid in the middle ear (the area behind the ear drum) is usually managed by the insertion of ear tubes. Many infants with profound hearing loss, who previously would have had significant difficulties with language, have been treated with cochlear implants (small electronic devices that are surgically implanted in the inner ear) that have allowed age-appropriate language development.

Middle ear infection (otitis media)

The most frequent reason for prescribing antibiotics in young children is otitis media, an infection of the middle ear, the small space located behind the eardrum.

Ear infections are most common between 6 months and 2 years of age, and by the time children are 2 to 3 years old, the majority will have had at least one ear infection. Young children are particularly prone to these infections because they catch viruses that cause upper respiratory infections, which can result in a buildup of fluid behind the eardrum.

The eustachian tube is a passage that connects the middle ear to the back of the throat and keeps the middle ear filled with air rather than fluid. Children have smaller and more horizontal eustachian tubes that become easily blocked and cause fluid to be trapped in the middle ear. This fluid becomes a fertile place for bacteria and viruses to multiply and produce an infection. In some children, large adenoids can contribute to ear infections. Signs that large adenoids might be present include snoring and mouth breathing.

Signs and symptoms of an ear infection

Most ear infections follow a common cold. Some signs that an ear infection is present include fever, pain, and ear rubbing or pulling. Children with ear infections will often have difficulty sleeping and will wake from sleep because the pain is more prominent at night.

Sometimes the pressure buildup behind the eardrum from the infected fluid causes a perforation (hole) in the drum, and fluid may be visibly draining out of the ear canal. This often leads to the child's feeling better because the pressure is relieved. The hole in the eardrum usually heals well on its own.

The diagnosis of an ear infection is confirmed by your doctor using an otoscope to look in the ear and examine the eardrum, looking for redness, swelling, or a perforation. Ear infections cannot be accurately diagnosed without a good look in the ear, and even then it can sometimes be difficult if the toddler is uncooperative and has a narrow ear canal or if the canal is obstructed with a lot of ear wax.

Red flags

Rarely, some children have a persistent buildup of fluid that can interfere with hearing. If fluid buildup is present for more than a few months, your doctor might discuss putting tiny ventilating tubes in the eardrums, a simple operation done by an ear, nose, and throat surgeon. This brief procedure is usually done as day surgery. Ventilating tubes may be inserted if infections keep recurring.

Treatment

Symptoms cased by an ear infection typically resolve within a few days without any specific treatment. However, in younger children and in persistent cases, treatment may be recommended.

- **Antibiotics:** In children younger than 2 years of age, or if the signs of the ear infection persist beyond 2 to 3 days, antibiotics are typically used. Fluid in the middle ear often takes weeks to drain, but it usually does occur by itself and does not require prolonged antibiotic treatment if there are no symptoms of an active infection.
- **Analgesics:** Medications for pain and fever are very helpful in keeping your child comfortable and should be used if your toddler appears uncomfortable. Options include acetaminophen (e.g., Tylenol, Tempra) or ibuprofen (e.g., Advil, Motrin).

Ear canal infection (otitis externa)

Otitis externa is an infection of the ear canal, the passage that leads from the outer ear to the eardrum. It is often called swimmer's ear because swimming is a risk factor for infection. Water in the ear irritates the ear canal and allows bacteria and fungi to flourish, potentially causing infection. It is more often associated with swimming in fresh water, particularly in the warm months when bacteria counts in lakes are typically highest. Otitis externa, however, can occur without swimming, after repeated irritation of the ear canal from using cotton swabs to try and remove wax (which is a 'no-no').

Signs and symptoms of ear canal infection

- Painful, red, swollen ear canal. This may not be visible without the use of an otoscope.
- Pain is typically aggravated by touching or moving the outer ear and may be worse when chewing.
- Discharge from the ear.
- Children might complain about their ear being "plugged."
- Fever is not usually present.

Treatment

Treatment of otitis externa involves prescription antibiotic drops in the ear, usually for 3 to 7 days. Measures that can reduce the chances of developing otitis externa include drying the ears well after swimming, avoiding earplugs if possible, and avoiding repeated and vigorous use of cotton swabs. For some children prone to swimmer's ear, cleaning the ears with rubbing alcohol or a mixture of equal parts white vinegar and water after swimming may be helpful.

Nosebleeds

Nosebleeds are very common in children. While the sight can be alarming and many caregivers become concerned that their child might have a bleeding problem, the majority of nosebleeds are caused by dryness of the nasal passages and nose rubbing and picking. Children with nasal allergies also frequently have nosebleeds because the nasal lining becomes inflamed and more fragile.

Prevention

Because dryness of the nasal passages is a common factor, particularly during the winter months, try to add humidity to the air. Using a humidifier in the room at night and applying a small amount of petroleum jelly (Vaseline) one or two times a day to the center wall inside the nose can help relieve dryness and irritation. If nasal allergies are present (see the discussion of hay fever, or allergic rhinitis, on page 389), treating the allergic symptoms is often helpful.

Stop nosebleeds

- Help your child sit up and lean forward to avoid swallowing blood.
- Provide a basin and cloth so your child can spit out blood that is draining into the throat. Swallowed blood is irritating to the stomach and not infrequently leads to vomiting.
- Tightly pinch the soft parts of the nose together and continue applying firm pressure for about 10 minutes.

- Do not squeeze the hard parts of the nose or apply ice packs or cold cloths to nose or forehead. These remedies are not effective.
- If bleeding is persistent, see your health-care provider.

Snoring

About 10% of preschool-age children snore. Most of these children are well, without any symptoms of illness.

Many children will snore transiently during colds or nasal allergy season, but it is estimated that about 2% of children have obstructive sleep apnea, which can have significant behavioral and health effects.

Signs and symptoms of obstructive sleep apnea

Snoring is likely to be a problem only if it is there all the time. Signs and symptoms that identify whether a preschooler's snoring may be caused by obstructive sleep apnea include

- Disrupted sleep with pauses, gasps, or snorting
- Restless sleeping
- Mouth breathing and nasal speech
- Excessive daytime sleepiness or inattention
- Poor growth or being overweight

Treatment

For children who snore because of nasal allergies, treatment is available (see the discussion of hay fever, or allergic rhinitis, on page 389).

If you have any concerns about persistent snoring with some of the signs and symptoms of sleep apnea, you should discuss them with your physician. Sleep apnea may be quite difficult to diagnose because disrupted sleep may be subtle. Your doctor might refer your child to an ear, nose, and throat surgeon or pulmonologist. Sometimes, a more sophisticated test of sleeping called an overnight sleep study is performed. This procedure combines video- and audiotaping of sleep with continuous monitoring measurements of breathing and depth of sleep.

Removing the tonsils and adenoids, if they are enlarged, may help some children.

Did You Know?

Enterovirus infection

Hand, foot, and mouth disease (enterovirus infection) is caused by a virus that can lead to sore throat and painful mouth sores that look like small blisters in young children. Despite its name, most children only get mouth sores from these viral infections, without necessarily getting the skin blisters on their hands and feet.

Sore throat (pharyngitis)

A sore throat (pharyngitis) is a very frequent complaint among toddlers. They may not complain specifically about their throat but may instead refuse to eat or drink because of throat pain.

Most sore throats are caused by self-resolving viral infections and generally last for about 3 to 4 days. If your child has a runny nose, nasal congestion, or cough, you can be fairly comfortable that the sore throat is the result of a viral infection, and if she is otherwise well, no further testing or visit to the doctor is usually necessary. Acetaminophen or ibuprofen are helpful in relieving discomfort, but throat sprays, lozenges, and over-the-counter cough and cold remedies are generally not helpful and may cause serious side effects in young children.

Guide to

Managing hay fever

AVOIDANCE

Because hay fever is generally a lifelong condition that tends to recur every season, avoidance of an allergen is the best prevention, but complete avoidance of pollen is practically impossible. Some ways to reduce the amount of exposure include

- Avoiding prolonged outdoor activities during times of high pollen counts
- Avoiding fresh-cut grass
- Washing hands and eyes after outdoor play and after playing with pets that may have lots of pollen on their fur

MEDICATIONS

For more persistent and troublesome symptoms, use antihistamine syrups and steroid nasal sprays. Oral antihistamines are available without prescription at drugstores and typically contain diphenhydramine (Benadryl). The main side effect is drowsiness. For children over the age of 6 years, there are prescription antihistamines that are less sedating. Nasal sprays containing a steroid are available by prescription and are particularly effective for nasal stuffiness because they decrease the swelling in the nasal passages.

Strep throat

If your child has a persistent sore throat in the presence of fever, particularly without a cold, strep throat is a possibility. By about 3 years of age, streptococcal bacterial infections (strep throat) become more common, accounting for about 10% of throat infections in children.

It can be impossible to distinguish strep throat from viral throat infections just by looking at the throat, so it is recommended that a throat swab or rapid strep test be done to confirm the diagnosis before antibiotics are prescribed. Other signs that may suggest a strep infection include a rash and stomach pain.

Red flags

Some throat infections are serious and require immediate attention. Your child should be seen immediately if she is

- Drooling or cannot swallow
- Having difficulty with breathing
- Lethargic or acting very unwell

Hay fever (allergic rhinitis)

Allergic rhinitis (hay fever) is very common, affecting nearly 20% of children. While hay fever is not a dangerous condition, it can cause discomfort and poor sleep for your child and for you.

Symptoms include watery and itchy eyes, nasal congestion, sneezing, and sore throat. These symptoms result from an allergic reaction of the nose and sinuses to an allergen in the air. When nasal passages become inflamed, nosebleeds may also occur.

Common allergens include pollen from trees (typically worst in the spring), grasses (summer), and weeds (fall). Ragweed pollen is the most common allergen. Less commonly, rhinitis can be a year-round symptom from indoor allergens, such as animal dander or mold.

Managing chest and breathing problems

Unless we breathe adequate oxygen into our lungs, the body cannot function. Toddlers are prone to a number of common respiratory problems, including asthma, croup, and chest infections (pneumonias). While the majority of these episodes are mild and easy to manage, it is important to know when to seek help.

Wheezing and asthma

Wheezing is a whistling or sighing noise made by air passing through narrowed small air passages in the lungs. Although usually detected by a stethoscope, wheezing may sometimes be heard by the unaided ear. Wheezing should be differentiated from the noises made by congested nasal passages that occur with colds. Wheezing is typically heard when breathing out (exhaling), while nasal congestion usually leads to snoring or noisy breathing while breathing in (inhaling). Wheezing is also often accompanied by more rapid and labored breathing than usual, which is not generally the case with nasal congestion.

Causes

In young children, wheezing is most often a reaction to respiratory viruses that are most prevalent during the fall and winter. Many infants and young toddlers will have a single episode of wheezing that doesn't recur. Some other children will develop wheezing with cold viruses but are well between episodes and tend to outgrow their tendency to wheeze as they become older.

Signs and symptoms of asthma

- Colds that tend to spread to the chest, with coughing, wheezing, and labored breathing
- Nighttime cough
- Coughing with exercise or in cold weather
- Allergic symptoms, such as environmental allergies, eczema, or hay fever
- Family history of asthma or allergic symptoms

Red flags

Your child needs to be seen by a physician if there are signs of breathing difficulty, such as

- Rapid breathing
- Visible use of the muscles to breathe (e.g., sucking in between the ribs)
- Anxious appearance
- Difficulty speaking

Treatment

Many children with asthma outgrow their symptoms. And while there is no cure, effective control of symptoms is achievable. Many individuals with asthma have been able to compete in the Olympics and at the highest level in all sports. Reducing the exposure to triggers, especially cigarette smoke, and using anti-inflammatory medications correctly is the best way to control symptoms.

Managing asthma

ASTHMA TRIGGERS

Avoid, if possible, the following common triggers for asthma:

- Cold viruses
- Secondhand smoke
- Allergens (e.g., pet dander and molds)
- Wood-burning stoves

MEDICATIONS

If wheezing is felt to be related to asthma or is recurrent and persistent, your physician may prescribe medication. Any child using a puffer will require a spacer device, such as an AeroChamber, with an appropriately sized mask or mouthpiece. This ensures adequate delivery of the medication into the lungs.

- **Bronchodilators:** Bronchodilator puffers contain medications used to treat symptoms immediately. A bronchodilator may be administered through a puffer and spacer device or a nebulizer to reverse the muscle spasm causing obstruction to airflow. They

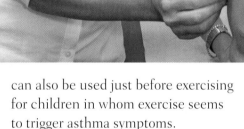

can also be used just before exercising for children in whom exercise seems to trigger asthma symptoms.

- **Steroids:** A steroid medication in an inhaled or oral form to reduce inflammation of the airways may be indicated. The puffer (inhaler) is mainly used for prevention, but the oral (liquid or pill) form is often used for acute asthma attacks. The concept is similar to brushing your teeth *every* day to prevent cavities. Your child may need to use these "preventers" on a daily basis to prevent the onset of

Did You Know?

Asthma

Repeated episodes of wheezing, particularly if symptoms tend to be persistent and recurrent, are often a sign of asthma. Asthma affects up to 10% to 15% of children, making it one of the most prevalent childhood conditions. Less common causes of wheezing include reflux of stomach contents up the gullet, with spillage into the lungs, and choking on an object that becomes stuck in the airway.

an asthma attack when exposed to various triggers.

- **Leukotriene antagonists:** Newer medications include the group of leukotriene antagonists, which are given by mouth, but are used mainly in older children.

Coughs

All children will develop coughs from time to time. A cold will often lead to coughing for 7 to 10 days before resolving. Some children, however, will have coughing that is much more persistent or frequent.

The most common causes of persistent or frequent coughing are repeated viral infections, particularly with young children in daycare, and asthma. Whooping cough (pertussis) can lead to fits of coughing that can be present for months before going away and can occur even in children who have been immunized. Toddlers who develop coughing without any cold symptoms may have choked on something that is now blocking the airway. This can occasionally lead to coughing even if your child has not had a witnessed episode of choking.

Red flags

You should speak to your physician about your child's coughing if

- She is coughing frequently at night or with active play (consider asthma)
- The coughing comes in spasms, especially if there is a whooping sound when breathing in (consider whooping cough)
- You are concerned that she might have choked on something (consider aspiration of a foreign body)
- You have concerns about her growth or energy level (consider an immune problem)
- She is otherwise unwell (consider pneumonia)

Croup

Many parents will experience the frightening experience of having their toddler suddenly develop a loud, barking, seal-like cough, often appearing in the middle of the night after a few days of cold symptoms. This is croup, a common condition usually caused by a viral infection that occurs most frequently in the fall months. The virus causes inflammation and swelling in the voice box and windpipe (larynx and trachea), leading to the characteristic hoarse, barking cough and sometimes to noisy and labored breathing.

Mild croup

While the noisy cough can be alarming, if your child is otherwise breathing comfortably and quietly between bouts of coughing and is swallowing normally, the croup is classified as mild. Simple measures, such as bringing the child into a steamy bathroom or outside into the cool air, may be helpful.

Serious croup

A child with any of the following symptoms, however, needs to be seen immediately by a physician:

- Harsh and high-pitched noise heard mostly when inhaling (called stridor)
- Anxious appearance
- Difficulty swallowing
- Obvious increase in effort to breathe, such as visible use of the chest muscles

Treatment

Inhaled epinephrine to reduce the swelling in the windpipe may be required. A dose of oral steroid medication may also be given to help reduce the inflammation. Most children recover quickly, but loud coughing can persist for days.

Pneumonia

Pneumonia is an infection of the air sacs in the lungs. It is common in young children but should be differentiated from a cold. Cold viruses cause nasal congestion and subsequent noisy breathing, cough, and fever but should not cause breathing difficulty. An X-ray is often done to confirm the presence and assess the extent of the pneumonia. In a clinic or office setting, a physician or nurse can check the oxygen level in the blood by using a sensor that is applied to a finger or toe.

Signs and symptoms of pneumonia

If these signs are present, be sure to consult your physician:

- Rapid breathing
- Visible use of the muscles to breathe
- Ill appearance
- Persistent fever
- Chest or sometimes tummy pain

Viral pneumonia

The majority of cases of pneumonia in toddlers are due to viral infections. The infection typically resolves on its own, but the cough can persist for up to a few weeks. Antibiotics are not helpful in the treatment of these viral pneumonias.

Bacterial pneumonia

It can be very difficult to distinguish viral from bacterial pneumonia. Antibiotics are often prescribed when a bacterial pneumonia is diagnosed based on the toddler looking unwell, with a high fever and abnormal sounds detected by listening to the chest with a stethoscope, or based on abnormal findings on a chest X-ray. Children can be expected to improve after taking an antibiotic for 24 to 48 hours.

Treatment

Most children with pneumonia can be cared for at home. Acetaminophen or ibuprofen helps relieve discomfort from pain and fever. However, cough suppressants and decongestants are not helpful; indeed, they are potentially harmful in treating pneumonia (see the discussion of these hazards on page 370). On occasion, toddlers may be ill enough to require hospitalization if oxygen is needed, if they cannot tolerate an oral antibiotic, or if they appear very unwell.

Treating heart conditions

Some babies are born with an inherited heart problem; for example, a hole in the heart. These conditions are usually identified in the first year of life. With the exception of this group, heart problems are unusual in this age category.

Heart murmur

"Heart murmur" is a worrisome term for many parents, but having a heart murmur does *not* necessarily mean your child has a heart disease. A murmur is simply a sound produced by blood flowing through the chambers and valves of the heart. This sound can be heard when listening to the heart using a stethoscope.

In fact, up to 50% of children may have a heart murmur during childhood, and in only a small fraction is a murmur a sign of heart disease. The rest are called innocent or functional heart murmurs. They may be accentuated or first heard when your toddler is ill and her heart is beating faster because of fever, pain, or anxiety. Sometimes it may be difficult to tell for certain by listening that a murmur is innocent, and your doctor might decide to investigate further with an electrocardiogram, heart ultrasound (echocardiogram), or referral to a pediatric cardiologist.

Kawasaki disease

While most people associate the name Kawasaki with high-performance motorcycles, Kawasaki disease is a relatively common condition in young children, affecting about 1 in 1,000 toddlers. It is more common in children of Asian ancestry but affects all ethnic groups.

While the cause is not known, the condition results in a characteristic cluster of symptoms, including prolonged and persistent fever (for 5 or more days), skin rash, reddened eyes, dry and red cracked lips and tongue, red and swollen hands and feet, and enlarged lymph nodes in the neck. Young children are usually particularly irritable and cranky. The inflammation can also affect the blood vessels of the heart.

There is no single reliable test to diagnose Kawasaki disease. Other conditions, such as viral infections, an infected lymph node in the neck, or allergic reactions, are usually thought of early on in the course of the illness. But Kawasaki disease should be at least kept in mind anytime a fever persists for more than 3 to 4 days and is accompanied by some of the other associated signs.

Fortunately, effective treatment is available. This involves being admitted to hospital for a few days of treatment with gamma globulin (an intravenous blood product) and Aspirin.

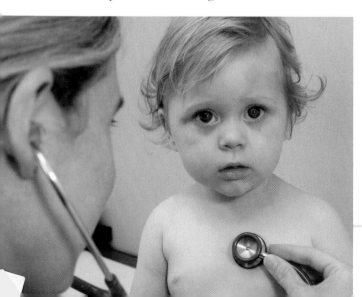

Taking care of stomach conditions

For some reason, as parents, we are often preoccupied with the bowel habits of our toddlers. Too infrequent stooling (constipation) or too frequent stooling (diarrhea), as well as tummy aches, are a common complaint among toddlers.

Constipation

Constipation is an extremely common issue in children, especially toddlers. There is a wide variation in the frequency of passing stools. Some children have three stools a day, while others have three stools a week. Both patterns may be normal.

Stools that are hard in texture, difficult to pass, and usually less frequent are typical of constipation. This can lead to stomach pain, decreased appetite, and bleeding from the rectum caused by small tears while passing hard stools, leaving bright red blood on the surface of the hard stool and on the toilet paper.

Long-standing constipation can make toilet training more difficult, because the fear of passing painful stools leads to withholding of stool, setting up a cycle of worsening constipation and sometimes even soiling.

Causes

In toddlers, the most important factor is usually a diet that is low in fiber and fluids. Fiber is found in grains, fruits, and vegetables. Constipation often begins when the change is made from breast milk and formula to cow's milk and when switching from baby food to solid food.

Ignoring the urge to have a bowel movement is another factor that can aggravate constipation. Children may not want to interrupt play or ask a teacher to use the toilet, or they may be fearful of public bathrooms. For children who are too busy to use the toilet, encourage them to sit on the toilet for 5 minutes after meals.

Remedies

If constipation is persistent despite adding fiber and water to the diet, there are many products available that can help. Lactulose, a non-absorbable liquid sugar, and mineral oil, which is available as a liquid or jelly spread, are widely available, effective, and don't result in a long-term "dependence." Mineral oil should not be used for children less than 2 years of age or those with swallowing difficulties, because it can cause pneumonia if it goes down the "wrong way."

If constipation is an ongoing problem, speak with your health-care provider about other options.

Diarrhea and vomiting

A self-limited episode — an episode that resolves on its own — of vomiting and diarrhea is common in young children and is usually due to viral intestinal infections

HOW TO
Increase dietary fiber

One of the most important ways to prevent and help manage constipation is to increase the amount of fiber in the diet:

- Serve high-fiber fruits, such as plums, peaches, prunes, apricots, and raisins, with the peel on.
- Add effective and easily hidden sources of fiber, such as wheat germ, to freshly baked goods.
- Try whole-grain breads instead of white bread.

- Provide higher-fiber cereals, such as bran, shredded wheat, whole grain, oatmeal, and granola, rather than refined cereals, such as corn flakes.
- Serve unbuttered, unsalted popcorn as a healthy, high-fiber snack for children older than 3 years.
- Limit cow's milk and juice intake to a combined 16 ounces (500 mL) a day to help encourage the intake of high-fiber foods and water.

(gastroenteritis), most prevalent in the winter and spring. These viruses are hardy, living on tabletops and objects for several days, and are very contagious, spreading easily among children in daycare and among family members. The infection causes fever, vomiting, cramping, loss of appetite, and frequent, watery stools. These symptoms may last several days to a week in most children, although the vomiting and fever usually resolve within 48 hours.

While most episodes can be managed simply at home, these infections can be distressing for families, particularly when several individuals are sick at once, and can lead to significant time away from school and work, with frequent visits to medical centers and emergency departments.

Small amounts of blood in the stool occur infrequently, and large amounts of blood in the stool are very uncommon and suggest a more serious bacterial infection. In these cases, stool will need to be collected for culture by your health-care provider.

Dehydration

The major risk to children from these infections is dehydration — the loss of water and salts from excessive vomiting or diarrhea. While mild dehydration can be managed at home with no change in diet, more significant dehydration can be dangerous and may even need to be treated in a hospital.

Red flags

Children who appear ill or exhibit these signs of dehydration should be seen by a physician:

- Inability to keep offered fluids down
- Lethargy, with a lack of interest in surroundings
- Dry mouth without saliva
- Dry, sunken eyes
- Lack of urine

Rehydration

Children who have persistent vomiting or who are dehydrated should be offered a commercially prepared oral rehydration solution (e.g., Pedialyte, Enfalyte, or Gastrolyte). These are available at most drugstores, and no prescription is required. Rehydration solution should be offered in frequent but small amounts every 10 to 15 minutes, even if vomiting is present.

These solutions tend to have a slightly salty taste, so it's a good idea to pick a flavored variety. Some of them are made into ice pops as well. Other fluids, such as flat soft drinks, juices, tea, rice water, and soup, do not have the appropriate mix of water and salts and should not be used to manage dehydration.

Stomach pains

"Mommy, my tummy is sore" is a common refrain during the toddler years. There are two main types of tummy pain: one is a fairly sudden and short-lived, acute pain; the other is a chronic pain that lasts for days and recurs quite often.

Acute stomach pain

Acute tummy pains are usually related to eating — eating too much, eating too quickly, or simply eating something that disagrees with you. But there are other, sometimes more serious causes:

- **Stomach flu (viral gastroenteritis):** Vomiting and diarrhea will usually be accompanied by painful cramps. Other family members or friends at daycare may also have an upset stomach. The toddler may also have a low-grade fever and feel generally under the weather, with decreased energy and appetite.

- **Constipation:** This condition can certainly cause some abdominal cramps.
- **Food poisoning:** A less common cause, food poisoning usually manifests within hours of eating the offending food. Others who ate the same meal will likely also be complaining!
- **Appendicitis:** Appendicitis usually affects school-age children but can occasionally occur in preschoolers as well. The pain usually starts around the belly button, is sharp and steady, and moves down to the right groin area over a matter of hours. Movement — for example, coughing or jumping — will usually make the pain more intense.
- **Intussusception and volvulus:** Intussusception occurs when a piece of the intestine telescopes into the adjacent piece and gets stuck. The pain is episodic and the stools may look like red currant jelly. Volvulus occurs when the intestine twists on itself, causing severe pain and dark green vomiting.

Chronic stomach pain

Recurrent or chronic tummy pains are more commonly seen in school-age children but can occur at a younger age as well. These pains can have various causes and symptoms.

- **Constipation:** Constipation can cause cramps at any age.
- **Heartburn (gastroesophageal reflux):** This condition can also occur at any age, after eating certain foods, and usually gives a burning sensation in the pit of the stomach that moves up behind the breast bone.

- **Inflammatory bowel disease (IBD):** This condition is usually first seen in teenagers but can occasionally affect preschoolers, in whom it may be associated with bloody diarrhea, poor growth and weight gain, mouth ulcers, and skin rashes.
- **Lactose intolerance:** A small percentage of children are intolerant to lactose sugars, and will get a bloated and gassy, uncomfortable feeling after ingesting dairy products.

Red flags

ACUTE TUMMY PAIN

- Vomiting, with minimal intake and decreased wet diapers and urine production
- Dark green bile or blood in the vomit
- Bloody stools
- Sharp, steady, increasing pain that moves from the belly button to the lower right side of the abdomen

CHRONIC TUMMY PAIN

- Pain that wakes her up in the night
- Pain that is specifically in one part of the abdomen, not generalized
- Chronic diarrhea or vomiting
- Poor growth and weight gain
- Strong family history of ileitis or colitis

Guide to

Treating stomach aches

Most commonly, there will be no clear reason for the child's tummy ache. These cases tend to settle down with time, distraction, and reassurance. However, be alert to these situations:

- If your toddler is constipated, there are a number of interventions you can try (see page 214).
- If you suspect that the cramps are a symptom of gastroenteritis, observe your toddler for signs of dehydration and rehydrate him as necessary (see page 397).
- If you suspect heartburn, avoiding certain foods that seem to exacerbate the pain or using a simple antacid may help.

- If you suspect IBD, seek an expert opinion to diagnose this condition or other disorders that will need specific treatment.
- If you suspect lactose intolerance, try stopping all dairy products for a few days to see if the symptoms settle. If the symptoms improve, consult your health-care provider, who can arrange testing. If lactose intolerance is confirmed, the appropriate enzyme treatment can be started.
- If no cause can be found by your doctor, and your toddler is growing well and not showing red-flag symptoms, reassure him and encourage him to continue with his regular activities as much as possible.

Addressing genitourinary problems

Infection of the bladder and kidneys may not always be easy to diagnose. A genital examination as part of your toddler's general physical examination is important to detect conditions such as undescended testicles in boys and vulvitis or labial adhesions in girls.

Urinary tract infections

Urinary tract infections are one of the most common reasons for antibiotic use in children. After infancy, they are more common in girls than boys — about 2% to 3% of girls will have a urinary tract infection during childhood. They are much less common in boys who are circumcised. These infections are caused by bacteria that normally inhabit the bowel. Bacteria can attach themselves to the urethral opening (the end of the tubular passage through which urine travels out from the bladder) and then travel up into the bladder and urinary tract, where they can multiply and cause infection.

Older children may complain of painful and frequent urination, and you might notice a foul odor to the urine. In young children, however, these symptoms and signs are often absent. Infections in young children might manifest with fever alone. Vomiting, abdominal pain, and irritability can also be present.

Antibiotic treatment

If an infection is present in the urine, antibiotics are required and can usually be given by mouth. If your child is quite ill, vomiting, and not able to tolerate fluids and oral medication, then intravenous antibiotics may be indicated.

Did You Know?

Clean urine sample

Diagnosing a urinary tract infection depends on being able to obtain a clean sample of urine that is examined and sent to the laboratory to see if an infection is present. In children who are toilet trained, voiding into a specimen collection container, after adequate cleaning around the genital area, is practical. In younger children, urine is often obtained by a health-care professional using a catheter that is passed through the urethra to collect urine and then removed. Specimens obtained by urine bags attached to the skin are not reliable in obtaining urine to determine if bacteria are present, because the samples are frequently contaminated with bacteria from the skin.

Further tests

Other investigations are often recommended in young children who regularly develop urinary tract infections. These may include an ultrasound to evaluate the size and structure of the kidneys and urinary tract. Your doctor might also discuss performing a test to determine if vesicoureteral reflux is present.

Vesicoureteral reflux

After urine is made in the kidneys, it flows down tubelike structures called ureters before entering the bladder, where it is stored until emptied through the urethra. Normally, the ureters are designed to prevent urine from flowing backward. Reflux occurs when this mechanism is faulty, allowing urine to move from the bladder backward into the ureter and sometimes all the way up to the kidneys. Reflux is associated with an increased incidence of urinary tract infections — approximately 25% of toddlers who have a urine infection have reflux.

Diagnosis

Vesicoureteral reflux is most commonly diagnosed and assessed with a voiding cystourethrogram (VCUG), a specific X-ray test of the urinary tract. This test involves placing a catheter through the urethra into the bladder and injecting dye through it. X-ray pictures are taken as the bladder is filled and then emptied to check if urine backs up through the ureters (reflux), and, if so, how far, and whether the urinary tract is swollen.

Treatment

Most children with reflux have a mild degree that is typically outgrown by school age. Your doctor should discuss the relative benefits and drawbacks of using a regular preventive dose of antibiotics to reduce the risk of recurrent urinary tract infections. Higher degrees of reflux are usually managed with preventive antibiotics and, in some children, surgery. In these cases, consultation with a pediatric urologist is recommended.

Undescended testicle

The testes develop inside the abdomen while the baby is inside the womb and normally descend into the scrotum during the last trimester of pregnancy. However, about 3% of boys born after a full-term pregnancy have a testicle that has not come down into the scrotum, while approximately 30% of premature boys have this problem. Most undescended testicles come down into the scrotum over the first several months of life, but about 1 in 150 boys has a testicle that remains undescended.

Did You Know?

Complications of an undescended testicle

Examination of your son's scrotum is an important part of routine physical examinations. The potential problems with an undescended testicle can include reduced sperm production and future infertility; increased risk of testicular cancer; twisting of the testis, causing loss of its blood supply; and the adverse psychological effects of appearing different with an empty or half-empty scrotum. Changes inside the testicle and their adverse effects on sperm development can be seen as early as 6 months of age. The risk of developing a tumor of the testicle is up to 10 times greater in males who have an undescended testis. This risk does not change with bringing the testis down into the scrotum, but it makes examination and detection of any mass easier.

This condition must be differentiated from a retractile testicle, which can appear undescended because of a reflex, usually from exposure to cold temperature or touch, that causes the testis to pull up from the scrotum. In these cases, the testis can easily be manipulated back down into the scrotum. This is normal.

Most true undescended testicles can be felt by your doctor higher up in the groin area. In 10% to 20% of cases, both sides are affected. If one or both of the testicles can't be felt by your health-care provider, an ultrasound is usually done to check for the presence of the testicles higher up inside the abdomen.

Treatment

If an undescended testicle has not come down into the scrotum by about 6 months of age, it is unlikely to spontaneously descend. The testis can usually be brought down into the scrotum with a simple outpatient surgical procedure (orchiopexy), which is usually performed between 9 and 15 months of age. Hormonal treatment has been tried but is generally not very successful.

Vaginal discharge

Redness, discomfort, and itching of the external genitalia are common in young girls. Known as primary vulvitis, this condition usually occurs because, prior to puberty, the lining of the genitalia is relatively thin and prone to irritation from feces and other irritants that can lead to discomfort and pain when urinating. Vulvitis is caused by a number of factors, including suboptimal hygiene (e.g., wiping from back to front after going to the toilet), chemical irritation by scented soaps or bubble bath preparations, and bacteria normally present on the body.

Differential diagnosis

Your daughter's reaction to vulvitis should not be confused with masturbation, pinworms, or yeast infections. Masturbation is a normal behavior in young girls (see pages 242–243). On the other hand, irritation around the anus can be caused by a number of different infections, but the most common is pinworms.

A large amount of discharge from the vagina does not usually occur with vulvitis alone and may indicate inflammation of the vagina due to a bacterial infection or the presence of a foreign object.

While yeast infection occurs commonly in very young infants, this infection is uncommon in older girls before puberty. Yeasts generally attach to genital lining that has been estrogenized, which only really happens at puberty.

Managing vulvitis

- Use oatmeal or bicarbonate of soda baths, which help soothe the inflamed area. Also use a zinc barrier cream.
- Pay close attention to hygiene, making sure that your daughter wipes from front to back after using the toilet.
- Avoid scented soaps and bubble baths.
- Avoid tight synthetic underwear.
- See your physician if the genital area is very red and inflamed or significant vaginal discharge is present. The doctor might prescribe a local steroid ointment. Severe pain and redness can be a sign of a bacterial infection (from streptococci, which also cause streptococcal throat infections). Swabs may be done to look for these bacteria, and oral antibiotics are usually prescribed.

Labial adhesions

Before puberty, the labia (external genitalia) are not affected by estrogen, so they remain thin and are more susceptible to irritation. Labial adhesions occur when the labia minora (the inner, thinner labia) become irritated and stick together in the middle. Irritation of the vulva, with associated redness, itching, and scratch marks, may be present as well. Predisposing factors are vulvitis and various irritants, such as scented soaps and bubble bath preparations.

Sometimes, labial adhesions may be mistaken for a hymen that does not have a normal opening. When labial adhesions are present, however, the urethra (the opening through which urine is passed) is difficult to see, whereas it is easy to see in children with an intact hymen.

Treatment

Often, no specific treatment is needed, beyond paying attention to hygiene, avoiding irritants and tight underwear, and regularly airing the area between diaper changes. If more than 75% of the labia minora are adhering to each other, your physician may prescribe an estrogen cream to apply to the area of attachment. Using a zinc barrier cream or petroleum jelly (Vaseline) once separation occurs is important to prevent recurrences.

Managing neurological conditions

Conditions affecting the brain are very worrisome for parents of young children. With such a wide range of normal variation in child development in the early years, these are often difficult to diagnose. Here is some information you may find helpful in this regard.

Autism

Due to considerable publicity over the past few years, you may well have heard a great deal about autism. Autism is a disorder of abnormal brain development, for which there is increasing evidence of a genetic basis, and it is part of a spectrum, known as autism spectrum disorder (ASD). ASD comprises autism, pervasive developmental disorder (not otherwise specified), and Asperger syndrome. These neurobehavioral disorders are characterized by impairments in socialization and communication skills and by stereotypic (repetitive) behavior patterns.

While a diagnosis of ASD is usually not made before the toddler years, there are early, "pre-speech" signs of this condition. In retrospect, many parents of children with ASD recognize that, as babies, their little ones did indeed demonstrate developmental differences from other children. If parents and health-care providers recognize these symptoms early on, a more timely diagnosis can be made and appropriate therapy can be implemented that much sooner.

Signs and symptoms of ASD

Because ASD is a spectrum, it may look very different from one child to the next. The following lists provide a few examples of the disordered behavior typical of children diagnosed with ASD. Many toddlers may exhibit a couple of these behaviors, but the more of them that are present, the more important it will be to obtain advice from your health-care practitioner.

Did You Know?

Prevalence of ASD

ASD affects approximately 27.5 in 10,000 children, though some estimates put it as high as 1 in 150. This prevalence has increased over time, though it isn't clear whether the disorder is truly becoming more common or whether the numbers appear higher due to a broader definition of autism and an increase in awareness of ASD symptoms among parents and health-care professionals.

Did You Know?

Autism and vaccines

There has been conjecture that vaccines are associated with the onset of autism. There is no evidence to support this. This concern dates back to a 1998 report, based on parental accounts of eight children, which linked the measles-mumps-rubella (MMR) vaccine to a form of ASD. However, since then, several large, population-based studies have failed to show any association between MMR and autism, and laboratory-based studies have not found any biological link. Subsequently, 10 of the 13 authors of that 1998 report have retracted their original interpretation.

A second vaccine-related concern has been raised in regard to thimerosal, a mercury-containing compound used as a preservative in vaccines. The evidence regarding thimerosal has been reviewed by experts, and no scientific evidence has been found for an association between thimerosal-containing vaccines and ASD.

SOCIALIZATION
- Exhibits poor eye contact
- Does not respond to facial expressions (e.g., a parent's smile)
- Does not point to objects or show objects to share interest
- Has difficulty making friends

COMMUNICATION
- Does not respond to her name, but does respond to sounds, such as a car horn
- Has trouble starting and continuing a conversation
- Does not use toys for their appropriate use in pretend play
- May lose previously achieved language milestones

BEHAVIOR
- Stereotypic behavior, such as rocking backward and forward or flapping hands
- Plays with parts of a toy (e.g., spinning the wheels of a truck) instead of the whole toy
- Likes routines, rituals, and order
- Does not cry if in pain

ASD Screening

By asking questions about your toddler's developmental milestones, health-care providers screen children for ASD at their 18-month and 2-year checkups. A formal diagnosis of ASD is made by a specialist in child development, but appropriate therapy can often be initiated while you're waiting for this referral.

Red flags

Not all children with these features will turn out to have autism, but they are indications for immediate referral to a specialist:
- No babbling or pointing or other gestures by 12 months
- No single words by 16 months
- No two-word spontaneous phrases by 24 months
- Repetitive behaviors
- Loss of language or social skills at any age

Treatment

Unfortunately, there is no cure for autism. While it is a lifelong disorder, children with ASD can progress developmentally and learn new skills, particularly when appropriate therapy is in place. Since ASD is a spectrum, the specific therapy for each child will be different. In general terms, there are two main branches of therapy for children with autism: focal behavioral techniques and intensive educational programs.

FOCAL BEHAVIORAL TECHNIQUES

These treatments are designed to target specific behaviors. For example, the goal of therapy may be to decrease self-injurious behavior or to increase eye contact. Sometimes, medication may also help control certain behaviors in children with ASD.

INTENSIVE EDUCATIONAL PROGRAMS

The goal of this therapy is global improvement in a child's symptoms, including an improved long-term outcome. These programs are intensive, costly, and require a significant commitment from parents and caregivers. As such, funding and resources for these programs have become significant public policy issues. Further research is needed to determine which educational program is optimal. However, there is evidence that successful programs should include a minimum of 15 hours a week of structured, individual teaching, family involvement, and ongoing program evaluation and adjustment to tailor the therapy to the individual child's needs.

Headaches

Headaches are probably more common in young children than is appreciated, partly because children may have difficulty describing their pain. It is estimated that more than half of all children will have experienced at least an occasional headache by the time they enter school.

Many things can lead to episodes of headache in children, such as hunger, viral infections, and strep throat. Like teenagers, toddlers and preschoolers can suffer from tension headaches and migraines, but preschool children in particular may not experience symptoms that we typically think of with migraines, such as flashing lights, but instead have upset stomachs and vomiting.

If your child is otherwise well, reassurance and simple steps to make her more comfortable are helpful. These may include rest, fluids, and pain medications, such as acetaminophen (Tylenol, Tempra) or ibuprofen (Advil, Motrin).

Red flags

While the majority of headaches in children are due to either self-limited or benign conditions, most parents will worry, at least at some point, that a headache is a sign of a serious condition. Symptoms that indicate a need to see a physician include

- Stiff neck, fever, or ill appearance
- Early morning vomiting
- Disturbed vision, balance, or strength
- Severe or persistent pain, especially in a preschool child

Meningitis

Few words are more frightening to parents than "meningitis," an inflammation or infection of the membranes and fluid surrounding the brain and spinal cord. Fortunately, the most serious forms of meningitis have become far less common in recent years with the introduction of immunizations against some of the most common bacteria responsible for this infection.

Meningitis caused by viruses is more common and generally much less serious than bacterial meningitis and does not usually lead to any long-term health problems. Even with timely antibiotic therapy for bacterial meningitis, brain injury can occur, potentially leading to hearing loss, seizures, visual impairment, and physical and mental handicaps.

Signs and symptoms of meningitis
- Stiff neck and headache
- Fever and ill appearance
- Vomiting

Treatment

Meningitis is diagnosed by performing a lumbar puncture, or spinal tap, to obtain spinal fluid to test for infection.

Viral meningitis resolves on its own without any specific therapy, but antibiotic treatment for bacterial infections may be given initially until the results of the spinal fluid analysis are complete.

Bacterial meningitis, the life-threatening form of this infection, is treated with intravenous antibiotics. But prevention is the most effective treatment. The recently introduced pneumococcal and meningococcal conjugate vaccines, in addition to the Hib (*Haemophilus influenzae* type B) vaccine, are very effective against several of the most common forms of bacterial meningitis.

Seizures

A seizure is an abnormal electrical discharge from somewhere in the brain. Because a seizure can be triggered from almost anywhere in the brain, the signs of a seizure will vary dramatically. Triggers for seizures include fever, injury, and infection.

Kinds of seizures
- Grand mal, or tonic-clonic, seizures involve an obvious loss of consciousness and stiffening or jerking of the limbs. Some seizures are much more subtle and might only manifest with staring spells or confusion.
- Febrile seizures are the most common type in young children (see the discussion of fever on pages 365–368). These are generally benign and disappear as children approach school age.

Diagnosis

Because seizures often occur in an unpredictable pattern and most children who experience them will otherwise appear completely well, the description of the episodes is very important in determining whether a seizure has occurred. Videotaping of the events, if possible, can sometimes be helpful.

Did You Know?

Definition of epilepsy

Epilepsy is defined as recurrent seizures that are not triggered by fever, infection of the brain, or immediate brain injury.

Some types of epilepsy lead to infrequent seizures and may be outgrown, while other types of recurrent seizures are very resistant to treatment and require lifelong medication.

Other conditions can be easily confused with a seizure in children, including breath-holding spells, tics, fainting, vertigo, migraine headaches, and sleep disturbances (restless legs or night terrors).

The most common test used in helping to diagnose seizures is an EEG (electroencephalogram), which measures the electrical activity of the brain by means of electrodes attached to the outside of the scalp. The test is painless but often requires a sedative in young children because movement interferes with the recordings. Depending on the circumstances, a picture of the brain from a CT (computerized tomography) scan or MRI (magnetic resonance imaging) may be requested.

TREATMENT

About half of all children who experience an unprovoked seizure will not experience a second one. Medication is usually only considered after a second seizure occurs. Treatment of seizures will depend on an assessment of the potential risks and benefits of medication — which usually needs to be taken regularly to prevent seizures — for each child.

Treatments for children with epilepsy that is difficult to control using anticonvulsant medications include specialized diets, brain surgery, and surgically implanted nerve stimulators.

ADMINISTERING FIRST AID FOR SEIZURES

- Try to remain calm.
- Leave the child where she is unless she is in danger.
- Remove objects that can cause injury.
- Do not put objects or your hand in the child's mouth. She will not "choke" on her tongue during a seizure.
- Do not attempt to remove food from the child's mouth. This can push it in deeper.
- Turn her on her side. Vomiting can occur, and this maneuver can help avoid choking.
- Never leave a child with a seizure disorder unsupervised while she is bathing or swimming.

Cerebral palsy

"Cerebral palsy" (CP) is a term used to describe children with a wide range of abnormalities, including abnormal muscle control that results from an injury or malformation of the brain as it is developing. CP may be caused by a host of conditions, including genetic events before or during pregnancy, infections acquired by the fetus in the womb, extreme prematurity, head trauma, meningitis, and strokes. In many children, the cause of the CP is unknown.

Signs and symptoms of CP

CP can appear as different types of movement problems involving a different number of limbs, from one leg or arm to all four limbs. The most common type is spastic CP, where the muscles are very stiff. This may sometimes make it difficult to change a diaper due to the stiffness of the legs. Other children with CP may be floppy, with low muscle tone. Still others may have jerking or writhing movements.

CP can range in severity from mild to severe. Some, but not all, children with CP may encounter cognitive problems. Difficulties with swallowing, leading to feeding problems, may be an early symptom. Symptoms can often change over the first several years of life, making it difficult to diagnose in the first 6 months.

TREATMENT

There is no cure for cerebral palsy, but many therapies and resources that aim to maximize the potential of each child are available for children and families:

- Early intervention programs are available for toddlers, as are special-education classes for children entering kindergarten.
- Physical and occupational therapists are integral in helping children adapt to their different movements and achieve independence in daily living skills, including feeding, toileting, dressing, and bathing. Therapists are invaluable in adapting seating, vehicles, and homes for children with special needs.
- Depending on the type of disability, orthotics, walkers, and wheelchairs may be necessary to help children and families get around.

Recognizing musculoskeletal conditions

To prevent chronic problems, it is important to be aware of common musculoskeletal complaints encountered in healthy growing toddlers and preschoolers.

Intoeing

As children start to walk, many parents become concerned that they stand or walk with their toes pointed inwards like a pigeon. Commonly referred to as pigeon toe, intoeing is usually caused by tibial torsion, a very common condition in toddlers where the shin bone (tibia) is turned inward toward the big toe. Intoeing often runs in families and may also be influenced by the cramped position of the baby while still inside the womb.

Complications

Intoeing does not cause pain or delayed walking, but some children may tend to trip more frequently as they begin to learn to run. You may notice that the outside part of the shoe gets worn out earlier than expected because it scuffs on the ground.

By school age, and usually earlier, the shin bone in most pigeon-toed toddlers gradually rotates outward as it grows. On rare occasions, the asymmetry is so pronounced that surgery may be considered. Braces and shoe inserts are expensive, often cumbersome, and not helpful. You might also be reassured that adult runners who intoe are often the fastest!

Did You Know?

Flat feet

Flat feet, or fallen arches, can affect one or both feet, and the arch visibly falls when the child stands. While infants normally have flat feet — the arch takes time to form as the ligaments, tendons, and bones in the feet develop and the baby fat disappears — arches should develop by 2 to 3 years of age. In many toddlers, this does not happen, but fallen arches are not usually a cause for any concern. Some older children and adults may experience foot or ankle discomfort with vigorous exercise, but even this is not clear.

Studies have shown that shoe inserts do not correct or reduce the chances of discomfort from flat feet. While some people have suggested that flat feet are less common in societies where wearing open sandals or walking barefoot is more common, specific exercises are also not of any help.

Growing pains

Growing pains are a common but poorly understood symptom that most often affects the calf or shin area. This condition typically affects children between 3 and 6 years of age rather than older children. Children characteristically complain of pain at night in both legs, sometimes after an active day.

Some children may in fact have restless leg syndrome (RLS), which is another common but often not recognized condition that affects children and adults. This leads to discomfort or a "creepy crawly" feeling associated with an urge to move the legs that may interfere with sleep.

Red flags

Growing pains can continue for several nights a week and last for months before resolving on their own. If any of the following symptoms accompany the leg pain, consult your health-care provider:

- Fever
- Limping
- Swelling
- Redness
- Affects one leg only
- Worse with regular daytime activities
- Increasing in frequency or severity

Treatment

There is no proven treatment for growing pains, though some parents suggest that massaging the legs may help. Pain relief medications, such as acetaminophen or ibuprofen, are sometimes effective. As long as your toddler doesn't show any red-flag signs, you can rest assured — and reassure your child — that the pain is temporary and that she will outgrow it.

Giving medicine to your toddler

As most parents only too readily discover, giving medications to your toddler can be a challenge. It can be doubly difficult if the medication has an unpleasant taste and texture or needs to be given as eye- or eardrops. Don't despair — with a little practice, you can become very proficient in administering medications.

Administering medications
Preparation

- Before giving the medication, carefully check the dosage recommendations on the label and any directions given by your health-care provider or pharmacist.
- Be careful not to confuse units of measure and ingredients. It is very easy to mix up mL and mg, and different formulations of the same medication — for example, acetaminophen (Tylenol and Tempra) or ibuprofen (Advil and Motrin) — may have different strengths and therefore require different dosages.
- Keep in mind that medications for children are based on weight. Take this into account if the product's recommendations are based on age and your child is larger or smaller than average.
- Check the storage directions. Some liquid medications, such as antibiotics, need to be stored in the refrigerator.

Oral liquid medication

Most medications come in oral form, to be given by dropper, syringe, or cup.

- If using a dropper or syringe, direct the tip of the dropper or syringe toward the cheek and slowly squeeze the dropper or press the plunger of the syringe.
- To help prevent gagging, avoid squirting liquid medication at the roof of the mouth or the back of the tongue. Small squirts into the space between the gum and cheek often work best.
- If the medication is vomited within 15 to 30 minutes, it may be appropriate to repeat the dose.
- If your child has problems with the liquid form of a medication, check to see if there is a chewable tablet option. Some medications, such as Tylenol, Advil, and Motrin, come in chewable tablets that some toddlers will swallow more easily.

Eyedrops

- When using eyedrops, first warm the bottle in your hands to avoid discomfort.
- Place your child on her back, resting comfortably.
- Gently pull the lower eyelid down with your thumb, forming a pocket for the drops.

- Do not touch the eye with the dropper.
- For some antibiotic eye medications, an ointment form may be better tolerated, so ask your physician or pharmacist if this is an option.

Eardrops

- When using eardrops, warm the bottle in your hands to avoid discomfort.

- Have your child lie down with the infected ear facing up.
- Gently pull her ear down and back to straighten the ear canal.
- Drop, don't squirt, drops into the ear.
- Keep your child lying down for a minute to prevent the drops from running out.

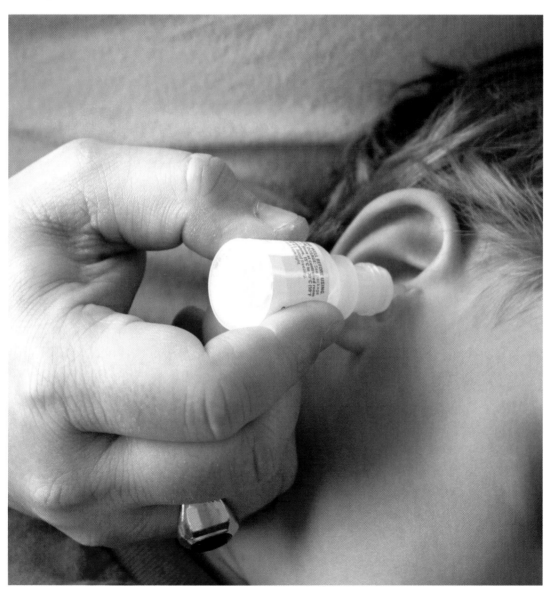

Preparing your child for surgery

A stay in the hospital can be a frightening experience for a young child who might have to deal with potentially uncomfortable procedures, an unfamiliar environment, and separation from family members. Preparing children beforehand for their hospitalization can help them talk about their fears, feel reassured that their parents will still be taking care of them, and feel some degree of control over their experience.

Before hospitalization

Because children under 6 or 7 years of age lack a concrete understanding of time, there is little sense in speaking to them about their surgery more than a few days before going to the hospital. Any further warning period will likely just increase their anxiety. Books and toys can be used to help an imaginative toddler understand what will likely happen. Many books involving favorite cartoon characters are appropriate for this age group. Allowing your child to express how the characters are feeling can be helpful, and demonstrating procedures on a doll or stuffed animal can correct misconceptions. Some children's hospitals offer a tour prior to the scheduled procedure to help your child feel more comfortable on the day she's admitted.

Guide to

Helping your hospitalized child
Once your child is admitted, there is much you can do to comfort him:

- Bring something from home, such as a photograph or favorite toy, to help your child feel more at home.
- Use simple but frank language when explaining procedures. Be honest, and certainly don't say that something won't hurt if it will!
- You know your child best, so make sure to tell your child's health-care providers about ways they can make him feel more relaxed and comfortable.
- Remain calm and try not to show your anxiety. Your child will be looking for his cues from you.

Caring for a child with a chronic illness

The day your child is diagnosed with a chronic illness is an unforgettable event that will change your child's and your family's life indefinitely. Having some tools and strategies at hand to cope with this lifelong challenge may be invaluable in parenting your child.

Diagnosis

Diagnosis of a chronic illness can be long in coming or can come out of the blue as a nasty surprise. Usually, parents are the first to recognize subtle differences in their children's health or behavior. As a parent, you may suspect that something is different about your child and may have already sought medical care for repeated illness. Then again, at a regular checkup, your health-care provider may detect a chronic illness. You may be given the particular name of your child's illness, or your health-care provider may still be searching for a diagnosis that fits your child's symptoms. Regardless, this is now an extremely difficult time, but you can rise to the occasion and help your child and her health-care providers by becoming better informed and cooperating with treatment plans.

Information sources

Once a diagnosis has been established, you can then start to look for disease-specific information. Knowledge is empowering, but where should you begin?

- Start with your health-care providers. They will be able to give you information or provide recommendations on where to go for information. If they have cared for a child with the same or a similar condition, they may be able to provide you with experiential advice. Keep in mind when seeking information that all children are different. Illnesses can present in a multitude of ways, and just because something happened to one child does not mean it will happen to yours.
- Contact health-related organizations. Sources of information can be

Did You Know?

Defining chronic illness

The term "chronic illness" refers to a very broad spectrum of disease. It can be an illness primarily affecting one body system, such as asthma, or many body systems, such as sickle cell anemia. It can affect your child's nervous system and the way he reaches his developmental milestones. A chronic illness may not be permanent, and is certainly not necessarily terminal, but it can last for months or years.

Educating others

If others are to ensure that your child receives the best care possible, then education is crucial. In simple terms, you should tell all your child's daycare workers, nannies, teachers, program providers, and relatives about his illness. They are often very interested, and you can help to dispel any myths they might have. If you feel this information is confidential or it might upset your child, then ask them to be discrete when discussing it around him and others.

child-specific (e.g., the American Academy of Pediatrics) or disease-specific (e.g., the Asthma Society of Canada). These reputable organizations will likely be a good starting point to find reliable and relevant information.

- Explore the Internet, but a word of caution: while this is an excellent place to seek a wide range of information, you also need to be able to separate the useful from the dubious. Try to visit sites that provide broad factual information on your child's illness, then move on to disease-specific sites. Many of the disease-specific sites have more detailed information and parent chat groups that can be very supportive. This is especially true if your child's illness is not very common. These chat groups may even lead to meeting other families and children who have had the same diagnosis as your child. Some families find this a rewarding and helpful experience. You will also inevitably find personal accounts of illness. These will either make you feel very hopeful or very scared. Remember that all children are different — the way in which your child's disease manifests will likely also be different.

Helping your family cope

The diagnosis of a chronic illness is a life-changing event for every member of the family. Immediate family members affected include siblings (who are often overlooked at this time), your partner, and you.

SIBLINGS

With so much attention directed to your sick toddler, a sibling may feel invisible or rejected. You will have to work hard to ensure that this does not happen. Try to involve them in caregiving. Can you involve a sibling by having her decorate a medication schedule? Can she help you with your ill child's journal, for example, by creating a sibling page?

Siblings may also have difficulty explaining things to their friends. They may worry that their friends won't like them anymore or may make fun of them. They may even have their own worries about your ill child — "Will my sister die?" and "Will I get sick too?" Discuss all these things with your children. Talk to them and prepare them to deal with potential situations that may arise. Speak to their teachers at school and let them know what the family situation is like and what they can do to help.

HOW TO
Care for a child with a chronic illness

A chronic illness adds another layer to the already complex and challenging process of parenting. You are now managing your child's illness in addition to common childhood issues. There are many things you can do to try to simplify this process:

1. Stay organized

You will have a multitude of things to remember, and you will need a comprehensive way of doing this. Here are some helpful tips:

- **Create a care plan:** Some health-care providers, in collaboration with you, will create a care plan. The plan outlines your child's medical diagnoses, how to manage emergencies, medication, feeding information, and any other relevant medical information. You should carry it with you at all times. Not all providers have the time or resources to create these documents, but it is worthwhile to inquire if yours does.

- **Keep a journal or notebook:** You will want to keep a journal or notebook of your child's illness. Many children's hospitals have specific templates for such a journal that you may find helpful. Alternatively, you may want to create your own. Document when your child is well and especially when your child is ill. Keep notes on things that concern you. Document symptoms and what you did (e.g., "Fever of 38.9°C at 8:00 a.m. Gave 120 mg of Tylenol at 8:30 a.m."). Share

this information at your next appointment. If an emergency trip to the hospital is needed, this information will be extremely important in the management of your child's acute illness. Do not be afraid to tell one person what another has said — especially if the information is contradictory. You need to ensure that everyone who is caring for your child is aware of the care plan and is working together.

- **Follow a schedule:** Keep a calendar to record all your child's appointments. If possible, arrive early or on time for appointments. This will decrease your stress level and increase the amount of time you will be able to spend with your health-care provider. If you can, try to schedule all your appointments at one location on the same day. Some hospitals may have systems to facilitate coordinating clinic appointments.

2. Be prepared for an emergency

There are situations when you may have to rush your child to the hospital. Be prepared.

- **Post emergency contacts:** Place emergency service telephone numbers by your telephone and program these numbers into speed dial on your land and cellular telephones.

- **Prepare an emergency bag:** Pack an emergency bag with things that you need to take with you. This list should include your care plan and observation notes, your child's medications (which is helpful in case it takes a while to get them in the emergency room or if your provider has questions about dosages), any medical equipment (such as feeding pumps, ventilator, tracheotomy tubes), a change of clothes for you and your child, cash for food, your mobile telephone and relevant telephone numbers, insurance cards, and possibly even pillows for positioning your child comfortably and safely.

3. Advocate for your child

You are your child's strongest advocate, so never be afraid to speak to your child's health-care providers about any issues you may have. Here are some helpful hints when interacting with the health care system:

- **Choose your child's providers:** Find providers that you trust. If you feel at ease asking questions and communicating with these people, it will facilitate collaboration, ultimately benefiting your child. You may form a strong relationship with your child's primary doctor or other providers, such as a social worker, nurse practitioner, or physiotherapist.

- **Write a list of questions:** Before your child's appointments, make sure you write down all the questions you may have. It's easy to forget these when you're being asked many different questions yourself.

- **Ask all your questions:** Even if your health-care provider is very busy or running out the door, make sure you let her know that you need to ask all your questions.

- **Record the answers:** Asking questions is extremely important, but recording the answers is equally important. It is very easy to forget what was said, especially if you're stressed or rushed, or the answers are surprising or shocking.

- **Don't go alone:** Take your partner or a friend to your child's appointments. Friends are always asking how they can help, and this is one way they can be very helpful. This person can remind you about all the questions you wanted to ask and record the answers. It is also useful to have a second person there because he may interpret things differently, providing more useful information. In addition, a second set of hands can be invaluable when your child is bored or fussy, giving you time to talk to your health-care provider.

- **Locate the hospital playroom:** Many children's hospitals have a playroom where your other children can play while you take your child to his appointment.

- **Trust your instincts:** You know your child best, and your intuition is likely right. You will notice subtle things that your health-care provider may not. If you're worried about something, ask about it. No question is stupid and no issue is too small.

4. Support your child

Depending on the age of your child at diagnosis, he may have many questions for you or he may just be learning to talk. Regardless of the developmental stage your child is at, the most important thing you can do for your child is to be a loving, caring parent. Although you will need to take care of your toddler's medical condition, try to make parenting your first priority.

- **Be honest with your child:** When facing a medical procedure, toddlers will typically ask, "Will it hurt?" and "Am I going to die?" One of the ways children learn and cope is by asking questions, so be sure to answer these as simply and honestly as possible. Never lie to your child to make it easier. If he will be getting a needle poke, answer honestly — "Yes, it will hurt, but only for a moment." Remember that a child's receptive language is often much better than his expressive language. Toddlers understand a lot more than we think. Make sure that you're comfortable with your child's diagnosis before you explain it to him. An anxious parent usually results in an anxious child. Explain it in terms he will understand.

- **Create outlets for expression:** You may want to find ways for your child to express his feelings other than by talking. Some children may want to draw pictures or listen to music. Try to continue to involve them with their peers. You may also be able to meet other families who have children with a chronic illness and have your child interact with these children.

- **Treat your child as normally as possible:** The worst thing you can do is to define your child by his illness. Keep his life as normal as possible. Allow him to participate in regular childhood activities, with modifications as needed. Children with a chronic illness still need proper routines, with behavior expectations outlined for them. Routines may need to be modified for them — for example, a child with cerebral palsy may have difficulty picking up toys as fast as other children, but this doesn't mean they should be exempt from doing it. If it's going to take longer, you will need to plan for this.

Did You Know?

Starting school

Aside from the time when your child is first diagnosed and just after his first discharge from hospital, if he was hospitalized, starting school is one of the most stressful events for parents of children who are chronically ill. This may be the first time that your child is separated from you. Before your child starts school, meet with the principal, as well as with your child's teacher. You need to provide them with information, including clear and concise details about your child's illness. Putting this information in a chart makes it easy to use in times of emergency. Try to use simple terminology and avoid too much "medical speak." You may also need to correct any myths they may believe about your child's illness. Also explain how your child should interact with other children. Socialization at school is critically important for your child's development.

PARTNERS

Parents often get so caught up in caring for their child that they forget each other. Support each other and remember to take time, even if it's only a few minutes, to talk to each other. Take proactive measures to ensure that you and your partner are communicating and spending time together. This means accepting help from family and friends to give you both a little respite.

YOURSELF

To take care of your child, you have to take care of yourself! Your needs are often last on the list and are usually neglected, but if you are exhausted, you run the risk of getting sick and, in turn, so does your child. You need to rest and let your body recover from the stress of taking care of your child.

Try to accept help from others. When people ask what they can do to help, let them know what you need. Maybe you don't want them caring for your child, but they could cook dinner or help you do laundry.

Find someone you can talk to. This may be your best friend or your partner. It may be the parent of another child with a chronic illness, or it may be someone who is involved in caring for your child. You will need to discuss issues and frustrations. You need someone to listen to you.

Social and financial support

Social supports for you and your child are essential. You will want to find a local play group or daycare center to promote integration with other children. Community service agencies may be able to help you locate specialized programs. These agencies may also direct you to sources of financial support.

Chronic illness can be costly, placing a significant financial burden on the family. Bills can add up very quickly, and if you don't have a good supplementary insurance plan, you may struggle. This is where a resourceful social worker can help. They may be aware of resources you can access. Speak with other parents and benefit from the research they've already done. They will know who to ask for funding and how to go about getting it.

Complementary and alternative medicine

Recent studies have shown that 20% to 40% of children are using complementary and alternative medicine (CAM) therapies for common acute illnesses and more than 50% of children with chronic illness use these therapies. Given the popularity of CAM, these therapies may have a place in the modern medical treatment of children. Although at this time there is limited conventional scientific research available to validate CAM therapies, investigation is ongoing.

Major kinds of CAM

The United States National Center for Complementary and Alternative Medicine (NCCAM) has classified all CAM therapies into five categories:

Whole medical systems

These systems of care may have a basis in either Western or Eastern medicine. They are holistic models of care that attempt to address the whole person. Examples based on Western medicine include homeopathy and naturopathy, while examples based on Eastern medicine include traditional Chinese medicine and ayurvedic medicine.

Homeopathy is based on the concept that to treat an illness, you use a small, diluted dose of a substance that in larger quantities would cause the patient to have the same symptoms that the illness is causing. The theory is that this will stimulate the body's own healing powers. There are questions about the efficacy of such treatments, as the dosages used are so small; at the same time, the small doses decrease the risks of the treatment.

Naturopathy uses therapies and natural treatments to stimulate the body to self-heal. The naturopathic doctor may use many different or eclectic therapies — for example, herbal medicine, diet adjustment, and acupuncture.

Did You Know?

Definitions

Complementary medicine refers to the use of treatment methods that are not traditional in Western societies in addition to using traditional Western methods — for example, using massage and acetaminophen together.

Alternative medicine refers to the use of treatment methods that are not traditional in Western societies instead of traditional Western medicine — for example, using acupuncture treatments (from traditional Chinese medicine) instead of acetaminophen to treat a headache.

Traditional Chinese medicine (TCM) is based on the principle of harmony and the belief that illness is related to an imbalance in the body's yin and yang complementary vital forces. TCM uses different treatments, including acupuncture, herbal medicine, massage, and manipulation.

Ayurvedic medicine is an ancient system of medicine from India. It involves the body, mind, and spirit and includes different therapies, such as meditation, herbal remedies, and massage.

Mind-body medicine

These CAM therapies focus on the interplay between the mind and body. Examples include hypnosis, meditation, yoga, biofeedback, qigong, and tai chi.

These therapies have minimal side effects, and research has shown that they influence immune, endocrine, and autonomic function. They have also been shown to work well for controlling some forms of pain.

Biologically based practices

These therapies include diet therapy, nutritional supplements (vitamins, minerals, amino acids, pre- and probiotics), and botanical (herbal) therapies. They are used for prevention and treatment of illness.

Manipulative and body-based practices

These therapies are based on movement of one or more body parts and chiropractic, osteopathy, and massage therapy. These therapies are widely used by many individuals and a high level of satisfaction is reported.

Chiropractic focuses on the neuromusculoskeletal system of the body, paying particular attention to the spine, nervous system, and joints. It not only diagnoses and treats certain illnesses, but is also used as preventive therapy.

Osteopathy identifies, via palpation, structural parts of the body that are not moving or flowing well. In the United States, a doctor of osteopathic medicine (DO) is considered a conventional provider of medicine, trained in manual osteopathic practice and in traditional Western medicine. In Canada, an osteopath is not a medical doctor and osteopathy is considered a CAM therapy.

Massage therapy involves a non-invasive manipulation of the soft tissues and joints of the body to improve functioning or prevent deterioration.

Energy medicine

This CAM practice includes biofield therapies such as reiki and therapeutic touch and bio-electromagnetic-based therapies, such as magnetic fields and pulsed fields. These techniques are based on the concept that all humans have an energy that runs through them, which can be manipulated by therapy to improve health. This is one of the most controversial areas of CAM because it is not easily measured by today's scientific standards. That being said, it is very popular and continues to be used frequently.

CAM cautions

There is nothing more important than being an educated consumer. If you are

Did You Know?

Nutritional supplement regulation

Supplements commonly found in your local drugstore or health food store are not regulated in the same way that prescription drugs or over-the-counter medications are, although the United States Department of Agriculture (USDA), the Food and Drug Administration (FDA), and the Natural Health Products Directorate (NHPD) in Canada are in the process of establishing new standards. Drugs are regulated to ensure that they're safe before being put on the market; supplements are regulated for safety after they're put on the market. Drugs are regulated to ensure that they do what they say they will do; supplement manufacturers are not required to substantiate their claims but at the same time cannot make unreasonable claims about what their product can do. Use caution in choosing biologically based therapies that may be appropriate for your children.

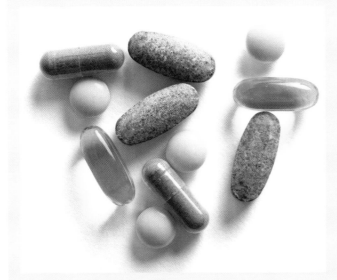

considering a CAM therapy for your child, discuss this with your regular health-care provider to see if she has any insight into current CAM therapies available for the problem. Keep your primary health-care provider in the loop of care.

You may also want to do your own research in the area to determine what therapy is most appropriate and how it works. Be cautious. Anything that sounds too good to be true usually is.

Limited pediatric research

It is important to recognize that your child's body functions differently from yours and that research done in adults is not necessarily applicable to children. Unfortunately, there has been very little good research done in children to this point.

Ingredients

Remember that natural does not necessarily mean safe. Know the ingredients of any supplement you are giving to your child and understand the reason why you are giving it.

Use caution when administering substances from countries outside of North America, because all the ingredients may not necessarily be listed on the package, and occasionally they may contain toxic materials or heavy metals.

Interactions

Some supplements and herbs may interact with traditional medicines, which can be dangerous. If you notice anything unusual, do not hesitate to contact your primary health-care provider.

Internet information

Be cautious about information posted on the Internet. Although the Internet is a great source of medical information, this medium is not without bias and error. Ask yourself these questions as you evaluate a website:

- Who runs the site? Is it a government, a university, or a reputable medical or health-related association? Or is it sponsored by a manufacturer of health products or drugs? The sponsor should be clearly identified.
- What is the purpose of the site? Is it to educate the public or to sell a product? The purpose should be clearly stated.
- What is the basis of the information? Is it based on scientific evidence with clear references? Advice and opinions should be clearly set apart from the science.
- How current is the information? Is it updated and reviewed frequently?

Adapted from the National Center for Complementary and Alternative Medicine (NCCAM), "10 Things to Know about Evaluating Medical Resources on the Web," at http://nccam.nih.gov/health/webresources.

Choosing a CAM practitioner

If you decide that your child would benefit from a particular CAM therapy, do your research to find the most qualified provider. First, ask your regular health-care providers if they have any recommendations. There are also many other places to look. Some CAM providers are licensed practitioners (e.g., chiropractors and massage therapists) and are regulated through a college or professional organization. These organizations may be able to help you find the best provider for your child. Schools that teach CAM therapies may also be able to provide you with guidance. Make sure that the provider you choose is comfortable working with children and has experience specific to kids. Before going to see them, write down any questions or issues you would like to discuss with them and bring this list to the appointment.

Frequently asked questions

As family doctors, pediatricians, and nurse practitioners, we answer many questions from parents. Here are some of the most frequently asked questions. Be sure to ask your health-care providers any other questions that may arise. If they don't have the answers, they will refer you to a colleague who does.

Q: My toddler always complains about feeling sick while in the car. She sometimes even vomits. Is there anything I can do?

A: What you are describing is a quite common complaint known as motion sickness. This tends to occur when the brain receives conflicting information from the eyes, inner ears, and nerves. The child will often experience some queasiness, becoming pale and restless, which is often followed by vomiting. Give her a light snack before the journey. Try to make sure that she looks at things out the window, rather than at books or games. If these suggestions and other distractions don't work, try using an anti-nausea medication, such as Gravol. The most common side effect is usually some drowsiness. Make sure to take some barf bags and an extra set of clothing, just in case!

Q: When I take my child to the doctor for his regular checkup, I'm always worried that he may pick up something from all the sick children in the waiting room. Am I being neurotic?

A: No, this is a reasonable concern because it is impossible to stop children from sharing toys and space while waiting. Some studies have shown that children are no more likely to pick up an infection in a doctor's office than in a daycare center or while playing with their siblings. Nevertheless, you could try for the first appointment of the day or after the lunch break — which means you're more likely to be in and out quickly. If this isn't practical, make sure that your child's immunizations are up to date and that he washes his hands frequently. Believe it or not, handwashing is still the best defense against germs.

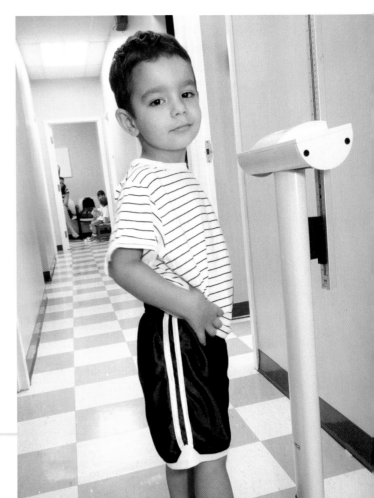

Sam's Diary

April 6 (50 months old)

We sold our house. We're excited about our new home but very sad to leave the house where we got married and had both you and Dani. It's been a great house and we've had lots of fun here. Dad and I hadn't directly said anything to you about the move yet, because it's only happening in August, but today you said, "When are we moving, Mom? I'm tired of our house." You've come with us to look at houses, so presumably you just worked out what is going on. So much for trying to protect you from the stress!

Today you told your teacher that when you're 19 you'll be able to chew bubblegum, walk to school on your own, and — you put both your hands in the air, rubbed them through your hair, and said, "I'll be bald!"

August 4 (54 months old)

While we were away on vacation, you learned to skip. You also sort of learned how to swim! At the beginning of the two weeks you wouldn't go into the water beyond your knees with all the pleading and coaxing in the world, and by the end of the holidays we couldn't get you out of the water! We got you water wings and goggles, and you were jumping into

the water, swimming under the water, and staying in for up to two hours at a time.

You also made friends with a teenage girl, with whom you spent ages in the water. When you gave her a chocolate at the end of the holiday, she was very appreciative.

September 7 (55 months old)

We've had a great summer and tomorrow you start JK! Where has the time gone and how did you grow so fast?

You've been excited about this for a long time and have been playing school games for quite a while now. You are going to love learning! We were reading Dr. Seuss's <u>Hop on Pop</u> at bedtime, and you decided that you wanted to try to read and YOU DID IT! You sounded out the letters and then put them together to make the word. It was such an exciting experience. Your first words after reading were, "I want to tell Judy" — your teacher from last year — "in the morning."

December 10 (58 months old)

It snowed the other day, and you commented that the houses were painted so beautifully in white. These days you're amazing with Dani, often comforting her with words if she's upset or helping her to get her things — shoes, pacifier, etc.

You are thriving at school and just loving it. You often almost forget to say goodbye when I drop you off because you're so excited to get in and see all your friends. It's wonderful to see you so happy.

Sam, you have grown up into this amazing, friendly, kind, warm-hearted, much more independent, happy little man — and Mom and Dad and Dani are completely in love with you! As is everyone else whose life you touch — you really are an incredible little almost-5-year-old. Thanks for being you and for making life such fun. We love you, Sam!!!

Toddler Care Resources

A word about reliable resources

The last decade has witnessed a dramatic transformation in the way people learn about things. The Internet and sophisticated search engines, such as Google and Yahoo, have put vast amounts of information at the disposal of millions of people. Simply pick a topic and hundreds, even thousands, of websites pertaining to a given subject become immediately available. We are now capable of informing just about everyone about pretty well everything.

But there's one catch. People can get misinformation on the Internet just as easily. There is no requirement demanding that websites be screened for accuracy.

Opinion can replace fact. What you read on any subject may or may not be either authoritative or true.

What, then, is a parent seeking advice to do when trying to filter all the available information? Seek answers from websites sponsored by well-respected professional organizations and official government sites. The advice on these websites is carefully researched and written. Even so, trust your instincts: any advice you are given should always make sense to you, regardless of the source.

We have provided here a short list of reliable and comprehensive international resources. However, your child's health-care providers remain your best source of information.

Parenting Corner
American Academy of Pediatrics (AAP)
PO Box 927, Dept C
Elk Grove Village, IL 60009-0927
Tel: 847-434-4000
www.aap.org/parents.html
Authoritative information in an American context, with links to other credible resources.

Caring for Kids
Canadian Paediatric Society (CPS)
2305 St Laurent Boulevard
Ottawa, ON K1G 4J8
Tel: 613-526-9387
www.caringforkids.cps.ca
Authoritative information in a Canadian context, with links to other credible resources.

National Institute of Child Health and Human Development
Bldg 31, Room 2A32
31 Center Drive
Bethesda, MD 20892-2425
www.nichd.nih.gov
Official site of the U.S. government office on children's health.

Canadian Institute of Child Health
Suite 300, 384 Bank Street
Ottawa, ON K2P 1Y4
Tel: 613-230-8838
www.cich.ca
An advocate for children's health in a Canadian context.

About Kids Health
The Hospital for Sick Children
555 University Avenue
Toronto, ON M5G 1X8
www.aboutkidshealth.ca
Comprehensive source of practical
guidelines for baby and child care.

Motherisk
The Hospital for Sick Children
555 University Avenue
Toronto, ON M5G 1X8
Tel: 416-813-6780 or 877-327-4636
www.motherisk.org
A reliable source of evidence-based
information about exposure to drugs and
chemicals during pregnancy and while
breast-feeding.

Child and Family Canada
www.cfc-efc.ca
A collective of more than 50 child health
agencies.

La Leche League International
1400 North Meacham Road
Schaumburg, IL 60173-4840
Tel: 800-LA-LECHE
www.lalecheleague.org
Support for mothers who choose to
breast-feed.

Other Authoritative Sources

IMMUNIZATION
National Advisory Committee on
Immunization (NACI), Public Health
Agency of Canada
www.phac-aspc.gc.ca/naci-ccni
A source of information, official
statements, and updates on vaccines used
in Canada.

NUTRITION
United States Department of Agriculture
www.mypyramid.gov
The USDA's MyPyramid food guide.

Food and Nutrition, Health Canada
www.hc-sc.gc.ca/fn-an/index-eng.php
A webpage called "Food and Nutrition,"
with links to Canada's Food Guide,
information on labeling, and other
resources.

SAFETY
Safe Kids Canada
http://www.safekidscanada.ca
A resource for current safety regulations
and information.

SLEEP
American Academy of Sleep Medicine
(AASM)
www.aasmnet.org
A source of accurate information on sleep
and sleep disorders.

TEETH
American Dental Association
www.ada.org

Canadian Dental Association
www.cda-adc.ca

TOILET TRAINING
*The American Academy of Pediatrics Guide
to Toilet Training* (New York: Bantam,
2003).
A useful book about toilet training.

Acknowledgments

I would not have been able to put this book together without the help of so many individuals. To all of you, I am sincerely grateful and hope that you share my pride in our finished product. This is by no means an exhaustive list, but I would like to specifically mention the contributions of

- My team of authors — Sherri Adams, Carolyn Beck, Stacey Bernstein, Catherine Birken, Sheila Jacobson, Michael Peer, Michelle Shouldice, and Michael Weinstein — many of whom are collaborating with me on a book project for the third or fourth time and probably get nervous when they pick up the telephone and hear my voice on the other end! I think that their expertise, compassion, and dedication comes across in the text they've contributed. Sherri, Carolyn, and Catherine were on maternity leave with their second or third child at the time of writing, so a special thanks for taking the time while balancing a couple of toddlers and a newborn! Although my friend and writing partner, Norman Saunders, passed away before we started on this book, his guidance and mentorship over the years played a major role in preparing me for this project.
- The great team at Robert Rose — Bob Hilderley, Bob Dees, and Marian Jarkovich — and, of course, Kevin Cockburn and Andrew Smith at PageWave Graphics. What a great group of professionals to work with! They have done a masterful job of presenting our material in an attractive, practical, and reader-friendly format.
- My colleagues at Sick Kids — Denis Daneman, the pediatrician-in-chief, Mary Jo Haddad, our CEO, and Ron Laxer, vice president of medical and academic affairs — for their mentorship, encouragement, and total dedication to children's health and the superb Hospital for Sick Children. Thanks to Tiziana Altobelli, my administrative assistant, for putting up with me for the last 10 years; to Susana Andres and Heidi Falckh and their team at Sick Kids Corporate Ventures for their help on the business side; and to Lisa Lipkin from Public Affairs and Michael O'Mahoney and his team at the Sick Kids Foundation for the great job they do, specifically for their help in promoting my books.
- Robert Teteruck and Diogenes Baena from Sick Kids, who did most of the photography for the book, as well as to Andrea Boysen, who also contributed some photographs. Thanks to all the photographic models, who for the most part were the offspring of the contributing authors or my colleagues from work or were patients at Clairhurst Medical Centre.

- Howard Leibovich, Lisa Gerstle, Carole Tylman, and Monica and Benjamin Taryan — thanks very much for your insightful contributions. Also thanks to Daina Kalnins, Joanne Saab, and the wonderful group of dietitians, as well as Shelly Weiss and Val Waters from Sick Kids, and the group at Safe Kids Canada for reviewing various sections of the book and for their constructive comments.
- My wife, Shelley, for once again letting me excerpt sections from Sam's collection of diaries, which she continues to maintain, as well as for her helpful reviews of the work in progress, thoughtful comments, and unrelenting support through the long process of putting this book together. And, of course, my children, Sam and Danielle, who continue to teach me about parenting every single day. Please go easy on me when you hit the tween and teenage years — I haven't had a chance to get started on that book!

— *Dr. Jeremy Friedman*

Photography Credits

All photos by Robert Teteruck and Diogenes Baena, © The Hospital for Sick Children, except: **5** © iStockphoto.com/Brian McEntire; **34** © iStockphoto.com/Jaimie Duplass; **48** © iStockphoto.com/Jeanne Hatch; **61** © Anita Patterson Peppers, 2009. Used under license from Shutterstock.com; **65** © Masterfile; **79** © iStockphoto.com/Douglas Allen; **90–91** © Shelley and Jeremy Friedman; **101** © iStockphoto.com/Nina Shannon; **106** © iStockphoto.com/Debi Bishop; **111** © iStockphoto.com/Morgan Lane Photography; **114** © iStockphoto.com/Emrah Turudu; **116** © iStockphoto.com/SK Designs; **118** © iStockphoto.com/Dan Harmeson; **120** © iStockphoto.com/Daniele Barioglio; **123** © iStockphoto.com/Achim Prill; **126** © iStockphoto.com/Tony Casanova; **128** © iStockphoto.com/Dion Widrich; **129** © Ami Beyer, 2009. Used under license from Shutterstock.com; **134–135** © Shelley and Jeremy Friedman; **150** © iStockphoto.com; **163** © iStockphoto.com/Marilyn Nieves; **175** © iStockphoto.com/Scott Espie; **191** © iStockphoto.com/Steve Cole; **196–197** © Shelley and Jeremy Friedman; **202** © Anita Patterson Peppers, 2009. Used under license from Shutterstock.com; **206** © Veer Incorporated; **210** © iStockphoto.com/Maya Kruchancova; **211** © iStockphoto.com/Tim McCaig; **212** © Masterfile; **215** © iStockphoto.com/Robert Bremec; **216–217** © Shelley and Jeremy Friedman; **242** © iStockphoto.com; **245** © iStockphoto.com; **247** © iStockphoto.com/Kais Tolmats; **250** © iStockphoto.com/Renee Lee; **252** © iStockphoto.com/Andrea Laurita; **254** © iStockphoto.com/Katya Monakhova; **263** © iStockphoto.com/Marilyn Nieves; **268–269** © Shelley and Jeremy Friedman; **272** © iStockphoto.com/Katya Monakhova; **274** © iStockphoto.com/Andrea Gingerich; **277** © iStockphoto.com/Leigh Schindler; **279** © iStockphoto.com; **281** © iStockphoto.com; **283** © iStockphoto.com/Karen Squires; **288** © iStockphoto.com/Thomas Perkins; **290** © iStockphoto.com; **295** © iofoto, 2009. Used under license from Shutterstock.com; **301** © iofoto, 2009. Used under license from Shutterstock.com; **302–303** © Shelley and Jeremy Friedman; **308** © iStockphoto.com/Graça Victoria; **309** © iStockphoto.com/Pabis Studio; **310** © iStockphoto.com/Curt Pickens; **311** © iStockphoto.com/Rich Legg; **313** © iStockphoto.com; **319** © iStockphoto.com; **321** © iStockphoto.com/Evelin Elmest; **323** © iStockphoto.com/Lisa Thornberg; **325** © iStockphoto.com/Mark Evans; **326** © iStockphoto.com/Lauri Wiberg; **327** © iStockphoto.com/Wendy Shiao; **330–331** © Shelley and Jeremy Friedman; **341** © iStockphoto.com/Yvan Dubé; **347** © iStockphoto.com/Nicholas Belton; **349** © iStockphoto.com/Kenneth C. Zirkel; **350** © iStockphoto.com/Nikki Lowry; **351** © iStockphoto.com/Suzanne Tucker; **352** © iStockphoto.com; **353** © iStockphoto.com; **354** © iStockphoto.com/Rebecca Ellis; **355** © iStockphoto.com/Dan Todd; **356** © iStockphoto.com/John Sartin; **357** © iStockphoto.com; **359** © iStockphoto.com/Bettina Baumgartner; **360–361** © Shelley and Jeremy Friedman; **364** © iStockphoto.com/Thomas Perkins; **366** (left) © iStockphoto.com/Jaimie D. Travis; **371** © iStockphoto.com/Olaf Loose; **374** © iStockphoto.com; **375** © iStockphoto.com/Jaimie Duplass; **379** (top) © iStockphoto.com/Ales Veluscek; **382** © iStockphoto.com; **385** © iStockphoto.com/René Mansi; **387** © iStockphoto.com; **396** © iStockphoto.com/Libby Chapman; **397** © iStockphoto.com/Alison Hausmann; **401** © iStockphoto.com; **403** © iStockphoto.com/Renee Lee; **409** © iStockphoto.com/Andres Balcazar; **411** © iStockphoto.com/Brian McEntir; **413** © iStockphoto.com/ Frances Twitty; **414** © iStockphoto.com/Judy Barranco; **419** © iStockphoto.com/Sheryl Griffin; **423** © iStockphoto.com/Paul Kline; **424** © iStockphoto.com/Peter Finnie; **426–427** © Shelley and Jeremy Friedman

Every effort has been made to obtain permission for the photographs in this book. If omissions and errors have occurred, we encourage you to contact the publisher.

Library and Archives Canada Cataloguing in Publication

Friedman, Jeremy
    The toddler care book : a complete guide from 1 to 5 years old / Jeremy Friedman.

Includes index.
ISBN 978-0-7788-0214-3

1. Toddlers. 2. Preschool children. 3. Child rearing. 4. Parenting.
I. Title.

HQ774.5.F754 2009   649'.123   C2009-900077-6

Friedman, Jeremy
    Canada's toddler care book : a complete guide from 1 to 5 years old / Jeremy Friedman.

Includes index.
ISBN 978-0-7788-0210-5

1. Toddlers. 2. Preschool children. 3. Child rearing. 4. Parenting.
I. Title.

HQ774.5.F753 2009   649'.123   C2008-907677-X

Index

A

academic skills, 228–29
accidents, 306. *See also* injuries; toilet
   training
acting out, 167
adaptive development
   in young toddlers, 27, 28
   in older toddlers, 142
   in preschoolers, 228, 232
adenoids, 384, 387
ADHD, 266–67
adhesions, labial, 403
adoption, 251–52
advertising. *See* television
aggression, 148–49, 240
   disciplining, 246
   preventing, 154
   toward new sibling, 167
airplane travel, 172–74
allergies
   anaphylaxis, 121, 353–54, 358
   to foods, 121–23, 358
   hay fever, 389
   hives, 376–77
alphabet, 188, 229, 256. *See also*
   reading
alternative medicine, 421–24
amblyopia (lazy eye), 381
anemia. *See* iron (as nutrient)
anger, 147, 148–49. *See also* aggression;
   temper tantrums
animal bites, 350–53
antibiotics, 371
antihistamines, 389
anxiety, 157. *See also* separation anxiety
apnea, 298, 387
appendicitis, 398
appetite, 101–2. *See also* eating

art, 228–29, 260
ASD. *See* autism
aspiration. *See* choking
aspirin, 368
asthma, 390–92
autism, 209–10, 404–6
ayurvedic medicine, 422

B

baby gates, 307, 308
baby walkers, 307
bathroom talk, 242
baths
   safety during, 50, 307–8, 322
   young toddlers and, 49, 86, 88
bedrooms, 82, 282
beds, 60–62, 312
bedtime. *See* sleep
bedwetting, 203
bee stings, 353–54
behavior. *See also specific behaviors;*
   discipline
   with diapers, 46
   in groups, 184
   illness and, 365–67, 419
   sadness and, 250
   sexual, 160, 242–43
   sleep, 284–90
   start, 154
   of young toddlers, 41–51
   of older toddlers, 145–49, 184
   of preschoolers, 240–47
beverages. *See* drinks
bicycles, 186, 262–63, 320–21
biofeedback, 422
birthmarks, 379–80
bites, animal, 350–53
biting, 149

bladder infections, 211–13, 215, 400–401
boating, 322
body mass index (BMI), 126–27, 235, 236–37
books. *See* reading
booster seats
  in cars, 317–18
  for eating, 65
bottle-feeding, 59, 108, 116
boundary setting, 190–91
bowel movements, 213, 394–99
breast-feeding, 116
breath holding, 41–42
breathing problems, 390–93
bubble bath, 88
burns, 309–10, 348. *See also* sunburn
bus travel, 172

C

caffeine, 282
calcium, 110–12, 120
"callbacks," 294–96
Canada's Food Guide, 95–97
car seats, 314–18
  traveling with, 172–74, 176
car travel, 171–72, 265. *See also* car seats
  motion sickness during, 173, 425
  safety during, 314–18
carbon monoxide, 310
cardiac disease, 127, 394
cardiopulmonary resuscitation (CPR), 340, 342–45
caregivers, 66–71, 178, 207. *See also* daycare
cavities (dental), 59
cerebral palsy, 209, 408–9
checkups, 425
  for young toddlers, 29–32
  for older toddlers, 143–44
  for preschoolers, 234–38
chest problems, 390–93

chicken pox, 36–37, 378–79
childproofing, 48, 177, 311
Chinese medicine, traditional 3, 422
chiropractic, 422
choking, 128–29, 335, 392
  first aid for, 336–39
  risks, 308–9
  seizures and, 359, 367
cholesterol, 127, 133
circadian rhythms, 274
climbing, 22
clothing
  getting dressed in, 51, 78
  as insect protection, 80
  as sun protection, 77
  for toilet training, 205–6
  in winter, 78
co-sleeping, 61, 283
cochlear implants, 384
cognitive development, 186–87
  delayed, 209
cold weather, 77–79
colds, 369–71, 388
comfort objects, 42–45
commercials. *See* television
communication, 23. *See also* language development
  about problem behavior, 247
  between parents, 248
complaining, 240, 241
complementary medicine, 421–24
computer use. *See* Internet; screen time
conjunctivitis (pink eye), 382
consistency
  in discipline, 150, 247
  in meal schedules, 100, 278
  in sleep schedules, 277–78, 281, 289
constipation, 213–14, 215, 395, 398
control (need for), 147
conversation, 255, 256
convulsions, 359, 367–68, 407

cooking safety, 309
coughs, 392. *See also* colds
counting, 229, 257
CPR (cardiopulmonary resuscitation), 340, 342–45
crawling, 22
cribs
  safety issues, 308–9
  transition from, 60, 62
croup, 358, 392–93
crying, 240
curiosity, 254
cuts, 350, 351

D

dads. *See also* parents
  and young toddlers, 85–87
  and older toddlers, 190–91
  and preschoolers, 262–63
day trips, 169–70
daycare, 70–71, 277–78. *See also* caregivers
death, 249–50, 267
DEET, 80
defiance, 102, 147, 209–10
dehydration, 176, 397
dental care. *See* teeth
development. *See also* checkups; developmental milestones
  adaptive, 27, 28, 142, 228, 232
  delayed, 209, 233, 258
  and discipline, 150–51
  motor, 22–23, 140, 185–86, 228
  and new siblings, 164
  play and, 73, 186–87
  and television viewing, 161–62
developmental milestones
  eating-related, 105
  for young toddlers, 15, 24–25, 26
  for preschoolers, 231–32
diapers, 45–46
  changing, 87, 174

diarrhea, 176, 395–97
diet, 94–98, 102. *See also* eating; food; nutrition
  adding foods to, 102, 106, 123
  and dental health, 181
  fiber in, 395, 396
  food preferences and, 105–6
  and portion size, 102, 106
  vegetarian, 119–20
diphtheria, 38
discipline, 150–54, 244–47. *See also* behavior; rules
  consistent, 150, 247
  counting method for, 152–54
  time out as, 152, 153, 240–42
divorce, 246–47
doctors. *See also* checkups
  choosing, 29, 424
  talking to, 418
  visits to, 30
dog bites, 350, 352
Down syndrome, 15
drawing, 228–29
dreaming, 273
dressing, 51, 78
drinks, 107–8
  before bed, 281
  at playtime, 87
drowning, 335
  first aid for, 340
  risks, 322, 327
DTaP-IPV, 38, 239
DVDs. *See* screen time
dyssomnias, 284, 287–96

E

ear tubes, 384, 385
eardrops, 413
ears. *See also* hearing
  cleaning, 386
  infections in, 383, 384–86
  piercing, 89

eating. *See also* diet; food; mealtimes;
     nutrition
   healthy, 100–103, 126
   implements for, 65
   issues around, 125–29
   messy, 47, 51
   of non-food items, 48–49
   picky, 100–102
   skills for, 105–6
   during travel, 177
   young toddlers and, 47, 48–49, 51, 65
eczema, 377–78
elbow, pulled, 347
emergencies (in chronic illness),
     417–18. *See also* first aid
emotional development
   in young toddlers, 27, 28
   in older toddlers, 142
   in preschoolers, 229–30, 232, 254, 258
encephalitis, 36
energy medicine, 422
enterovirus (hand, foot, and mouth
     disease), 388
epilepsy, 407–8
eustachian tube, 384
exercise. *See* physical activity
eyedrops, 412–13
eyes. *See also* vision
   injuries to, 354
   problems with, 381–82

F

failure to thrive, 127–28
falls, 307–8, 320
family members. *See also* dads; parents;
     siblings
   activities with, 246
   as caregivers, 66–68
   and chronic illness, 416–20
   eating with, 100, 102, 191
   multicultural, 252
   and nudity, 160

and physical activity, 102, 126
   and sleep schedules, 284, 300–301
fantasy, 161
farm safety, 312–13
fast foods, 131
fat
   in bloodstream, 127
   in diet, 133
fathers. *See* dads
fears, 42, 43, 265, 280
feelings (expressing), 147, 156
feet, 410
fetal alcohol syndrome, 209–10
fevers, 365–68
   convulsions during, 359, 367–68,
     407
fiber (dietary), 395, 396
fires, 310. *See also* burns
first aid, 334–59
   for choking, 336–39
   for drowning, 340
   kit for, 357
   for major injuries, 346–48
   for minor injuries, 350–56
   for poisoning, 341
flu. *See* influenza vaccine; stomach
     flu
fluoride, 180
folate, 109
food, 117–18. *See also* diet; eating;
     nutrition
   allergies to, 121–23, 358
   as choking hazard, 128
   throwing, 47
food guides, 95–98
food poisoning, 398
foreskin, 88
formula, 108, 116
fractures, 346–47
friends, 256, 267
   imaginary, 139
frostbite, 78, 327
fruit, 117. *See also* juice

frustration, 146–47. *See also* temper tantrums
funerals, 267
furniture hazards, 311–12

G

games, 228. *See also* sports
   adapting, 186
   educational, 257
   for toilet training, 203
gastroenteritis, 395–97, 398, 399
gates, baby, 307, 308
genitals
   exploration of, 159, 160
   problems with, 401–3
goodbyes, 178. *See also* separation anxiety
grief, 250, 267
growing pains, 411
growth. *See also* checkups; growth charts
   and appetite, 101
   of young toddlers, 14–21, 29
   of older toddlers, 138–41
   of preschoolers, 220, 222–27
growth charts, 128
   for young toddlers, 15–21
   for older toddlers, 138, 143–44
   for preschoolers, 222–27
guns, 267

H

hair
   cutting, 56
   lice treatments for, 373
   washing, 88–89
hand, foot, and mouth disease (enterovirus), 388
handedness, 23
handwashing, 207, 369, 425
harnesses, 83
hay fever, 389

head
   circumference of, 14, 20–21
   injuries to, 346
head lice, 373–74
headaches, 406
health. *See* checkups
hearing. *See also* ears
   concerns about, 143
   loss of, 383–84
   and toilet training, 208
heart disease, 127, 394
heart murmur, 393
heartburn (gastroesophageal reflux), 398, 399
height. *See also* growth charts
   as adult, 133
   of young toddlers, 15, 18–19
   of older toddlers, 138
   of preschoolers, 224–25
Heimlich maneuver, 337–39
helmets, 186, 321
hemangioma, 380
hepatitis, 39
herpes, 382
Hib vaccine, 38, 407
hiking, 171
hitting, 149
hives, 376–77
homeopathy, 421
hospitalization, 414
hotel rooms, 177
hyperactivity, 286. *See also* ADHD
hypnosis, 422

I

identity, 229
illness, 364–425. *See also specific illnesses*; fevers; infections
   chronic, 415–20
   recognizing, 364
immunization. *See* vaccinations
impetigo, 378

independence
    need for, 102
    and safety, 328
    in young toddlers, 27
    in older toddlers, 145, 214
    in preschoolers, 228
infants
    hearing tests for, 383
    Heimlich maneuver for, 338–39
infections
    bacterial, 37–38
    ear, 383
    signs of, 351, 352
    throat, 388–89
inflammatory bowel disease (IBD),
        399
influenza vaccine, 39, 143
injuries. *See also* accidents
    major, 346–48
    minor, 350–56
insects, 79–80, 353–54
insurance, travel, 175
International Association for Medical
        Assistance to Travelers, 176
Internet
    children and, 164
    as information source, 416, 424,
        428–29
interruptions, 193
intoeing, 410
intussusception, 398
iron (as nutrient), 102, 110, 114–16
    food sources of, 115, 119

J
jet lag, 177
jewelry, 89
juice, 59, 102, 107–8, 116

K
Kawasaki disease, 393

L
labial adhesions, 403
lactose intolerance, 123–24, 132–33, 399
language. *See also* language development
    bathroom talk, 242
    for toilet training, 204
    word and tone management, 191
language development
    and expressing feelings, 147, 156
    play and, 186–87
    and temper tantrums, 146
    in young toddlers, 23, 26
    in older toddlers, 141, 157–58,
        186–88
    in preschoolers, 231, 256–57
laxatives, 213
leashes, 83
length. *See* height
lice, head, 373–74
life stories, 251
lifejackets, 322
limit-setting disorder, 294–96
literacy, 257. *See also* alphabet; reading
loss, 248–50, 267
love, 151

M
malaria, 79
manners, 193. *See also* behavior
massage therapy, 422
mealtimes, 47
    as family times, 100, 102, 191, 246
    routines for, 100, 254, 278
    television and, 163
measles, 36
medications
    administering, 412–13
    for allergies, 389
    for asthma, 391–92
    for colds, 370, 388
    for ear infections, 385

medications (*continued*)
  for fever, 368
  herbal, 423–24
  over-the-counter (OTC), 370, 388
  as poisoning cause, 310
medicine, complementary and
    alternative (CAM), 421–22
meditation, 422
meningitis, 37, 383, 407
meningococcal conjugate vaccine,
    37–38
milestones, 140. *See also* developmental
    milestones
milk, 102, 107, 116. *See also* lactose
    intolerance
minerals, 109–12
MMR vaccine, 36, 239
mobility, 22. *See also* motor skills
Mongolian spot, 379
mornings, 254
mosquitoes, 79, 80
motion sickness, 173, 425
motor disabilities, 209
motor skills
  for eating, 105
  play and, 185–86
  for school readiness, 253
  of young toddlers, 22–23, 26
  of older toddlers, 141, 185–86, 194
  of preschoolers, 228, 231
mouth injuries, 348
mouth-to-mouth rescue breathing, 340
mumps, 36
musculoskeletal conditions, 410–11
music, 188, 193–94, 260
MyPyramid food guide, 95, 98

N

nannies, 68–70. *See also* caregivers
naps, 275, 276–77, 278, 282. *See also*
    sleep
naturopathy, 421

neurological conditions, 404–9
neuromuscular disorders, 209
night
  feedings during, 277, 278, 300
  wetting during, 45, 203
night terrors, 296–97
nightlights, 280
nightmares, 296–97, 300
"no," 102, 147
nose
  injuries to, 354–55
  picking, 194, 355
nosebleeds, 355, 356, 386–87
nudity, 159–60
numeracy, 229, 257
nutrition, 31, 94–135, 429. *See also* diet;
    eating; food
  needs, 94–98
  television and, 162

O

obesity, 95, 103, 125–27, 162. *See also*
    overweight
object permanence, 27
obstructive sleep apnea, 298, 387
older toddlers (2–3 years), 138–97
  behavior of, 145–49, 184
  dads and, 190–91
  development of, 140–42
  group behavior in, 184
  language development of, 141,
    157–58, 186–88
  motor skills of, 141, 185–86, 194
  play for, 182–87
  problem-solving by, 141
  psychosocial development of, 142
  and reading, 187–89
  sleep needs of, 276
  social development of, 142, 187
omega 3 fats, 133
1-2-3 Magic, 152–54, 242
oppositional defiant disorder, 209–10

osteopathy, 422
otitis (ear infections), 383, 384–85, 386
overeating, 100, 103, 162. *See also* obesity
overprogramming, 260
overweight, 125–27, 235. *See also* obesity

P

pacifiers, 52–54, 181
pain, 411. *See also specific injuries*
    reducing (vaccinations), 34, 239
parasomnias, 284, 296–98
parents. *See also* dads
    absences by, 177–78
    of chronically ill child, 417–19
    conflict between, 248–49, 258
    conversation with, 255, 256
    death of, 267
    and nudity, 159–60
    quiet time with, 245–46
    self-care for, 420
    support for, 168, 240, 420
    time out for, 154
    and toilet training, 201–2
parks, 85, 87
passports, 174–75
PCV (pneumococcal conjugate vaccine), 37–38, 407
peanuts. *See* allergies
pediatricians. *See* doctors
penis, 88
pertussis (whooping cough), 38
pets, 89
pharyngitis (sore throat), 388–89
phobias. *See* fears
phonetics, 256. *See also* reading
physical activity, 102, 126. *See also* sports
    options for, 259–63, 328–29
picky eaters, 100–102
pigeon toes, 410
pink eye (conjunctivitis), 382

pinworms, 402–3
play, 72–75, 88, 182–87
    cooperative, 156
    creative, 185
    and development, 73, 186–87
    functional, 23, 25
    in groups, 72
    imaginary, 25, 139, 184, 187
    interactive, 184, 230, 255–56
    learning through, 184–85, 186–87
    parallel, 88
    sexual, 160, 243
    solo, 73, 88
    symbolic, 25
    unstructured, 260, 263
play dates, 73, 88, 155, 182–84, 230, 256
playgrounds, 185–86
    building, 325
    safety in, 83, 324–25
pneumonia, 393
poisoning, 310–11, 341
polio, 38
pools. *See* swimming
port wine stain, 380
potties, 204–5
praise, 151, 156, 207, 245
preschoolers (4–5 years), 220–67
    behavior of, 240–47
    dads and, 262–63
    development of, 220, 228, 231–232
    emotional development of, 229–30, 232, 254, 258
    language development of, 231, 256–57
    lunches for, 131
    motor skills of, 228, 231
    programs for, 260–61
    psychosocial development of, 232
    and reading, 229, 253, 256
    sleep needs of, 276, 277
    social development of, 229–30, 232, 255–56
problem-solving, 25, 26, 27, 141

protein, 120
psychosocial development
  of young toddlers, 27–28
  of older toddlers, 142
  of preschoolers, 232
pull-ups, 206
punishment. *See* discipline

Q

qigong, 422
quiet time, 245–46, 278

R

rabies, 352
rashes, 372, 377
reading
  young toddlers and, 74, 75
  older toddlers and, 187–89
  preschoolers and, 229, 253, 256
recreation, 259–63, 321. *See also*
  physical activity; sports
reflux
  gastroesophageal (heartburn), 398
  vesicoureteral, 401
regression, 167, 213
rehydration solutions (ORSs), 397
reiki, 422
respect, 150, 154, 255
restless leg syndrome (RLS), 411
rewards, 151, 207, 245–46
Reye's syndrome, 368
rhythmic movements, 298
ringworm, 374–76
roseola, 377
routines
  bedtime, 280, 281, 286, 295
  caregivers and, 178, 207
  in chronic illness, 419
  for meals, 100, 254, 278
  and new siblings, 168
  for schooldays, 254

and separation anxiety, 44
  for toilet training, 206–7
  while traveling, 177
rubella (German measles), 36
rules, 163, 193. *See also* discipline
running, 22

S

safety, 306–29, 429. *See also* supervision
  in bath, 50, 307–8, 322
  bicycling, 186, 320–21
  discipline about, 151
  with food, 117, 128
  at home, 307–13
  Internet, 164
  in park, 87
  sleepwalking and, 298
  swimming, 176, 322
  with toys, 48, 73, 187
  during travel, 176–77, 320
  for young toddlers, 31, 48–49, 50, 87
salmon patch, 379
Sam's diary
  as young toddler, 90–91, 134–35,
    196–97, 216–17
  as older toddler, 268–69, 302–3,
    330–31, 360–61
  as preschooler, 426–27
scalds, 309–10
scalp. *See* hair; head lice
school, 253–58, 420
school buses, 320
scooters, 320–21
scrapes, 350, 351
screen time, 74, 126, 164. *See also*
  television
scrotum, 401–2
seat belts (cars), 316, 317
seizures, 359, 407–8
  febrile, 367–68, 407
self-care
  for parents, 420

by young toddlers, 51
separation, 248–49
separation anxiety
  in parents, 44, 66
  preschoolers and, 228, 258
  in young toddlers, 42, 44
sexual behavior, 160, 242–43
shampoo, 88–89
sharing, 155–56
shoes, 62, 63
shopping carts, 320
siblings
  and chronic illness, 416
  fighting between, 265
  new, 165–68
skateboarding, 321
skating, 259, 320–21
skiing, 259
skin problems, 372–80. *See also specific problems*
sleep, 60–62, 272–301, 429. *See also naps; sleep problems*
  associations with, 282–83, 287–89
  cycles in, 273–74
  environment for, 280–82
  need for, 275–77
  routines for, 280, 281, 286, 295
  and school, 254
  during travel, 177, 295, 304
  types of, 272–73
sleep problems, 284–90
  apnea, 298, 387
  chair-sitting method for, 291, 293
  dyssomnias, 284, 287–96
  extinction method for, 291–95
  medical, 284, 298
  parasomnias, 284, 296–98
  sleep-onset association disorder, 287–90
  sleepwalking, 298
  solving, 287–98
  timed-waiting method for, 291–92
slivers, 355

smoke inhalation, 309–10
snacks
  for outings, 87, 169, 183
  for trips, 172, 174
snoring, 387
social development
  eating-related, 105
  of young toddlers, 27, 28
  of older toddlers, 142, 187
  of preschoolers, 229–30, 232, 255–56
soft drinks, 108
soothers. *See* pacifiers
sore throat (pharyngitis), 388–89
spanking, 152. *See also* discipline
spinal cord problems, 209
splinters, 355
sports, 228, 259, 260, 262. *See also games*
  organized, 328–29
  winter, 327
squint (strabismus), 381
stairs, 22
stings (insect), 353–54
stomach flu (viral gastroenteritis), 398
stomach pains, 398–99
stools. *See also* bowel movements
  blood in, 395, 397
  withholding, 213
strangulation hazards, 309, 321, 324, 327
streptococcus, 37
  strep throat, 389
stress, 157
strollers, 62–64, 172, 318–20
stubbornness, 102
stuttering, 157–58
sudden infant death syndrome (SIDS), 54
suffocation hazards, 308–9
sun
  protection from, 76–77, 78, 87, 327, 375
  and vitamin D, 113
sunburn, 374, 375

supervision, 83, 324. *See also* safety
supplements
  herbal, 423–24
  in vegetarian diet, 120
support
  for behavioral problems, 240
  for chronically ill children, 420
  with new sibling, 168
surgery, 414
swimmer's ear, 386
swimming, 85–86, 259
  lessons in, 322, 328
  safety issues, 176, 322

T

tai chi, 422
TCM (traditional Chinese medicine),
  422
teeth, 429. *See also* teething
  care of, 51, 58–59, 179–81
  first, 15, 57
  flossing, 181
  injuries to, 348
  pacifiers and, 54
teething, 57–59, 367
television, 74, 161–64, 193
  and eating habits, 100, 102, 162
  violence on, 161, 162
temper tantrums, 146–48, 184, 240,
  242
temperature taking, 365, 366
terrible twos, 41–51. *See also* defiance; "no"
testicles, undescended, 401–2
tetanus, 38
therapeutic touch, 422
thermometers, 366
thirst, 107. *See also* dehydration; drinks
throat, sore (pharyngitis), 388–89
thumb sucking, 54–55, 181
time out, 152, 153, 240–42. *See also*
  discipline
  for parents, 154

toilet training, 200–215, 429
  accidents during, 211, 212
  equipment for, 204–5
  readiness for, 200–202, 214
  special needs and, 208–10
  strategies for, 203–7
tonsils, 387
toothpaste, 59
toys, 73
  for bath, 50
  boxes for, 311
  for older toddlers, 184–85, 194–95
  safety of, 48, 73, 187
  for young toddlers, 23, 25, 48, 73
train travel, 172
training pants, 206
trampolines, 329
trans fats, 133
travel, 169–77
  by air, 172–74
  by car, 171–72, 173, 265, 314–18, 425
  documents needed for, 174–76
  by parents, 177–78
  to tropical countries, 79
tricycles, 186, 194, 262–63
trust, 150, 151, 154
turn taking, 82, 156
Turner syndrome, 15
twins, 81–83, 312

U

underwear, 206
underweight, 127–28, 235
undressing, 51
urinary tract infections, 211–13, 215,
  400–401

V

vacations, 295, 304. *See also* travel
vaccinations, 31–39, 143, 239, 429
  and autism, 405

for influenza, 39, 143, 239
  pain reduction for, 34, 239
  for travel, 175
vaginal discharge, 402–3
varicella. *See* chicken pox
vegetables, 106, 117
vegetarianism, 119–20
vesicoureteral reflux, 401
videos. *See* screen time; television
vision, 143, 193. *See also* eyes
  and toilet training, 208
vitamins, 109–10, 132
  vitamin B$_{12}$, 119
  vitamin D, 110, 113–14, 120
volvulus, 398
vomiting, 395–97
vulvitis, 402–3

W

walkers, baby, 307
walking, 171, 410
  safety issues, 318, 319
  young toddlers and, 22, 62–63, 86
warts, 372–73
water. *See also* baths; swimming
  for drinking, 108
  temperature of, 50, 309
weight, 101. *See also* growth charts;
    obesity; underweight
  as adult, 133
  of young toddlers, 15, 16–17
  of older toddlers, 138
  of preschoolers, 222–23, 226–27
West Nile virus, 79

wheelchairs, 209
wheezing, 390, 391
whining, 240, 241
whooping cough (pertussis), 38, 392
window safety, 308, 309
winter clothing, 78, 327
writing, 229, 253, 256

Y

yeast infections, 403
yoga, 422
young toddlers (12–24 months), 14–89
  adaptive development of, 27, 28
  bathing, 49, 86, 88
  behavior of, 41–51
  dads and, 85–87
  developmental milestones for, 15,
    24–25, 26
  emotional development, 27, 28
  growth of, 14–21
  language development of, 23, 26
  motor skills of, 22–23, 26
  play for, 72–75, 88
  problem-solving by, 25, 26, 27
  programs for, 68, 72
  psychosocial development of, 27–28
  and reading, 74, 75
  safety for, 31, 48–49, 50, 87
  sleep needs of, 275–76
  social development of, 27, 28

Z

zinc, 110

Better Baby Food

Second Edition

Your Essential Guide to Nutrition, Feeding
& Cooking for All Babies & Toddlers

Daina Kalnins, MSc, RD, and Joanne Saab, RD

The Hospital for Sick Children

ISBN 978-0-7788-0195-5

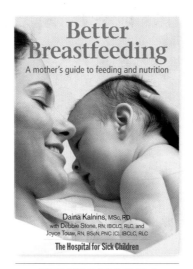

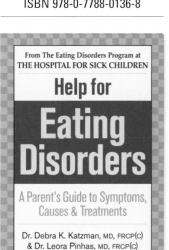

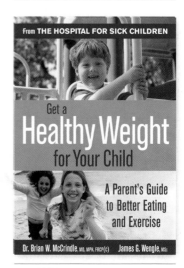

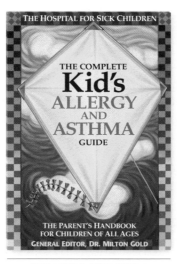

Also Available

Canada's Baby Care Book

ISBN 978-0-7788-00160-3 USA

the baby care book

A Complete Guide from Birth to 12 Months Old

Dr. Jeremy Friedman MB.ChB, FRCP(C), FAAP
Dr. Norman Saunders MD, FRCP(C)

The Hospital for Sick Children

Complete Guide
...rth to 12 Months Old

...y Friedman MB.ChB, FRCP(C), FAAP
...rman Saunders MD, FRCP(C)

Hospital for Sick Children

ISBN 978-0-7788-0156-6 CAN

For more great books, see previous pages

Robert **ROSE**